SPORT AND LEISURE IN THE CIVILIZING PROCESS

Sport and Leisure in the Civilizing Process

Critique and Counter-Critique

Edited by

Eric Dunning

and

Chris Rojek

University of Toronto Press
Toronto and Buffalo

Published in Great Britain by
MACMILLAN ACADEMIC AND PROFESSIONAL LTD
Houndmills, Basingstoke, Hampshire RG21 2XS
and London
Companies and representatives
throughout the world.

First published in Canada and the United States by
UNIVERSITY OF TORONTO PRESS
Toronto and Buffalo

ISBN 0–8020–2804–7 (cloth)
ISBN 0–8020–7679–3 (paper)

Printed in Hong Kong

Canadian Cataloguing in Publication Data
Main entry under title:
Sport and leisure in the civilizing process
Includes index.
ISBN 0–8020–2804–7 (bound)   ISBN 0–8020–7679–3 (pbk.)
1. Sports – Social aspects.   2. Leisure – Social
aspects.   I. Dunning, Eric.   II. Rojek, Chris.
GV706.5.S66   1992   306.4'83   C91–095401–1

Contents

Contents

Preface

Although, for a long time, it was generally neglected as an area of theorizing and research and still rarely merits a mention in work carried out within the dominant paradigms in the subject, during the 1970s and 1980s the sociology of sport began to expand and emerge as one of the most lively areas in sociology overall. In that period, too – as part of the expansion – the 'figurational' or 'process-sociological' study of sport came increasingly to be a focus for critical discussion and debate. Usually, the debate centred around the theory of 'civilizing processes', the basis of which had originally been laid down by Norbert Elias in the 1930s. As is often the case in circumstances of this kind, the debate was stimulating and exciting but, at the same time, in many ways frustrating. It was frustrating largely because the protagonists on all sides showed distinct signs of retreating behind the protective cover of entrenched positions, accusing one another – not always without justification – of misrepresentation, misconstrual and even caricature.

It was in the hope that it might contribute to breaking the impasse and help this area of the sociology of sport to return to constructive debate and research that we conceived the idea for *Sport and Leisure in the Civilizing Process*. We contacted a number of well-known scholars from different countries and asked them to contribute chapters on themes worked out in discussion with us. They were divided, more or less equally, between those who had expressed mainly positive opinions on the figurational sociology of sport and those whose judgements inclined more towards the negative pole. We are very pleased with the result. *Sport and Leisure in the Civilizing Process* is, we feel, a good and lively book. We are reasonably confident that it will play a part both in moving the debate on to a higher and more constructive plane and in contributing to the generation of fruitful research.

Sadly, Norbert Elias died as our work on the book was nearing completion. Towards the end of his long and productive life, Norbert came increasingly to feel puzzled, even to an extent bitter, over the fact that the reception of his work in Britain had come nowhere near to equalling its reception in continental countries. After all, he was a naturalized British citizen and spent almost half his life living and working in this country. We share his puzzlement. However, we would like to think that *Sport and Leisure in the Civilizing Process* shows that Norbert's readership in Britain – and, indeed, in the United States and the rest of the English-speaking world – was at least somewhat wider and more sympathetic than was suggested by his own most pessimistic judgement. That is the case, we think, particularly among younger sociologists and those working in such fields as sport, leisure, the body and the sociology of 'culture'.

We hope that *Sport and Leisure in the Civilizing Process* will help to clarify what Norbert Elias had to say on the subjects of sport and leisure, and that it will add momentum to the growth of his reputation in the English-speaking countries. Norbert was an outstanding sociologist. He was, in our opinion, one of the twentieth century's greatest figures in the subject. Dirk Käsler of the University of Hamburg recently had this to say: '[Norbert Elias was] a potential founding father of a European Sociology, which in turn might provide a model for a World Sociology for the 21st century'.[1] We agree with Professor Käsler. We only want to add that one measure of Norbert's greatness is the fact that he was among the first to see the relevance of and need for a sociology of leisure and sport.

Thanks are due to all our contributors for the lively, pointed, incisive and scholarly chapters they have written. Although we have sometimes been more or less critical of what they have had to say, it is obvious that, without them, we could not have produced this book. Thanks are also due to Johan Goudsblom, Richard Kilminster, Stephen Mennell, Patrick Murphy and Ivan Waddington for their helpful advice on some of the material. Last but not least, we are extremely grateful to Janet Tiernan for undertaking with unflagging patience and unfailing cheerfulness the onerous typing, word-processing and photocopying tasks that producing a book like *Sport and Leisure in the Civilizing Process* inevitably entails.

Leicester and London

CR
ED

Note

1.   Dirk Käsler, 'Norbert Elias: European Sociologist for the 21st Century', unpublished speech delivered at the Memorial Meeting for Norbert Elias held at the University of Amsterdam, Saturday, 3 November 1990.

Notes on the Contributors

Alan Clarke is Lecturer in the Centre for Leisure and Tourism, North London Polytechnic.

Eric Dunning is Professor of Sociology, Department of Sociology, Leicester University.

Allen Guttmann is Professor of American Studies, Amherst College, Mass.

Jennifer Hargreaves is Reader in Sport Studies, Roehampton Institute, London.

Grant Jarvie is Lecturer in the Department of Physical Education, Warwick University.

Joe Maguire is Lecturer in the Department of Physical Education and Sport Science, Loughborough University.

Patrick Murphy is Senior Lecturer in Sociology, Leicester University.

Ruud Stokvis is Lecturer in Sociology, Amsterdam University.

Chris Rojek is Senior Editor in Sociology, Routledge, London.

Ivan Waddington is Senior Lecturer in Sociology, Leicester University.

John Wilson is Associate Professor of Sociology, Duke University.

For Anna and Gerry

Introduction: Sociological Approaches to the Study of Sport and Leisure

ERIC DUNNING and CHRIS ROJEK

I

Social life is about interdependence and interaction. It is therefore about display, confrontation, exhibition and questions of tolerance. In his autobiography, P. T. Barnum (1869: 103), the legendary American showman of the nineteenth century, described some of the attractions exhibited in his 'American Museum', New York, in the 1840s and 1850s:

> Automatons, jugglers, ventriloquists, living statuary, tableaux, gypsies, albinoes, fat boys, giants, dwarfs, music, singing and dancing in great variety, dioramas, panoramas, models of Niagara, Dublin, Paris and Jerusalem; Hannington's dioramas of the Creation, the Deluge, Fairy Grotto, Storm at Sea, the first English Punch and Judy in this country, Italian Fantoccini; mechanical figures, fancy glass-blowing, knitting machines and other triumphs of the mechanical arts; dissolving views; American Indians, who enacted their warlike and religious ceremonies on the stage – these, among others, were all exceedingly successful.

Is there not, in this exuberant collection of 'peculiarities', an insight to be gained into the forms of what we relate to 'naturally' today as 'amusing' and 'pleasurable'? For one thing that can be said about Barnum's museum is that most of the human exhibits – the albinoes, the fat boys, the giants and the dwarfs would not now be seen as acceptable objects of display in the amusement industry. Somewhere along the line our tolerance to these things has changed. From the very first, the branch of sociology which has grown up from the writings of Norbert Elias[1] – the 'developmental', 'figurational' or 'process-sociological' approach – concerned itself with understanding the structure and history of our tolerance to things in the human world. In examining 'the civilizing process', Elias claimed to have discovered a number of interlinked changes in the personality structure of people and the structures of the societies which they form. The growth of manifold chains of interdependence between people, together with the monopolization of taxation and the legitimate use of physical force by the state, correlated with changes in what people 'naturally' found to be 'acceptable' and 'tolerable' in their relations with each other.

Elias pursued this thesis in many areas of human behaviour: from changes in the balance of power between the sexes to transformations in our attitudes to death; from institutional changes in the organization and testing of knowledge to questions of perceptions and misperceptions between the superpowers. But it was perhaps inevitable that sport and leisure should emerge as important areas of enquiry.[2] After all, modern culture values sport and leisure as areas of social life in which many of the normal everyday rules are relaxed. Here we can give vent to the passions which are subdued in work, education and the daily course of family and community life. It is precisely for this reason that sport and leisure activity is often associated with behaviour which is rougher and more aggressive than other areas of social life. Might there not be grounds, then, for holding that sport and leisure activity does not conform to the standards of self-control and restraint that obtain elsewhere in modern society? Is one to conclude that sport and leisure activity is beyond 'the civilizing process'?

Questions like these formed the backdrop to a variety of studies into sport and leisure conducted by process sociologists. Topics of study included the development of football, the history of fox hunting, the excitement content of leisure activity and the dynamics of football hooliganism.

We do not propose to attempt to summarize the findings of these various studies here – the work was, and continues to be, diverse; and in any case, several contributions later in this volume focus on specific research matters at some length. However, it is perhaps helpful to remark upon two meta-themes which soon emerged to guide research and debate. The first dwelt on the 'mimetic' character of much of the excitement that is generated in sport and leisure. Process sociologists investigated the proposition that a great deal of sport and leisure activity is permeated with staged tensions, artificially induced fears and imaginary dangers. As spectators we savour the conflicts on the football field or the cinema screen, knowing that the probability is high that no real harm will come to the players or ourselves. The second meta-theme relates so closely to Elias's original analysis in *The Civilizing Process* that it is perhaps best to let him explain it in his own words. He (1986: 23) wrote:

> The competitive bodily exertions of people in the highly regulated form that we call 'sport' have come to serve as symbolic representations of a non-violent, non-military form of competition between states.

The insistence upon linking the structure of 'interpersonal conduct' to the structure of society is again very evident here. Together with an emphasis upon the unanticipated aggregate consequences of intended actions, this sensitivity to the *interdependence* of human actions is the hallmark of the 'figurational' or 'process sociological' approach to the study of social life.

II

The first wave of these arguments about sport and leisure reached the sociological community in published form in the 1960s and 1970s. It was not an auspicious time for them.[3] Sociology was dominated by the crumbling edifice of structural-functionalism.[4] Favouring metaphors drawn from biology, structural-functionalists argued that society is akin to a giant organism. Each of its specialized parts – education, work, the family, the military, sport and leisure – was seen as functioning to preserve the stability of the whole. Such an approach assumed that individuals are bound together by a common value system. Although it was recognized that values vary between societies – above all, between societies at different 'evolutionary stages' – it is limited or 'patterned' in finite, and hence predictable, forms and arrangements. According to structural-functionalists, harmony and order are the 'normal' states in society; conflict and change are read as abnormal states which require correction.

As is clear from the 'Introduction' to *The Civilizing Process* (1978), Elias had little time for structural-functionalism. He (1978: 228) abhorred the tendency of structural-functionalists to use concepts like 'common value system' and 'pattern variables' on the grounds that they reduce 'everything variable to something invariable' and simplify 'complex phenomena by dissecting them into their individual components'. Similarly, he (1978: 230) argued that structural-functionalism tends to reduce processes to states. Change, insisted Elias (ibid.), is not external or accidental to normality, as the structural-functionalists imply. On the contrary, it is the omnipresent, normal condition of social life.

It would be misleading to claim that all these arguments are or were unique to process sociology. On the contrary, the 1960s and 1970s witnessed a ferment of criticism against structural-functionalism in which similar arguments were made by conflict theorists, Marxists, ethnomethodologists and feminists. However, process sociologists can justifiably refer to the 1939 edition of *The Civilizing Process* to show that the recognition of change as a normal part of life and the rejection of 'static' concepts were original and integral features of the process approach. Yet in the 1960s, 1970s and 1980s this approach often met with suspicion and scorn. Where process sociologists argued that today's social problems could only be understood by taking a long-term perspective, radicals clamoured for immediate solutions to immediate problems; where process sociologists pursued a research strategy aimed at maximizing 'detachment', Marxists and feminists called for a politically committed sociology and rejected the idea of detachment as yet another 'functionalist' evasion; finally, where process sociologists wrote of 'destroying myths' and enhancing our 'orientation to reality', phenomenologically-based sociologists cast doubt on shared notions of 'reality', 'identity' and 'meaning'.

It was not until the late 1970s and early 1980s, with the publication of the English language translations of the two volumes of *The Civilizing Process* and Elias's major position statement on the subject, *What Is Sociology?,* that the process approach began to break free from its peripheral position in sociology. However, before this time there was one area of sociology in which the process approach was acknowledged as a major influence: the sociology of sport. Traditionally, sociologists had ignored sport and leisure as the less serious sides of life. At the start of the 1960s there were hardly any academic studies available. Even fewer sociologists would admit to a professional interest in the subject. Process sociology, in fact, encountered a fallow field made up of only one or two historical classics on sport, together with a handful of biological and psychological treatises on play. Process sociology, with its emphasis on the body and the emotional content of human relations was well-equipped to make its mark. Indeed, by the 1980s there is some evidence to suggest that the process approach was seen by some commentators as the dominant position in the field. Certainly, some authors expressed themselves vehemently that its influence was too great and that it should be curtailed (Curtis, 1986; Jary and Horne, 1987).

III

Given the rediscovery of Elias in mainstream sociology in the late 1970s[5] and the larger numbers of scholars and students who now study sport and leisure, this seems an opportune moment to publish a critical assessment of the contribution of process sociology in the field of sport and leisure. One of the themes that emerged independently for both of us in working upon this volume is the extraordinary extent to which discussion in the field has been marred by stereotyping, polarization and caricature. It seemed to us that process sociologists, Marxists, exponents of the cultural studies approach, functionalists, Weberians, Freudians and feminists occupied the same field but inhabited different worlds. Doubtless this lack of communication reflects the state of our field of study. We take this to be one of multi-paradigmatic rivalry in which different research traditions compete to 'explain' sport and leisure.[6] In any event, both of us see stereotyping, polarization and caricature as enormously counterproductive. It was in this spirit that we prepared our plans for the book and began to commission contributions.

Anyone acquainted with the sociology of sport and leisure will recognize that half the contributors to this volume are well-known critics of the process approach, while the other half are known to be sympathetic parties. By this means we hope to showcase the main sides, *pro* and *contra*, regarding the contribution of process sociologists to the field of sport and leisure studies.

The first chapter of the volume is by Chris Rojek. It aims to give the reader an overview of the field. The author discusses why sociologists have taken sport and leisure more seriously in the 1970s and 1980s. He guides the reader through the leading positions in the field. Special attention is paid to the stereotyping and polarization of arguments. The author maintains that in many cases the points of agreement between competing positions are at least as important as the points of disagreement. The observation is illustrated with a comparison between some of the central tenets in the cultural studies approach and the process approach.

Ivan Waddington and Patrick Murphy are the authors of the second chapter. It examines drugs, sport and ideologies. Both authors are members of the Department of Sociology at Leicester University – the Department where Elias taught and where several members of staff retain strong connections with his approach. They seek to explore the relevance of Elias's ideas by the method which he himself advocated as being superior to all others: theoretically informed concrete analysis in which neither the theoretical nor the empirical has precedence over the other. More specifically, the authors use Elias's concept of 'sportization' to examine certain moral ideologies in sport, notably those relating to 'fair play' and 'justice'. They also break new ground by combining insights from the sociology of medicine with those from the figurational sociology of sport. The paper is an important contribution to understanding the reasons why some sportsmen and sportswomen resort to drugs in today's competitions.

Chapter 3 is a spiky and challenging assault upon the central tenets of the process-sociological approach to sport and leisure. John Wilson begins by comparing the process approach with its Marxist and Durkheimian competitors. He argues that a major defect of process sociology is that it lacks a convincing theory of the state. As a result, he maintains, many of the assumptions and propositions made in the theory of the civilizing process are unrealistic and one-sided. Wilson illustrates his argument that the state is essential for understanding the history and structure of modern sport by means of an account óf the state in regulating sports activity in the USA. This forceful and lucid critique raises several crucial questions for process sociologists and, for that matter, any sociologist interested in sport and leisure.

In Chapter 4 Joe Maguire considers the contribution of process sociology to understanding the place of the emotions in sport and leisure. The author commends process sociologists for recognizing that an historical dimension is essential for any convincing understanding of the emotions; and also for submitting that sport and leisure practice cannot be explained in terms of a single, isolated determining force such as 'the economy' or 'the class struggle'. At the same time, Maguire holds that there is room for a wider dialogue between process sociologists and the advocates of other approaches to the study of the emotions. He backs up this argument with a discussion of what can be learned from three research traditions: symbolic interactionism; studies of commodification; and work on the body in consumer culture.

The fifth chapter of the book is written by Ruud Stokvis. He proposes that process sociology is wrong to maintain that the key feature of modern sport is its relatively low level of tolerated violence. The author sees this as simply one factor relevant tǫ the structure and history of certain sports. Other factors, he continues, such as the formal organization, standardization and commercialization of sport are of more importance. The case is developed by a critical examination of Elias's interpretation of the development of fox-hunting. Wide-ranging and powerfully argued, the author concludes that process sociologists must critically review many of the basic assumptions upon which their application of the theory of the civilizing process to the development of modern sport is based.

Chapter six is written by one of the most distinguished academic commentators on sport in the USA, Allen Guttmann. Guttmann goes to the roots of the theory of the civilizing process by considering the historical evidence for a civilizing process in antiquity, the Middle Ages and the Renaissance. In a rich and compelling account he explores data from Roman and Byzantine chariot races and medieval and Renaissance tournaments. Guttmann comes down as a qualified supporter of the theory that a civilizing process has occurred. His discussion pinpoints many areas in which the historical evidence is equivocal. He also suggests that process sociologists are at fault for being too descriptive in their work on the civilizing process and too weak in explanatory analysis. Measured and probing, Guttmann's piece praises many features of the process approach in sport and leisure studies without conceding that it has given us a complete or satisfactory answer.

The theory of the civilizing process 'focuses on male experiences, marginalizes females, and says very little about gender relations'. This, expressed in her own words, is the central theme of Jennifer Hargreaves's contribution to the volume in Chapter seven. Written with her customary verve, insight and pungency, Hargreaves looks at what process sociologists have actually written about gender and finds it to be woefully deficient. Process sociology is attacked for reproducing male bias and treating women as invisible actors in the male game of 'society'. Hargreaves discusses gender bias in state policy and the persistence of male aggression against women. Such facts, she concludes, prompt feminists to ask: in what sense is it meaningful to speak of a civilizing process in relation to the status and rights of women?

Questions of common rights and citizenship empowerment under the civilizing process are taken up by Grant Jarvie in Chapter eight. He examines the politics of sport in South Africa. In an informative and up-to-date guide, he builds on the analysis developed in his important book on racial and political sociology, *Class, Race and Sport in South Africa's Political Economy.*[7] Jarvie criticizes neo-Marxist approaches to the subject of race and sport on the grounds that they place too much emphasis upon the explanatory value of concepts of 'class' and 'cultural domination'. The author maintains that Elias's wider, more all-embracing concept of 'figuration' is more useful and accurate in explaining the roots of racism in South Africa and what is actually happening politically in South African sport today. Accomplished and penetrating, Jarvie's chapter is not a piece of agitprop in favour of process sociology. In arguing that the concept of 'figuration' has technical advantages over neo-Marxist concepts in getting to grips with issues of race and politics in South Africa, he is careful to conclude that Marxist cultural analysis need not see process sociology as anathema. On the contrary, his argument is for more exchange and cross-fertilization between the two approaches in order to make our theories fit more accurately with the facts.

In Chapter nine, Alan Clarke criticizes the process-sociological approach to the study of football hooliganism. The author argues that the historical analysis of process sociology into the question of football hooliganism has been too narrow. What is missing, he contends, is a convincing account of why football is popular in the community. By ignoring the cultural history and meaning in soccer, Clarke continues, the theory of the civilizing process is unable to understand the passions which it purports to 'explain'. In particular, it ignores the role of the commercialized sport and leisure industries in perpetuating stimuli which lead to outbursts of aggression.

The final chapter of the volume is written by Eric Dunning. It is the most detailed attempt that the author has made to indicate what is different about the process-sociological approach in comparison with leading cognate sociological research traditions. Here Dunning offers some personal reminiscences of what attracted him to the figurational approach as a student at the University of Leicester in the 1950s. He goes on to articulate his objections to Marxism and structuration theory. These approaches have often been presented as the way forward for sport and leisure studies. In a principled and systematic account Dunning shows why, in his view, neither approach is suited to this role. The author concludes with an appraisal of some of the principal issues raised by the contributors in this volume.

IV

The essays collected here were specially commissioned for this volume. None of them has appeared in any other published form. In no final sense can they be said to confirm or falsify the propositions made by process sociologists. How could they? For one of the disarming arguments made by process sociologists is that theoretical arguments, like all human beings, are themselves *in process*. What seems to be true and obvious in one historical period often seems to be false and unbelievable in another. Barnum's museum of living exhibits is a case in point. Who today would dream of displaying albinoes, fat boys, giants or dwarfs as 'museum' objects? Practices which Barnum took to be 'natural' and 'acceptable' now strike us as tasteless and cruel. And the most cursory reading of *The Civilizing Process* will supply the reader with a fund of additional examples.

However, we believe that the volume does contribute to a more accurate understanding of what process sociologists actually hold to be correct, and that it will help in revealing what the genuine strengths and weaknesses are in their theory of the civilizing process and their approach to studying sport and leisure. We would be best pleased if readers used this volume as a resource for further discussion and research. On the other hand we would think that the book had failed if our readers fell upon it as commensurate with the automatic opinions and knee-jerk reactions that, for too long, have passed for 'debate' in so many areas of our field.

Notes

1. The key work here is, of course, Elias's 2 volumes of *The Civilizing Process*: (1978), *The History of Manners* (Oxford: Blackwell) and (1982) *State Formation and Civilization* (Oxford: Blackwell). Originally published 1939 as *Über den Prozess der Zivilisation,* 2 vols (Basle: Verlag Haus zum Falken).
2. See, for example, E. Dunning and K. Sheard (1979), *Barbarians, Gentlemen and Players* (Oxford: Martin Robertson); N. Elias and E. Dunning (1986), *Quest for Excitement* (Oxford: Blackwell); E. Dunning, P. Murphy and J. Williams (1988), *The Roots of Football Hooliganism* (London: Routledge & Kegan Paul).
3. See Dunning's chapter in this volume for an account of the situation at the start of the 1960s.
4. Tony Giddens gives an on-the-spot account of the situation, albeit from a non-process sociology standpoint in the 1960s in his 'Notes on the Concept of Play and Leisure', *Sociological Review* (1964) 12(1): 73–89.
5. References to Elias's work are now regularly made by authors like Zygmunt Bauman, Richard Sennett, Pierre Bourdieu, Mike Featherstone, Philip Corrigan, Derek Sayer and many other sociologists of world rank currently at work. For a useful publication which conveys the rediscovery of Elias's work in the late 1970s and 1980s see 'Norbert Elias and Figurational Sociology', *Theory, Culture and Society,* vol. 4, nos 2–3 (special edition) 1987.
6. For more on this see C. Rojek (1985), *Capitalism and Leisure Theory* (London: Tavistock) pp. 4–9.
7. London: Routledge & Kegan Paul, 1985.

References

Barnum, P. T. (1869), *Struggles & Triumphs* (Harmondsworth: Penguin).

Curtis, J. (1986), 'Isn't It Difficult to Support Some Notions of "The Civilizing Process"? A Response to Dunning', in C. R. Rees and A. Miracle (eds), *Sport and Social Theory* (Champaign, Ill.: Human Kinetics) 57–66.

Elias, N. (1978), *The Civilizing Process,* vol. 1: *The History of Manners* (Oxford: Blackwell).

Elias, N. (1986), 'Introduction', in N. Elias and E. Dunning (eds), *Quest for Excitement* (Oxford: Blackwell) pp. 19–62.

Jary, D. and Horne, J. (1987), 'The Figurational Sociology of Sport and Leisure of Elias and Dunning and its Alternatives', *Loisir et société,* 10(2): 563–70.

1 The Field of Play in Sport and Leisure Studies

CHRIS ROJEK

This chapter aims to answer three questions. What is the situation of theory in the field of sport and leisure studies in the 1990s? How is the figurational approach placed in this field? And what are the prospects for the figurational approach in the years leading up to the end of the century?

However, I want to preface my remarks on these matters with a brief discussion of the traditional position of sport and leisure studies in the Academy. Giddens (1964), who surveyed the field over a quarter of a century ago, asserted that biological and psychological approaches held sway. He found both wanting. Biological approaches were criticized for wrongly assuming that play performed similar functions in animals and humans and for underestimating the diversity of human play activity. Psychological approaches were taken to task for displaying naïve functionalism. That is, they were accused of presenting sport and leisure in one-dimensional terms as reinforcing the stability and harmony of the social system. Consideration of the role of sport and leisure in producing control or conflict was held to be insufficient. The only sociological theory which Giddens commented upon in any detail was Huizinga's (1949) discussion of *homo ludens*. However, Giddens argued that this exercise in historical sociology was too fragmentary and diffuse to pass muster. As for the rest of the sociological heritage, Giddens (1964: 84) concluded that it amounted to nothing but 'gross statistical surveys of relative participation in particular kinds of leisure activities'.

The general impression that one gets from reading Giddens's commentary is that sport and leisure are major areas of human activity which have been massively neglected by the Academy. Giddens does not speculate very deeply on the reasons for this state of affairs. However, it is not hard to find the major reason if one examines a few of the classic texts in the human sciences. Sport and leisure are consistently presented as being peripheral to the main business of life: work. Self-consciousness and self-realization are positively associated with the workplace, not the field of play. Indeed, one finds a strong belief that to have too much sport and leisure in one's life is self-destructive. Even the author of one of the indisputable classics on leisure, Thorstein Veblen[1] (1925: 170) asserted that 'the addiction to sports

1

marks an arrested development of man's moral nature'. He (1925: 171) went on to cite the 'make-believe', 'histrionic' elements in sport and leisure as evidence of the inherent childishness of these activities.[2]

The picture was not all one-sided. Huizinga's (1949) discussion of the play element in Western culture may have been flawed, but it made a powerful case for taking sport and leisure seriously. Similarly, Riesman's (1961) work on 'the other directed' personality argued that leisure and sport were becoming more important in the organization of identity, association and practice. One should also mention the Frankfurt School's work on the repressive effects of modern leisure forms,[3] and Goffman's (1967: 149–207) brilliant, but maddeningly underdeveloped, phenomenology of 'action places' in modern societies. Nevertheless, taking everything into account, these were simply exceptions that proved the rule.

Since the 1970s the situation has been transformed. In both Western Europe and North America there has been a steady expansion in student numbers and academic resources devoted to sport and leisure studies. The professional profile has been raised through the foundation of new specialist journals and professional associations.[4] A growing number of academic monographs and textbooks have appeared with the avowed aim of taking sport and leisure seriously. What has brought all of this about? The most obvious factor has been the economic growth of the leisure and sport sector. The expansion of the pleasure industry has multiplied career opportunities and elevated the impact of sport and leisure in the organization of social life. However, this economic development is itself bound up with wider social changes. In particular, the belief that self-consciousness and self-realization are centred on work experience has declined. Sociologists can no longer assume that work is the central life interest of individuals. On the contrary, many authors maintain that work is now seen as the means of financing other interests which lie beyond the doors of the workplace in 'free time' experience.[5]

The argument also connects with certain themes that have emerged from the debate about modernism and post-modernism. Briefly, it is argued that modern culture, the culture of bourgeois society, was work-centred. Bourgeois ideology emphasized rationalism over irrationalism, and respectability over freedom. It assumed that individual conduct was bound by an innate, rational order of things. For example, in bourgeois society it was held to be self-evident that there was a correct way of dressing and a proper way of speaking and behaving for all social occasions. This was expressed institutionally in the divisions between private and public life, work and leisure, civilization and primitivism, and so on. Bourgeois ideologies preached that it was the responsibility of the higher orders to impart the principles of self-help to the lower orders and, through this, to advance the cause of 'progress'. In contrast, it is argued that post-modern culture rotates around images and spectacles. Instead of the absolutism of modernism, post-modernism emphasizes diversity, difference, irrationalism, emotionalism and fantasy in identity, practice and association. Received modernist ideas that work and family define who one is or that there is a 'correct' way of behaving are treated ironically. Where modernists profess to observe the wheels of society running to an intricate order, post-modernists see only the voracious disorder of things. This is not the place to speculate on whether the post-modernist arguments are accurate.[6] However, it is important to point out that post-modernists assume that practice, meaning and association now revolve around relations of consumption, relations of leisure experience and commodities. It would be wrong to deduce from this that post-modernism holds that social life is now centred on leisure, not work. For post-modernists treat notions of centred meaning, centred subjects, with unconcealed disdain. On the other hand, the proposition that leisure and sport must be taken as serious topics of enquiry is an obvious and prominent feature of post-modernist discussion.

So much for suggesting why leisure and sports studies have attained a higher profile in the Academy since the 1970s. Let me now come to the question of the situation of sport and leisure studies in the 1990s.

THEORY IN SPORT AND LEISURE STUDIES

Among sociologists and philosophers it is generally accepted that most attempts to define and study social phenomena can be classified in terms of a central dualism between agency and structure theories.[7] Agency approaches commence with the atomized individual. Practice, meaning and development are studied as the product of individual action. Agency theories attribute freedom, choice and self-determination to the individual. Although society is recognized as a real thing it is defined in pluralistic terms; that is, as an association or loose community of small groups. While power differentials between these groups are recognized, agency theories maintain that there is no necessity for any one group to dominate. Agency theories adhere to the view that scientific method is value-free and that the proper application of scientific method will produce 'objective' knowledge.

Structure approaches take issue with agency approaches at almost every point. Thus, they commence with society and regard the views and practices of the individual as an aspect or reflection of social structures, such as class, gender, race or status groups. Social development is not regarded as a product of individuals acting solely in pursuit of their voluntarily chosen ends. On the contrary, it is regarded as the outcome of ascertainable structural influences such as the class struggle, racial discrimination or men's oppression of women. Pluralistic divisions in society are viewed as nothing but surface variations which, in the end, can be reduced to the determinate social forces which animate the social system. Structure approaches hold that scientific knowledge is not necessarily value-free. They maintain that what is presented as science in society at any one point in time often, on inspection, amounts to nothing more than the prejudices of the ruling class, race or sex. However, structure theories also insist that knowledge shaped by these prejudices – ideological knowledge – can be demystified and that, through demystification, objective knowledge is produced.

Of course, I appreciate that interesting and relevant criticisms have recently been made by writers who call into question the validity of the agency/structure framework.[8] These criticisms are part of a wider attack on the nature of Western rationality which is, in itself, of some moment in explaining the positions which agency and structure theorists have articulated. However, for two reasons I do not propose to go into the substance of these criticisms here. In the first place, these matters are complicated; to enter into them in any serious way would require me to embark upon considerable additional exposition, for which there is insufficient space in this chapter. In the second place, the agency/structure theories in sport and leisure studies which I shall examine show little evidence of being concerned with, or indeed even registering, the epistemological issues raised by the criticisms of Western rationality which are in question.[9] Be that as it may, let me come to the matter of agency/structure approaches in the sport and leisure field.

(1)   Agency Approaches[10]

Many of the first contributions to sport and leisure studies were made by researchers and authors working in the humanist tradition (Wilensky, 1960, 1964; Kaplan, 1975; Parker, 1983; Ruskin, 1984). They believed that 'Man'[11] has essential needs which must be fulfilled to achieve personal well-being and collective order. They associated the growth of leisure and sport with human progress. Indeed, some of them suggested that the term 'life satisfaction' should be used to define the meaning of leisure and sport in contemporary society.[12]

Agency approaches (Parker, 1981, 1983) continue to emphasize that choice, flexibility and freedom are integral features of sport and leisure practice. Although social and economic inequalities are recognized, the ultimate reality is viewed to be the individual. Change continues to be seen in broadly progressive terms. For example, a review of leisure trends in the 1980s by Olszewska and Roberts (1989: 47–61), emphasizes the continuity of improvements.[13] By way of evidence, Olszewska and Roberts (1989: 60) cite the growth of leisure time and spending power for the leisure poor.[14] Similarly, agency approaches continue to present their arguments as 'scientific', 'objective' and 'impartial'. Surveys and other quantitative methods continue to be defended as the best guides to the central questions posed in sport and leisure studies.

(2) Structure Approaches

Structure approaches in sport and leisure are critical of many aspects of agency approaches. However, they also share some of the main assumptions of agency theory. The most notable shared assumption is that human beings have universal needs which must be fulfilled in order to achieve personal well-being and social progress. However, this essentialist idea is presented and developed in strikingly different ways. Broadly speaking, three versions of the idea can be distinguished: Marxist, feminist and ethnic. Let me briefly work through each of these positions in turn.

Marxist writers on sport and leisure have identified the mode of production as the key structural influence upon individual consciousness and practice (Hoch, 1972; Brohm, 1978; Rigauer, 1981; Van Moorst, 1982). Sport and leisure are seen as vehicles of social control. Both are used to replenish the worker's exhausted energies and to expand the consumer market for capitalist accumulation. Moreover, both are seen as defusing the worker's critical consciousness of the class mechanism which produces lifelong enslavement. 'Physical leisure activities', remarks Brohm (1978: 90), 'in fact constitute the best way of dulling and intellectually neutralizing the masses.' The essentialist, humanist assumption which underpins most Marxist analysis is that human beings have universal needs. Capitalism is attacked for frustrating the realization of human needs through class exploitation. Marxists dismiss the proposition that progressive reform of the system is possible. They maintain that capitalism cannot be stripped of its class character, because class exploitation is the foundation of the entire system. Accordingly, Marxists conclude that the way to produce genuine freedom and social progress is to sweep away the structure of exploitation through concerted working-class action.

Feminist approaches to sport and leisure mirror Marxist positions in treating capitalism as a system of exploitation and oppression (Deem, 1985;

Green *et al.*, 1987; Wimbush and Talbot, 1988). However, their identification of the key structure of exploitation is rather different. Instead of examining class, they concentrate upon patriarchy. As Hargreaves (1989: 130) puts it:

> Without doubt, men possess greater cultural power than women. In leisure activities in general, and in sport in particular, men spend more time and have access to a wider range of opportunities than women, and sport is a unique feature of cultural life in which women are seriously disadvantaged and where sexism is fostered.

Some feminist authors (Wimbush and Talbot, 1988: 179; Ramazanoglu, 1989), have warned against essentialist models of female oppression which invoke the idea of the homogeneity of women's and men's experience. Nevertheless, there is a strong essentialist tone to many feminist contributions to sport and leisure studies. Bialeschki and Henderson (1986) reflect this unequivocally in their concept of 'the common world of women'. 'Regardless of their employment status', they (1986: 307) write, 'where leisure activity occurs and with whom, women seem to perceive similar criteria as important to the leisure experience.'

Ethnic approaches illustrate the third main application of the concept of structure in sport and leisure studies (Cashmore, 1982; Lapchick, 1984). They use the concept to refer to organized racial exploitation and oppression. Although the origins of racism are traced to the rise of capitalism, and especially the institution slavery, the present-day structure of racism is presented as irreducible to the capitalist system. Ethnic approaches note the higher levels of achievement by blacks in the sporting field. However, they maintain that this is not biologically but socially determined. Sport is presented as an escape route of upward mobility for blacks in a society which systematically restricts their general life chances. The social structure of racism is therefore seen as exerting two universal effects in contemporary society: it defines black lifestyle and morally impoverishes white culture.

These, then, are the main ways in which the concept of structure has been applied in sport and leisure studies. In at least two ways they are of more value than agency approaches. In the first place, they demonstrate the situated character of social action. Participation in sport and leisure is rather more than a matter of personal choice, spontaneity and free will. The kind of choices that people make, and the relative freedom which they exercise, depends upon their social position. This brings me to the second positive feature of structure approaches; that is, their insistence that sport and leisure relations must be understood as relations of power. Social structures of class, sexism and racism are present on the field of play and in leisure space and leisure time.

However, in other respects structure approaches are open to fundamental objections. Three points must be made. To begin with, their treatment of the concept of social structure tends to be somewhat one-sided. Class, sexism and racism are presented as determining individual consciousness to the point that individuals have little or no choice in the actions which they take. The interactive aspects of the relations between consciousness and structure, individual and society are neglected. In the second place, structures are often presented in static terms as a sober fact of social life which brooks no change. For example, Marxists often dismiss the political moves toward democratization and civil rights in capitalist society as nothing more than window-dressing which leaves the fundamental class system intact. Thirdly, structure approaches have done little to examine how structures of power interact with each other. One searches in vain among structure approaches to sport and leisure for an account which explores the relations between class, sexism and racism and the contingencies attached to these relations in sport and leisure practice. Instead, structure approaches to sport and leisure tend to reinforce the idea that sport and leisure practice, in the last instance, obeys a primary structure of motivation: class, sexism and racism.

The figurational approach to sport and leisure is opposed to false dichotomies, such as individual and society or work and leisure. It also dismisses static thinking and insists on exploring the interactive aspects of power relations. In these senses it offers a way forward from the impasse of agency and structure thinking. On the other hand, it is far from being alone in offering this option. Before coming to the place of the figurational approach in the field of sport and leisure studies it is necessary to say a few words about competing approaches which claim to go beyond the agency/ structure dualism. What unites them with the figurational approach is a concern with the interactive aspects of power relations, a concern with process rather than structure or agency. For this reason I want to refer to them collectively as process approaches. However, there is also much which divides these approaches and I shall come to the divisions which relate to the figurational approach later in the chapter. If one sets the figurational approach aside for the moment there are three fronts on which process-type approaches to sport and leisure have been developed: neo-Marxist cultural studies, structuration theory and Kelly's social existentialism. Let's look briefly at each of these in turn.

The neo-Marxist cultural studies approach attempts to apply certain ideas drawn from leading Marxist thinkers on culture – notably Gramsci and Raymond Williams – to matters of leisure and sport. Its principal exponents in sport and leisure studies are Hall and Jefferson (1976); Clarke and Critcher (1985); Griffin (1985); Hargreaves (1986); Tomlinson (1990). All these writers are critical of agency approaches to sport and leisure. They borrow from Marxian structure approaches the proposition that the class system is of fundamental importance in understanding the organization of sport and leisure. However, they exhibit much discomfort with traditional Marxist treatments of base/superstructure relationships. Instead of positing a causal relationship between base and superstructure, the neo-Marxist approach emphasizes interplay and dialectics. For example, sport and lei-sure activities are seen as heavily conditioned by the accumulation re-quirements of the capitalist commodity market. In the work of Hargreaves (1986: 207) sport and leisure are presented as playing an ideological role in unifying dominant classes while defusing critical consciousness in sub-ordinate ones. On the other hand, the capacity of social actors to demystify the meanings of the capitalist commodity market is never doubted by neo-Marxist cultural-studies authors. Even if this capacity is not typically routinized in everyday life, it is stipulated as a constant potential of the capitalist system. Youth subcultures have been examined as one prominent area of popular resistance to capitalist commodification (Hall and Jefferson, 1976; Robins, 1982: 136–51; Clarke and Critcher, 1985: 82–8). The media and the state are identified as two influential institutions in society where capitalist values can be contested and exposed. Jary and Horne (1987: 188), in a sympathetic account of the cultural studies approach, argue that its main strengths are threefold: it takes seriously the idea that sport and leisure practice must be understood as relations of power; it emphasizes the role of the state and the economy in structuring sport and leisure activity in con-temporary society; and it applies an open-ended approach to sport and leisure studies so that new developments can be investigated in a non-dogmatic fashion. To this must be added the acute sense of history which reverberates through the publications of cultural-studies authors. Sport and leisure practices are correctly explored as deeply rooted social processes. On the other hand, Jary and Horne (1987) are rather lightweight in taking stock of the manifest weaknesses of the neo-Marxist cultural-studies view-point. Three points, in particular, must be made.

In the first place, the concern of cultural-studies writers to be relevant often boils down to nothing more than the recording of contemporary events. Discussions of consumerism read like bulletin boards of the latest or most prominent commodity brand-names in the market (Tomlinson, 1990: 21–35). Commentaries on subcultures rattle off cast lists of actors who bound on to the stage of history and then fade away (Willis, 1978). Certain themes are apparent in all this: the versatility of capitalist culture in separating pleasure-seekers from the goal of pleasure; the capacity of subordinate classes to modify and, in some cases, subvert commodification; and the transformation of market-led needs into 'natural' desires. However, this hardly amounts to a theory. Cultural studies offer hardly any testable propositions or hypotheses.

The second problem with the cultural-studies approach relates to its much vaunted openness. Cultural studies arose, as I have already remarked, from a sense of discomfort with the traditional Marxian treatment of the relationship between base and superstructure. Subcultures were theorized as forms of identity, practice and association which were not necessarily coterminous with class distinctions. The attraction of the approach lay in its potential to free neo-Marxists from the dogmatic received ideas buzzing around class analysis. On the other hand, by conceding the reality of pluralism, neo-Marxists risked being mistaken for new-wave pluralists, losing the authority attached to the fundamental Marxian proposition that the class struggle is the secret of history. The tension has been expressed in the *non sequiturs* and illogicality which abound in the cultural studies attempts to make sense of sport and leisure. Consider Clarke and Critcher's (1985) study of leisure. It is a book which richly displays many of the positive aspects of the cultural studies approach: it consistently explores leisure relations as relations of power; it reveals how many features of leisure identity and practice which we take to be 'natural' are, in fact, historically organized by social, economic and political forces; and it is steeped in a strong appreciation of history. However, the fastidious attention which the authors pay to recording the historical facts does not extend to the subject of theoretical interpretation. After recording the changes in state provision which oppose class domination, they (1985: 217–9) introduce the Gramscian notion of hegemony to support the argument that the changes in state provision simply reinforce class domination at a new level of integration. Transformations in the power structure of capitalist societies which other social scientists have documented[15] – the decline of traditional working-class communities; the rise of flexible accumulation; the emergence of a huge service class which does not fit in with traditional Marxian models of class structure – all this is triumphantly dismissed by Clarke and Critcher. 'Class', they (1985: 190) write, 'stubbornly refuses to be buried. Each announcement of its death has, so far, been premature.'[16] I leave it to the reader to judge how open, undogmatic and relevant this statement is.

The third point I want to make about the cultural-studies approach to sport and leisure refers to its parochialism. Cultural-studies authors may pay lip-service to the importance of global capitalism in organizing choices and participation in sport and leisure activity (see Tomlinson, 1990: 30). However, in practice their published work is a monument to the Little Englander mentality. Europe, America and Australasia rarely figure in the cultural studies scheme of things, to say nothing of Scotland, Wales and Northern Ireland. There is, of course, always a balance to be struck between the particular and the general, the local and the global, in sociological enquiry. But cultural studies comes nowhere near to being even-handed.[17]

This brings me to the second main example of process approaches in leisure and sport studies that I want to examine: structuration theory. The term 'structuration theory' is today most closely associated with the sociology of Anthony Giddens.[18] In a series of theoretical works, he (1979; 1981; 1982; 1984) has attempted to establish a new way of studying society which overcomes the problems of the agency/structure dualism. Structuration theory aims to treat structure as both the medium and outcome of social actions. Giddens formulates a daunting number of neologisms and hypotheses to develop this idea. However, he (1981: 19) expresses the crux of the matter in fairly simple terms:

> All social action consists of social practices, situated in time-space, and organized in a skilled and knowledgeable fashion by human agents. But such knowledgeability is always 'bounded' by unacknowledged conditions of action on one side, and unintended consequences of action on the other.

Structuration theory, then, acknowledges the situated character of individual conduct. However, it is also militantly antagonistic to determinism and is committed to cultivating sensitivity to the contingencies, the 'unacknowledged (time/space) conditions' and the 'unintended consequences' of individual action. In sport and leisure studies the principal exponents of structuration theory have been Gruneau (1983), Bramham (1984) and Mommas and Van der Poel (1987).

The strengths of structuration theory are considerable. For example, Gruneau (1983) powerfully conveys the sense in which sport and leisure activity is simultaneously liberating (facilitating political and cultural bonds of recognition, belonging and membership) and constraining (reflecting the accumulation requirements of capitalist society). Structuration theory also insists that sport and leisure relations must be unequivocally situated in the general power-structure of contemporary society. It is therefore diametrically opposed to the ambition, expressed by some professionals in the sport and leisure industries, to formulate a pure science of sport and leisure which enforces an ethically neutral attitude to social, political and economic issues in society.

However, as one might expect of a theory which depends so much on the synthesis of existing ideas, neither of these strengths is unique to structuration theory. For example, the proposition that 'men make their own history, but not under circumstances of their own choosing' is a central tenet of classical Marxism. Similarly, the Frankfurt School (1973: 9) attacked the idea that human activities can be studied as if they were independent of social conditions. The originality of structuration theory is therefore a moot point in determining its significance. More deeply, the articulacy which Giddens and his followers display in defining concepts and formulating hypotheses has not been matched by fastidiousness in applying these concepts and hypotheses to the study of concrete social problems. Structuration theory's place is largely on the drawing-board. Very few empirical applications have been attempted. This, of course, makes it very difficult to judge if it is superior to competing models in the field as a tool of enquiry. As regards questions of sport and leisure, even on the drawing board one can locate inherent practical problems with the use of the approach. Chief among these is the neglect of the emotions. Structuration theory inclines rather too much to a rational view of human conduct in which knowledge means rational understanding and capability means the rational, intentional power to realize one's will. Against this, much activity in sport and leisure is obviously driven by passion. The arousal of deep emotions in, for example, spectator sports or heavy drinking or drug use, usually has very little to do with rational consciousness. Indeed, rational consciousness is often powerless in the face of deep emotions. Here, the problem with structuration theory can be traced to its premise. Giddens and his followers start from the position of the situated activities of actors *vis-à-vis* one another. For other authors, notably Elias (1978a, 1982a), Foucault (1975, 1981) and Turner (1984), this is the wrong place to start. In their view the situated body is the starting point of analysis. Before human beings can act they have to gain awareness and control of their bodily processes. This suggests a whole agenda of research relating to the constitution and disciplining of bodies, meanings of bodily containment and excess, personal identity and difference, which structuration theory is incapable of generating.

The third main example of process theory that I want to comment upon is Kelly's (1987) theory of social existentialism. Unlike neo-Marxist cultural studies or structuration theory, Kelly's theory is a direct response to conceptual and practical problems encountered in studying sport and leisure.

Although it is highly derivative, drawing freely from aspects of Marx's historical materialism, Heidegger's ontology and the methodology of social psychology, it makes a genuine attempt to produce a testable theory of sport and leisure.

Kelly argues against essentialism and determinism in the study of sport and leisure. He calls for a dialectical approach to phenomena. As he (1987: 235) puts it:

> Leisure is no either/or: decision or state of being, immediate experience of personal development, relaxed or intense, flow or creation, separate or engaged, problematic or structured. Leisure is act and an environment for action, of the culture and creating the "not yet", developmental and community and building.

In another passage he (1987: 237) defines leisure as 'a possibility of situated freedom'.

Kelly, then, follows cultural studies and structuration theory in submitting that sport and leisure activity is never entirely free or wholly constrained. He appreciates the situated character of sport and leisure practice, and therefore recognizes that questions of power and inequality must be at the heart of sport and leisure studies. He also appreciates that self-criticism is a necessary condition for any plausible social theory, and therefore discounts dogmatism and fundamentalism in theoretical practice.

On the other hand, Kelly's theory of social existentialism is not distinguished by a keen sense of history. Leisure identities are examined, but without much attention to leisure biographies; leisure interaction with other systems of action is explored, but without much interest in the historical emergence and development of these systems. Also, Kelly's discussion of social existentialism and his definition of leisure are truisms.[19] Of course, individual conduct has a situated character; of course, leisure offers possibilities of 'situated freedom'. The question is what theorems and predictions can be extrapolated from these insights. Kelly's theory is low in the very attributes which it sets great store by: testable propositions and predictive content.

So far the discussion has set out the main agency and structure approaches in the field of sport and leisure studies. It has also considered the claims of three of the most important examples of process approaches which claim to transcend the agency/structure dualism. It is now time to come to the second question which I set myself at the beginning of the chapter: How is the figurational approach placed in the field of sport and leisure studies?

THE FIGURATIONAL APPROACH IN THE FIELD OF SPORT AND
LEISURE STUDIES

Elsewhere, I (1986b: 65–77) have argued that it is revealing to think of
contributions to a given field of enquiry in the social sciences in terms of a
gladiatorial paradigm. By the term 'gladiatorial paradigm' I mean an
adversarial state of affairs in which contributions to knowledge are presented and developed as participants in a competitive struggle to command
the terrain.[20] Discussion tends to proceed in a confrontational way by highlighting the differences between positions, rather than recognizing the
similarities.[21] As a result, positions get stereotyped and arguments polarized. This makes it difficult to cross-fertilize research findings and theoretical
insights in order to construct propositions which have higher explanatory
value in getting to grips with the main research issues.

These comments are certainly germane to understanding the reaction to
the figurational approach in the field of sport and leisure studies. While
many commentators have praised the power and originality of the figurational
approach (Sica, 1984; Guttmann, 1986; Kilminster, 1987), just as many
have argued that it is a blind alley for sport and leisure studies to pursue
(Curtis, 1986; Hargreaves, 1986; Taylor, 1987; Jary and Horne, 1987). Here
I want to concentrate, in particular, on the criticisms made by associates of
the neo-Marxist cultural studies approach. I want to do so for three reasons.
First of all, some of these criticisms illustrate very clearly how positions get
stereotyped and arguments polarized in the gladiatorial paradigm of sport
and leisure studies. Secondly, cultural-studies writers have produced the
most detailed criticisms of the figurational approach in the field. Thirdly,
while stopping short of asserting leadership in the field, cultural-studies
writers have gone a long way towards claiming that their approach transcends the alleged weaknesses of rival positions (Jary and Horne, 1987;
Tomlinson 1989; Critcher 1989 (a) and (b)).

Cultural-studies writers acknowledge that the figurational approach was
one of the first sociological approaches to argue that sport and leisure must
be studied historically. A highly developed sensitivity to history is, of
course, inherent in Elias's (1978a, 1982a) theory of 'the civilizing process'.
It is carried over into the various studies of the dynamics of sports collected
together in Elias and Dunning (1986). It is also richly demonstrated in the
full-length studies of the development of rugby football in Britain produced
by Dunning and Sheard (1979), and football hooliganism in Britain produced by Dunning, Murphy and Williams (1988). Cultural-studies writers
also acknowledge that the concept of 'figuration' was one of the first
sociological concepts to emphasize that relations of power are both enabling

and constraining. The concept shows that sport and leisure relations are rule-governed and that, simultaneously, rules constitute resources for critical departures in the expression of identity, practice and association (Jary and Horne 1987: 179–82).

In addition, two further points, not usually formulated by cultural-studies writers, need to be made. First of all, the figurational approach was for a long time unique in insisting that social scientists should take the body seriously.[22] Long before Foucault (1975, 1981), Elias (1978a, 1982a) examined the body as a nexus of power, and unequivocally related historical transformations in bodily appearance and self-discipline to transformations in the social structure. The second point is that the figurational approach breaks rather sharply with the received language and conventional styles of thought associated with traditional and critical forms of social science. One of Elias's most iconoclastic arguments is that traditional and critical social science are blighted by the twin scourges of reductive metaphysics and reification. The conventional distinctions between the individual and society, materialism and idealism, base and superstructure, culture and class, work and leisure, may all be cited as examples. Figurational sociology has sought to develop a terminology of concrete references which attempts to pursue the pattern of social processes as it develops, rather than to conform to the foundational principles of a governing theory. As Kilminster (1987: 215–6) puts it:

> [figurational sociologists] will talk of party-establishments when others prefer "the political"; or economic specialists rather than "the economic sphere"; or social specialists of violence control instead of "repressive state apparatus"; or means of orientation rather than "ideological practice."

I shall come back to these questions of language and styles of thinking later in the chapter. I think they help to explain how the figurational approach has been stereotyped by critics working in the cultural studies tradition and why similarities between the two traditions have, on the whole, been ignored. However, having reviewed some of the widely acknowledged strengths of the figurational approach, let me now proceed to examine the central criticisms of the approach made by cultural-studies writers. Broadly speaking, the criticisms fall into three groups: presentational issues relating to the status of the figurational approach; methodological issues relating to the self-reflexivity of the figurational approach; and theoretical issues pertaining to the alleged 'functionalism' and 'evolutionism' of the figurational approach. Let me deal with these matters in turn.

Jary and Horne (1987: 183–4) argue that the figurational approach has presented itself as enjoying 'special status' in the field. They contend that Elias and his followers have claimed that the concept of figuration is the key to a reorientation in social study which more accurately conveys the dynamic, contingent qualities of human relationships. Citing Bauman (1979: 118–19), they assert that there is little difference between the concept of figuration and the more traditional sociological concepts of 'pattern' and 'situation'. It is tiresome to get embroiled in semantic disputes. However, it must be pointed out that the *Oxford English Dictionary* defines 'pattern' as 'an excellent or ideal example; model or design or working instructions from which a thing is made; decorative design as executed on paper'. None of these nuances quite embraces the habitual, constantly moving, routine, unfinished, ordinary qualities of human relations which the concept of figuration embodies.

As for 'situation', the *Oxford English Dictionary* entry is: 'place, with its surroundings, occupied by something; set of circumstances, position in which one finds oneself'. Again, the emphasis here is rather on the static side of things. The concept of situation does not convey the mobile, unfinished qualities of human relations as unequivocally as the concept of figuration. However, semantic issues apart, Jary and Horne are right to argue that the figurational approach has no unique status in claiming that social study must pay attention to the dynamics and contingencies of human interaction. The question is whether figurational sociologists would accept that the proposition that figurational sociology has presented itself as unique is an accurate statement of their position. On this there is much evidence to show that Jary and Horne's criticism is excessive. At least two points must be made. First of all, Elias (1978b: 33–49) has argued at length that the awareness of the dynamic, contingent qualities of human interaction was one of the pivotal achievements of Enlightenment thought. However, his appreciation of this achievement is tempered. To be sure, he never follows Adorno and Horkheimer (1944) in positing the dialectic of Enlightenment. On the other hand, he does recognize that the Enlightenment quest to understand social processes emerged side-by-side with a managerial interest in controlling social life 'rationally' for the good of 'Man'.[23] In his (1974, 1982b) commentaries on scientific theory and scientific establishments, Elias quite clearly associates reductive metaphysics and reification with radical modernist systems of social intervention and the management of society. However, the point that needs to be stressed is that Elias quite plainly states that the Enlightenment posed many accurate questions with regard to studying social processes, and that the figurational approach should, in part, be seen as an attempt to exploit and develop these questions.

The second general point that I want to make regarding Jary and Horne's criticism is that it fails to recognize that any claim to unique status in social life would be regarded as fundamentally suspect by figurational sociologists. For figurational sociologists, nothing comes of nothing. Each event, each development, is interconnected with other events and developments in the figuration. The idea of a unique or isolated development is not only anathema to figurational sociologists, it is quite explicitly rejected as an impossibility.

There are grounds for criticizing the presentational status of figurational sociology, but they are not the grounds which Jary and Horne cover. The issue here refers to the conspicuous failure of figurational sociologists systematically to compare and contrast their position with competing positions in the field. Elias himself has been confronted with the charge. He shrugged it off using terms which recall Weber's (1918) defence of science as a vocation. 'It is more productive', asserted Elias (quoted in Kilminster, 1987: 215), 'if I go on working in the laboratory as I have done before, like a physicist who would go to his labour every day and do his stint instead of criticizing other physicists.' Sympathetic commentators find in such an attitude evidence of the integrity and single-mindedness of the figurational approach; on the other hand, critics find Elias's position to be merely imperious, because it ignores well-supported alternative research traditions without even bothering to investigate them. I think that the omission of figurational sociology to situate itself clearly in the field by thoroughly comparing and contrasting its arguments with the arguments of competing positions has been a major tactical error.[24] It has left figurational sociologists vulnerable to the objection that they are incapable of relating to competing positions except through caricature.[25]

This brings me to the second main group of criticisms that cultural-studies writers mobilize against the figurational approach: those relating to the self-reflexivity of figurational sociology. Every academic approach to the study of social life requires a methodology to attempt to separate fact from fiction, and to defend itself against charges of partiality and prejudice. According to Tomlinson (1989: 105–6) the methodological strengths of the cultural-studies approach rest upon its alleged realistic view of the power struggle in capitalist society, and its sense of the continuity of struggle in social processes. The latter, Tomlinson argues, prevents cultural-studies writers from having a closed mind or adopting a blinkered approach to social questions. It means, in Tomlinson's (1989: 106) words, that the academic concepts formulated and applied by cultural-studies writers will be commensurate with '"experience", with how popular subjectivities are constituted from below'. This identification with 'popular subjectivities . . . constituted from below' is a crucial matter for cultural-studies writers, for they eschew sympathy with the notion of ethical neutrality. Instead, they declare commitment with the struggles of subordinate groups and oppressed classes. 'Cultural Studies', trumpets Tomlinson (1989: 106), 'has produced cultural analysis and cultural commentators whose form of praxis has been cast in more aspirantly transformational form, often linked to projects designed to mobilize collectivist strategies and ideals.'

In contrast, figurational sociologists adhere to a methodology of detachment, a methodology of self-consciously distancing oneself from the object of study. Despite appearances, detachment is not a simple concept. Figurational sociologists use it in two senses. On the one hand, they refer to it as the self-disciplined practice of science which enables one to study a given object dispassionately. On the other hand, they use it to refer to a condition of social development. In this latter sense, detachment means an unplanned, unintended state in human development where individuals separate themselves from 'Nature' and 'Society'. Cultural-studies writers do not recognize the distinction; rather, they see in the concept of detachment a synonym for ethical neutrality. Figurational sociologists are castigated for failing to declare a commitment with subordinate cultures and classes. Their silence is interpreted as an apologist stance on the question of the inequalities which are specific to capitalist society (Jary and Horne, 1987: 185–6).

The issues raised here are complex. Cultural-studies writers are quite right to complain that there is no manifesto for a better society in figurational sociology. In part this absence is due to the German realist tradition in epistemology from which Elias emerged. Elias, let us remember, studied medicine as well as philosophy at Breslau and came under the influence at Heidelburg and Frankfurt of Rickert, Jaspers, Husserl, Mannheim and Alfred Weber. It was a liberal education which combined a breadth of factual knowledge from the natural and social sciences which is unimaginable today. At its heart was a Kantian respect for phenomena over noumena (Sica, 1984: 50). Elias was taught never to present any argument until he was completely sure of his facts. In contrast, the strong emphasis which the cultural studies tradition places upon political engagement militates against a Kantian respect for phenomena over noumena. Before a problem is fully investigated, the tradition provides a set of arguments to frame it and sometimes even a solution to deal with it. For example, Critcher (1989a: 160), responding to the new lifestyles associated with the growth of the tertiary sector in the 1970s and 1980s asserts that 'such expressions seem to some of us no more than labels for the changing cultural forms assumed by middle class life'. While Tomlinson (1990: 26), writing on marketing strategies in consumer culture, contends that:

> The marketeer has begun to move more and more seducingly, flattering the punter, coaxing in the consumer. The act of purchase or consumption then becomes an invitation rite – *yes*, you choose X rather than Y. And of course that's because you're quite as discerning and in-the-know as those other discriminating consumers whom you're now joining.   (emphasis in the original)

Both passages prompt the reader to ask if the cultural-studies tradition is prepared to recognize that there is anything new under the sun? They also raise doubts on the question of how successful the tradition has been in transcending the base/superstructure dogmatism of classical Marxism.[26] Critcher's comment reduces sub-cultural distinctions to epiphenomena of the class struggle. Material distinctions between workers in the secondary and tertiary sectors are skipped over with ease; cultural differences are effaced by the brute fact of property relations. As for Tomlinson's words on marketing, they reveal a one-sided vision which treats marketing only as an instrument of manipulation and not as the focus for activating and radicalizing consciousness.[27] It is a vision which accomplishes the remarkable feat of simultaneously recalling the bleak determinism evinced by Adorno and Horkheimer (1944) in their discussion of 'the culture industry', and also Garfinkel's (1967) lament that the greatest mistake of sociologists is to treat the individual, the consumer, as 'a cultural dope'.

Although there is much to dissent from in the stereotyping of the figurational approach to method by cultural-studies writers, it is important to avoid the move of polarization which spoils so much research and writing in the gladiatorial paradigm of sport and leisure studies. Cultural-studies writers may be wrong on the alleged ethical neutrality of the figurational approach. After all, the closing pages of Elias's (1982a: 332–3) *magnum opus* on the civilizing process state clearly that we will never be 'more truly civilized' until the tensions between nation-states have been mastered by 'a central political institution' with 'a worldwide monopoly of physical force' capable of 'pacifying the earth'; until the monopolistic order of the free market is properly regulated; until the control of opportunities 'ceases to be the hereditary and private preserve of an established upper class and becomes a function under social and public control'. It is for the reader to decide whether statements like these either confirm or falsify the charge that figurational sociologists are apologists for the existing power structure in capitalist society. However, moving on, cultural-studies critics are certainly right to maintain that there are problems with the concept of detachment. Hargreaves, in this book (pp. 162–6), argues that the concept of detachment is implicitly sexist because it does not take account of the unequal power-ratio between the sexes. While figurational sociologists might respond that there is nothing inherent in the concept of detachment to bar taking account of this matter, it is certainly true that they have not exercised the method very widely to explore sexism in their accounts of the civilizing process.[28] In addition, as I (1986b) have argued at length elsewhere, the epistemological soundness of the concept of detachment is questionable on two further counts. In the first place, figurational sociologists have produced no rules, no drill, to accomplish self-distancing from the object of study. Beyond historical distance, there is little in figurational sociology to calibrate degrees of involvement and detachment with objects in the present. This brings me to my second point. If it is correct to argue that the self-reflexivity of the figurational approach regarding objects in the present is low, what does figurational sociology do which social history does not do? Bauman (1979) in a typically incisive review, recognized Elias as 'a great sociologist'. None the less, he (1979: 124) made the pertinent comment that figurational sociology is in danger of confining itself to 'the role of wise outsider finding out what people have done while doing what they thought they were doing'. The question here is one of integrity. Sociology must be historical. For, as Adorno (1989: 267) remarked, 'society is essentially process'. However, as Marx, Durkheim and Simmel and their followers have argued, one of sociology's distinctive tasks is also to theorize about the future.[29] To be sure, figurational sociologists do maintain that they are seeking a reorientation of consciousness regarding process and control issues in society. However, the concept of detachment does not illuminate the substantive basis upon which agreement about process and control issues in society might be constructed. One can hardly contemplate the history of this, the bloodiest of all centuries, with much equanimity about the prospects for rational, corporatist solutions to social problems. From Passchendaele to the Stalinist terror, from the Nazi death-camps to the massacre at Tiananmen Square, the twentieth century confronts us with a brutal gallery of irrationality and *Macht*. It is ridiculous and, I think, insulting, to accuse Elias of ignorance or indifference about these matters (his mother perished in Auschwitz) (Dunning, 1989: 38). However, the crypto-rationalist, universalistic overtones of the concept of detachment hardly add up to a convincing foundation for achieving the reorientation which is so obviously needed.

The third set of criticisms which cultural-studies critics have exploited and developed in relation to the figurational approach refer to its alleged 'functionalism' and 'evolutionism'. For example, Jary (1987: 568) asserts that

> the 'civilizing process' is formulated as serving central power and 'explains' in functionalist terms. Essentially, the same functional argument explains the leisure forms found in modern societies. In practice what this often means is that empirical instances of changes in sport-games are presented as either fitting or not fitting the civilizing process and these functional needs.

The criticism is not unique to the cultural-studies tradition. It is also made by Curtis (1986) and Taylor (1987). What does functionalism mean? Most people take it to mean the proposition that causal relationships obtain between objects. Propositions of the order that the red billiard ball moves because of a transfer of energy when struck by the white billiard ball belong to this order. In this sense, functionalism is very common in investigations of social life. For example, it is a widespread feature of the cultural-studies approach. Thus, Clarke and Critcher (1985: 232) argue that 'leisure is now central to capitalist economic and cultural domination'. Similarly, Tomlinson (1990: 32) submits that 'it is the marketing strategies of market-men and media-programmers that determine much of our consumption'.

However, this is not the sense in which most critics have attacked functionalism in the social sciences. They use the term to mean something else: that is, the doctrine that society can be compared to a biological organism. Just as parts of a biological organism are functional to the survival of the organism, it is argued that functionalists in the social sciences maintain that parts of society (education, industry, leisure) are functional for the survival of the social system. Critics object to this because it is an excessively harmonistic way of studying social life. For example, conflict or disorder tend to be explained in terms of disequilibrium in the system. The solution is to engineer re-equilibrium rather than to pursue the contradictions that will produce the collapse of the system. More generally, functionalists are criticized for not recognizing that change is produced through opposition and that the conflict generated by a given system cannot necessarily be contained by that system.

This, broadly speaking, is the line which cultural-studies critics follow in their allegations of functionalism in the figurational approach. Elias and his followers are held to assume that the civilizing process is an evolutionary process which is both necessary and irreversible (Jary and Horne, 1987:

184). They are also held to overestimate the controlling aspects of the civilizing process and to see in sport and leisure only the performance of compensatory functions (Stedman Jones, 1977: 168).[30]

How accurate are these criticisms? To take the question of evolutionism first: figurational sociologists certainly argue that deep-rooted tendencies towards the self-control of aggressive and sexual impulses and emotions can, unequivocally, be demonstrated in the development of Western societies between the twelfth and twentieth centuries. However, they also reject the evolutionist idea that these tendencies are inevitable or necessary. For example, Elias (1978b: 160–4) warns against attributing inevitability to social processes. He argues that to apply concepts drawn from the natural sciences, which study mechanical causal connections, to the social sciences, which study the relations between people, is inadmissible. Similarly, Dunning (1989: 39), in a direct answer to the charge of evolutionism, declares:

> While the sequence of biological stages through which an individual human being or any other organism passes on its way from birth to death is necessary and inevitable, the compulsions involved in a process of social development do not have the same character of inevitability and irreversibility.

Even allowing for the lack of ambiguity in these summary statements, critics might still respond that figurational sociologists have ignored their own advice in the practice of concrete analysis.

What is the evidence here? Let us turn first to the seminal influence in figurational sociology: Elias's (1978a, 1982a) theory of 'the civilising process'. What Elias claims is that, from the Middle Ages to the twentieth century, a structured yet unplanned development towards greater self-control of bodily functions and violent emotions can be demonstrated. Elias insists that the civilizing process should not be seen as a unilinear process. 'The civilizing process', writes Elias (1982a: 251), 'moves along in a long sequence of spurts and counter spurts.' One can hardly take this as a sign of enthusiasm for evolutionary doctrine. He (1982a: 333) even closes his two-volume study with a quotation from Holbach: '*la civilization . . . n'est pas encore terminée*'. Similarly, Dunning *et al.* (1988: 243) in their study of football hooliganism in Britain, refer to 'reverse' development in the growth of civilizing standards. However, critics of figurational sociology might respond that while the civilizing process does allow for regression as well as progress, the emphasis in the theory is upon the civilizing process moving *forward*. Comparatively little systematic analysis has been devoted to reverse developments. This is not an accident. Figurational sociologists avow that the civilizing process is a learning process. 'Since all social processes', observe Dunning *et al.* (1988: 223), 'depend upon the learning of more or less knowledgeable and reflexive actors any [counter civilizing] change, however great its duration and extent, is unlikely to replicate in reverse the details and phasing of its counterpart.' As I have already intimated (see p. 19), one can argue the toss over the supposed rationality of human behaviour against the historical record of horror and brutality in the twentieth century. The point is that it is not an argument which figurational sociologists enter into. Furthermore, the emphasis on learning inevitably suggests not merely growth, but evolution. There is undoubtedly a tension between the terminology used by figurational sociologists to represent patterns of process and their insistence that they depart from evolutionist precedents.

In summary, having considered the evidence, the criticism of evolutionism cultural-studies writers make in respect of the figurational approach is not warranted. Demonstrably, the theory of the civilizing process allows for counter-civilizing as well as civilizing movements. On the other hand, the emphasis which figurational sociologists place upon examining human behaviour with a long-term historical perspective can be criticized for endorsing a rationalistic, universalistic model of human learning.

Turning now to the charge of functionalism in respect of the figurational approach: functional propositions are certainly widespread in figurational sociology. For example, Dunning *et al.* (1988: 241–2) maintain that, among the factors which have shaped football hooliganism in Britain since the mid-1950s have been: social and economic policies, especially as they have affected the material conditions of the lower working class; the growth of a youth leisure market and concomitant youth subcultures; the increased sophistication of the media in orchestrating moral panics over the hooligan phenomenon; the changing balance of power between the sexes; the relative decline in the cost of travel which makes it easier for fans to attend fixtures abroad; and the recent slump in the youth-labour market. All these factors assume functional relationships with the phenomenon of football hooliganism. However, Dunning *et al.* are careful not to make the classic error of functionalist analysis by assigning priority to any single factor, such as the economic base or the system of patriarchal rule. As Dunning *et al.* (1988: 242) put it, 'football hooliganism . . . has to be approached, in our view, as a socially produced form of behaviour that takes place as part of a *developing social configuration*' (emphasis in the original).

So much for what one might refer to as the weak sense of functionalism as it applies to the figurational approach. What of the strong sense of the term, that is, the view that society should be studied as an organic system in which the parts contribute to the well-being of the whole? It is certainly true that figurational sociologists use terms like 'controlled excitement', 'tension excitement' and 'tension tolerance' to describe some forms of sport and leisure activity (Elias and Dunning, 1986: 25, 28, 43, 88–90). These terms undoubtedly invoke organic analogies. However, it is not the case that figurational sociologists see compensatory functions in sport and leisure everywhere and resolutely ignore conflict and contradiction. For example, Elias and Dunning's (1986: 80–4) discussion of mimetic leisure forms clearly maintains that events which exploit 'controlled excitement' can get out of hand. Similarly, Dunning *et al.*'s fastidious analysis of the historical pattern of football hooliganism in Britain can hardly be taken as a paean to the power of sport to enhance harmony or stability in society. Nor is there much purchase in the criticism that figurational sociologists take a complacent line on the power of the dominant groups in society to orchestrate equilibrium.

Elias (1982a: 327–33) in the closing pages of his study of the civilizing process expresses the hope that the tensions between nation-states will be controlled through international agreement; but there is also a strong undercurrent of misgivings in his discussion. For their part, Dunning *et al.* (1988: 242) submit that social-control policies designed to curb crowd disorder in sport have, on the contrary, often tended to aggravate it. In sum, neither of these arguments gives much comfort to those who wish to present figurational sociologists as purveyors of complacency. The remarkable thing is that critics never acknowledged the radical backbone at the heart of figurational sociology. Elias and his followers assert that the conventional methods of traditional and critical sociology are fundamentally flawed. In particular, they maintain that the field is blighted by the errors of essentialism, reification, false dichotomies and static metaphysics. They call for a profound reorientation in thinking and research which conveys the mobile, contingent, unfinished qualities of human relationships. The arguments that figurational sociologists have formulated to support these propositions may themselves be open to objections. This chapter has pointed to some of the main objections, notably in respect of the concept of detachment, and the rationalistic, universalistic overtones in the theory of the civilizing process. However, it cannot be said of figurational sociology that complacency is its *métier*.

This completes my discussion of the principal criticisms made by authors working in the cultural-studies tradition of the figurational approach to the study of sport and leisure. Although I have been sceptical of many of the criticisms made by these writers, I have not attempted to whitewash figurational sociology. Indeed, I am firmly of the opinion that many of the methodological criticisms that Elias makes of traditional and critical sociology also apply to the figurational approach in sport and leisure studies. For example, while few of Elias's followers have struggled with more determination or distinction to 'think processually' than Eric Dunning,[31] there is more than a whiff of 'static metaphysics' in his (1988: 218–9) charge that the cultural-studies tradition involves 'historical amnesia'. One may disagree with the interpretation that writers like Clarke and Critcher (1985) make of historical data. But there is no doubt that their account of the development of leisure practice in Britain never deviates from expressing the central importance of history in explaining the 'natural', 'obvious' leisure forms of the present day. Similarly, Dunning *et al.*'s (1988: 218) complaint that cultural-studies reifies social life by insisting that, in the last instance, the economic base is the key to identity, practice and association, ignores the genuine interest that cultural-studies writers have shown in learning from feminist critiques of power, masculinity and male order.[32]

If these criticisms are correct they suggest that figurational sociologists are themselves guilty of stereotyping competing positions. The result is that common points between positions tend to be overshadowed by exaggerated differences. This is very different from affirming that there are no real differences between the figurational approach and the cultural-studies tradition, or between structuration theory and social existentialism. Rather, the essential argument is that the points of agreement between competing positions are as analytically significant as the points of disagreement. This has a bearing not only upon the current position of the figurational approach in the field, but also upon its prospects for the years leading up to the end of the century and beyond. In the closing section of the chapter I want to examine how points of contact between competing positions are obscured; that is, I want to consider how the gladiatorial paradigm in sport and leisure studies operates.

THE PROSPECTS FOR THE FIGURATIONAL APPROACH IN THE 1990S AND BEYOND

What pushes contributors in the field into exaggerated and polarized positions? The answer to the question cannot be reduced to a matter of language, for the positions pursued by contributors comprise of more than language alone. On the other hand, since language is a crucial signifying system through which experience is shared and meaning differentiated, it is of evident importance in approaching the question at hand. The ideas and practices of writers like Foucault (1970, 1974), Barthes (1973, 1975, 1977), Lacan (1977) and Pêcheux (1982) have emphasized the importance of language in organizing identity, association and practice. Although the arguments of these writers differ in many respects, they all insist that discourse is power. By the term discourse is meant a language and an institution with distinct conventions and practices. Examples abound in advanced industrial societies. Thus, anyone who has passed through academic or professional training will know that the process is heavily ritualized. The outsider is accepted by members of the established group by conforming to agreed rituals of accreditation.[33] One of the most vital rituals symbolizing membership and belonging is demonstrating proficiency in the language of the established group. To become accepted by figurational sociologists or members of the cultural-studies tradition one must learn the in-house language. Discourse theory argues that language is more than a vehicle of communication. Crucially, it orders the professional and academic world and symbolizes authority. The point is not to deny the existence of a real, objective world independent of consciousness which is, however, ascertainable by consciousness. Rather the point is to maintain that no object or process of knowledge is independent of discourse systems. As Tagg (1988: 24) puts it: 'Particular bodies of discourse and practice can and do develop their own appropriate criteria of adequacy and effectivity, specific to their objectives and to the technologies they deploy, but not valid beyond their domains.'

What is the relevance of all this for accounting for the polarized positions adopted by contributors to sport and leisure studies? If it is correct that specific research traditions, such as cultural-studies and the figurational approach, are discursive formations, it follows that the objects which they study are open to question. For, from the standpoint of discourse analysis, the way in which these research traditions represent the real world is as meaningful as the object of enquiry which they claim to define. The point is germane both to the evident stereotyping which widely occurs in sport and leisure studies and to the testability of given theories of sport and leisure. Take the question of stereotyping first: if the research conventions and authority hierarchy in the cultural-studies tradition propose that property relations are the key to understanding sport and leisure, what incentive is there for members associated with the tradition to take an incommensurate view? Rejection of the proposition is tantamount to rejecting the rites of passage that signify membership within the established group and authority to outsiders. In short, one rejects a little bit of oneself. It does not follow from this that those who adhere to the tradition, despite their misgivings, must be *ipso facto* guilty of duplicity. This brings me to the matter of the testability of theories. Both the cultural-studies approach and figurational sociology are vulnerable to the Popperian objection that they cannot be falsified. For example, cultural-studies writers insulate themselves from the criticism that class relations in the post-war period have become less important in explaining sport and leisure relations and that lifestyle has become more important, by dismissing lifestyle as an epiphenomenon of class (Critcher, 1989a: 160). Similarly, the acceptance by figurational sociologists of 'reverse developments' in the civilizing process means that it is impossible to disprove the theory of the civilizing process. For viewed from a long term perspective upsurges in the rate and intensity of violence can be seen as temporary aberrations in 'the civilizing curve'.

Enough has been said about the way in which knowledge is organized and institutional power is mediated in the field of sport and leisure to indicate that it is unlikely that any single theory will win over the competition. Nor, given the disagreements about the object of enquiry and epistemological standards of authentic knowledge, is there much prospect of the emergence of a transcendent theory which will revolutionize the field, in the way that the Copernican or Einsteinian revolutions transformed the world of science. For the foreseeable future leisure and sport studies seem set to develop under a gladiatorial paradigm in which theories are compared according to their differences rather than their similarities. However, that in itself is no reason to abandon the attempt to show continuities between theories, to focus on principles of convergence as well as principles of divergence. After all, viewed from a long term perspective, few theories in the social sciences have managed to pursue a bunker mentality very successfully. As figurational sociologists and cultural-studies barrack one another with taunts that each is inflexible and domineering, it is worth remarking that Dunning *et al.*'s (1988: 199–204) work on football hooliganism has, in fact, drawn heavily on Suttle's work on 'ordered segmentation', while much of the most productive work in the cultural-studies tradition has borrowed from feminist critiques of male power (Clarke and Critcher, 1985: 220–5). In other words, transference between theories is already occurring in the field.

What room is there for transference between cultural studies and the figurational approach? Tomlinson (1989: 97–106), in a rather flatulent state-of-the-art review, produced a hit list of 'cultural tenets' in the cultural-studies tradition which, he alleged, identified that tradition as superior to all comers. In an ascending series of claims, Tomlinson marched his men[34] to the top of the hill in leisure and sport studies. His review contrived to leave the reader with the impression that the *aficionados* of Gramsci, Williams and Stuart Hall were masters of all they surveyed. This is, perhaps, a suitable occasion to march Tomlinson and his men back down the hill, by comparing his list of central tenets in cultural studies with those of the figurational approach.

First, Tomlinson (1989: 105) claims that cultural studies does not separate the present from the historical. What is taken to be 'natural' and 'obvious' in contemporary leisure and sport practice must be understood as historically constructed. Given the emphasis on process, historical contingency and the unfinished qualities of social life in figurational sociology, there is nothing that any figurational sociologist would object to in Tomlinson's position on this matter.

Secondly, Tomlinson (ibid.) claims that cultural studies refuses to take phenomena at face value. In contrast to less plausible positions, cultural studies is alleged to 'see the familiar as strange' and to approach 'the at first-sight as redolent with significant meaning'. It is, I think, safe to say that most figurational sociologists would find the obligation always to see the familiar as strange to be an onerous requirement. From the figurational standpoint the familiar is nothing but familiar. The strangeness lies in investing it with a significance that it does not have. However, on the broader point, Tomlinson's second claim is really no more than a restatement that the 'natural' and 'obvious' must be understood as historically constructed. The reader has already been advised of the fundamental agreement of figurational sociologists with the cultural studies view on this matter.

Thirdly, Tomlinson (ibid.) claims that cultural studies recognizes that there is no single culture and that researchers need to address the relations between cultures. Again, no figurational sociologist would disagree with this. Indeed, Elias (1978a: 3–10) makes exactly the same point in the opening pages of his study on the civilizing process, where he compares German, French and English meanings of the term 'civilization'. However, here a real difference between the two approaches can be pinpointed. Cultural studies tends to conflate every aspect of social practice into culture.[35] Other universals in society may be acknowledged but the only one written about in any detail is the economy. In contrast, figurational sociology recognizes cultural plurality but counterposes this against not merely the economy but also civilization. The latter term is understood in its broadest sense as stretching from 'the level of technology, to the type of manners, to the development of scientific knowledge, to religious ideas and customs . . . to the type of dwelling or the manner in which men and women live together, to the form of judicial punishment, or to the way in which food is prepared' (Elias 1978a: 3).[36] Figurational sociology therefore maintains that social as well as economic universals obtain in the integration of society. Furthermore, social universals cannot be read as a reflection of the economy, as the expression of mere property relations. On the contrary, they must be understood as being irreducible to economic forces.

Fourthly, Tomlinson (ibid.) claims that cultural studies is alert to the range, diversity and richness of the cultural. It rejects 'dominant culture' models of society as selective, political and inaccurate. So does figurational sociology. For example, Dunning *et al.* (1988: 212–6) castigate received models of working-class life which neglect to take account of the material and cultural distinctions which apply around the division between the 'rough' and the 'respectable' working class. The same authors (1988: 214–49) decry the policies of the dominant culture to stamp out hooliganism as they are articulated through the state apparatus. These policies, argue Dunning *et al.*, will fail because they do not understand the real material and cultural conditions of working-class life. In sum, there is nothing in figurational sociology which induces a blinkered vision on either the range, diversity and richness of culture, or the selectivity, partiality and inaccuracy of dominant culture models.

Fifthly, Tomlinson (ibid.) claims that cultural studies 'has been concerned with struggle and intervention, in which the analytical itself is a form of practice, or more accurately, praxis'. There are views about what sociology should be and there are views about what sociology should be. On the question of social and political involvement, figurational sociologists and cultural studies exponents, really are poles apart. As we saw earlier (see p. 19), figurational sociologists maintain that scientific enquiry should aspire to the condition of detachment, a methodology of self-consciously distancing oneself from the object of study. They regard 'praxis', in the sense in which Tomlinson uses the term, as the betrayal of science because it continuously involves political values muddying the quest for objectivity. This then is a genuine point of polarization between the two approaches.

But what of the other tenets which Tomlinson asserts are the hallmark of the cultural-studies approach? Three out of four would be regarded by figurational sociologists as not only acceptable but as matters of routine practice. It is for the reader to decide whether the point of difference, the point regarding the prominence which cultural-studies writers assign to the economy as the most significant societal universal, reflects the realism and accuracy of that approach over figurational sociology. Beyond that the common points between the two approaches to which I have drawn attention are hardly negligible. The common respect for history, the common emphasis on the historical and social dimensions of the 'natural' and the 'obvious', the common application of cultural diversity and richness – these are not insignificant common denominators. They do not cancel the differences between the cultural-studies tradition and figurational sociology. On the other hand, they do show that the two approaches are much closer in key respects than the received view of polarization would allow.

Theories in a given field of social enquiry are bound together by similarities, by principles of integration, as well as being divided by differences. Examining these principles may not produce a theory which transcends points of difference. However, it can correct the misleading view that theories are wholly antithetical and that progress in the field means demolishing the theoretical foundations of competing theories. Such a course of action may strike the reader as anodyne when compared with Elias's (1978b: 50–70) assertion that the vocation of the sociologist is to 'destroy myth'. However, critical thought is not necessarily restricted to a destructive role. Indeed, by revealing the continuities as well as the discontinuities between theories, critical thought will become more critical, because it will be more accurate.

Notes

1. Veblen's *Theory of the Leisure Class* was originally published in 1899.
2. Veblen (1925: 171) mentions the examples of the behaviour of huntsmen and athletes: 'Huntsmen are prone to a histrionic prancing gait and to an elaborate exaggeration of manners. . . . Similarly, in athletic sports there is almost invariably present a good share of rant and swagger and ostensible mystification – features which mark the historionic nature of those employments. In all of this, of course, the reminder of boyish make-believe is plain enough.'
3. Notably, Adorno and Horkheimer (1944), Adorno (1975), and Marcuse (1955, 1964).
4. For example, the Leisure Studies Association was established in 1975; the *Leisure Studies* journal first appeared in 1982; *Loisir et société* first appeared in 1978. As regards sport, the International Committee for the Sociology of Sport was founded in 1965; the International Review of Sociology of Sport in 1966.
5. See, for example, Gorz (1976, 1980).
6. For full-length commentaries on the matter, see Harvey (1989) and Rojek (forthcoming ch. 3).
7. See Giddens (1982: 28–40; 1984: 5–28). For an application of this classification to leisure and recreation theory, see Rojek (1989: 69–88).
8. The works of Foucault, Derrida and Lacan spring to mind.
9. For example, they do not appear in the field surveys written by Clarke and Critcher (1985); Deem (1985); Wimbush and Talbot (1988).
10. My discussion here is deliberately brief. The objections to agency theory in sport and leisure are well known: see Rojek (1985: 85–105); Moorhouse (1989: 15–35); Hargreaves (1989: 130–49).

11. The sexist connotations of agency theory have been commented upon by several feminist writers. See, for example, Deem (1985), Wimbush and Talbot (1988) and Hargreaves (1989).

12. The suggestion was made by John Roberts at one of the plenary sessions at the 1984 Leisure Studies Association conference at Sussex University.

13. The somewhat complacent tone of the book is well shown by the editors in two propositions which they make in the 'Introduction'. In the first place Olszewska and Roberts (1989: 8) speak of the economic crisis in Britain and Belgium as having 'passed into recent history' – a somewhat precipitate statement given the high levels of unemployment throughout the 1980s and the balance of payments crisis which depressed the British economy at the start of the 1990s. The second proposition has to do with leisure in Eastern Europe. The editors (1989: 13) rather blithely remark that 'by the end of the decade there seemed little reason for any major change of course. Even the Polish crisis appeared capable of solution by suppressing or incorporating reform movements, and by restoring growth through some combination of absorbing new technology and persuading and enabling people to work harder and longer' – unfortunate words written and published at precisely the time when the forces of change in Eastern Europe were already gathering to transform the post-war situation.

14. Significantly, Roberts writes little about the quality of experience for the 'leisure poor'.

15. See esp. Lash and Urry (1987) and Harvey (1989).

16. Clarke and Critcher (1985) is, in part, an attempt to demonstrate the central importance of class for understanding sport and leisure.

17. Perhaps this is one reason why the cultural-studies approach has not been diffused very widely outside Britain. Most of the enthusiasts outside the UK are, in fact, émigrés, for example, Ingham in the USA and Bennett in Australia.

18. The term 'structuration' was, to my knowledge, first used by Lucien Goldmann (1964: 156) in his account of 'genetic-structuralist method'. Giddens (1984: xvi) has acknowledged the 'Gallic roots' of the term. However, he has not commented in detail its origins.

19. This is not necessarily a criticism. As De Swaan (1990:3) remarks: 'Most, maybe all, of the basic tenets of social science are truisms. Almost everybody agrees at first sight, almost everyone knew it all along – except that most people all along have also held the opposite to be true. . . . Social science is based upon platitudes, good social science is based upon true platitudes, and what is difficult is to abandon the equally familiar false ones.'

20. For a more detailed discussion of the 'gladiatorial paradigm, see Rojek (1986a: 65–77).

21. See, for example, the hostile, reactionary dismissal of Veal's (1989) 'pluralist framework' for leisure studies by Scraton and Talbot (1989) and Critcher (1989b).

22. Elias's view of the body as a self-controlled, self-restrained entity reflects the discipline and training required by bourgeois society. In some respects this 'closed' view of the body is inadequate – especially when contrasted with phenomenological approaches to the subject which emphasize the protean, 'always conceiving' aspects of bodily form (for an example of a pheno-

menological approach which contrasts sharply with that of Elias's, see Bakhtin, 1968: 1–59).

23. However, he does not fully pursue the irrationality of bureaucratic systems of management, and therefore overestimates the rationalistic effects of rational-legal rule.

24. On the rare occasions when Elias has compared the figurational approach with competitors in the field, he has too often lapsed into caricature (see Elias, 1978a: 221–63: a frosty denunciation of Parsons' sociology); and his eccentric treatments of the sociology of Marx and Weber in Elias (1978b: 115–16; 139–44).

25. Jary (1987) makes the same point in a commentary on Elias and Dunning's work on leisure. Jary (1987: 569) writes: 'It is disingenuous of them to suggest, simply on the grounds of "object adequacy", that they are in a position to exclude other perspectives and theories: notably of course alternative theories of the distinctive role of leisure in specifically "capitalist" societies, together with theories making altogether more negative assessments of social power than their own.'

26. This is especially so when taken in conjunction with Clarke and Critcher's (1985: 190) comment that 'class stubbornly refuses to be buried. Each statement of its death has, so far, been premature' (already cited on p. 9 of this chapter).

27. Tomlinson (1990: 29) contends that marketing prioritizes 'individualism over collectivism, status over class, consumption over production'. This is surely a specious argument. It ignores the obvious fact that marketing has been used by political organizations which prioritize collectivism over individualism, class over status, and production over consumption, for example, the Labour Party, the trade union movement, the ANC and so on. More seriously, Tomlinson prejudges the issue in a way which recalls Elias's strictures regarding 'static metaphysics': instead of a concrete examination of marketing processes as they develop, Tomlinson comes to the matter with a set of fixed principles which automatically define 'reality'.

28. Dunning's (1986) paper, 'Sport as a Male Preserve', is an exception to the rule. However, feminists argue that he takes an inadequate position on the question of male power (see Hargreaves, 1986).

29. Marx, Durkheim, Simmel and their followers, of course, also insist on the requirement for sociologists to theorize about the present.

30. Interestingly, Stedman Jones (1977: 168) identifies functionalist thinking in both the figurational approach and the neo-Marxist tradition: 'We may think of sport, for example, as a healthy release for spontaneity and freedom, like the sociologist Eric Dunning; or we may think of it as a diversionary use of leisure time reinforcing the alienated consciousness engendered by the workplace. But there is no challenge here to the functionalist analysis of sport.'

31. Here Dunning's pedagogic influence in shaping the sociological imagination of a generation of sociologists now working in the sport/leisure field should be recognized, for example, Grant Jarvie, Joe MacGuire, John Williams and myself. Eric's capacity to make the significance of 'thinking processually' come fully alive has left an indelible mark on all of us. Even if some of us are now more critical of the figurational approach than we were as students, very

few, I would imagine, have lost the sense of the intellectual excitement and moral purpose in sociological enquiry which Eric generated then and continues to generate now.

32.   At the same time there is considerable equivocation in the cultural-studies tradition as to whether patriarchy should be regarded as a by-product of capitalism or vice versa. The question is of no mere scholastic interest. Between the neo-Marxist and feminist traditions there is a rather acrid debate on the question of whether analytic priority should be assigned to patriarchy or capitalism. For example, in an argument which many feminists find sinister, Anderson (1983: 92–3) asserts: 'Universal though the cause of women's emancipation may be, one so radical that men too will be freed from their existing selves by it, it is insufficiently operational as a collective agency, actual or potential, ever to be able to uproot the economy or polity of capital. For that, a social force endowed with another strategic leverage is necessary. Only the modern "collective labourer", the workers who constitute the immediate producers of any industrial society, possesses that leverage – by reason of their specific "class capacity", or structural position within the process of capitalist machinofacture as a whole, which they alone can paralyze or transform.'

33.   These are generally institutionally based, that is, within the academy.

34.   The word 'men' is used advisedly: Tomlinson mentions hardly any female writers.

35.   Simon Frith makes the same point in a comment on Willis *et al.*'s (1990: 153) study of 'common culture'.

36.   The emphasis in this passage on 'the manner in which men and women live together' tends to support the view that there is no inherent sexism in the theory of the civilizing process.

References

Adorno, T. (1975), 'Culture Industry Reconsidered', *New German Critique,* 6: 12–19.

_____ (1989), 'Society', in S. Bronner and D. Kellner (eds), *Critical Theory and Society: A Reader* (London: Routledge) pp. 267–75.

_____ and Horkheimer, M. (1944), *Dialectic of Enlightenment* (London: Verso, 1979 edn).

Anderson, P. (1983), *In the Tracks of Historical Materialism* (London: Verso).

Bakhtin, M. (1968), *Rabelais and his World* (Cambridge, Mass.: MIT Press).

Barthes, R. (1973), *Mythologies* (St Albans: Paladin).

_____ (1975), *The Pleasure of the Text* (New York: Hill & Wang).

_____ (1977), *Image–Music–Text* (Glasgow: Fontana).

Bauman, Z. (1979), 'The Phenomenon of Norbert Elias', *Sociology,* 13(1): 117–25.

Bialeschki, M. D. and Henderson, K. (1986), 'Leisure in the Common World of Women', *Leisure Studies,* 5(3): 299–308.

Bramham, P. (1984), 'Giddens in Goal: Reconstructing the Social Theory of Sport', in P. Bramham *et al., New Directions in Leisure Studies* (Bradford and Ilkley Community College) pp. 5–30.

Brohm, J. (1978), *Sport: A Prison of Measured Time* (London: Interlinks).

Cashmore, E. (1982), *Black Sportsmen* (London: Routledge & Kegan Paul).

Clarke, J. and Critcher, C. (1985), *The Devil Makes Work* (London: Macmillan).

Critcher, C. (1989a), A communication in response to 'Leisure and Status: a Pluralist Framework for Analysis', *Leisure Studies,* 8(2): 159–62.

_____ (1989b), 'The Future of Leisure: Breaking with Old Distinctions', *Leisure Studies*, 8(2): 201–8.

Curtis, J. (1986), 'Işn't it Difficult to Support some Notions of "The Civilizing Process"? A Response to Dunning', in C. Roger Rees and A. Miracle (eds), *Sport and Social Theory* (Champaign, Ill.: Human Kinetics Publishers) pp. 57–66.

Deem, R. (1985), *All Work and No Play*, (Milton Keynes, Beds. Open University Press).

De Swaan, A. (1990), *The Management of Normality* (London: Routledge).

Dunning, E. (1986), 'Sport as a Male Preserve', *Theory, Culture and Society,* 3(1): 79–98.

_____ (1989), 'The Figurational Approach to Sport and Leisure', in C. Rojek, (ed.), *Leisure for Leisure: Critical Essays* (London: Macmillan) pp. 36–52.

_____ and Sheard, K. (1979), *Barbarians, Gentlemen and Players* (Oxford: Martin Robertson).

_____ , Murphy, P. and Williams, J. (1988), *The Roots of Football Hooliganism* (London: Routledge & Kegan Paul).

Elias, N. (1974), 'The Sciences: Towards a Theory', in R. Whitley (ed.), *Social Processes of Scientific Development* (London: Routledge & Kegan Paul) pp. 21–42.

_____ (1978a), *The Civilizing Process* (Oxford: Blackwell). Originally published 1939 as *Über den Prozess der Zivilisation,* 2 vols (Basle: Verlag Haus zum Falken).

_____ (1978b), *What Is Sociology?* (London: Hutchinson).

_____ (1982a), *The Civilizing Process,* vol. 2: *State Formation and Civilization* (Oxford: Blackwell).

_____ (1982b), 'Scientific Establishments', in N. Elias, H. Martins and R. Whitley (eds), *Scientific Establishments and Hierarchies* (Dordrecht: Reide).

_____ (1987), *Involvement and Detachment* (Oxford: Blackwell).

_____ and Dunning, E. (1986), *Quest for Excitement* (Oxford: Blackwell).

Foucault, N. (1970), *The Order of Things* (London: Tavistock).

_____ (1974), *The Archaelogy of Knowledge* (London: Tavistock).

_____ (1975), *Discipline and Punish* (Harmondsworth, Middx: Penguin).

_____ (1981), *The History of Sexuality* (Harmondsworth, Middx: Penguin).

Frankfurt Institute for Social Research (1973), *Aspects of Sociology* (London: Heinemann).

Garfinkel, H. (1967), *Studies in Ethnomethodology* (Englewood Cliffs, N.J.: Prentice-Hall).

Giddens, A. (1964), 'Notes on the Concept of Play and Leisure', *Sociological Review,* 12(1): 73–89.

_____ (1979), *Central Problems in Social Theory* (London: Macmillan).

_____ (1981), *A Contemporary Critique of Historical Materialism* (London: Macmillan).

_____ (1982), *Profiles and Critiques in Social Theory* (London: Macmillan).

_____ (1984), *The Constitution of Society* (Cambridge: Polity Press).

Goffman, E. (1967), 'Where the Action Is' in his *Interaction Ritual* (New York: Pantheon) pp. 149–270.

Goldmann, L. (1964), *Towards a Sociology of the Novel* (London: Tavistock).

Gorz, A. (ed.) (1976), *The Division of Labour* (Brighton, Sussex: Harvester).

_____ (1980), *Farewell to the Working Class* (London: Pluto).

Green, E., Hebron, S. and Woodward, D. (1987), *Women's Leisure in Sheffield* (Sheffield: Dept of Applied Social Studies, Sheffield Polytechnic).

Griffin, C. (1985), *Typical Girls* (London: Routledge & Kegan Paul).

Gruneau, R. (1983), *Class, Sports and Social Development* (Boston, Mass.: University of Massachusetts Press).

Guttmann, A. (1986), *Sports Spectators* (New York: Columbia University Press).

Hall, S. and Jefferson, T. (eds) (1976), *Resistance through Rituals* (London: Hutchinson).

Hargreaves, J. (1986), 'Where's the Virtue? Where's the Grace? A Discussion of the Social Production of Gender Relations in and through Sport', *Theory, Culture and Society*, 3(1): 109–21.

_____ (1989), 'The Promise and Problems of Women's Leisure and Sport', in C. Rojek (ed.), *Leisure for Leisure: Critical Essays* (London: Macmillan) pp. 130–49.

_____ (1991) 'Sex, Gender and the Body in Sport and Leisure: Has there been a Civilizing Process?', in E. Dunning and C. Rojek (eds), *Sport and Leisure in the Civilizing Process* (London: Macmillan).

Harvey, D. (1989), *The Condition of Postmodernity* (Oxford: Blackwell).

Hoch, P. (1972), *Rip Off the Big Game* (New York: Anchor Doubleday).

Huizinga, J. (1949), *Homo Ludens* (London: Routledge & Kegan Paul).

Jary, D. (1987), 'Sport and Leisure in the "Civilizing Process"', *Theory, Culture and Society*, 4(2–3): 563–70.

_____ and Horne, J. (1987), 'The Figurational Sociology of Sport and Leisure of Elias and Dunning and its Alternatives', *Loisir et société*, 10(2): 177–94.

Kaplan, M. (1975), *Leisure: Theory and Policy* (New York: John Wiley).

Kelly, J. (1987), *Freedom to Be* (New York: Macmillan).

Kilminster, R. (1987), 'Introduction to Elias', *Theory, Culture and Society*, 4(2–3), 213–22.

Lacan, J. (1977), *Ecrits* (London: Tavistock).

Lapchick, R. (1984), *Broken Promises* (New York: St Martin's Press).

Lash, S. and Urry, J. (1987), *The End of Organized Capitalism* (Cambridge: Polity Press).

Marcuse, H. (1955), *Eros and Civilization* (London: Abacus).

_____ (1964), *One-Dimensional Man* (London: Abacus).

Mommas, H. and van der Poel, H. (1987), 'New Perspectives on Theorizing Leisure', *Loisir et société*, 10(2): 161–76.

Moorhouse, H. (1989), 'Models of Work, Models of Leisure', in C. Rojek (ed.), *Leisure for Leisure: Critical Essays* (London: Macmillan) pp. 15–35.

Olszewska, A. and Roberts, K. (eds) (1989), *Leisure and Life-Style* (London: Sage).

Parker, S. (1981), 'Choice, Flexibility, Spontaneity and Self Determination', *Social Forces*, 60(2): 323–31.

_____ (1983), *Leisure and Work* (London: Unwin Hyman).

Pêcheux, M. (1982), *Language, Semantics and Ideology* (London: Macmillan).

Ramazanoglu, C. (1989), *Feminism and the Contradictions of Oppression* (London: Routledge).

Riesman, D. (1961), *The Lonely Crowd* (New Haven, Conn.: Yale University Press).

Rigauer, B. (1981), *Sport and Work* (New York: Columbia University Press).

Robins, D. (1982), 'Sport and Youth Culture', in J. Hargreaves (ed.), *Sport, Culture and Ideology* (London: Routledge & Kegan Paul) pp. 136–51.

Rojek, C. (1985), *Capitalism and Leisure Theory* (London: Tavistock).

_____ (1986a), 'The "Subject" in Social Work', *British Journal of Social Work*, 16: 65–77.

_____ (1986b), 'Problems of Involvement and Detachment in the Writings of Norbert Elias', *British Journal of Sociology*, 37(4): 584–96.

_____ (1989), 'Leisure and Recreation Theory', in E. Jackson and T. Burton (eds), *Understanding Leisure and Recreation* (State College: Venture Publishing) pp. 69–88.

_____ (forthcoming), *Ways of Escape: Transformations of Leisure and Travel under Modernity and Postmodernity* (London: Macmillan).

Ruskin, H. (1984) (ed.), *Leisure* (London: Associated University Presses).

Scraton, S. and Talbot, M. (1989), 'A Response to "Leisure, Lifestyle and Status: a Pluralist Framework for Analysis"', *Leisure Studies*, 4(2): 155–8.

Sica, A. (1984), 'Sociogenesis and Psychogenesis', *Mid-American Review of Sociology*, 9: 49–78.

Stedman Jones, G. (1977), 'Class Expression versus Social Control? A Critique of Recent Trends in the Social History of Leisure', *History Workshop Journal*, 4: 162–70.

Tagg, J. (1988), *The Burden of Representation* (London: Macmillan).

Taylor, I. (1987), 'Putting the Boot into Working Class Sport: British Soccer after Bradford and Brussels', *Sociology of Sport Journal*, 4: 171–99.

Tomlinson, A. (1989), 'Whose Side Are They On?: Leisure Studies and Cultural Studies in Britain', *Leisure Studies*, 8(2): 97–106.

_____ (ed.) (1990), *Consumption, Identity and Style* (London: Routledge).

Turner, B. S. (1984), *The Body and Society* (Oxford: Blackwell).

Van Moorst, H. (1982), 'Leisure and Social Theory', *Leisure Studies*, 2: 157–69.

Veal, A. J. (1989), 'Leisure, Lifestyle and Status: a Pluralist Framework for Analysis', *Leisure Studies*, 8(2): 141–54.

Veblen, T. (1925), *The Theory of the Leisure Class* (London: Allen & Unwin).

Weber, M. (1918), 'Science as a Vocation' (129–58), in H. Gerth and C. Wright Mills (eds) (1948), *From Max Weber* (London: Routledge & Kegan Paul) pp. 129–58.

Wilensky, H. (1960), 'Work, Careers and Social Integration', *International Social Science Journal*, 4: 543–60.

_____ (1964), 'Mass Society and Mass Culture', *American Sociological Review*: 173–97.

Willis, P. (1978), *Profane Culture* (London: Routledge & Kegan Paul).

_____ (1990), *Common Culture* (Buckingham: Open University Press).

Wimbush, E. and Talbot, M. (eds) (1988), *Relative Freedoms* (Buckingham: Open University Press).

2 Drugs, Sport and Ideologies

IVAN WADDINGTON and PATRICK MURPHY

INTRODUCTION

In November 1989 Steve Pinsent, a British former Commonwealth Games weightlifting champion, was jailed for three months at Aylesbury Crown Court, near London, for supplying anabolic steroids. In passing sentence, Judge Morton Jack told Pinsent (*The Times,* 18 November 1989) that the use of drugs in sport to improve performances 'is an evil which is prevalent and growing'. Judge Jack's comment nicely points up two of the three interrelated issues which form the subject matter of this paper. The first of these concerns the question of whether the use of drugs in sport is indeed 'prevalent and growing'. The second problem to be examined arises from the fact that what is often described as 'drug abuse' in sport frequently arouses strong and immediate condemnation – as expressed, for example, in Judge Jack's use of the word 'evil' – and that this condemnation is frequently accompanied by demands for swingeing punishments, such as life bans, for athletes found guilty of using prohibited substances. But what is the basis of this opposition to the use of drugs in sport? In seeking to answer this apparently simple question, not from a moralistic but from a sociological perspective, we may be able to shed light on some aspects of the development and contemporary structure of modern sport. The third and final issue of this chapter is to examine some of the major processes, both within sport and within the structure of the wider society, which have been associated with the use of drugs in recent years. In this connection, particular attention will be focused on developments in, and changes in the inter-relationship between, sport and medicine.

THE EXTENT OF ILLICIT DRUG USE IN SPORT

The use by athletes of substances believed to have performance-enhancing qualities is certainly not a new phenomenon. At the Ancient Olympic Games and in Ancient Egypt athletes had special diets and ingested various substances believed to improve their physical capabilities, whilst Roman gladiators and knights in mediaeval jousts used stimulants after sustaining injury to enable them to continue in combat. In relation to modern sports, swimmers in the 1865 Amsterdam canal races were suspected of taking some form of dope, but the most widespread use of drugs in the late nineteenth century was probably associated with cycling, and most particularly with long distance or endurance events such as the six-day cycle races (Donahoe and Johnson, 1988: 2–3).

It is, of course, impossible to arrive at any very precise estimate of the extent of illicit drug use in contemporary sport for, since the use of many drugs is prohibited under the rules of the International Olympic Committee and other sporting bodies and since the possession of such drugs may also constitute a criminal offence, those who use performance-enhancing substances will almost inevitably seek to do so without being detected. Nevertheless, there are grounds for suggesting that the illicit use of drugs by athletes has increased very markedly in the post-war period and more particularly in the last three decades. This is certainly the view of Donahoe and Johnson who have suggested that the 'production of amphetamine-like stimulants in the thirties heralded a whole new era of doping in sport', and they go on to suggest that in recent times 'a massive acceleration in the incidence of doping in sport has occurred', a development which in their view is largely associated with further improvements in chemical technology (Donahoe and Johnson, 1988: 2, 4). Mottram (1988: 1–2) dates the increase in drug use from about the same time as Donahoe and Johnson and, perhaps not surprisingly since all three are pharmacists, he attributes it to largely the same causes. Thus he writes: 'Around the time of the Second World War, the development of amphetamine-like central stimulant drugs reached its peak. . . . Not surprising by the 1940s and 1950s amphetamines became the drugs of choice for athletes.' He goes on to claim that the 'widespread use of drugs in sport . . . began in the 1960s' and, like Donahoe and Johnson, he links this with the 'pharmacological revolution' of the 1960s which resulted in the development of more potent, more selective and less-toxic drugs.

Although we cannot know precisely how widespread the use of drugs is amongst sportsmen and -women, it is clear that many people with an intimate knowledge of sport – competitors, coaches, managers and others – are of the view that the use of drugs has increased to the point where it is now very widespread. Perhaps the most striking claim in this respect came from Dr William Standish, the chief physician to the Canadian Olympic team for the Seoul Olympics of 1988. Speaking a few months prior to the Games, Dr Standish (*The Times,* 7 April 1988) claimed that the ideal of a drug-free Olympic competition was no longer possible. He claimed: 'We have solid information that the use of drugs to enhance performance is really an epidemic. There is rampant use of anabolic steroids and other performance-enhancing drugs among young athletes. . . . I think we have to look at the traditional Olympic charter and understand that to have a clean Olympics is no longer possible.' John Goodbody, the sports correspondent of *The Times* and someone who has for several years campaigned against the use of drugs in sport, has claimed (*The Times,* 28 May 1987) that in weightlifting 'drug-taking has been notorious for years', and that it is now 'more than 20 years since anabolic steroids first became readily available in London gymnasia'. Goodbody also points out (*The Times,* 27 October 1988): 'Drug-taking in athletics is a widely recognised problem, and in the past 10 years dozens of athletes have been banned from the sport for it. Rumours are rife that many more athletes are taking drugs and that officials are conniving at the practice.' Giving evidence under oath to a Canadian government inquiry following the disqualification of the Canadian sprinter Ben Johnson at the Seoul Olympics, Johnson's coach Charlie Francis (*The Times,* 2 March 1989) said that the use of drugs in sport was pervasive and that the spiral of record-setting would be impossible without them. When he was chairman of the International Athletics Committee in 1985, Paul Dickenson (*The Times,* 18 November 1989), a hammer thrower who now works as an athletics reporter for BBC television, estimated that 'sixty per cent of the full range of international athletics events were likely to include some competitors who had taken drugs'.

Outside athletics there have been many drugs scandals involving other sports, with cycling in particular having what Goodbody has called a 'history of deceit'. In 1966 the first five men in the world road race championship all refused to take a drugs test: the five included Jacques Anquetil (*The Times,* 21 July 1988), five times winner of the Tour de France, who later admitted to taking stimulants and said: 'Everyone in cycling dopes himself and those who claim they do not are liars.'

Whilst many of the most famous drugs scandals – most notably, perhaps, the drugs-related death of the British cyclist Tommy Simpson in the 1967 Tour de France and more recently the disqualification of Ben Johnson at the 1988 Olympics – have involved Western competitors, there have also been persistent rumours for many years alleging the widespread use of drugs amongst East European athletes. Recent evidence from East European sources suggests that there may well be some substance to these rumours. For example, in June 1989 two East Germans, a former Olympic ski-jumping champion and a former sports official who defected separately to the West, claimed that all East Germans who competed for their country were using drugs. Hans-Juergen Noozenski (*The Times,* 27 June 1989), the former head of the East German Judo Association, claimed: 'Every athlete that competes internationally for East Germany is doped, every one.' More recently, Sergei Vachekovsky (Independent, 1 December 1989), the Soviet swimming head-coach from 1973 to 1982, has admitted that he personally administered drugs to his swimmers.

One should not, of course, accept without question all such allegations concerning the frequency of drug use in sport, particularly when they are made by people seeking to defend themselves against charges of doping, for such people might seek to exaggerate the degree of drug use in an attempt to mitigate their own offence, for example by claiming that what they did was only 'normal practice'. Nevertheless, it is suggested that allegations of the kind outlined above have to be given some credibility for a variety of reasons. The first of these relates to the sheer number of such allegations, those cited above constituting just a small proportion of the very many similar allegations which have been made in recent years. The second consideration relates to the fact that broadly similar allegations have come from a wide variety of sources – that is to say, from competitors, coaches, managers, doctors and sports commentators, from a wide variety of sports and from a number of different countries – and many of those who have made such allegations are widely respected both for their knowledge of sport and for their integrity; indeed, several of those who have made such allegations have been in the forefront of the campaign against the use of drugs in sport. The third and final consideration relates to relatively 'hard' evidence in the form of the results of testing for drug use by athletes.

At an international conference on doping in sport held in June 1989. Professor Raymond Brooks revealed that during 1987 he had tested a number of urine samples from sportsmen competing in Britain. The test was for a particular drug, human chorionic gonadotrophin (HCG), a hormone drug which raises the level of testosterone, so helping a competitor to recover more quickly from intensive exercise. HCG was not banned by the International Olympic Committee until 1989, and prior to this time there were reports that competitors stopped taking anabolic steroids a month before an event in order to avoid detection, and switched safely to HCG for the last few weeks of preparation. Professor Brooks indicated that, of 740 samples tested, 21 samples taken from thirteen sportsmen had proved positive. It should be emphasized that the test was not designed to identify a wide range of drugs but just HCG, and Professor Brooks concluded that the results of his tests indicated 'a very high rate of abuse of a single drug'.

Professor Arnold Beckett (*The Times*, 7 June 1989), a leading member of the IOC medical commission concurred, arguing that 'According to these facts . . . then at least in the UK there is a serious problem'.

On an international level, the most recent large-scale testing for drug use by athletes came at the 1988 Seoul Olympic Games. The most celebrated drugs scandal at the Games was, of course, that involving Ben Johnson who was disqualified after failing a drugs test following his victory in the 100 metres. In addition to Johnson, nine other competitors were banned during the Games for taking drugs. Clearly, however, these ten represented only the tip of a much larger iceberg. Before the start of the Games, four Canadian weightlifters were pulled out because they were found to have taken anabolic steroids, whilst three more weightlifters, two from Egypt and one from Iraq, were also found positive in the random pre-Games testing. In addition, three Tunisians refused to undergo tests. In the Games themselves, two Bulgarian gold-medal-winning weightlifters were disqualified, following which the whole of the Bulgarian team – the premier force in the sport in recent years – was withdrawn. Following these events, the International Weightlifting Federation announced that it was to launch its own investigation into drug-taking in an attempt to restore the credibility of the sport (*The Times*, 26 September and 3 October 1988).

Further evidence that illicit drug use was much more widespread than the ten suspensions during the Games would suggest came from research involving the retesting of urine samples taken from 1100 male competitors at the Games. The retesting was carried out some time after the Games by Professor Manfred Donike, one of the world's leading authorities on drug abuse, and the results, which were accepted by the IOC medical commission, indicated that more than 50 competitors had used anabolic steroids during training. No action could be taken against the athletes concerned because the names identifying the athletes' samples are destroyed after the Games (*The Times*, 28 August 1989).

Although none of this evidence is sufficiently conclusive to enable us to make very precise statements about trends in, and current levels of, illicit drug use in sport, the evidence does strongly suggest, first, that there has been a significant increase in the level of drug use particularly in the last three decades or so; and second, that the illicit use of drugs is now by no means uncommon; indeed there is no reason to disagree with Professor Beckett's view that the use of drugs is now sufficiently common for it to constitute a 'serious problem'.

THE ACHIEVEMENT OF PROBLEM STATUS

The characterization of illicit drug use in sport as a 'serious problem' does however immediately raise the question of why the use of drugs to enhance sporting performance is seen as a 'problem'. Speaking at the Olympic Congress in 1981, Sebastian Coe, the 1500 metres gold medallist in the 1980 Games, said: 'We consider this [doping] to be the most shameful abuse of the Olympic ideal: we call for the life ban of offending athletes; we call for the life ban of coaches and the so-called doctors who administer this evil' (see Donahoe and Johnson, 1988: 1). Why should the use of drugs evoke from many people within the world of sport such strong condemnation, coupled with demands for swingeing punishments for those found to be using drugs?

The two most usual grounds for objecting to the use of drugs in sport are clearly set out in a leaflet entitled *Doping Control in Sport: Questions and Answers,* published in Britain by the Sports Council in 1987. In this leaflet, the Sports Council set out their objections to the use of drugs in the following terms:

> Drugs and other substances are now being taken not for the purposes they were intended [sic], but simply to attempt to enhance performances in sport. It puts the health of the athlete at risk. *It can be dangerous.* It undermines the foundation of fair competition. *It is cheating.* (Italics in original)

The position could hardly be stated more clearly. The Sports Council is opposed to the use of drugs, first, because it may be damaging to health, and secondly, because it is a form of cheating. It may be useful to consider each of these objections in turn.

The first objection – that the use of drugs may be harmful to health – is considerably elaborated in another, undated, leaflet produced by the Sports Council, entitled *Dying to Win.* The leaflet contains on the front cover a health warning reminiscent of the government health warning on cigarette packets: 'Warning by the Sports Council: taking drugs can seriously damage your health'. The leaflet details some of the side-effects which, it claims, are associated with the use of stimulants, narcotic analgesics and anabolic steroids, and refers on several occasions to the possibility of death as a result of drug abuse. The leaflet concludes by advising coaches, teachers and parents to 'warn athletes of the great dangers of these drugs. . . . Tell them that by taking drugs, what they would be doing would literally be DYING TO WIN.'

It might be noted that bodies such as the Sports Council have recently been accused of exaggerating the health risks associated with drugs such as anabolic steroids (*The Times,* 18 September 1987). However, it is not our intention to become embroiled in this debate. Our concerns are sociological rather than pharmacological and, as such, our aim here is not to evaluate the validity of these pharmacological arguments about drugs and health but to locate that debate within the context of broader social processes.

That at least part of the objection to the use of drugs should rest upon grounds of health is, perhaps, not altogether surprising, for as Goudsblom (1986: 181) has pointed out: 'in the twentieth century, concern with physical health has apparently become so overriding that considerations of hygiene have gained pride of place among the reasons given for a variety of rules of conduct'. Moreover, this is the case even where – as is by no means uncommon – those rules had, at least in the first instance, little or nothing to do with considerations of health. This point may, perhaps, be most clearly illustrated by reference to the work of Norbert Elias on which Goudsblom has drawn.

In *The Civilizing Process* Elias analyzes the development and elaboration over several centuries of a variety of rules of conduct relating to bodily functions such as eating, drinking, nose-blowing and spitting. In relation to the way in which such bodily functions are managed, Mennell has noted that, since the way in which these functions are performed clearly has important implications for health, there is a tendency on our part to assume that these functions must have been regulated largely in the interests of health and hygiene. As Mennell (1986: 46) puts it, to

the modern mind it seems obvious that considerations of hygiene must have played an important part in bringing about higher standards. Surely the fear of the spread of infection must have been decisive, particularly in regard to changing attitudes towards the natural functions, nose-blowing and spitting, but also in aspects of table manners such as putting a licked spoon back into the common bowl?

In fact, however, as Elias (1978: 115–16) demonstrates, a major part of the controls which people have come to impose upon themselves has not the slightest connection with 'hygiene', but is concerned primarily with what Elias calls 'delicacy of feeling'. Elias's argument is that over a long period and in conjunction with specific changes in human relationships, the structure of our emotions, our sensitivity – our sense of shame and delicacy – also changes, and these changes are associated with the elaboration of controls over the way in which bodily functions are carried out. It is only at a later date that these new codes of conduct are recognized as 'hygienically correct', though this recognition may then provide an additional justification for the further elaboration or consolidation of these rules of conduct.

In many respects Elias's analysis provides a good starting point for a re-examination of the debate about sport, drugs and health. Could it be that what Elias argues in relation to codes of conduct relating to such things as nose-blowing or spitting or washing one's hands is, at least in some respects, also applicable to a rather different set of rules of conduct, namely, those relating to the use of drugs in sport? In other words, is the ban on the use of certain drugs in sport based primarily on a concern for the long-term health of athletes? Or is it the case that the arguments about health are essentially secondary or supporting arguments which, because of the cultural status of medicine and the value generally placed upon health, lend particularly useful support to a code of conduct which is based primarily on considerations having little, if anything, to do with health? We do not claim to be able to provide a definitive answer to this problem. However, a preliminary exploration of this question is worthwhile, not least because it raises a number of other interesting problems concerning the relationship between sport and health.

THE LIMITS OF THE HEALTHY BODY ETHOS

If the concern for health constitutes the principal objection to the use of drugs in sport, then we might reasonably expect a similar concern for health to inform other aspects of the organization of sport. Is this in fact what we find? It is undoubtedly the case that, at least at an ideological level, there is a strong link between sport and health. The idea that sport is health-promoting and even life-enhancing is one which is frequently stressed by those involved in sport – to quote Sebastian Coe (foreword to Mottram, 1988): 'Sport is an integral part of a healthy lifestyle in today's society.' Though the ideology linking sport and health is a very powerful one – and one which is probably widely accepted – an examination of certain aspects of the organization of sport casts some doubt on the assumed closeness of the relationship between sport and the promotion of healthy life-styles. From amongst several relevant features of modern sport which could be examined, we limit ourselves, for reasons of space, to just two: namely, sponsorship in sport and the widespread but legal use of drugs for the management of sports-related conditions.

Perhaps the area which casts doubt most publicly on the assumed relationship between sport and the promotion of healthy life-styles is that of sports sponsorship. In the 1970s overall business sponsorship of sport and the arts in Britain grew at around 20 per cent a year, from £15 million in 1973 to over £50 million by 1981. Roughly 90 per cent was spent on sports and the rest on the arts, with the tobacco companies being by far the biggest spenders (Taylor, 1985: 99). Sports sponsorship is a relatively cheap and highly cost-effective means of advertising for the tobacco companies, not least because in Britain it enables them to circumvent the 1965 ban on the advertising of cigarettes on television; in 1981 three of the four top sporting events which gained most television exposure were sponsored by tobacco companies, these being the Embassy and State Express snooker tournaments and John Player cricket (Taylor, 1985: 103). Sponsorship of sporting events by tobacco companies is now very widespread; amongst the sports sponsored in Britain are motor racing, powerboat racing, cricket, speedway, snooker, darts, bowls, horseracing, tennis, rugby union, rugby league, badminton, show-jumping, motor-cycling and table-tennis.

Sponsorship of sporting events by the tobacco companies is, of course, not confined to Britain. In 1982 Dr Thomas Dadour introduced in the Western Australian Parliament a bill to ban all forms of cigarette advertising and promotion. Had the bill been passed, one of the first casualties would have been the advertising at the Australia versus England Test Match, which was sponsored by Benson and Hedges who have been the Australian Cricket Board's main sponsor for more than ten years. The bill was narrowly defeated. The following year, the state government of Western Australia introduced another bill similar to Dr Dadour's. This bill was also defeated following intensive lobbying by, amongst others, those associated with the cigarette-sponsored sports under threat (Taylor, 1985: 48–9).

Such sponsorship would not, at least in the context of the present argument, be of any significance were it not for the fact that, by the early 1980s, cigarette smoking was estimated to be responsible for more than 300,000 premature deaths a year in the US, and nearly half a million deaths a year in Europe. In a 1982 report the US Surgeon-General described cigarette smoking as 'the chief, single, avoidable cause of death in our society, and the most important public health issue of our time', whilst in Britain the Royal College of Physicians, in their 1971 report *Smoking and Health Now* referred to the annual death-rate caused by cigarette smoking as 'the present holocaust' (Taylor, 1985: xiv, xvii). Without labouring the point, one might reasonably suggest that the ideology which associates sport with healthy life-styles sits uneasily with the widespread acceptance of sports sponsorship by tobacco companies.

The issue of whether the banning of certain drugs in sport reflects a primary concern with health issues may, however, be approached rather more directly. In particular, a brief examination of the use of several drugs which are not banned and which are widely used in the treatment or management of sports-related conditions is quite revealing.

One of the most common sights in many sports is that of the trainer running on to the field of play to treat an injured player, often by the application of an aerosol spray to a painful area, thereby enabling the player to continue. However, as Donahoe and Johnson (1988: 94) point out, one of the functions of pain is to '"warn" us that we need to rest the damaged area', and they suggest that most athletes and coaches 'fail to recognize the damage that can be caused by suppressing pain'. This issue is part of the more general concern about overuse injuries, a growing problem which is clearly associated with the increasing constraints placed upon sportsmen and women to compete and more particularly to win with, one suspects, often scant concern for the potential longer-term health risks. It has been noted (Donahoe and Johnson, 1988: 93) that, 'To succeed in modern sport, athletes are forced to train longer, harder, and earlier in life. They may be rewarded by faster times, better performances and increased fitness, but there is a price to pay for such intense training.' Part of the price of such intense training and of the readiness – often encouraged by coaches and medical advisers – to continue training and competing despite injury, is unquestionably paid in the form of overuse injuries, which are now a serious problem. It should also be noted that, as Donahoe and Johnson (1988: 93) point out, the 'long-term effects of overuse injuries are not known, but some concerned doctors have asked whether today's gold medallists could be crippled by arthritis by the age of 30', and they cite examples of world-class competitors who have, in their words, 'been plagued by a succession of overuse injuries'.

It is, however, not simply the problem of overuse injuries which is of relevance. Since, as we have seen, part of the case against the use of drugs such as anabolic steroids rests on the possible health risks associated with those drugs, it is of some interest to note that several drugs which are very widely – though perfectly legally – used within sport also have a variety of potentially serious side-effects. Prominent amongst these drugs are several painkillers. Injections of local anaesthetic drugs, for example, can produce cardiac disorders and should not be used 'on the field'. In very large doses they cause central nervous system stimulation, convulsions and death. The IOC permits the use of local anaesthetics only where there is 'medical justification' – by which is presumably meant only where there is an injury which would otherwise prevent a competitor from taking part – and 'only with the aim of enabling the athlete to continue competing' (Donahoe and Johnson, 1988: 95). One might reasonably ask whether these regulations express a primary concern for the health of the athlete or whether considerations relating to the value of competition are ranked more highly?

Several painkilling drugs which are widely used for the treatment of sports injuries are known to have a variety of side-effects, with prolonged use leading to possible gastrointestinal effects such as ulceration or perforation of the stomach or intestines, whilst diarrhoea is a commonly reported side-effect. In addition to effects on the liver and blood cells, they also affect the central nervous system causing headaches, dizziness or disorientation. Most concern has, perhaps, been expressed about the use of phenylbutazone, commonly known as 'bute'. Introduced in 1949 for the treatment of arthritis, phenylbutazone is a powerful anti-inflammatory drug which has a large number of toxic side-effects, some of which have had fatal outcomes. The most serious side-effects are the retention of fluid, which in predisposed individuals may precipitate cardiac failure, and interference with normal blood cell production most commonly resulting in aplastic anaemia and agranulocytosis which can occur within the first few days of treatment. A Washington consumer group recently called for bans on phenylbutazone and another anti-inflammatory drug, oxyphenbutazone, claiming that their side-effects may have led to 10,000 deaths worldwide. Many physicians argue that phenylbutazone is too dangerous to use for the treatment of self limiting musculoskeletal disorders, and in Britain it is now indicated only for use in hospitals under careful supervision. However, in the US it is still widely used in the sports context to reduce pain and swelling in joints and ligaments, most notably in the National Football League (Donahoe and Johnson, 1988: 97; Elliott, 1988: 103). Phenylbutazone is not on the list of drugs banned by the IOC.

From what has been said it is clear that, whilst there may indeed be potentially dangerous side-effects associated with the use of certain banned drugs, much the same may also said about many drugs which are not banned and which are widely used within the sporting context. The fact that several potentially dangerous drugs are used perfectly legally within sport suggests that – whatever the ideological rhetoric linking sport and health – considerations of health may not constitute the primary basis underlying the decision to ban certain drugs but not others. To return to the question raised earlier, could it be the case that health considerations – though they may not be entirely irrelevant – provide a convenient and useful but essentially secondary justification for a ban which rests primarily on other values having little or nothing to do with health? If this is the case, then what might these other values be?

'FAIR PLAY' VERSUS 'CHEATING'

It will be recalled that the Sports Council, in the leaflet cited earlier, give a second reason for their opposition to the use of drugs, namely, that using drugs 'undermines the foundation of fair competition'. In a word, it is cheating, and it is this, we suggest, rather than a concern for health, which constitutes the primary objection to the use of drugs. That this is so is suggested by the relatively tolerant attitude taken by many sporting bodies towards the 'social' use of drugs such as marijuana and cocaine, the latter of which may have potentially dangerous side-effects and both of which – unlike many of the drugs banned by the IOC – are illegal in many countries.

Let us consider first the case of marijuana. Prior to the Seoul Olympic Games the IOC was asked by several countries to test for marijuana 'to see whether there was a problem among top-class competitors'. A small number of competitors were found to have smoked marijuana recently. The possession of marijuana is a criminal offence in Korea, but the names of the athletes involved were not released because cannabis is not banned by the IOC. In the words of the president of the IOC's medical commission: 'Marijuana does not affect sporting performance.' A similar position was expressed by Professor Arnold Beckett (*The Times,* 14 September 1988), another leading member of the IOC medical commission, who argued that 'If we started looking at the social aspect of drug-taking then we would not be doing our job.'[1]

Some sporting bodies – it should be noted that not all sporting bodies have the same rules in this respect – appear to have taken a similar position in relation to the use of cocaine which, though technically a stimulant and therefore on the list of drugs banned by the IOC, is also very widely used for 'recreational' purposes. It is presumably the latter consideration which has led the tennis authorities at the Wimbledon Championships to adopt a relatively tolerant attitude towards tennis players found to be using cocaine. Thus in 1986 it was revealed (see *The Times,* 14 September 1988) that tests for cocaine were to be carried out on male tennis players at Wimbleton, although no action would be taken against those who tested positive; instead, psychiatric help would be offered.

What we are suggesting, therefore, is that the major basis of differentiation between those drugs which are banned and those which are not banned is to be found not in the fact that the former pose a threat to health whilst the latter do not – such an argument, we would suggest, is exceedingly difficult to sustain – but in the fact that the former are perceived as being taken in order artificially to boost performance, thereby giving the competitor who uses drugs an unfair advantage over those who do not. The more fundamental objection to the use of drugs, then, lies in the fact that, in the words of the Sports Council, 'it is cheating'.

But why should the practice of cheating be regarded as so objectionable? Why should drug-taking evoke calls for swingeing punishments against those who are tested positive? At first glance the answer may seem self-evident, for such is the strength of feeling against cheating that we might be tempted to think that the idea of cheating 'naturally' arouses strong hostility. The matter is, however, considerably more complex than this, for an analysis of the development of the concept of cheating and of the associated notion of 'fair play' raises some interesting questions about the civilizing process and the development of modern sport.

It is essential to see the development of concepts such as 'cheating' and 'fair play' as an integral part of the development of a broader configuration of relationships. More specifically the development of these concepts – at least in the sense in which they are used within modern sport – can be seen as part of that process which Elias has termed 'sportization'. Though the concept of 'sportization' may jar upon the ear it does, as Elias notes, fit the observable facts relating to the development of modern sports quite well. Elias's (1986: 151) argument is that, in the course of the nineteenth century – and in some cases as early as the second half of the eighteenth century – with England as the model-setting country, some leisure activities involving bodily exertion assumed the structural characteristics which we identify with modern sports. A central part of this 'sportization' process involved the development of a stricter framework of rules governing sporting competition. Thus the rules became more precise, more explicit and more differentiated whilst, at the same time, supervision of the observance of those rules became more efficient; hence, penalties for offences against the rules became less escapable. One of the central objectives – perhaps *the* central objective – of this tightening up of the rules was to ensure that sporting competitions were carried on with proper regard for what we call 'fairness', the most important element of which is probably the idea that all competitors must have an equal chance of winning.[2] As part of the 'sportization' process, the idea of 'fairness' – and therefore the abhorrence of cheating – has come to be regarded as perhaps the most fundamental value underpinning modern sporting competitions. In this context one might, for example, compare the relatively highly rule-governed character of modern sports with the relative absence of rules governing many traditional folk-games in pre-industrial Europe, many of which had few, if any, rules governing such things as physical contact or even the number of players permitted on each side (Dunning and Sheard, 1979: ch. 1). The importance of the sportization process and its relationship to the concept of cheating may be brought out very simply: where there are no rules one cannot cheat. The development of the concept of cheating, therefore, is closely associated with the development of a body of relatively clearly defined rules; in this sense, the development of our modern concepts of 'cheating' and of 'fair play' can only be adequately understood as part of the sportization process to which Elias has drawn our attention.

Thus far we have examined some of the evidence relating to the use of drugs in sport, and we have considered some of the social processes underpinning specific objections to the illicit use of drugs. We now turn to our third and final problem; namely, how do we account for what, as we noted earlier, does indeed appear to have been a significant increase in the use of drugs in sport in recent years? In order to shed some light on this issue, it is necessary to examine recent developments not merely in sport but also in medicine. We begin with the latter.

THE MEDICALIZATION OF LIFE

In an influential essay published in 1972, Irving Zola (1972: 487) argued that in modern industrial societies medicine is becoming a major institution of social control. This process, he argued, was a largely insidious and often undramatic one which was associated with the 'medicalizing' of much of daily living, a process which involves 'making medicine and the labels 'healthy' and 'ill' *relevant* to an ever increasing part of human existence'. The medicalization process has involved an expansion of the number and range of human conditions which are held to constitute 'medical problems', a label which, once attached, is sufficient to justify medical intervention. Zola cites four such problems: ageing, drug addition, alcoholism and pregnancy, the first and last of which were once regarded as normal processes and the middle two as human foibles and weaknesses. This has now changed and medical specialities have emerged to deal with these conditions, one consequence of which has been to expand very considerably the number of people deemed to be in need of medical services. A similar process has occurred as a result of the development of 'comprehensive' and psycho-somatic medicine, both of which have considerably expanded that which is held to be relevant to the understanding, treatment and prevention of disease. The development of preventive medicine, in particular, has justified increasing medical intervention in an attempt to change people's lifestyles, whether in the areas of diet, sleep, work, marital relationships, exercise, tobacco and alcohol consumption, or in the areas of safer driving or the fluoridation of water supplies.

The theme of the medicalization of life has subsequently been taken up by a number of other writers. Waitzkin and Waterman (1974: 86–9), for example, have attempted to analyze this process in terms of what they call 'medical imperialism'. However, perhaps the most famous thesis of this kind is that associated with Ivan Illich. Illich argues that the medicalization of life involves a number of processes, including growing dependence on professionally provided care, growing dependence on drugs, medicalization of the life-span, medicalization of prevention and medicalization of the expectations of lay people. One of the consequences has been the creation of 'patient majorities' for, argues Illich (1975: 56), people 'who are free of therapy-oriented labels have become the exception'. Large numbers of people are now regarded as requiring routine medical attention, not because they have any definable pathology, but 'for the simple fact that they are unborn, newborn, infants, in their climacteric, or old' (Illich, 1975: 44). In other words, the expansion of that which is deemed to fall within the province of medicine has expanded to the point where, as de Swaan (1988: 243) puts it, 'there remain only patients and those not yet patients'.

Although several of those involved in developing the medicalization thesis have made some pertinent observations on recent social developments relating to medicine, it is probably fair to say that, on the whole, these analyses have not involved a great deal of theoretical sophistication, whilst some – the work of Waitzkin and Waterman and, even more so, that of Illich comes to mind here – are notable for their polemical character and their relative lack of detachment. The early essay of Zola (1972: 487) is in many respects more satisfactory, though it is largely descriptive, and his analysis of the process – that it 'is rooted in our increasingly complex technological and bureaucratic system' – is too vague to be of any real value. In this respect, we would suggest that de Swaan's work, which draws upon the work of Elias, is particularly valuable. Specifically we would argue that it is his use of an Eliasian framework which enables de Swaan to make a series of relatively precise and very fruitful connections between the medicalization process – or what he calls the reluctant imperialism of the medical profession and the collectivizing of welfare services, state forma- tion and development and the civilizing process. Though we cannot here enter into a detailed consideration of de Swaan's work – this would take us on a lengthy detour away from the main subject matter of this chapter – we suggest that de Swaan's analysis offers considerably more, by way of explanatory purchase, than do the other approaches outlined above, and that it provides further evidence of the fruitfulness of an Eliasian approach.

It is an important part of our argument that, particularly in the last three decades or so – very roughly, the period coinciding with the most rapid growth in the illicit use of drugs – the medicalization process has encompassed sport. This process has been most evident in the rapid development, particularly since the early 1960s, of what is now called sports medicine, an area of practice which has been described by two of the leading British exponents (Williams and Sperryn, 1976: ix) as 'an integrated multidisciplinary field embracing the relevant areas of clinical medicine (sports traumatology, the medicine of sport and sports psychiatry) and the appropriate allied scientific disciplines (including physiology, psychology and biomechanics)'.

Some of the processes involved in the medicalization of sport – and in particular the development of an ideology justifying increasing medical intervention – can be illustrated by reference to textbooks in the area of sports medicine. This ideology is clearly expressed in one of the early British texts in the field – J. G. P. Williams's *Sports Medicine,* published in 1962 – in which the author argues that the intensity and diversity of modern competitive sport 'has resulted in the emergence from the general mass of the population of a new type of person – the trained athlete'. Williams goes on to argue – some may feel not very convincingly – that the trained athlete 'is as different physiologically and psychologically from "the man in the street" as is the chronic invalid'. This argument is, however, important in establishing a justification for medical intervention, for he goes on to suggest: 'Just as extreme youth and senility produce peculiar medical problems, so too does extreme physical fitness' (Williams, 1962: vii). One can see here the development of the idea, now very widespread, that athletes require routine medical supervision not because they necessarily have any clearly defined pathology but, in this case, simply because they are athletes. This position is, in fact, spelt out quite unambiguously in the foreword to Williams's book by Arthur (later Lord) Porritt, who was at that time the president of the Royal College of Surgeons of England and the chairman of the British Association of Sport and Medicine. Porritt's (in Williams, 1962: v) position could hardly have constituted a clearer statement of what is involved in the medicalization process, for he argued quite baldly that 'those who take part in sport and play games are essentially patients'. Athletes have thus become yet one more group to add to Illich's list of those – the unborn, newborn, infants and so on – who are held *by definition* to require routine medical supervision, irrespective of the presence or absence of any specific pathology.

One consequence of the development in recent years of the discipline of sports medicine, and of closely associated disciplines such as exercise physiology, biomechanics and sports psychology, has been to make traditional methods of training for sporting events increasingly outmoded. At least at the higher levels of sport, both amateur and professional, the image of the dedicated athlete training alone or with one or two chosen friends no longer corresponds to reality. Instead, the modern successful athlete is likely to be surrounded by – or at least to have access to – and to be increasingly dependent upon, a whole group of specialist advisers, including specialists in sports medicine. Moreover, this dependence on those who practise sports medicine goes far beyond the treatment of sports injuries; as Williams and Sperryn (1976: 1) point out, as 'practice for the competitive event takes place . . . sportsman [sic] seeks systematic methods of preparation. He examines such technical and scientific information as is available about the way his body performs its athletic function and turns to the doctor as physiologist.' One consequence of these developments has been to make top-class athletes more and more dependent on increasingly sophisticated systems of medical support in their efforts to run faster, to jump further or to compete more effectively in their chosen sport. As the former Amateur Athletics Association national coach, Ron Pickering, notes in his foreword to Sperryn's *Sport and Medicine* (1983: vi), few would deny that 'nowadays medical support is essential for the realization of the athlete's natural capacity for optimum performance'; indeed, at the highest levels of competition the quality of the medical support may make the difference between success and failure. Just how sophisticated modern systems of medical back-up have become is illustrated by Pickering's admittedly tongue-in-cheek comparison between the limited amount of scientific knowledge which was available to coaches at the start of his career and the vast amount of knowledge which has subsequently been gained from experiments on athletes 'who have given blood, sweat, urine, muscle biopsies and personality inventories, have often been immersed in tanks, and photographed naked in three dimensions at altitude'.

It would, however, be quite wrong to suggest that athletes are simply unwilling 'victims' of medical imperialism for, as de Swaan (1988: 246) has noted, professionals – in this instance, doctors – 'do not simply force themselves with innocent and unknowing clients'. In the case of sport, a number of developments, particularly in the post-Second World War period, have led sportsmen and -women increasingly to turn for help to anyone who can hold out the promise of improving their level of performance. The most important of these developments are probably those which have been associated with the politicization of sport, particularly at the international level, and those which have been associated with massive increases in the rewards – particularly, but not exclusively, the material rewards – brought by sporting success. Both these processes, it is suggested, have had the consequence of increasing the competitiveness of sport, and one aspect of this increasing competitiveness has been the downgrading, in relative terms, of the traditional value associated with taking part whilst greatly increasing the value attached to winning.

Although the trend towards the increasing competitiveness of sport has been particularly marked in the post-1945 period, the trend itself is a very much longer-trend which can be traced back over two or more centuries and which has been associated with the processes of industrialization and state development. Before we examine the relatively recent developments associated with the politicization and commercialization of sport, it may be useful to outline briefly the social roots of this longer-term trend towards the increasing competitiveness of sport or, what is the same thing, towards the 'de-amateurization' of sport.

THE 'DE-AMATEURIZATION' OF SPORT

The long-term trend towards the increasing competitiveness of sport is a good example of what Elias (1987: 99–100) calls a 'blind' or 'unplanned' long-term social process; that is, this trend is not the intended outcome of the acts of any single individual or group but, rather, the unintended outcome of the interweaving of the purposive and often conflictual actions of the members of many interdependent groups over several generations. In his analysis of the 'de-amateurization' of sport, Dunning (1986: 205–23), drawing upon an earlier paper by Elias and himself (Elias and Dunning, 1966), argues that the overall social figuration of pre-industrial Britain was not conducive to the generation of intense competitive pressure in sporting relations. The relatively low degree of state centralization and national unification, for example, meant that 'folk-games', the games of the ordinary people, were played in regional isolation, competition traditionally occurring between adjacent villages and towns or between sections of towns. There was no national competitive framework. The aristocracy and gentry formed a partial exception in this respect for they were, and perceived themselves as, national classes and did compete nationally among themselves. However, their high degree of status security – that is, their power and relative autonomy – meant that the aristocracy and gentry were not subject, in a general or a sporting sense, to effective competitive pressure either from above or below. As a result, the aristocracy and gentry, whether playing by themselves or with their hirelings, were able to develop what were to a high degree self-directed or egocentric forms of sports participation; put more simply, they were able to participate in sport primarily for fun and, in this sense, came close to being amateurs in the 'ideal-typical' sense of that term.

Dunning argues that the growing competitiveness of sporting relations since the eighteenth century has been associated with the development of the pattern of inter-group relationships characteristic of an urban-industrial nation-state. Inherent in the modern structure of social interdependencies, he suggests, is the demand for inter-regional and representative sport. Clearly no such demand could arise in pre-industrial societies because the lack of effective national unification and poor means of transport meant that there were no common rules and no means by which sportsmen from different areas could be brought together. In addition, the 'localism' inherent in such societies meant that play-groups perceived as potential rivals only those groups with which they were contiguous in a geographical sense. However, modern industrial societies are different on all these counts. They are relatively unified nationally, have superior means of transport and communication, sports with common rules, and a degree of 'cosmopolitanism' which means that local groups are anxious to compete against groups which are not geographically contiguous. Hence such societies come to be characterized by high rates of inter-area sporting interaction, a process which leads to a hierarchical grading of sportsmen, sportswomen and sports teams with those that represent the largest social units standing at the top.

Dunning suggests that one consequence of these processes is that top-level sportsmen and -women are less and less able to be independent and to play for fun, and are increasingly required to be other-directed and serious in their approach to sport. That is, they are less able to play for themselves and are increasingly constrained to represent wider social units such as cities, counties and countries. As such, they are provided with material and other rewards and facilities and time for training. In return, they are expected to produce high-quality sports performances which, particularly through the achievement of sporting victories, reflect favourably on the social units which they represent. The development of the local, national and international competitive framework of modern sport works in the same direction and means that constant practice and training are increasingly necessary in order to reach and to stay at the top. In all these ways, then, the social figuration characteristic of an urban-industrial nation-state increasingly undermines the amateur ethos, with its stress on sport 'for fun', and leads to its replacement by more serious and more competitive forms of sporting participation.

THE POLITICIZATION OF SPORT

Although the relationship between politics and sport is by no means exclusively a post-World War Two phenomenon – witness the Munich Olympics of 1936 – there can be little doubt that sport has become increasingly politicized in the period since 1945. To some extent, this process has perhaps been associated with the development of independent nation-states in Black Africa and elsewhere and with the emergence in many of those states of several outstanding athletes whose international successes have been a major source of pride in new nations struggling to establish a national identity and a sense of national unity.

Of rather greater importance, however, was the development – although they have recently begun to change in fundamental but as yet uncertain ways – of state socialist societies in many parts of Eastern Europe and, associated with this, the emergence of the Cold War and of superpower rivalry. Within this context, international sporting competition took on a significance going far beyond the bounds of sport itself, for sport – at least within the context of East–West relations – became to some extent an extension of the political, military and economic competition which characterized relationships between the superpowers and their associated blocs. Thus comparisons of the number of Olympic medals won by the United States and the Soviet Union or the medals won by the two Germanies took on a new significance, for the winning of medals came to be seen as a symbol not only of national pride but also of the superiority of one political system over another. As many governments came to see international sporting success as an important propaganda weapon in the East–West struggle, so those athletes who emerged as winners came increasingly to be treated as national heroes with rewards – sometimes provided by national governments – to match.

SPORT AND COMMERCIALIZATION

If the politicization of sport has been associated with an increase in the competitiveness of international sport, this latter development has also been facilitated by the growing commercialization of sport in the West. Whilst the winning of an Olympic medal has doubtless been considered a great honour ever since the modern Olympics were founded in 1896, it is indisputably the case that in recent years the non-honorific rewards – and in particular the financial rewards – associated with Olympic success have increased massively. For example, successful athletes are not only in a position to demand substantial appearance fees for competing in major meetings but, much more importantly, they can also earn huge incomes from sponsorship, from television commercials and from product endorsement. Although this development appears to be a fairly general one within Western societies, the financial rewards associated with Olympic success are probably greatest in the United States. Dr Robert Voy ('On the Line', 1990) the chief physician to the US team at the 1988 Seoul Olympics, recently estimated that in the US the average Olympic gold medal was worth around $1 million in sponsorship, television advertisements and product promotion. He went on to point out, however, that such fabulous rewards are available only to those who come first for, as he put it, 'second place doesn't count'.

As the rewards to be gained from sporting success have increased, so the emphasis placed on winning has also increased. This process has, according to the leading US athletics coach, Brooks Johnson ('On the Line', 1990), resulted in a situation in which many top-class international athletes 'wake up with the desire and the need and the compulsion and the obsession to win, and they go to sleep with it. . . . Make no mistake about it, an Olympic champion is clinically sick.' A not-dissimilar point has been made by Angella Issajenko, a world-record-holder over 50 metres indoors who, like Ben Johnson, was coached by Charlie Francis and who, also like Johnson, has recently admitted to taking steroids. Issajenko (*The Times*, 14 March 1989) said she took the decision to use steroids after being beaten by East German sprinters and, in explaining her decision ('On the Line', 1990), she said that most people 'had no idea of what goes on in the mind of an elite athlete. Nobody wants to be mediocre. Nobody wants to be second best.'

The importance which has become attached to winning was particularly clearly expressed in an interview with Zoe Warwicke, a former British bodybuilding champion, following the disqualification of Ben Johnson at the Seoul Olympics. Although bodybuilding is not officially recognized as a sport, it may be regarded as a sport-like activity which has much in common with sport, not least, it would seem, in terms of the importance attached to winning. Commenting on Johnson's disqualification, Warwicke (*The Times*, 29 September 1988), who admits to having used anabolic steroids, said: 'I am not going to say whether Johnson did right or wrong. He did what he thought was necessary to win for both his country and himself and I empathize with that.' Speaking of her own use of steroids, Ms Warwicke, who is reported to suffer from kidney and liver disorders as a result of her use of the drugs, said that she does not regret taking them and would do so again under medical supervision for 'that one moment of glory, that feeling of being blessed all athletes seek'. The experience of winning was, she said, 'the best high you can have in life. The moment I won the national championship elevated me into something else for ten minutes or so. Just to win made it worth all the pain.' Warwicke almost certainly echoed the sentiment of a great many athletes when she said: 'I would not want to compete unless I had a chance of winning', and she went on to suggest: 'What we are asking athletes to do is very unfair. We are asking them to get slapped for being clean and losing. No one remembers losers even if they were clean of drugs.'

THE SPORT/MEDICINE AXIS

At this stage it might be useful to summarize briefly our argument thus far. We have suggested that what appears to be a significant increase in the illicit use of drugs in recent years has been associated with two major processes. The first of these relates to what has been called the 'medicalization of life' or 'medical imperialism', whilst the second relates to the increasing competitiveness of sport and to a growing emphasis on the importance of winning. More specifically, it is suggested that certain developments within the medical profession have meant that medical practitioners have been increasingly prepared to make their professional knowledge and skills available to athletes at the very time when athletes, as a result of other developments within sport, have been increasingly eager to seek the help of anyone who can improve the level of their performance. The conjuncture of these two processes, it is suggested, has been associated with two closely related developments. One of these developments – and one which is generally viewed as wholly legitimate – involves the emergence of sports medicine; the other – which is normally regarded as illegitimate – involves the increasing use by athletes of banned substances to improve their per-formance. The close association between these two developments has been clearly noted by Brown and Benner (1984: 32), who have pointed out that, as increased importance has been placed on winning, so athletes have turned to mechanical (exercise, massage), nutritional (vitamins, minerals), psychological (discipline, transcendental meditation), and pharmacological (medicines, drugs) methods to increase their advantage over opponents in competition. A major emphasis has been placed on the nonmedical use of drugs, particularly anabolic steroids, central nervous system stimulants, depressants and analgesics.

In other words, the very processes which have been associated with the development of sports medicine have also been associated with a rapid growth in the illicit use of drugs. The relation between illicit drug use and processes of medicalization has also been noted by Donahoe and Johnson (1988: 126–7):

> we live in a drug-oriented society. Drugs are used to soothe pain, relieve anxiety, help us to sleep, keep us awake, lose or gain weight. For many problems, people rely on drugs rather than seeking alternative coping strategies. It is not surprising that athletes should adopt similar attitudes.

It should be noted, that since our analysis stresses the conjuncture of these two processes, one within the world of medicine and the other within the world of sport, it follows that the increasing use of drugs in sport cannot be explained simply by reference to the changing patterns of behaviour amongst athletes. Indeed, we would suggest that the increasing use of drugs has been associated with the emergence, in both the world of sport and the world of medicine, of those who may be described as innovators or entrepreneurs. Referring first to the world of sport, it is hardly surprising that, given the increased emphasis which has come to be placed on winning, some athletes – and almost certainly a growing number – have been prepared to innovate by making illicit use of the fruits of medical and pharmacological research, or by themselves acting as 'brokers' who provide these fruits for others. Equally, however, it is a clear implication of the above analysis that there are doctors – and again the probability is that their number is growing – who may be regarded as medical 'entrepreneurs' in the sense that they are prepared to stretch the boundaries of 'sports medicine' to include the prescribing of drugs with the specific intention of improving athletic performance.

This point is of some importance for it suggests that the increasing use of drugs in sport has been associated with the development of a network of co-operative relationships between innovators or entrepreneurs from the two increasingly closely related fields of sport and medicine. In this respect, our analysis is rather different from that of some other writers. Goodbody (*The Times*, 27 May 1987), for example, has argued:

> Each generation of competitors uses the experience of its predecessors to find new illegal methods of improving performances. Each generation of administrators and doctors tries to stop every loophole, extend the number of banned drugs and become more sophisticated in its testing and trapping of offenders.

We would suggest that Goodbody's argument is far too simplistic, primarily because it posits an unreal dichotomy or opposition between two groups – competitors and doctors – one of whom, it is suggested, seeks to use and the other to prevent the use of illicit drugs. As indicated above, we would argue in marked contradistinction to Goodbody, that all too frequently the illicit use of drugs is actually premissed upon a significant degree of co-operation between 'innovating' athletes and 'entrepreneurial' doctors. There are, we believe, good grounds in support of this contention.

Donahoe and Johnson (1988: 62), in a phrase which is reminiscent of Goodbody's argument, have suggested: 'Athletes are enterprising people; as soon as detection methods are developed for one anabolic agent they move on to another.' No doubt there are many athletes who are indeed enterprising people, though one might reasonably doubt whether many of them are sufficiently well-informed about recent developments in medicine and pharmacology to devise their own drug programmes – and more particularly, to avoid detection, as many undoubtedly do – without professional advice. In this context, it is worth noting that many drug regimens, such as those involving 'stacking', are very complex. 'Stacking' is a technique which is particularly used by weightlifters and involves the use of several different types of anabolic steroid concurrently. A typical 'stacking' programme has been described as follows (Donahoe and Johnson, 1988: 46):

> The athlete may start a drugs programme by using a low dose of an oral anabolic steroid. The dose would be increased after a week or so and supplemented with a weekly injection of one of the long-acting steroids such as nandrolone decanoate. Over the next few weeks, the doses and frequency of these treatments would be increased. A month before competition, the athlete might be taking about ten times the therapeutic dose of oral steroids, plus about six or eight times the therapeutic dose of injectable long-acting steroids. In an attempt to avoid detection, for the few weeks prior to competition the synthetic drugs would be dropped, to be replaced by testosterone.

Without overstating the argument, it seems improbable that complex drug programmes of this kind have been worked out by the athletes themselves, without access to specialized advice, whilst it seems even more improbable that athletes have the specialized technical knowledge required to avoid detection, for this necessarily involves keeping one step ahead of what are becoming increasingly sophisticated testing procedures.

The case of so-called 'blood-doping' provides another instance of a form of cheating in which the critical technological breakthrough, as well as the administration of the treatment, clearly involves medical personnel. Blood-doping involves the removal of a few hundred millilitres of blood which is stored for a few weeks and then reinfused into the athlete, a process which boosts the oxygen-carrying capacity of the blood, and thus the quantity of oxygen available to the muscles. This process once again points to a significant degree of co-operation between competitors and doctors for, as Donahoe and Johnson (1988: 119) note, blood-doping 'obviously requires the aid and skills of medical staff'.

In addition to the above considerations, there is also a good deal of direct evidence relating to the involvement of doctors in the use of drugs in sport. We now know, for example, that for several years prior to his disqualification at the Seoul Olympics, Ben Johnson had been taking anabolic steroids under the direction of his physician, Dr Mario Astaphan. Giving evidence under oath to a Canadian government inquiry, Astaphan (*The Times*, 26 May 1989) claimed that 32 athletes representing twelve countries and several sports had sought his help. Such examples of medical involvement in the use of drugs are not difficult to find. Dr Robert Kerr, a Los Angeles physician whose surgery is said to have become a 'takeaway for Olympic athletes', has claimed that in the Los Angeles area alone there are between 60 and 70 doctors who prescribe steroids for athletes ('On the Line', 1990). There is also evidence that at the Los Angeles Olympics of 1984 at least some team doctors were involved in blatantly exploiting a loophole in the doping regulations. Although beta-blockers were not at that time banned by the IOC, team doctors had to fill in declarations for all athletes using beta-blockers and state the doses used. If competitors produced a doctor's certificate stating that they needed the drugs for health reasons, they would not be disqualified if drug checks proved positive. However, when urine specimens were screened there were several positives in the modern pentathlon contest. To the amazement of officials, team managers came forward with doctors' certificates covering *whole teams*. In October 1984 Colonel Willy Grut, the secretary-general of the world body governing the modern pentathlon, challenged the IOC to reveal the names of those athletes who 'clearly took dope, not for medical reasons, but to improve performance'

(Donahoe and Johnson, 1988: 85–6). What is of importance in the context of the present argument is not the fact that these athletes took drugs but that the drugs appear to have been taken with the knowledge of team doctors who then protected the athletes against disciplinary action.

Such examples are not, of course, confined to the Olympic Games or to Olympic sports. One of the most celebrated cases in the US involved an eminent psychiatrist, Dr Arnold Mandell. Mandell was the founding chairperson of the Department of Psychiatry at San Diego, is a recognized expert on neurochemistry, is the recipient of millions of dollars in research grants and is the author of several books and hundreds of scientific papers. Mandell also worked with the San Diego Chargers in the National Football League. In 1974 he was dismissed after the NFL accused him of giving the team 1750 amphetamine pills over a three-month period. Mandell conceded that he wrote very large prescriptions and subsequently carried out research on amphetamine use by NFL players; in September 1978 at a national conference on amphetamine use he presented a paper called 'The Sunday Syndrome', in which he claimed that players typically took a high dose of amphetamines once a week during the game on Sunday (Donahoe and Johnson, 1988: 28–9).

Several other examples implicating doctors in the non-medical use of drugs could be cited from athletics, cycling and association football (Donahoe and Johnson, 1988: 161; *The Times*, 18 October 1982). These cases all come from Western Europe, but it seems probable that in Eastern Europe the medical profession is even more closely involved in the illicit use of drugs in sport than is the case in the West. There are, as we noted earlier, many allegations concerning the organized abuse of steroids, particularly in East Germany, some of them based on information from international athletes who have defected to the West. There is at least one advantage to what seems to be 'official' involvement in the use of drugs: it does mean that the athletes concerned do at least get regular and systematic medical monitoring. As Donahoe and Johnson (1988: 69) note: 'While official involvement in doping is often attacked as state control by Western critics, and certainly cannot be condoned, there are probably many American or European athletes who would welcome the medical backup that accompanies tacit state approval of drug abuse.'

CONCLUSION

In this chapter we have suggested that if, as seems probable, sportsmen and -women have in recent years increasingly turned to the illicit use of drugs, then this development can only be adequately understood by analyzing the changing network of relationships in which they are involved. In this regard, we have suggested that, as a result of changes within the structure of sport – changes associated particularly with structurally generated competitive pressures and with political and commercial developments – the pressure on sportsmen and -women to win, and the rewards of winning, have greatly increased. As a consequence, sportsmen and -women have increasingly been prepared to turn to a variety of specialists able to hold out the promise of helping competitors to improve the level of their performance. These developments within the structure of sport have coincided with another, largely autonomous development – the medicalization process – which has involved the extension of medical intervention into more and more areas of social life and which, particularly from the early 1960s, has increasingly involved doctors in the systematic use of medical and pharmacological developments in an effort to improve sporting performances. These developments have resulted in a coming together of two groups, sportspeople and doctors, one of whom has increasingly demanded, and the other of whom has increasingly been prepared to supply, specialist medical advice in the search for improved performances. The conjuncture of these developments in sport and in medicine has had two closely related consequences, one of which is normally seen as legitimate, the other as illegitimate. Thus it is suggested that the increasing competitiveness of sport and the medicalization process have been associated, on the one hand, with the rapid development of sports medicine, but that these very processes have also been associated, on the other hand, with the increasing use of prescribed drugs.

This analysis thus suggests that the increased use of drugs in sport in recent years is a process which is closely interrelated with a number of other major processes of social change on both the national and international levels. If this is indeed the case, it suggests that, for as long as those broader processes of change continue on their present lines of development, then the constraints on sportsmen and -women to use drugs illicitly may also continue to grow. If this proves to be the case, and if those sportspeople who use drugs are able to continue to rely on the network of co-operative relationships with those whom we have described as 'entrepreneurial' doctors, then the illicit use of drugs in sport may well prove extremely difficult to control.

Notes

1. It should be noted that since this chapter was written the IOC has added marijuana to the list of banned drugs, not because it affects sporting performance but on the grounds that it is apparently held to be 'damaging to youth and a threat to world peace'. This decision is not consistent with the earlier position taken by the IOC and it is difficult to see it as anything other than part of a 'moral panic' associated with an attempt to 'clean up' the image of athletics, particularly in the wake of the Ben Johnson affair. See *The European,* 8–10 June 1990.
2. We are aware of the fact that the idea of 'fairness' is one which, in practice, is imperfectly applied. The reality of the upper levels of sporting competition is that it often involves individuals or teams which are highly differentiated in terms of their access to resources and support systems.

References

Brown, T. C. and Benner, C. (1984), 'The Nonmedical Use of Drugs' in W. N. Scott, B. Nisonson and J. A. Nicholas (eds), *Principles of Sports Medicine* (Baltimore, Md, and London: Williams and Wilkins).

De Swaan, A. (1988), *In the Care of the State: Health Care, Education and Welfare in Europe and the USA in the Modern Era* (Cambridge: Polity Press).

Donohoe, T. and Johnson, N. (1988), *Foul Play: Drug Abuse in Sports* (Oxford: Basil Blackwell).

Dunning, E. (1986), 'The Dynamics of Modern Sport: Notes on Achievement-Striving and the Social Significance of Sport', in N. Elias and E. Dunning, *Quest for Excitement* (Oxford: Basil Blackwell) pp. 205–23.

_____ and Sheard, K. (1979), *Barbarians, Gentlemen and Players* (Oxford: Martin Robertson).

Elias, N. (1978), *The Civilizing Process* (Oxford: Basil Blackwell).

_____ (1986), 'An Essay on Sport and Violence', in N. Elias and E. Dunning, *Quest for Excitement* (Oxford: Basil Blackwell).

_____ (1987), *Involvement and Detachment* (Oxford: Basil Blackwell).

_____ and Dunning, E. (1966), 'Dynamics of Sports Groups with Special Reference to Football', *British Journal of Sociology,* 17(4): 388–402. Also in Elias and Dunning (1986), *Quest for Excitement* (Oxford: Basil Blackwell).

Elliott, P. N. C. (1988), 'Drug Treatment of Inflammation in Sports Injuries', in D. R. Mottram (ed.) *Drugs in Sport* (London: E. & F. N. Spon).

Goudsblom, J. (1986), 'Public Health and the Civilizing Process', *Millbank Quarterly,* 64(2): 181.

Illich, I. (1975): *Medical Nemesis* (London: Calder & Boyars).

Mennell, S. (1989), *Norbert Elias: Civilization and the Human Self-Image* (Oxford: Basil Blackwell).

Mottram, D. R. (1988), 'Introduction: Drugs and their Use in Sport', in D. R. Mottram (ed.), *Drugs in Sport* (London: E. & F. N. Spon).

On the Line, 'Drugs, Lies and Finishing Tape' (1990), BBC2 TV, 24 January.

Sperryn, P. N. (1983), *Sport and Medicine* (London: Butterworth).

Taylor, P. (1985), *The Smoke Ring* (London: Sphere Books).

Waitzkin, H. B. and Waterman, B. (1974), *The Exploitation of Illness in Capitalist Society* (New York: Bobbs-Merrill).

Williams, J. G. P. (1962), *Sports Medicine* (London: Edward Arnold).

_____ and Sperryn, P. N. (eds) (1976), *Sports Medicine*, 2nd edn (London: Edward Arnold).

Zola, I. K. (1972), 'Medicine as an Institution of Social Control', *Sociological Review*, n.s. 4: 487.

3 Cleaning up the Game: Perspectives on the Evolution of Professional Sports

JOHN WILSON

This essay considers the grounds for claiming that figurational sociology provides a distinctive and innovative perspective on sport. After a brief review of the general theory of societal development formulated by Norbert Elias, the relation of that theory to those formulated by Marx and Durkheim is described. I argue that there is much of Marx in the figurational account of societal development. However, there is much more of Durkheim, a fact I seek to demonstrate by examining the concept of 'interdependency' and its relation to the evolution of codes of conduct. I then describe a competing theory of the history of manners which, I believe, provides a more accurate picture of the civilizing process, at least as it is found in the United States today. This competing theory attaches more significance than does figurational sociology to the peculiar 'logic' of capitalism. The increasing regulation of play, I contend, does not so much represent the permeation of courtly values as the imposition of a rationality upon play such as to make it amenable to commodification. Codes of conduct are thus interpretable as a means of imposing order upon activities and thus excluding from those activities elements of conduct which would disturb exchange relations. These elements include communal and democratic impulses. To explore these themes I examine the rise of the 'commissioner system' in American team sports. This system of private government introduced an extra note of 'civility' into the conduct of commercial sports, closely regulating all aspects of the game that might impugn its 'integrity', such as violence, gambling and cheating, and could therefore be seen, from the point of view of figurational sociology, as an 'evolution' in the social organization of the game. Figurational sociology accounts for the emergence of this new governance structure only partially, however, and a political-economy perspective must be used to explain its timing and function. The commissioner system was to be expected under the 'franchise' government which had formed since the turn of the century as a way of dealing with the conflicting demands of economic freedom for business and political sub-ordination for workers. Democratic rights could be legitimately denied in the interest of economic progress.

The events upon which I have chosen to focus are particularly well-suited to an examination of Elias's theory of sports development because they revolve around the issue of gambling. Elias's writings are most often associated with a description of breaches in civility which do not have strong connotations of moral culpability. Their range is limited to what is considered 'bad form'. However, figurational sociologists have made serious efforts to extend the reach of the theory to account for developments in the interpretation and treatment of what we can only consider vices, such as drunken brawling at soccer matches and destruction of public property; acts, that is, for which people should be held morally accountable. But, as shown in the case of the disorderly behaviour of sporting crowds, the line between mere incivility and shocking vice is difficult to draw in real life. Gambling sits astride this line, for it is characteristically viewed with ambivalence, a person enjoying it and deploring it at the same time. Controlling gambling in association with sporting events is, in one sense, simply 'playing fair'; it is also, in another sense, a means of eliminating vice and organized crime.

THE CIVILIZING PROCESS

The figurational sociology of sport is part of a larger theory of social development formulated by Norbert Elias (1982: 236), who sees human history as the story of a more or less continuous

> moderation of spontaneous emotions, the tempering of affects, the exten-sion of mental space beyond the moment into the past and future, the habit of connecting events in terms of chains of cause and effect – all these are different aspects of the same transformation of conduct which necessarily takes place with the monopolization of physical violence, and the lengthening of the chains of social action and interdependence. It is a 'civilizing' change of behaviour.

With increasing structural differentiation, people who were formerly in-dependent of each other become more and more dependent and are thus forced to curb their desires and instincts. 'As more and more people must attune their conduct to that of others, the web of actions must be organized more and more strictly and accurately, if each individual action is to fulfill its social function' (Elias, 1982: 232). A world where other people are likely to be dangerous predators gives way to a world where other people are dependent on each other. At first, close surveillance and retributive punishment are necessary to curb conduct, but self-control gradually becomes more deeply internalized, lessening the need for external constraint. It might be noted here that the theory simply predicts that the *standards* of violence-control will become stricter. It is a moot point whether actual rates of violence will fall, although the implication is that the standards and their sanctions will have the desired effect.

The civilizing process is also the result of the growing monopolization of force held by the central authority, which attempts to insure that conflict within its own domain will be expressed through peaceful forms. 'Physical violence is confined to barracks' (Elias, 1982: 238). Thus, for example, during the eighteenth century the 'cycle of violence' that had characterized the previous century 'gradually calmed down and political conflicts came to be conducted more in terms of a set of non-violent rules and rituals, the rules and rituals of Parliament' (Dunning, 1989: 45). The self-same ruling groups simultaneously devised means for reducing the violence of their pastimes; for example, fox-hunting become more 'civilized' in that the hunters no longer killed the fox themselves nor used the carcass for food.

Rules of conduct are set by powerful élites. They are 'the principal standard-setting groups . . . from whom standards have subsequently diffused' (Dunning, 1989: 43). The 'strict code of manners' promulgated by the élite is a prestige symbol, 'but it is also an instrument of power' (Elias, 1982: 313). Political rule, wherever it occurs, requires a 'civilization of the colonized'. Codes of conduct are thus a clue to the 'fears' and 'anxieties' of 'the custodians' of a society's 'precepts'. Writing in the 1930s, Elias (1982: 329) explains how the middle class of that time lived among 'tensions and entanglements', 'a mounting work pressure and also a profound insecurity which never ceases'. This condition gives rise to 'fear of dismissal, of unpredictable exposure to those in power, of falling below the subsistence level, of loss of prestige and status', fears which 'are particularly disposed to internalization'. Elias (1982: 330) associates the rules imposed on sexual life and the 'automatic anxieties' now surrounding the erotic sphere with 'the fear of losing opportunities or possessions and prestige, of social degradation, of reduced chances in the harsh struggle of life'.

Over the course of social development, the transmission of codes from the élites to the lower orders changes as the division of labour and interdependence become more extensive: 'everywhere small leading groups are affected first, and then broader and broader strata of Western society'

(Elias, 1982: 248). Civilization thereby spreads 'outward' with democratization as élites come to constitute a larger proportion of the general population. Although the *History of Manners* (the first volume of Elias's *Civilizing Process*) describes a unilinear trend toward 'more civilized' societies, there is nothing in the logic of the theory that would deny 'decivilizing spurts' and 'counter civilizing developments', when the trend toward state monopoly, increasing differentiation, or social levelling reverses itself.

FIGURATIONAL SOCIOLOGY AND MARXISM

The relation of figurational sociology to both Marxism and Durkheimian sociology is of considerable interest and has generated much debate. In this part of the essay I should like to position figurational sociology, with an eye to gauging its possibilities for making a distinct contribution to the sociology of sport.

Figurational sociology is structural but sets itself off from Marxism, which is also structural, because of the latter's belief in the primacy of the mode of production. Unfortunately, this effort to carve out a perspective on social development distinct from Marxism is not altogether successful. One reason for this is that the figurationists' efforts to avoid what they see as 'single cause' explanations for social development result in a 'vacuous interactionalism', where 'everything is as important as everything else'. Dunning's (1986b: 11) answer to this criticism is to assert that 'the question of relative importance is an empirical issue' (Dunning, 1986b: 11). This is not, however, a theory of society at all, merely a conceptual mapping replete with methodological exhortations to observe process and watch interaction. As a result, I believe, real theories are smuggled in when actual research problems are dealt with. I shall illustrate this below.

A second reason why I find figurationists' efforts to position themselves with respect to historical materialism unsatisfactory is that their portrayal of it is a caricature, a highly simplistic vision of society which figurationism can then repair. The result, however, is considerable overlap between the real Marxism and the theory presented by Elias and his colleagues. Marxists need to be told, it appears, that 'the economic sphere and the mode of production are manifestly not the same in all types of social figuration'; and that the 'political' and the 'religious' spheres vary in their relative autonomy from epoch to epoch. Marxists are also reminded that they should not treat 'particular societies as if they existed on their own and developed solely according to their own endogenous dynamics'.

It would consume too much space to refute each of these notions in sufficient detail. However, a cursory glance at Marxist sociology would be enough to remind the reader that the crux of the theory is precisely that 'the mode of production' will not be the same in each social formation. Furthermore, each social formation will contain several modes of production, although one will tend to dominate: 'real capitalist societies always contain subordinate modes of production other than the capitalist mode of production itself' (Wright, 1978: 74). It will also reveal that Marxist sociology rejects a mechanistic notion of economic determinism: Marx notes in *Capital* that there will be 'infinite variations and gradations in appearance, which can be ascertained only by analysis of the empirically given circumstances' occasioned by the interplay of 'natural environment', 'racial relations' and 'external historical influences' and the mode of production. As Miliband (1977: 8) suggests in connection with the passage just quoted, the mode of production must be treated as 'a starting point', and not that to which all other aspects of society should be 'reduced'. Furthermore, Marxist sociology recognizes that the 'autonomy' of institutions such as politics and religion from the economic base will vary historically. One problem here seems to be a too-narrow definition of economics on the part of figurationists. Marx's political economy sees economic elements as pervaded by political, social and even religious elements. If the entire mode of production gives an economic cast to the materialist view of history, it is because it is organized around the overriding necessity of production, not because economic motives or activities dominate all others. Finally, an inspection of Marxist sociology, dating back to the writings of Hilferding and Luxemburg, would reveal the considerable amount of attention paid to the process of the internationalization of capital and its consequences for developed and underdeveloped societies.

The point of these remarks is not to try to demonstrate that Marxist sociology is better than figurational sociology. Quite the contrary; for a recognition of the true character of Marxist sociology and of figurational sociology reveals how much overlap there is between these two approaches. When Maguire (1986: 219), in his figurational study of football spectating, argues 'that social processes are structural and . . . their structure is an unplanned consequence of the interweaving of the intended acts of innumerable interdependent individuals', he does not distinguish himself from the structuralism at the heart of Marxism. Marxism's 'relational' approach to classes is also replicated in Elias's (1982: 289) contention that codes of conduct 'do not "originate" in one class or another, but arise in conjunction with the tensions *between* different functional groups in a social field and *between* the competing groups within them'. When Maguire goes on to add that 'Critical in this regard . . . are the ways in which the structurally generated balance of power between groups creates pressures and constraints on people to modify their behaviour', he is saying no more and no less than would Marx or the current generation of 'critical theorists'. Compare, for example, Whitson's (1989: 60) assertion that 'leisure practices are always historical products, whose specific character has consistently reflected the power of dominant élites to establish their own practices as norms, while proscribing or taming practices they consider threatening'.

Maguire traces variation in the 'respectability' of football crowds between 1880 and 1985. Until the First World War the middle class was very concerned about the rowdy behaviour of football crowds and considered many means for bringing these crowds under control. Spectating was perceived to be both morally and physically debilitating. Maguire attributes this to the growing militancy of the working class and the beginning of a loss of status on the part of the middle class, increasing the amount of tension between them. Between the wars 'the crowds appear to have grown more "respectable"'. With a lessening of class anxiety bourgeois values spread throughout society as a whole. The implication here is that the working class were rendered passive and quiescent by the Depression (not mentioned) and the hegemony of the middle class was reasserted. After 1945 a process of *embourgeoisement* divided the working class. The more affluent portion adopted a more 'privatized and individualistic outlook' and largely ceased attending soccer matches. They reacted in a manner not unlike the late-Victorian middle classes to the increasing attendance at matches of those working-class groups excluded from the benefits of the post-war boom (Maguire, 1986: 233). Class tension was once again heightened and with it a preoccupation with rules of conduct among spectators as they became, once more, disrespectable.

This account of the history of football spectating, reproduced in *The Roots of Football Hooliganism* (Dunning *et al.*, 1988), is plausible and convincing, but what unique insight has the figurational perspective contributed to it? Marxist and Weberian accounts of sport all acknowledge the role class plays in determining the appropriateness of pastimes. No other groups are identified by Maguire. Marxists, in particular, would wish to draw attention to resistance to middle-class efforts to colonize the leisure of the working class in the interest of 'decency' and 'order'. Maguire (1986: 220) likewise acknowledges that the working class 'sought to retain their traditional codes of conduct' and notes that they were particularly successful in doing this where they could easily escape surveillance, in the 'less gregarious, more privatized forms'.

Dunning and Sheard's (1979: 279) story of the evolution of rugby, football and the different path taken by soccer, also uses class analysis. Rugby split openly and formally into amateur and professional organizations while soccer did so much less cleanly and formally. One reason is that, while soccer began to professionalize in the 1880s, rugby's professionalization was postponed until the 1890s: the 1880s were a decade of relative peace in the class struggle, while the 1890s were less so. A second reason is that soccer was run by aristocrats secure in their status and relatively tolerant of the working-class professional; rugby was run by regional élites and upper-middle-class men less sure of their superiority over the working man.

The overlap between figurational sociology and Marxist analysis is the more pronounced because, despite the fact that Elias (1982: 315) believes that the 'class model is too narrow; one needs a broader concept to deal with the varieties of group oppression and group rise', it is not clear what groups he has in mind other than social classes. It is well known that he developed his own conceptual distinction between 'established' and 'outsiders' as a substitute for class analysis; but that conceptual scheme is so abstract as to be meaningless – and useless – for research. Thus, although Elias himself has maintained that by 'groups' he does not merely mean classes, his followers usually do.

Only more recently has gender been identified as another axis of tension. In his article 'Sport as a Male Preserve' Dunning (1986a: 80) describes the interdependency between men and women as being one in which the 'balance of power' favours men because of their superior physical strength and women's incapacitation during pregnancy. This theory he attributes to Elias and contrasts it with that of 'those Marxists who would attribute the *macho* complex largely to the demands and constraints of performing manual work'. Dunning goes on to argue that sports such as rugby developed and accrued their 'macho' rituals during a time when the balance of power between males and females was beginning to shift in the direction of the latter. He interlaces his argument with a class analysis: working-class men attending their football matches were less likely to degrade women because they were less fearful of losing status to them. This analysis is unobjection-able on the face of it. However, it is curious to find a figurationist publishing claims in the 1980s that place Elias at the forefront of writing on patriarchy. There is also, once again, a caricatured version of the Marxist analysis of the interplay of gender and class in the determination of social relationships (cf. Hartmann).

Despite these convergences between Marxism and figurational sociology, I do not wish to argue that they are identical. Take, for example, the sociology of time, a subject with which every sociologist of leisure must deal. Sociologists agree that the modern age stresses punctuality and synchronization, that the tempo of modern life is different from that found in pre-industrial societies. Elias, as we might imagine, traces the growing importance of synchronization to interdependence.

> This may show itself in the case of an official or businessman in the profusion of his appointments or meetings, and in that of a worker by the exact timing and duration of each of his movements; in both cases the tempo is an expression of the multitude of interdependent actions, of the length and density of the chains composed by the individual actions, and of the intensity of struggles that keep this whole interdependent network in motion.   (Elias, 1982: 248)

Apart from the hint delivered in the last clause of this sentence, there is no suggestion made in this account that the new tempo might be unequal in its effects, no glimpse of the class struggle over the definition, distribution, indeed the ownership of time which ensued with the advent of capitalism and the factory system. Therefore no glimpse of the class, and gendered, nature of the definition of 'free time' as leisure. Elias's description does not deny these facts, it simply fails to introduce them. There is fairly widespread agreement among historians (Cross, 1988) that rules governing use of free time, and therefore participation in sport, arose in conjunction with changes in the industrial and familial order which accompanied the rise of capitalism.

> The social integration of sport into the realm of necessity was itself a response to the great upsurge of rationalization in late capitalist society. That is, the rationalization of work, which emptied it of whatever charm it had by uncoupling thinking from doing; the rationalization of the family, which transformed it from refuge from economic reality to simply another vocational unit; the rationalization of politics, which undermined its communicative, consensual basis; and the rationalization of leisure, which denounced spontaneous expression in favor of the prudential (i.e. productive) use of free time, collectively created the need for diversions – for a release from the harsh effects of ubiquitous rationalization.   (Morgan, 1985: 66)

If, as Elias implies, civilization meant the segregation of playtime and worktime, then it did not result from 'interdependence' but was intended to permit work to go on uninterrupted. It follows that uncivilized behaviour remixes worktime and playtime. Thus, those who engage in 'schmoozing' (a Yiddish term whose basic meaning is 'nothing talk') at work, those workers who engage in idle gossip while on the job rather than waiting until their break, are disorderly. The 'schmoozers', on the other hand, are re-asserting a holistic definition of life that integrates worktime and playtime. 'Schmoozers' have no need for breaks.

FIGURATIONAL SOCIOLOGY AND DURKHEIM

I believe, then, that while there is more convergence between figurational sociology and Marxist sociology than is pretended by Elias and Dunning, some significant differences remain. This is because figurational socio-logists, despite their wish to distance themselves from his work also, are much closer to Durkheim than their claim to propound a new theory of societal development would lead one to expect. Elias, after all, sees the social relations of capitalism as simply an extension of the money economy, which lengthens the chain of human interdependency, reflecting a develop-mental tendency toward greater complexity and abstraction. This theory is very similar to that of Durkheim, who saw the division of labour, more broadly conceived as the differentiation of social functions, as resulting from morphological factors (changes in the size and density of the popula-tion), not from changes in the economic structure. Durkheim believed that a higher form of human community could be achieved if the various functions and the relations among them could be properly regulated and adjusted. This would require knowledge, patience and a moderation of appetites. Healthy adjustment requires self-mastery.

Figurational sociologists would be reluctant to accept this imputed kinship. They have dismissed Durkheim's vision of organic solidarity as 'Utopian' (Dunning and Sheard, 1979: 278). Dunning (1986b: 56) points out that the concept of interdependence 'is used in a nonharmonistic sense and without a connotation of equality; that is, interdependencies tend to involve a conflictual element and they can vary along a symmetry–asymmetry con-tinuum'. This disclaimer notwithstanding, the very same essay repeats the idea that the 'functional democratization' accompanying structural differ-entiation results in 'decreasing power-differentials within and among groups' and a society of 'multipolar controls'. The performers of specialized roles are dependent on others and can, therefore, 'exert reciprocal control'. In short, 'the division of labour exerts an equalizing or democratizing effect' (Dunning, 1986b: 53).

It is also worth pointing out here that Dunning (1986b: 54) subscribes to the view enunciated first by Durkheim and then by Parsons that the division of labour is associated with 'a tendency for roles to be allocated on the basis of achievement rather than ascription'. Parkin (1979: 71) tartly comments on this line of reasoning:

> For many sociologists it would seem that the shift from ascription to achievement values is tacitly understood as a mark of moral progress, heralding the arrival of the good society. But to refer to the reward system of modern capitalism as one stressing the virtues of individual achievement shows an alarming confusion of thought, by suggesting as it does that a fairly close relationship exists between the level of personal effort and the level of reward. Clearly, a girl from the black ghetto who succeeds via high school and college in becoming a junior school teacher will have demonstrated far more in the way of individual achievement and effort than, say, the son of a doctor who enters the medical profession. Yet every 'achieving society' will lavish more benefits and honours on the latter than on the former.

Not only do Durkheim, Parsons and Dunning underestimate the importance of a quasi-ascriptive credentialism in reproducing social inequalities, they also overlook the manner in which a sexual division of labour is replicated in the economic division of labour. When women become caught up in the increasing division of labour they are very likely to do the kinds of jobs they used to do at home, such as food preparation and service, cleaning of all kinds, caring for other people and so on. The division of labour does not abolish the connection between ascription and work but exploits it all the more efficiently. In the United States today, four categories of female workers (those in peripheral manufacturing industries, in retail trade, in clerical occupations, and in the health and educational sectors) account for 95 per cent of all female employment.

Figurationists might argue that further structural differentiation will eliminate these vestiges of ascription. Not only does this argument ignore the manner in which ascriptive criteria such as sex and race are used to put the division of labour into effect (less-skilled jobs can be created if there is a cheap, low-skilled labour force ready to fill them), it also overlooks the fact that no amount of functional specialization and rationalization of the division of labour will overcome the sexual division of labour in the family. The consequences of these debates for the sociology of sport are obvious. Sport has ostensibly banished ascription; but it is a sham meritocracy, where blacks and women were for many years excluded from participation altogether and where today they are confined to the most menial positions. Sport also continues to be governed by rules of conduct which privilege white males and make it difficult for other groups to be taken seriously as athletes.

Despite their disclaimers, then, figurationists use a functionalist theory of the division of labour very similar to that of Durkheim. They appear to confuse the social division of labour, the distribution of tasks, crafts or specialities of production throughout society with the division of labour in detail, the manufacturing division of labour. Specialization of occupational roles takes on very different forms if it occurs within an organization and under the control of others instead of among self-employed, autonomous actors. 'While the social division of labour subdivides society, the detailed division of labour subdivides humans' (Braverman, 1974: 73). The latter is inevitably hierarchical. The subdivision of humans does not simply occur as the result of the increasing density of society: 'in a society based upon the purchase and sale of labour power, dividing the craft cheapens its individual parts' (Braverman, 1974: 80). This in turn creates not equality, but a structure that polarizes those whose time is infinitely valuable and those whose time is worth almost nothing. Figurationists, however, insist on the power of density alone when explaining the popularity of sports like wrestling, football and boxing: given the size and complexity of modern states people find themselves in competition with adversaries whom, 'if they are aware of them at all, they recognize only dimly' (Dunning and Sheard, 1979: 276); the 'aggressive fantasies' stimulated by the resulting anxiety are acted out vicariously in 'the mimetic sphere'. It is the 'sheer number of people involved' in modern sport that leads to one of its most striking features: the 'high achievement-motivation, long-term planning, strict self-control and renunciation of short-term gratification'.

These undeniable trends are not, however, the result of increasing density. The rationalization of sports participation is the result of the commodification of the body and the logic of capitalist production. It has its analogue in the scientific management of the labour process. The division of labour alienates men from one another and from themselves; the division of labour creates a condition in which men are unfree, deformed mentally. The new 'affect economy' which rewards high achievement-motivation and strict self-control is the result, not of the gradual spread of court behaviour to wider and less exclusive circles as interdependency chains lengthen, but of a new mode of production which requires not only self-control and asceticism but also rationalization and the systematization of social relations in a way fundamentally different from the regulation of relations at court. This new epoch does indeed foster self-development, but it is a form of development restricted and distorted by the needs of capital. Only marketable skills are developed. Modern sports, indeed modern leisure in general, provide myriad ways in which people are exploited psychologically and emotionally as well as physically. Elias (1986: 23) acknowledges that modern competitive sport can lead to self-abuse through over-exertion, specialization and drug-abuse, but he sees this as an aberration, part of a 'long-term trend in the course of which the swing of the pendulum, instead of remaining moderate, sometimes reaches an extreme form'. It is curious that figurationists, who claim for their perspective a particular sensitivity to historical context, here ignore the historical specificity of the nature of the division of labour and write about it as if it were something that varies only in quantity and not quality. But the differentiation of structures in the interest of efficiency begs the question of whose efficiency is meant, for it is always bound up with specific preference structures and the power resources of the actors variously affected by differentiation.

In his later formulations of the figurational sociology of sport, Dunning (1986b: 47; 1988: 236) seems to want to acknowledge that, not only has the actual occurrence of violence in sport not fallen, but that violence can take many forms, such that Elias's theory might well account for the decrease of certain kinds but seems unable to account for the persistence, or increase, of others. Thus he distinguishes between 'affective' or 'expressive' and 'rational' or 'instrumental' violence. 'This distinction hinges on whether violence is rationally chosen as a means of securing the achievement of a given goal, or whether it is engaged in as an emotionally satisfying and pleasurable end in itself.' This quite Weberian notion is then tied to the Durkheimian distinction between mechanical and organic solidarity. Expressive violence is more characteristic of societies in which bonding is 'segmented'. Instrumental violence is more characteristic of societies in which bonding is 'functional'. The more differentiated societies, according to Dunning, generate intense competitive pressures. In the presence of a state that has monopolized the legitimate use of physical force, this competition 'generates a tendency for illegitimate violence and other forms of rule violation to be used rationally in specific social contexts, such as in highly competitive combat sports'. Rational violence is, presumably, more civilized in that it depends upon and calls for greater self-control foresight on the part of the individual. Leaving aside what this says about the concept of civilization, Dunning's modification of the theory, while perhaps phenomenologically accurate, does not meet the criticism that his theory of the causes and consequences of the division of labour is wrong. The concept of 'rational' violence brings the theory closer to that of Marx or Weber without, however, using their more plausible theories of the nature of the division of labour and its causes.

My argument against figurational sociology, then, does not hinge upon the notion that the division of labour has been increasing and that this has had an effect on ideas of the self and on codes of interpersonal conduct. This much is undeniable. Rather, I assert that the codes of conduct are shaped by a *capitalist* division of labour and by the subsumption of social relations to the logic of the commodity form. I can illustrate the difference this makes by drawing on the work of Richard Sennett. Like Elias, Sennett sees the modern world as one of increasing interdependence, but its chief result, for him, is to 'mystify' that world such that social relations become ideologically opaque.

At issue here is the image of modernity propounded by Durkheim as opposed to Marx. For the latter, the modern world brings not so much the solidarity of 'interdependence' as

a constant revolutionizing of production, the uninterrupted disturbance of all social relationships, everlasting uncertainty and agitation. . . . All fixed, frozen relationships . . . are swept away. . . . All that is solid melts away, all that is holy is profaned. . . .   (Marx, quoted in Berman, 1982: 95)

The result is an impersonal world, from which people flee into a private sphere, seeking solace in an ideology of intimacy: 'social relationships of all kinds are real, believable, and authentic the closer they approach the inner psychological concerns of each person' (Sennett, 1976: 259). In assuming that civilization will see people govern overt emotional display, Elias miscalculates the 'affect economy', for in the United States at least, 'warmth is our God'. As a consequence, he overlooks the profound political consequences of this ideology of intimacy, the way in which it transmutes political categories into psychological categories.

Sennett, describing the death of public culture, agrees with Elias that people have become fearful of betraying their emotions to others involuntarily, that people don a mask of self-control and circumspection. But he recognizes, as Elias does not, that we attempt to liberate ourselves from this repression not by challenging the conditions that cause it but by intensifying the terms of personality, by being more straight, open and authentic in our relationship with others. This recourse has consequences that are especially important for the sociologist of leisure. It means that we lose all self-distance and, with it, the ability to play. We cannot imagine playing with our environment because we have internalized it. 'This ability to play with social life depends on the existence of a dimension of society which stands apart from, at a distance from, intimate desire, need and identity' (Sennett, 1976: 267). The more people think their social position in life is a product of their personal qualities and abilities, the harder it is for them to conceive of changing that condition.

Dunning's theory of sport does not so much explain as replicate this ideology. In his view, sport is part of the private sphere, an escape that offers us mimetic excitement to compensate for its lack in everyday life, especially work. For its heavily male participants, sport also compensates for the loss of opportunities to express and validate masculine ideals of aggressiveness and physical prowess. Sport is thereby relegated to a secondary position in social life, much as religion might be were that portrayed solely as compensation for deprivation. What is lost is any prospect of sport leading to social change, or sport being an opportunity for groups to escape or overthrow the conditions which induce the need for compensation.

Sennett's theory of civilization, written from the Left and by a writer exposed to American codes of conduct, is thus almost exactly the opposite of Elias's, although their analyses of nineteenth-century developments are quite similar. Sennett believes that the interdependence of which Elias writes has indeed led to a refinement of manners, but this, in turn, has led to a flight into the private sphere and a denuding of the public sphere. The resulting effort to measure social reality in psychological terms actually robs society of its civility. If 'civility has as its aim the shielding of others from being burdened by oneself' and incivility is 'burdening others with oneself', then our age is less, not more, civil. The reason is that capitalism has robbed us of 'impersonal space', of a public sphere where people can be judged by their actions rather than their feelings (Sennett, 1976: 264). The public world is now one in which people encounter each other as buyers and sellers. The market has replaced the forum as the focus of public life. The shopping mall has replaced the town hall. Public life is treated as merely the pursuit of private gain. At the same time, the older conception of the public realm as a source of moral inspiration and enlightenment has disappeared. Conversely, capitalism's competitiveness impels us to believe that people will be fully human only at home, and we come to look upon the private sphere as the place where meaning truly resides in the revelation of one's innermost emotional secrets. This does not mean that the private sphere is a shelter, however, for when intimacy takes on unprecedented ethical importance, it becomes the object of the same attention formerly reserved for public life. The daily maintenance of life, formerly assigned to the household, is now an important object of public policy (Lasch, 1985).

THE POLITICAL ECONOMY OF SPORT

In this second part of the essay, I should like to point out some of the ways in which a sociological analysis of sport and leisure must address the issues raised by figurational sociologists. I would also like to argue, however, that their perspective does not focus sharply enough on the interplay of economic and political forces in the construction of modern leisure ideas and practices.

Sport and the Economy

Despite their voluminous writings on sport, figurational sociologists are curiously silent about the business of sport. For example, in his account of the evolution of the soccer crowd in England and increasing concerns among the middle class about its conduct, Maguire does not point out that the enemy of the middle-class reformers of the late Victorian and Edwardian era was not so much the working-class spectator as 'professionalism' or, more accurately, commercialism. The enemy, in other words, was another segment of the bourgeoisie, the entrepreneur anxious to exploit the interest of the working class in sports for the purposes of profit. Maguire (1986: 225) notes that the founder of the Football League, William McGregor, sprang to the defence of football against what he probably saw as old-fashioned critics. Maguire, in common with other figurationists, pays little attention to the capitalization of sport and the attendant changes in the economy – such as transportation and communications – which made the sports industry possible.

Figurational sociology is by no means ignorant of the impact of a different business ethos on sport rules. Dunning and Sheard (1979: 271) remark on the greater commercialization of sport in the United States and use class analysis to account for it: 'industrial capitalism in Britain developed within the framework of an established system of dominance by the aristocracy and gentry, whereas, in the United States, no serious or lasting barriers to the establishment of bourgeois dominance existed'. In this section, I should like to take this argument much further than they choose to do and argue that, to the extent that civilizational changes have occurred, they have done so in such a way as to make the activity more predictable and less offensive *for the purpose of sale*. This need not be consciously done. The marketplace has its own logic which rises above the interest of this or that person or group. What is good for General Motors probably *is* good for the country, so long as the general standard of living, people's employment prospects and the fiscal health of the state are tied to the profitability of major corporations.

It is the economic constraints of the market under the conditions of competitive capitalism that demand rationality and the control of instincts on the part of human beings. The terms of civilization are thus set by a capitalist logic, by capitalists seeking an orderly market, the exact meaning of this phrase depending on the activity in question, those participating in it, that fraction of capital most threatened and offended by it and the success with which capital can mobilize the forces of local and national states to see the activity as wrong. The introduction of weight classes into boxing, for example, might well coincide with the rise of greater sensitivity, but the cry went up for 'greater equality of chances' in boxing because managers desired to protect their investment, because customers expected to see their money's worth, and because most gamblers wanted a sporting chance.

Civilization, in the sense of orderliness, rationality and forward plan-ning, could mean a number of things in sport and leisure, but capitalism emphasizes one of them. It could mean that people at leisure are encouraged to think of themselves as 'members' with an active commitment to the institution which is run on their behalf and over which they exercise collective control; as 'customers' with some kind of contractual relationship with the provider of the leisure experience; or as 'consumers', who look to the institution to provide immediate satisfaction but have no commitment to it. Capitalism, of course, encourages people to adopt the third role. In this case the sanctions they possess are entirely negative – the option not to buy. Condemned to the role of consumer, individuals soon lose faith in their ability to judge, their sense of themselves as active forces. They will cease to be witnesses and become spectators (Sennett, 1976: 261). The logic of capitalism sees 'membership' as costly and inefficient, and is likely to encourage codes of conduct that inhibit 'membership'-type behaviour. Unbusinesslike conduct is not respectable conduct. Thus Clarke and Critcher (1985: 105) interpret the 'civilization' of the English public house, the modernization of the decor and interior layout, the standardization of beers offered for sale (touted as means of making the pub more respectable), as simply a means to yield additional profits by promising no surprises. This example suggests that, in the logic of the market place, 'uncivilized' be-haviour is a mismatch between producers, product and consumer.

The connection between a certain kind of civility and capitalism's rationality is revealed in the modern city and its efforts to deal with disorderly life. Urban planners, city officials and merchants have been for some time seeking to bring order to street life. Much of this effort focuses on leisure and sports. Parks have been built to encapsulate play, ordinances passed to regulate noise and obstruction of sidewalks. Buildings and thoroughfares have been designed to regulate the flow of traffic and prevent congestion and milling. Many of these efforts have been successful: the downtown areas of many American cities, at street level and especially after work is over, are barren of life.

William H. Whyte, in his book *City: Rediscovering the Center,* laments the decline of street entertainment, the phoney pitchmen for good causes, the three-card-monte players and their skills, the prostitutes and their pimps, the drug dealers, the actors. Most are students, unemployed actors and the like, working part-time for voluntary contributions. The street becomes a kind of disorderly vaudeville. There is 'lots of life to see'. According to Whyte, it is largely owing to the complaints of merchants that city councils have passed repressive ordinances against street entertainment. It is now legal only if not much noise is made, the sidewalk is not obstructed and there is no solicitation of money. Whyte comments on the oddity of these champions of the free marketplace being so opposed to the pure expression of it. The street performers are the true entrepreneurs, the true risk-takers, dwelling in a world of extreme uncertainty. It actually helps if the goods they sell are thought to be stolen.

Whyte puts forward the heretical idea that 'disorder' on the street, a 'lively street life', might even be good for the merchants' business, did they but know it. Of course, they themselves know little about street life and exaggerate its threat and chaos. It is of little comfort to them that the street people are very frequently recent immigrants or of 'strange ethnic stock'. To Whyte, street people are a harmless sign of urban vigour. Ironically, raids by the police help demonstrate this vitality, for they succeed in dissipating this threat only temporarily, frequently for no more than 20 minutes. Whyte reminds us that street entertainment has in the past been caused by the actions of the very city officials who now seek to exterminate it. The construction of faceless office buildings, complete with inutile plazas, left a vacuum that the vendors were quick to fill. Gone, too, are the low-priced delicatessens, the cafeterias with occasional music, the bars, the small theatres, the front stoops. The entertainers and hucksters, in a revenge of the street, restore disorder. Berman (1982: 318), following the same logic, calls for a halt to slum clearance, freeways, suburbs, parks and malls, all of which are more civilized but all of which equally impose a barren and inhuman order on city life and constitute barriers to face-to-face communication and communion.

Sport and the State

An important feature of the figurational sociology of sport is that civilization is made possible by the centralization of power, and particularly the monopolization of the legitimate use of physical force, in the hands of the state. The powerful state, in conjunction with the interdependencies created by structural differentiation, induces people to restrain their impulses and behave civilly toward each other. The role of the state is portrayed in neutral terms. Thus, Dunning (1986b: 54) believes that structural differentiation leads to increased rivalry and aggressiveness in social relations. However, in modern societies this 'cannot be expressed in the form of openly violent behaviour because the state effectively claims a monopoly on the right to use physical force'. The state does not directly control sport in this theory, but exercises its civilizing role indirectly. Thus, in the growth of modern rugby an important development is the legitimation not only of referees or umpires but also a governing body to set and oversee the rules, including eligibility to play.

Dunning cannot be unaware of the social determination of the state's powers and functions and must, therefore, have speculated on their effect on the structure of modern sport. But there is no development of this theme in the work of figurational sociology. How is control of sport shaped by the larger governmental unit within which it must operate? To what degree does a theory that anticipates the centralization of fiscal and physical power in the hands of the state and the increasing division of labour in society explain the modern governance of sport?

One immediate problem is that figurational sociology has no theory of the state as such. We are simply led to assume that population growth and the growing division of labour will be accompanied by the growth of the state. Nothing is said about which groups in society might play the major role in forming the state and filling its positions: nothing is said about the state being structurally or politically beholden to one group or another. Nothing is therefore said about the state perhaps seeing some acts as disorderly and others not; or being more severe on some kinds of disorder than others.

The perspective of political economy provides an alternative view of the relation between sport and politics. It assumes that political forces are continuously impinging upon the operation of the sports economy. Furthermore, it does not regard the state as a passive reactor to sports developments but, rather, assumes that government policy toward the regulation of the economy has its own dynamic which necessarily affects the conduct of sport. For example, regulatory policy changes continuously with swings of political mood and fortune, each time with important consequences for sport.

Modern capitalist societies seek the twin goals of individual freedom and democratic decision-making, of liberty and equality. Liberty can be realized, however, only at the expense of equality. Historically, democracy stands for participation in decision-making; capitalism requires a state prepared to remove encumbrances to the market, especially the market for labour-power. While one emphasizes equality, the other emphasizes liberty. So long as a society remains capitalist, the state must ensure the liberties (with respect to property) believed to facilitate capital accumulation, at least to some degree; but at the same time, in order for capitalist decisions to be acceptable to the citizenry at large, democratic desire must in some way be taken into account.

In the United States the market system, or capitalism, is more powerful and democracy is 'vowed to the cause of liberty'. The egalitarian tradition in democracy has been subordinated to the libertarian. Furthermore, liberty has been defined principally in terms of freedom to engage in trade, establish enterprises, to move about, to keep one's earnings and assets, and to be secure 'against arbitrary exactions' (Lindbloom, 1977: 164). Public policy is chiefly concerned with issues of fostering individual initiative, removing economic bondage, avoiding coercive monopolies.

The relation between sport and government in the United States, since the formation of this relationship one hundred years ago, is that which would be expected in a liberal democratic regime. By and large, the sports entrepreneurs have favoured policies which guarantee capital accumulation. Politicians (and judges) have also favoured liberty over equality. In their eyes the purpose of government, and the need of government itself, is to promote economic growth and opportunity. For example, businessmen lobbying for a tax reduction or arguing for exemption from government statutes do not appear as representatives of a special interest but as functionaries performing socially indispensable tasks whose welfare is paramount. The egalitarian impulse has not been completely stifled: the electorate and their representatives are quite capable of reasoning that justice is sometimes served by placing curbs on individual freedom (for example, to close a plant), that some 'goods' (such as clean air) are in their nature collective and must be secured collectively, that some things (for example, beaches) should not be regarded as private possessions, that some inequalities place insuperable burdens on people's abilities to enjoy basic human rights. Accordingly, in conjunction with, and in reaction to, the commercialization of sport there has arisen the idea that sport is a 'public trust', a collective good, subject to political as much as economic determination.

This tension between liberalism and egalitarianism might be said to underlie virtually every sports policy debate. The sides in these debates tend to have occupied different positions with respect to this tension, one side defending (or seeking more) liberty while the other seeks more (or defends) equality. An increase in liberties might well imply less equality; just as more equality typically means restrictions on liberty. Granting individual professional athletes more contractual freedom – a liberty issue – might well make it more difficult to perform 'public' functions of, for example, ensuring franchise stability. On the other hand, granting leagues monopoly privileges in the interests of industry profitability might make it harder for individual athletes to enjoy rights of participation that other workers take for granted. For one party the cause to be championed is that of liberty, for the other equality is in danger. They disagree not about the solution so much as the problem. There is a general tendency for owners (and their political supporters) to favour policies to protect and enhance liberties and for players, excluded groups and fans (and their advocates) to favour policies to protect and enhance equality.

Of course, the institutional gulf between sport and the state is quite wide, but the state does not stand above sports developments in quite the way figurational sociologists imply. The development of sport and of politics (itself closely allied with powerful economic interests) go hand in hand. Thus Riess (1974: 42) shows how professional baseball was in many ways the creation of local political élites:

> Ball clubs with political allies secured preferential treatment from city governments with regards to assessments and various municipal serv- ices; inside information about real estate and traction developments; and protection against competition and community opposition. Politicians benefited because the ball clubs were fine investments which provided them with sources of honest and dishonest graft, patronage for their supporters, traffic for their traction routes, and favorable publicity.

Politicians came to believe that a city with a baseball franchise would appear progressive and modern. As Riess points out, while the public image of baseball's business side was that it epitomized the free-wheeling entrepreneurialism of 'the American Way', its success depended heavily on the support of elected, but often corrupt, politicians. These politicians, ironically, had quite a strong vested interest in civilizing baseball. They worried about crowd control and about gambling. But these were political concerns. The utility of baseball for political purposes declined the costlier it became to control and the dirtier its image became. Here, owners and political allies spoke with one voice, concerned above all that fans would believe that the product was tainted.

The political economy of sport, then, demands that we examine closely the relation of the governance of sport, its economic base and the larger structure, or configuration, within which it is located. In the United States this configuration has been liberal democracy at both local and national levels. The industrialization and urbanization which provided the raw material for the growth of sports occurred in the context of an economic and political system which emphasized above all individual freedom in the marketplace. Thus far, this account looks very much like that given by figurational sociology. The division of labour and democratization go hand in hand. To the extent that the division of labour civilizes play, it will therefore democratize it. From a Marxist perspective, of course, the division of labour means hierarchy and a lack of democracy. When play becomes sport levelling ceases. The kind of argument to which the second perspective leads can be seen if we examine the growth of the commissioner system in professional sports in the United States. We shall see that the commissioner system was a form of private government that, in the name of order, defended the liberties of the owners and denied those of the players.

Sociologists agree that sport assumes some kind of regulation – rules of eligibility, of play and of means of determining championships. To move beyond this rather vacuous level, however, we must ask what kind of regulation sport is subject to. Western democracies, for a variety of reasons, relegate sport to the private sphere, outside the pale of acceptable government interference. The issue, therefore, is not whether sports activities should be regulated but whether the regulation should be public or private. The very first national baseball league was unregulated in either respect since players could leave teams at the conclusion of the season. However, owners soon imposed their own regulation on trade in players (and competition with non-league teams) thus imposing a system of private regulation.

The line drawn between the private and the public sphere is not fixed but is the object of considerable and often bitter conflict. Sports are caught up in this struggle as much as any other sphere of life such as entertainment or family matters. In the United States the tendency has been to restrict the size of the public sphere and guard very jealously the sanctity of the private. Private associations, ranging from the family to multinational corporations, still have large claims to autonomy from public regulation. Those advocating greater accountability are met with opposition from those who see a threat to individual liberty, economic efficiency and other values.

Throughout the nineteenth century it was taken pretty much for granted that private activity, including the right of association, should be free of government restraint, subject only to the boundaries set by the law of property, contract, tort, crimes and similar legal categories. These private associations were touted as a valuable counterbalance to government and to each other. Nor was there much fear that they would be undemocratic. Being essentially voluntary associations, the threat of exit would be enough to constrain leaders to temper authoritarianism. The government thus adopted a 'hands-off' posture, on the understanding that private institutions were basically good for society and should be left to run themselves except under the most unusual circumstances.

With the rise of the welfare state and government intervention into the working of the capitalist economy, the state began to play a more intrusive role in the private sphere, gradually redefining its boundaries. Although private enterprise was still sacrosanct, public regulation was to be used as an adjunct to help it reach its societal goals. At the same time, private associations, most notably business corporations, began to grow in size and economic strength, assuming what to many people seemed to be public functions, thus blurring the line between the private and the public.

With this tendency, the distinction between private and public organization shifted again. A business corporation, despite the fact that it was privately owned, might be regarded as public. This led people to place their confidence more in the distinction between non-profit and for-profit organizations. Thus, the anti-trust Sherman Act was not seen as applicable to non-profit entities. It would not have been considered appropriate, for example, to apply this law to the National Colleges Athletics Association (NCAA). Profit-orientated entities, on the other hand, were considered liable to regulation and inspection because of their intricate involvement in the welfare of the economy and their effect on the national interest. Government dealings with professional sports leagues have tended to emphasize issues of 'public trust'. As the status of the NCAA has changed – that is, toward a more profit-oriented body – its treatment by the state has changed commensurately.

It is no accident that the growth of sports coincides with the emergence of a large number of professional groups. In the 1890s there was a great rush to pass occupational licensing laws: for plumbers, barbers, lawyers, pharmacists, midwives, nurses and the like. Greater competition for 'turf' placed a premium on getting the state to 'franchise' control over some of that turf so that others could not occupy it. Thus arose the idea of voluntary associations undertaking non-public action, thereby wielding considerable power in the name of public policy. While a sports league might not look much like the American Bar Association or the Chicago Board of Trade, in law and politics it did operate in much the same way. In certain respects, then, a sport came to resemble a franchise granted by the state. An essentially public power had been granted to an essentially private agency. They were granted in areas which, although in reality heavily politicized, were popularly considered nonpolitical. Franchises became the watchdogs of the national conscience in their respective areas. In return for acting in a mature and responsible manner, and on condition that it conduct its internal affairs with circumspection and some consideration for constitutional rights, the franchise was granted a mandate to provide services on a monopolistic basis, to make available collective goods for the purposes of private profit.

The idea of the franchise makes a lot of sense when discussing utilities, but professional sports leagues would not at first glance appear to fit into this category. The leagues, however, have never hesitated to claim special powers – a public mandate – because of the peculiar role of sports in American life. The state, for its part, has been willing to grant sports special privileges on these grounds, rights which lack the force and reach of those granted to professional associations, but which nevertheless had a major impact on the profitability of professional sports and the distribution of sports opportunities.

A franchise is rather like a private government. In the idea of 'private government' we assume that sports are essentially private but we acknowledge that they enforce government-like powers which are effective only in so far as they have the tacit backing of the 'real' government. As early as 1913 the state court of New York was approving the state Athletic Commission's power to ban a boxer, Robert Fitzsimmons, in 'the best interests of the game'. Fitzsimmons had become, in the opinion of the commission, too old to fight and had to be protected from himself. The courts thus set a precedent for state action in the case of sports (Sammons, 88: 66). The powers of private government are crucially dependent on this mandate from the state. For example, the politics of allowing sports leagues to operate as virtual monopolies gives them much greater internal control over member teams and players.

In professional team-sports in the United States, the private government is known as 'the commissioner system'. Originating in baseball, it worked so well that it has been imitated in football, ice hockey and soccer. Where a sport lacked a commissioner, such as boxing or tennis, its problems were sure to be traced to the absence of such a position. Professional baseball developed quite early the model of a powerful and energetic President of the League: 'Ban' Johnson, creator of the American League, is the best known.

In the National Agreement, signed in 1903, organized baseball (that is, the National League, the American League and the Minor Leagues) instituted the National Commission to regulate the sport, a troika consisting of the two league presidents and a third person. The true commissioner system did not come into force, however, until 1921, when a new agreement provided for a single Commissioner with the broadest authority over the game, backed up by 'the power to take punitive action, including fining or blacklisting, against Leagues, clubs, officers or players found guilty of . . . detrimental conduct' (Seymour, 1971: 322). Most important of all, the Commissioner was publicly charged with preserving the integrity of the game: it is not without significance that, although many of the Commissioner's powers would be whittled away after the Second World War, this one responsibility has remained.

The first Commissioner, Judge Kenesaw Mountain Landis, had a deep affection for baseball and looked upon the players more as heroes than as employees. However, he brought to baseball 'a disdain for law and due process' (Tygiel, 1983: 31). He banned for life the seven Chicago White Sox players accused of throwing the 1919 World Series, despite the fact that the players were acquitted in court of all charges of fraud, thus 'completely ignoring the players' civil liberties' (Sullivan, 1987: 8), and included for good measure two other players who were not even indicted but who, Landis became convinced, had known about the fix in advance and failed to warn the authorities (Seymour, 1971: 338). Landis actually used the acquittal of the accused players to argue that the Commissioner's extraordinary powers were necessary.

With the development of the commissioner system it might be said that professional team sport entered the modern age. Did it signal the kind of equalizing trend the figurationists would have predicted or the kind of increasing inequality and hierarchization that Marxists would have predicted with the increased capitalization of the industry? Did baseball, and those sports that imitated its system of private government, become more or less democratic with the development of the commissioner system? Although the system did not cause the players to be denied the freedom to choose where they worked (this had been effectively prohibited by collusion between the owners), once it was in place the players were bound to find it more difficult to obtain more equality. Although the commissioner system did not cause baseball to be exempted from the anti-trust laws, the fact that the sport had a judge to look after it made it all the more difficult for opponents to break up the cartel. Although the commissioner system did not, by itself, forestall unionism, the fact that the Commissioner claimed to speak for the 'good of the game', all the while being in the pay and serving at the mercy of the owners, made the formation of unions that much more difficult.

It could be argued, of course, that the setting up of the commissioner system and the appointment of Landis signalled a desire to clean up the game and defend its integrity. It was a civilizing spurt, part of a more general effort to retain the image of baseball as a pastoral pastime despite the fact of its increasing commercialization. Through the commissioner system baseball could become a thoroughly capitalized industry and yet appear to have no capitalists and no proletarians. It could cleverly produce and package a product and yet, with the Supreme Court's *imprimatur,* not appear to be commerce at all. In short, it could retain much of the 'civility' of the amateur tradition while at the same time becoming thoroughly professionalized.

The new single commissioner system, as practiced by Landis, *was* something in the nature of a purity crusade. From the perspective of figurational sociology, it represented a 'civilizing spurt' because it articulated and enforced higher standards of conduct for both owners, players and fans. These standards had been seriously undermined by the Black Sox[1] scandal because the fixing of a sporting event seemed to undermine fatally the integrity of the game. *Sporting News* columnist John Sheridan could not believe the rumours that the 1919 World Series had been fixed. It was not credible that such core values of personal conduct could be violated. For a player to throw a game would be 'a terrible thing'; such a man would die 'of his own self-contempt' (Crepeau, 1980: 10). The grand jury that indicted the Black Sox players saw an equally potent threat to the game's 'civility'. Baseball, it wrote, is a game that 'promotes respect to proper authority, self-confidence, fair-mindedness, quick judgement and self-control' (Crepeau, 1980: 42) and must be defended from those who do not share this code of conduct.

Figurational sociology prompts us to look at the wider society for an increase in tensions which might have prompted this crusade. There is no doubt that the period following the First World War was one in which inter-group tensions were very high. The decline of a way of life associated with traditional American Protestantism and of the social status of those most closely associated with that life, caused a backlash. Lipset and Raab (1970: 110) refer to a 'quickening of the monistic impulse' during the 1920s, 'the last desperate protest of a nineteenth-century Protestantism in the course of eclipse'.

In the period immediately following the war, drastic limitations were imposed on the immigration of nationality groups of non-WASP origin; legislation to outlaw the teaching of evolution was introduced in many states; the Prohibition Amendment was passed; laws were enacted to restrict the rights of political dissent; and membership in nativist movements such as the Ku Klux Klan rose dramatically. Anti-Semitism reached unprecedented heights. Jews were blamed for everything from socialism to jazz.

It is not a trivial matter, then, that Henry Ford's *Dearborn Independent* ran a headline, 'Jewish Gamblers Corrupt American Baseball', blaming the fixing of the 1919 World Series on Jews. Nor is it without significance that the *Sporting News* initially described the gamblers behind the fix as 'a lot of dirty, long-nosed, thick-lipped, and strong smelling gamblers' (Asinof, 1963: 21). Public reaction also betrayed status anxieties. Many fans wished to believe the national pastime incorruptible precisely because it was the national pastime, and allocated the blame to the high-rolling gamblers. These gamblers were not, of course, 'true Americans', but were of 'ethnic' stock: Irish, Italian or Jewish. The gamblers symbolized the threat to the 'American way' of playing the game, an approach to sport that placed good clean competition for its own sake at centre-stage. The commissioner system, a method of policing the sport more stringent than any seen before, would get the message across that the old values were still important, and that an 'instrumental' approach to the game would not be tolerated.

The figurationists' focus on the use of rules of conduct as prestige instruments during periods of societal upheaval and tension therefore seems warranted here. The new commissioner would clean up the game from the excesses of commercialism and greed that had entered by the back door. There is another perspective on the origins of the commissioner system, however, that does not attribute quite so much importance to the defence of status as such. First, the owners' cries of outrage at the immediate cause of the restructuring, the fixing of the 1919 World Series, must be taken with a pinch of salt. While there can be no doubting the sincerity of the owners' desire to distance baseball from gambling (they refused to allow boxing contests at baseball stadiums because of the bad reputation of the sport), it is also true that many owners were themselves notorious gamblers. Gambling had been a part of baseball for many years, and 'some owners thought [betting] pools stimulated interest in baseball' (Seymour, 1971: 280). Their greatest fear with respect to gambling was not that it infringed some abstract principle of fair play but that they would lose money. If there was something crooked about the national pastime, 'Who, then, would pay to see a game?' (Asinof, 1963: 14).

The owners had fears other than gambling on their mind. The 1918–21 period was one of considerably heightened union activity. It is possible to see the commissioner system as a movement against organized labour in a time of considerable capital–labour struggle. Union membership doubled between 1913 and 1920 (Gordon *et al.*, 1982: 154). Baseball owners were apprehensive about the possibility of the unionization of professional athletes. Not without cause, for the Fraternity of Professional Baseball Players, first organized in 1912, managed to enlist 1215 members by its peak in 1916. The Fraternity secured recognition from the National Commission by exploiting the on-going competition with the 'outlaw' Federal League. While the Fraternity's accomplishments were minor and while the union lost most of its leverage with the collapse of the Federal League in 1915, the lesson was not lost on the owners.

Many owners and not a few others connected to the game must have known how great was the temptation not to respect the game's 'integrity'. Although the better players did earn more than the average working-class man, most, especially those in the minor leagues, did not. Furthermore, the *relative* rewards of the players declined steadily as baseball became more commercially successful. Throughout this period, the relative position of players worsened; players' salaries comprised a declining proportion of clubs' outgoings, falling from 50 per cent in 1890 to 35 per cent in 1929 (Seymour, 1971: 174). Chicago White Sox owner, Comiskey, was 'tight-fisted and penny-pinching', his men the worst-paid in baseball. It is no wonder they were 'embittered by financial ill-usage' (Seymour 1971: 334). 1918 had seen baseball attendances fall because of the war, and the owners had agreed to cut the ballplayers' salaries 'to the bone' (Asinof, 1963: 15). The White Sox players, whose salaries were about 40 per cent less than those of players in other clubs, had threatened to strike at the beginning of the 1919 season.

Landis had a reputation as a foe of labour. A vocal opponent of unionism who had handed down harsh verdicts against International Workers of the World (IWW) members accused of hindering the war effort, Landis had been one of several prominent figures to be sent a parcel bomb in 1919, allegedly by anarchists (Leuchtenberg, 1958: 72). 'Landis is reported to have referred to the IWW as scum, filth, and slimy rats' (Crepeau, 1980: 21). He was a supporter of the 'American Plan', a campaign by business to bust the unions, that was eventually successful enough virtually to eliminate such gains as were made by labour during the First World War.

Landis launched an immediate campaign of his own to bring the players into line. He refused to reinstate the players acquitted in the Black Sox trial, expressing his scorn for 'the verdict of juries'. He was later to ban players accused of crimes (such as auto theft), even though they had been acquitted (Spink, 1974: 89) and he permanently blacklisted others for negotiating with leagues that had not signed the National Agreement. Three years after taking office Landis had placed 53 players on the ineligible list (Seymour, 1971: 388). In setting up the position of Commissioner and appointing Landis to fill it, the owners 'rescued the ballplayers from the clutches of the law, only to make victims of them on their own terms' (Asinof, 1963: 275).

The class nature of this conflict is suggested by the reactions to the court verdict in the Black Sox trial. When the indicted players were found not guilty by a court of law, the owners and many sports reporters expressed their dismay. But the ties between the media and the clubs were very close during this period: 'newspapermen were Comiskey's boys' (Asinof, 1963: 22). The decision was greeted in the courtroom, however, with 'a bedlam of rousing cheers' (Asinof, 1963: 272) in which the judge joined. There was considerable popular support for those suspected of throwing the games. 'Cleaning up the game' seems to have been more important to the owners than to the players or the fans. The targets of public anger and blame were the gamblers who fixed the games and the owners. People saw baseball as increasingly taking on the antidemocratic values associated with the organization of industrial firms, where democracy, and democratic rights, were surrendered at the factory gates.

The intensification of class conflict within the sport would not have been so threatening to the owners had they been more united. But the downfall of the old National Commission was prompted by 'a series of unpleasant disputes' among major league executives, chiefly over the rights to ball players (Seymour, 1971: 259). The National League had been riddled with disunity for some time, caused by owners not respecting each other's 'reserve' of players, but the end of the First World War saw the American League also in a state of 'armed truce' as owners fought with each other and with League President Johnson (Seymour, 1971: 270). In 1919 the Minor Leagues withdrew from the National Agreement. The Black Sox scandal might thus have provided the proximate cause of the restructuring and functioned as a convenient symbol, but it 'very likely would have come about in some form anyway' (Seymour, 1971: 312).

It is no coincidence that this restructuring took place in the shadow of the court decision handed down in 1919 by the District of Columbia Supreme Court, which marked baseball as a combination in restraint of trade. This decision was currently under appeal, and it does not take much imagination to see its impact on organized baseball's desire to have some dramatic means of getting its own house in order. Ironically, of course, the restructuring was to have the effect of solidifying the cartel. It did so, however, by making baseball appear to be a 'natural monopoly' in which complicit action was necessary for the existence of the game.

While it is often supposed, then, that the commissioner system was an outgrowth of the Black Sox scandal, the collapse of the National Commission preceded, if not the occurrence at the 1919 World Series, at least the public charges that the Series had been fixed. The crisis was used by American League President 'Ban' Johnson's foes to render him powerless and, in turn, Landis used the scandal to establish power and become the first czar of sport. In so doing, the owners secured a strong mandate from the government to police a very important social institution according to their own standards, including those governing management–labour relations.

In creating a Commissioner to rule over them, the owners in effect established the first 'industrial doctor' in America (Seymour, 1971: 323). Soon after Landis's appointment, the movie industry hired Harding's Postmaster-General, Will Hays, to be 'the Judge Landis of the movies' (Leuchtenberg, 1958: 169). The motive appeared to be the same in both cases, both industries seeking to head off closer government regulation. The sports industry was plagued with gambling, the movie industry accused of purveying obscenity. In both cases the governance structure was to prove troublesome and unstable. But perhaps more revealing than the analogy with the movie industry was another model for the commissioner system that was explicitly used when it was being devised, the juvenile justice system. The juvenile courts had only recently emerged in recognition of the special rights and protections flowing to children by virtue of their special status in society. Invoking this model, 'Landis treated players not as adults, able to make intelligent decisions on their own, but as PINS, persons in need of supervision and fatherly guidance' (Rosenberg, 1987: 142). The new code of conduct would be a patrimony, where players would be 'boys' well into the 1960s.

Note

1. 'White Sox' and 'Black Sox' both refer to the Chicago White Sox baseball team. The 'Black Sox' label was attached to them following a scandal involving bribery and match-fixing in 1919.

References

Asinof, Eliot (1963), *Eight Men Out: The Black Sox and the 1919 World Series* (New York: Holt, Rinehart & Winston).

Berman, Marshall (1982), *All that is Solid Melts into Air* (New York: Simon & Schuster).

Braverman, Harry (1974), *Labor and Monopoly Capital* (New York: Monthly Review Press).

Buck-Morss, Susan (1978), 'Review of Norbert Elias, *The Civilizing Process*', *Telos*, 37: 191–8.

Clarke, John and Critcher, Chas (1985), *The Devil Makes Work: Leisure in Capitalist Britain* (Urbana, Ill.: University of Illinois Press).

Collins, Randall (1975), *Conflict Sociology* (New York: Academic Press).

Crepeau, Richard (1980), *Baseball America's Diamond Mind: 1919–1941* (Orlando, Fla: University of Central Florida Press).

Cross, Gary (1988), 'Worktime and Industrialization', in Gary Cross (ed.), *Worktime and Industrialization* (Philadelphia, Pa: Temple University Press) pp. 3–19.

Dunning, Eric (1986a), 'Sport as a Male Preserve: Notes on the Social Sources of Masculine Identity and its Transformations', *Theory, Culture and Society*, 3: 79–90.

_____ (1986b), 'The Sociology of Sport in Europe and the United States: Critical Observations from an "Eliasian" Perspective', in C. Roger Rees and Andrew Miracle (eds), *Sport and Social Theory* (Champaign, Ill.: Human Kinetics Publishers) pp. 29–56.

_____ (1986), Preface to N. Elias and E. Dunning, *Quest for Excitement: Sport and Leisure in the Civilizing Process* (Oxford: Blackwell).

_____ (1989), 'The Figurational Approach to Leisure and Sport', in Chris Rojek (ed.), *Leisure for Leisure* (New York: Routledge) pp. 36–52.

_____ and Kenneth Sheard (1979), *Barbarians, Gentlemen and Players: A Sociological Study of the Development of Rugby Football* (New York: New York University Press).

_____ , Patrick Murphy and John Williams (1988), *The Roots of Football Hooliganism* (London: Routledge & Kegan Paul).

Elias, Norbert (1982 [1939]), *Power and Civility* (New York: Pantheon Books).

_____ (1986), Introduction to N. Elias and E. Dunning, *Quest for Excitement: Sport and Leisure in the Civilizing Process* (Oxford: Blackwell).

Gordon, David, Edwards, Richard and Reich, Michael (1982), *Segmented Work, Divided Workers* (New York: Cambridge University Press).

Hargreaves, Jennifer (1986), 'Where's the Virtue? Where's the Grace? A Discussion of the Social Production of Gender Relations in and through Sport', *Theory, Culture and Society*, 3: 109–21.

Horne, John and Jary, David (1987), 'The Figurational Sociology of Sport and Leisure of Elias and Dunning: an Exposition and Critique', in John Horne, David Jary and Alan Tomlinson (eds), *Sport, Leisure and Social Relations* (New York: Routledge & Kegan Paul) pp. 86–112.

Lasch, Christopher (1985), 'Historical Sociology and the Myth of Maturity', *Theory and Society*, 14: 705–20.

Leuchtenberg, William (1958), *The Perils of Prosperity* (Chicago, Ill.: University of Chicago Press).

Lipset, Seymour Martin and Raab, Earl (1970), *The Politics of Unreason* (New York: Harper & Row).

Maguire, Joe (1986), 'The Emergence of Football Spectating as a Social Problem, 1880–1985: a Figurational and Developmental Perspective', *Sociology of Sport Journal*, 3: 217–44.

Miliband, Ralph (1977), *Marxism and Politics* (Oxford: Oxford University Press).

Morgan, William (1985), '"Radical" Social Theory of Sport', *Sociology of Sport Journal*, 2: 56–71.

Parkin, Frank (1979), *Marxism and Class Theory: A Bourgeois Critique* (New York: Columbia University Press).

Riess, Steven (1974), 'The Baseball Magnates and Urban Politics in the Progressive Era: 1895–1920', *Journal of Sport History*, 1: 41–62.

Rosenberg, Norman (1987), 'Here Comes the Judge: the Origin of Baseball's Commissioner System and American Legal Culture', *Journal of Popular Culture*, 20: 129–46.

Sammons, Jeffrey (1988), *Beyond the Ring* (Urbana, Ill.: University of Illinois Press).

Sennett, Richard (1976), *The Fall of Public Man* (New York: Vintage Books).

Seymour, Harold (1971), *Baseball: The Golden Age* (New York: Oxford University Press).

Spink, J. G. Taylor (1974), *Judge Landis and Twenty-Five Years of Baseball* (St Louis, Mo.: Sporting News Publishing Company).

Sullivan, Neil (1987), *The Dodgers Move West* (New York: Oxford University Press).

Tygiel, Jules (1983), *Baseball's Great Experiment: Jackie Robinson and his Legacy* (New York: Oxford University Press).

Wehowsky, Andreas (1978), 'Making Ourselves More Flexible than We Are: Reflections on Norbert Elias', *New German Critique*, 15: 65–80.

Whitson, David (1989), 'Discourses of Critique in Sport Sociology: a Response to Deem and Sparks', *Sociology of Sport Journal*, 6: 60–5.

Whyte, William H. (1989), *City: Rediscovering its Center* (New York: Doubleday).

Wright, Erik Olin (1978), *Classes, Crisis and the State* (London: New Left Books).

4 Towards a Sociological Theory of Sport and the Emotions: A Process-Sociological Perspective[1]

JOE MAGUIRE

Sociological explanations both of social life in general and of sport in particular have failed to take seriously the task of finding an analysis which integrates 'social structure', 'social relations' and the 'emotions'. There are a number of reasons why this should have been the case and these will be discussed in due course. But for now I am more concerned to spell out the value that a sociological theory of emotions can be to the study of social life, sport and leisure. Two main advantages spring to mind. The development of a sociological theory of emotions will arguably help to ensure that human beings are studied 'in the round', capturing them as 'whole selves' and not as isolated physiological or psychological units who happen to live their lives out in 'society' (Goudsblom *et al.*, 1979). It will be argued here that there is an urgent need to study people 'in their totality', be it in a 'sports setting' or, indeed, elsewhere. The idea of viewing people 'in the round' stands in stark opposition to the dominant conception of 'sportspeople' provided by the sports sciences, and indeed, by the mainstream of the disciplines on which that group of subjects draws (Maguire, 1991). It seeks to avoid decomplexifying human beings by eschewing both biological and/or psychological determinism. But in doing so, it does not intend to replace one form of determinism by another. Cultural determinism can be just as misleading in the problem under investigation. It is in this connection that the other advantage in adopting the approach advocated emerges.

In going beyond some narrow vision of the sociology of sport and leisure, clarification of what Norbert Elias has termed 'the hinge' (Elias, 1987: 35) may prove possible. That is, a probing of the connection between biological changes and social development could be undertaken. Indeed, as will be argued, by adopting the approach proposed by Elias not only would the incremental knowledge of the sub-disciplines of the sociology of sport

96

and leisure be increased but also our understanding of social life would be based on a more adequate footing. What Elias has to say with regard to this connection is worth quoting at some length:

> The dominance of learned over unlearned characteristics in humans provides a biological framework for a social development which can occur without any biological changes, that is to say, independently of the process of evolution. The two concepts refer to processes which are different in kind. At present they are frequently confused. It has become customary to use the term indiscriminately for both. Some people present social development in the monistic manner as part of the unitary biological process. Others, dualistically, present biological evolution on the one hand and social development under the name of history on the other, without giving any thought at all to the problem of *the hinge,* to the question of their connection with each other. . . . Starting from the postulate that humans not only can but must learn in order to become fully human I have clarified the problem of the hinge.　(Elias, 1987: 351–2)

This is not to suggest that the exploration of 'the hinge' in analyses originating in the sociology of sport or leisure could be pursued in isolation from more conventional 'problems' such as political economy, stratification or deviance. Far from it. Studies of the emotions and the political economy of culture need to proceed in conjunction with each other. But the question arises of how best to conduct an exploration of 'the hinge'?

Elias suggests that monistic and dualistic thinking have prevented a clear grasp of 'the hinge' emerging (Elias, 1987). Let me discuss this in a little more detail. For Elias, in the human sciences there exist two opposing tendencies. In one, the focus is on the properties which human beings share with other species. Ethologists, for example, overlook the evolutionary innovations characteristic of the human species and select as relevant what they regard as unvarying human characteristics shared with other species. A form of 'reductionist monism' thus pervades in which there is an over-emphasis on the similarities with other species. The uniqueness of human beings is lost. In contrast, for Elias, in almost all the social sciences a dualism is evident: its subject matter is set apart from nature. The emphasis is on the uniqueness of humanity. No attempt is made to show how these uniquely human characteristics are connected with those which humans share with other species. Such opposing tendencies are no less evident in the study of the emotions. In physiological and psychological research human beings are treated as 'isolated units' with no past or present (Kemper, 1981; Scheff, 1983). Humans' 'thoughts' are cut off from their 'feelings'; their 'bodies' are cut off both from their 'consciousness' and from the 'society' in which they reside. Much the same tendency is evident when sport and the emotions have been examined (Biddle, 1985).

Though opposing this tendency, much social scientific research on the emotions also rests on dualistic thinking. The probing of the self and the 'lived consciousness' leads to a deliberate eschewing of the need to study human beings' physiological make-up. It also leads to the adoption of what Elias describes as a '*homo clasus*' model. That is, the emphasis in symbolic interactionist and phenomenologically inspired research is on the 'subject', a single thinking mind inside a sealed container, from which she or he looks out at other 'subjects' in the 'external world' (Shott, 1979; Denzin, 1984). The 'agency' of the individual, distinct from the 'society' in which he or she is located, underpins this position. Again, such thinking has found expression in the study of sport and the emotions (Zurcher, 1982; Gallmeier, 1987). While research conducted within this latter tradition is not without value, and indeed, further discussion of a symbolic interactionist perspective on the emotions will be undertaken in the concluding section of this chapter, it has to be stated at this point that such work is still locked into the dualistic trap which Elias (1978a; 1987) has effectively critiqued. The question remains, therefore, how best to conduct the discovery of 'the hinge' and the sociological study of the emotions?

In order to map out the approach on which the present chapter rests, a number of steps need to be undertaken. Initially, a review of the Eliasian perspective on the emotions will be attempted. Reference will be made in this connection to the work of its originator, Norbert Elias, and to one of Elias's more recent advocates, Cas Wouters. Next, the application of this perspective to the study of sport and leisure will be considered. Here, reference will be made to the collaborative work of Elias and Dunning. On this basis an overall assessment of the value of this perspective will be attempted. Having both noted the fruitfulness of such a perspective and suggested some areas of deficiency, the chapter will conclude by outlining some future lines of enquiry and dialogue with other work on the emotions and the body in consumer culture. In tackling the issue in this way, what is recognized is the need for a 'detached' critique, rather than one ideologically predisposed to reject the Eliasian approach outright (Hargreaves, 1982; 1986).

ON HUMAN BEINGS AND THE EMOTIONS: A PROCESS-SOCIOLOGICAL PERSPECTIVE

In his work, 'On Human Beings and their Emotions' (1987), Elias argues that the process-sociologists' concern with human emotions centres on both the emotional characteristics which humans share with non-human species and on others which are uniquely human and which have no equivalent in other species. In addition he argues that, while this does not imply any disregard of the evolutionary continuity linking humans to their non-human ancestors, it does represent a 'determined break with a tradition which induces human biologists and psychologists either to disregard or to blur structural differences between human emotions and those of non-human species' (Elias, 1987: 339). Existing accounts, he argues, tend to dichotomize the study of the emotions. Both tendencies, he suggests:

> suffer from an inability to understand the nature of processes. They are still trapped by a powerful conceptual heritage which forces people to represent in static terms sets of events that can be recognised and understood only if they are perceived as parts or aspects of processes, as events in a condition of continuous structured flux.   (Elias, 1987: 341)

In contrast to these tendencies, Elias proposes three interconnected hypotheses regarding a theory of human beings and their emotions. These hypotheses have to be located within the discussion which Elias is trying to promote, namely, how can the fact that the human species has certain unique characteristics be reconciled with the continuity of the evolutionary process?

First, he argues, human beings as a species represent an evolutionary breakthrough; that is, the balance between learned and unlearned conduct tilted decisively in favour of the former as the human species evolved. Secondly, human beings not only *can* learn far more than any other species, they also *have to learn*. The repertoire of unlearned ways of behaviour has become so softened and weakened in *Homo sapiens* that human beings cannot orientate themselves or communicate with others without acquiring a great deal of knowledge through learning. Thirdly, no emotion of a grown-up human person is ever an entirely unlearned, genetically fixed reaction pattern. Human emotions result from a merger of an unlearned and a learned process.

On the basis of these hypotheses Elias argues that the steering of human conduct is always the result of an intimate interweaving of learned and unlearned processes. This, he suggests, raises the problem of 'the hinge', the need to explore the 'connectedness' or interweaving of learned and unlearned processes. An important task facing the human sciences is, accordingly, to find out more about the way in which the uniquely large unlearned human potential for learning is activated and patterned by the learning process itself (Elias, 1987: 347). As Elias observes, a child's learning of a language is made possible by the intertwining of two processes: a biological process of maturation and a social process of learning. Indeed, for Elias (1987: 348):

> The dovetailing of a biological process of maturation and a social process of learning in a human child brings to light the hinge connecting human nature with human society, human culture and other aspects of what is traditionally set apart from nature as a second world existing in isolation from it.

On this basis, Elias proceeds to clarify further the concept of the emotions. He argues that, as with most attributes and properties of a human being, emotions must be understood in relation to people's relationships with existences other than themselves. While noting that emotions contain three component aspects – a physiological, a behavioural and a feeling component – Elias emphasizes the need to recognize the importance of the latter, but not to the preclusion of the other components. Noting that the 'feeling vocabulary' may be more differentiated in one country than another, Elias argues that such differences in the vocabularies of different peoples also confirm the hypothesis that learning plays a part in the feeling component of emotions. Interestingly, Elias's observations in this regard are supported by the work of Harre (1986) when the latter argues for a social constructionist view of the emotions. Elias (1987: 360–1) summed up his own approach to the study of emotions in the following way:

> the study of the emotions must remain unproductive as long as their connection with other aspects of human beings is not clearly taken into account. In the case of human beings, unlearned emotional impulses are always related to a person's learned self-regulation, more specifically to learned control of emotions. The changeable balance between emotional impulses and emotion-controlling counter-impulses shows itself in a person's movements, in their gestures and in their facial expressions which are signals by means of which people communicate involuntarily

or with intent the condition of the self-regulation of their emotions to other people. . . . Emotions and the related movements or 'expressions' are, in short, one of the indications that human beings are by nature constituted for life in the company of others, for life in society.

Cas Wouters (1989) argues in similar fashion. In taking exception to much of the symbolic interactionist and phenomenological work on the emotions, Wouters uses Hochschild's (1983) work on the 'managed heart' as illustrative of the problems associated with such approaches. Wouters argues that Hochschild hardly considers learned, internalized controls of emotions. She has overlooked the fact that, while human beings are born with very little natural self-regulation, they do have a natural disposition to learn to regulate themselves, but they also have to learn to regulate themselves according to the social habitus. On every level, therefore, this learned self-regulation takes the form of a tension balance between emotional impulses and emotion controlling counter-impulses (Wouters, 1989: 103). With regard to mapping out a process-sociological theory of the emotions, the importance of Wouters's observations lies not only in his implicit critique of recent work on the sociology of the emotions, but also in his stress on how emotions are both ingredients and instruments for managing life and how closely intertwined this is with the civilizing process. This observation also relates to the study of sport and leisure.

Elias's work on the emotions is complemented by research he conducted with Eric Dunning in the 1960s (Elias and Dunning, 1986). Again, the details of their analysis need not detain us at this point. Further discussion will be attempted shortly. What in essence they are arguing is that it is not possible to work out an adequate theory of leisure, or indeed, the emotions, within the framework of any single human science, whether it be human physiology, psychology or sociology. What they write on this issue is worth citing at some length:

> The problems of leisure, in fact, belong to that large class of problems which, at the present stage in the development of scientific specialization, fall not merely between two but between several stools. They do not fit wholly into the frame of reference of any one of these sciences as they are at present constituted, but rather belong to the unexplored no-man's land between them. If sociology is considered as a science which abstracts from the psychological or the biological aspects of human beings, if psychology or human biology are regarded as sciences which can proceed on their own without taking account of the sociological aspects of people, the problems of leisure will be left out on a limb. In fact, they

indicate in the clearest possible manner the limitations inherent in the compartmentalization of human beings as a subject of scientific study. (Elias and Dunning, 1986: 108)

At the present stage in the development of the scientific study of sport and leisure, disciplinary analyses suffer from the defect that they deal with aspects of people as if they in fact exist independently of each other. A relative advance in the adequacy of the scientific study of sport and leisure would be gained if an overall framework within which to place both disciplinary and multidisciplinary analyses could be devised.

It is therefore suggested that aspects of leisure, and people's experience of it, require a multidisciplinary synthesis. The study of socially structured processes and that of emotions cannot be pursued in separate compartments. To argue this is not to advocate the dissolving of sociological questions into biological and psychological ones. In this regard, as Elias and Dunning observe, sociology's struggle for autonomy for its own problems has been well justified. What is required is a thinking-through of the problems which need to be tackled and the relative contribution that existing disciplines can make in the collective endeavour. For Elias and Dunning (1986: 110):

The study of leisure . . . is one of the many instances in which it is not possible to disregard the problem of the actual relationship between phenomena on the sociological level and those on the psychological and physiological levels. Here, one cannot escape from the task of a multi-level analysis, from the task of considering, at least in broad outlines, how in the study of leisure the three levels – the sociological, the psychological and the biological – connect.

At this stage it is appropriate to discuss the perspective which Elias and Dunning offer on sport, leisure and the emotions in greater detail.

TOWARDS A THEORY OF SPORT AND THE EMOTIONS

Based on this general model of human relations – with what Elias (in Elias and Dunning, 1986) terms the civilizing process at its core – the sportization of English folk pastimes was, he argues, an example of the 'civilizing spurt' which occurred during the eighteenth century. From an Eliasian perspective, examination of this process is seen as crucial to understanding present day patterns of sport and leisure. That is because, in order to understand the present, the analysis has to trace how it emerged out of the past. The principal question which Elias (in Elias and Dunning, 1986) asks in this connection appears at first sight to be deceptively simple. Why, he asks, did modern sports – that is, highly regulated contests requiring physical exertion and skill – make their appearance first of all during the eighteenth century among the English upper classes, the landed aristocracy and gentry?

In examining the sports of cricket, fox-hunting and the early forms of modern football, Elias and Dunning (1986) conclude that all these cultural forms mark attempts to prolong the point-like pleasure of victory in the mock-battle of a sport and are symptomatic of a far-reaching change in the personality structure of human beings and that this in turn was closely connected with specific changes in the power structure of society at large. For Elias, these changes were bound up with the civilizing process to which he has directed our attention (Elias, 1978b; 1982).

But why did this 'civilizing' of game contests and the restraint on violence to others through social rules which required a good deal of individual self-control develop first in England? For Elias, the emergence of sport as a form of physical combat of a relatively non-violent type was connected with a period when the cycle of violence which had characterized English society in the seventeenth century had begun to calm down. This same period allowed groups to settle conflicts of interest increasingly by non-violent means, for example, the party rituals of parliamentary government began to emerge. For Elias it is not a question of whether parliamentarization caused sportization. Rather, his explanation is that the same people were caught up in two aspects of a broader process of development. As he himself expresses it:

> It was simply that the same class of people who participated in the pacification and greater regularization of factional contests in Parliament were instrumental in the greater pacification and regularization of their pastimes. . . . Sport and Parliament as they emerged in the eighteenth century were both characteristic of the same change in the power structure of England and in the social habitus of that class of people which emerged from the antecedent struggles as the ruling group. (Elias and Dunning, 1986: 40)

For Elias and Dunning (1986) it is no surprise that it was the aristocracy and gentry who were central in the sportization of traditional pastimes.

Among the upper classes it became a mark of distinction to refrain from using violence in certain spheres. The development of cricket between the owners of landed estates was symptomatic of this (Brookes, 1978). While it is not necessary to examine this process in detail, it should be observed that this sportization process was connected both to a civilizing spurt and to the right of assembly, that is, the ability of sections of the population to form their own clubs and associations, privileges which were denied even to the members of ruling groups in absolutist France.

The importance of these observations lies in the fact that the early stages of this sportization process set the tone of future sporting developments. Indeed, the fact that the demand for such activities arose in the first place and continued to command the interest of an increasing number of people was a sign of changes taking place within English society as a whole. It is here that the function of sport and leisure forms becomes more evident.

For Elias and Dunning (1986) a principal function of leisure is the 'arousal of pleasurable forms of excitement'. One feature of the civilizing of English society in this period was a marked narrowing of what was acceptable in public life. As a direct corollary of this, the need for a social enclave in which socially approved moderate excitement could be aroused and expressed increased. That is, the function of leisure activities has to be assessed in relation to the ubiquity and steadiness of excitement control. What is the significance of this?

The function which sport and leisure are seen to serve, from an Eliasian perspective, is based on a view of people whereby they have a socially conditioned psychological need to experience a kind of spontaneous, elementary, unreflective yet pleasurable excitement. The precise function of leisure activities is assessed in relation to a number of interrelated criteria. These include: the degree of controlled decontrolling of emotions that is evident; the degree to which emotions flow freely; the degree of eliciting or imitating excitement akin to that which is generated in 'real-life' situations; the nature of the tension-balances created; and the degree to which the activity serves to counteract stress tensions. Here we are dealing with tension-balances of varying blends. But the perpetual tension between routinization and deroutinization within leisure activities is the principal source of their dynamics: this is the 'shift to risk' which is integral to the activity being experienced (Gaskell and Pearton, 1979). Indeed, as society grows 'more serious', the cultural centrality of leisure sport increases.

In rejecting conventional work–leisure analyses, Elias and Dunning (1986) map out what they term the spare-time spectrum. The details of this need not concern us here. Rather, it is important to note that leisure activities are seen to fall into three forms: purely or mainly sociable activities; activities involving motility; and 'mimetic' activities. While sociable activities have the potential to serve important *gemeinschaft* functions, an examination of which would also prove fruitful in an overall study of the emotions, in this context attention will focus on 'mimetic' activities.

'Mimetic' activities vary considerably both in terms of their intensity and style but have basic structural characteristics in common; that is, they provide a 'make-believe' setting which allows emotions to flow more easily and which elicits excitement of some kind imitating that produced by real-life situations, yet without its dangers or risks. 'Mimetic' activities thus allow, within certain limits, for socially permitted self-centredness. Excitement is elicited by the creation of tensions: this can involve imaginary or controlled 'real' danger, mimetic fear and/or pleasure, sadness and/or joy. This controlled decontrolling of excitement lies, for Elias and Dunning (1986), at 'the heart of leisure sport'. The different moods evoked in this make-believe setting are the 'siblings' of those aroused in real-life situations. This applies whether the setting is a tragedy enacted at the Old Vic or a soccer match played at the Stadium of Light. They involve the experience of pleasurable excitement which is at the core of most play needs. But whereas both involve pleasurable excitement, in sport, but especially in 'achievement sport', struggles between human beings play a central part. Indeed, some sport forms resemble real battles between hostile groups.

For Elias and Dunning, sport-games need to be understood as a 'single configuration' in which the configuration on one side and that of the other are interdependent and inseparable. It is the fluctuating configuration of players itself upon which, at any given point in the game process, individuals base their decisions and moves. Sport-games are therefore conceptualized as figurations which have a hierarchy of several 'I', 'Me', 'We' and 'They' relationships. Sport-games involve a complex of interdependent polarities built into the game pattern which provide the *raison d'être* for game dynamics. Each of these polarities contributes to the maintenance of what Elias and Dunning call the 'tone' or 'tension-balance' of the game. The details concerning these polarities need not concern us here. It is important simply to recognize that these polarities are not mutually exclusive. Rather, they form a matrix of cross-cutting tensions within the fluctuating network of interdependencies of a game, and it is upon them that the decisions and moves of individuals depend. There are, however, additional polarities, notably between the interests of players and those of spectators and other powerful outsiders and between 'seriousness' and 'play'. For Dunning (1979: 334) tension-balances in games are:

Partly a consequence of the relatively autonomous dynamics of specific game-figurations and partly a consequence of the manner in which such figurations are articulated into the wider structure of social interdependencies.

The tension-balances to which Dunning is drawing attention here are also closely connected to the socially conditioned psychological need to experience the kind of spontaneous, elementary, unreflective yet pleasurable excitement referred to earlier, and the 'quality' of the tension-balance, the ebb and flow of the game dynamics, influences the nature of the participants' emotional experience.

Reference also needs to be made to several other key features of the Eliasian perspective on leisure, sport and the emotions. The mimetic sphere, though creating imaginary and staged settings, forms a distinct and integral part of social reality. It is no less real than any other part of social life. The manner in which this quest for enjoyable excitement finds expression in social institutions and customs also varies greatly over time and space. Nevertheless, the 'mimetic' sphere does contain elements which are integral to all leisure forms, namely sociability, motility and imagination. There is no leisure activity where all these elements are absent; more usually two or three elements combine with varying intensity.

In studying the problems of leisure, therefore, attention must focus on two interdependent questions: what are the characteristics of the personal leisure needs developed in the more complex societies of our time, and what are the characteristics of the specific types of leisure events developed in societies of this type for the satisfaction of these needs? Analysis of these dimensions and questions requires a multidisciplinary approach. The study of social structure and that of the emotions cannot be pursued in separate compartments. According to Elias and Dunning (1986) biological, psychological and anthropological research as well as sociological research is required.

AN EVALUATION OF THE ELIASIAN PERSPECTIVE ON SPORT, LEISURE AND THE EMOTIONS

There is much to commend this approach. In adopting a developmental and comparative perspective, and not simply tacking on a 'historical' dimension in the manner which is characteristic of some so-called 'historical sociology', the figurational approach allows for the substantive exploration of how leisure forms have assumed their characteristic patterns in modern societies. In addition, by formulating the idea of the 'spare-time spectrum', the rigid work–leisure dichotomy so beloved of both the 'conventional wisdom' in leisure studies and the neo-Marxist alternative promoted by Clarke and Critcher (1985), is thoroughly shredded.[2] Furthermore, the notion that leisure is synonymous with 'freedom' is also seen as inadequate. Instead, it is argued that modern leisure is characterized by a historically specific 'affect economy' (*Affektshaushalt*) of balances and restraints which have both enabling and constraining elements. For Elias and Dunning, leisure does not fulfil a 'compensatory function' associated with some general need to release tension. Rather, it involves the creation of tension as well as its release and the 'function' which leisure serves for individuals or social groups has to be viewed from the perspective of the long-term figurational shifts in patterns of economic, political and emotional bonding (Rojek, 1985: 164).

This point needs emphasizing, given the apparent confusion in the minds of some researchers who have encountered the work of Elias and Dunning. What Ferguson (1981) and Gallmeier (1987) have written on the emotions, for example, fundamentally misunderstands the figurational perspective when they suggest that the expression of emotions by players or spectators is interpreted by Elias and Dunning as a release for personal frustrations or social strains. Let us hope that the review so far provided in this chapter has laid to rest that particular portrayal of Elias and Dunning's work.

Of crucial importance to Elias and Dunning's analysis of sport, leisure and the emotions is the theory of the civilizing process. For Rojek (1985), who argues that leisure relations today are more privatized, individuated, commercialized and pacified than ever before, it is the concept of the civilizing process which draws all these themes together. It also provides, in Rojek's words 'a powerful rationale for explaining why [sport and leisure] have assumed their characteristic form in modern society' and a 'unifying problematic for leisure studies'. The present chapter does not argue with the overall thrust of Rojek's evaluation, though certain re-emphases will be detailed in due course. What I want to restate at this stage is that the concept of the mimetic sphere is interwoven with the rationale referred to and is of particular significance in developing a sociology of the emotions. It is this sphere that provides an enclave within which a controlled and pleasurable decontrolling of restraints on emotions is both possible and socially permitted.

Elias and Dunning are also to be commended for providing an analysis of sport-game dynamics and tension-balances in leisure activities more generally, which avoids the dichotomy between the 'micro' and 'macro' dimensions of emotional experience. Such a fault characterizes symbolic interactionist work on sport and the emotions (for example, Gallmeier, 1987). By virtue of the elasticity and fixity of rules, written or otherwise, quasi-autonomous networks of interdependent action emerge. Yet these networks can only be fully understood if it is recognized that they form interdependent parts of a wider social structure. In teasing out the nature and extent of the emotional experiences involved, reference to the interconnections between game-dynamics, the mimetic sphere and the civilizing process thus becomes essential.

The observation which Elias and Dunning (1986) make regarding the striking similarity between modern sport and the functions of religious customs of earlier periods is of relevance in this connection. An examination of this dimension is crucial to understanding both the emotional experience of sport for individuals and for assessing sport's social significance. The emotions engendered may be amplified and/or controlled both through processes of ritual and taboo and through the excitement generated by sports encounters and can thus lead to the experience of sport as 'sacred' and radically separate from the flow of 'profane' life. Durkheim's (1976) examination of Australian Aboriginal rites, for example, highlights not only the element of excitement in these activities but also the quest for sacred significance.

While I have concentrated in this section on detailing what I regard as the strengths of the Eliasian perspective, a number of re-emphases are also arguably necessary. The insights provided by Elias and Dunning regarding the sportization of folk-customs have undoubtedly broadened our understanding of the emergence of modern sport. Unfortunately, however, Elias and Dunning have tended to focus mainly on specific sports, particularly in their detailed studies, and have neglected others. Of course, there is only a certain amount that any one group can do and indeed a call is being made here for further substantive analyses of other sport and leisure forms. But the re-emphasis required is more than simply a question of more work needing to be done.

The sports that Elias and Dunning have focused on have tended to be those which best confirm the linkages with their theoretical model of sport. That is, sports where a high degree of 'battle excitement' is recurrently generated and where the emphasis of identity formation is on forms of manliness. The relevance of this for an analysis of the balance of gender power is not doubted. It has proved useful, for example, in teasing out the significance of different forms of manliness over time (Maguire, 1986). However, this does not exhaust the identity formation qualities of sport. This requires spelling out.

The functions which Dunning (in Elias and Dunning, 1986) attributes to sport, with his emphasis on the quest for excitement and manly identity, capture only a part – albeit an important part – of the character of the sports and leisure experience. My point is that sport involves the quest for 'exciting significance'. This is not merely a question of semantics. Such an assertion is based on a re-reading of Elias's own work on the emotions and on research which probes the 'symbolic' nature of sport. To repeat, in the Eliasian scheme the three main elements of leisure are identified as sociability, motility and imagination. As we also noted earlier, there is no sport form where all these elements are absent; more usually, two or three elements combine with varying intensity. Significantly, however, while Elias and Dunning (1986) note that sport and art-forms share the same mimetic function in producing an enjoyable and controlled decontrolling of emotions, they distinguish between them in terms of the fact that sport has the character of a battle which resembles real battles fought between rival groups. The quest is for battles enacted playfully in a contrived context which can produce enjoyable battle excitement with a minimum of injuries to the human participants. Compared with the arts, the scope for the exercise of the imagination involved appears to be of a rather restricted and heavily rule-bound kind.

This observation relates to a rethinking of how the Eliasian concept of the emotions has been applied to sport. In sport as elsewhere we are dealing with the social construction and presentation of emotions. Emotions are seen to involve cognitive and affective dimensions. An understanding of how various emotional vocabularies are used and how some aspects of emotions are culturally relative and others culturally universal is required. Our ability to describe feelings varies between cultures and may be more sophisticated than the actual physiological processes involved. Although Elias and Dunning (1986) are right to point to differences within and between mimetic events, in doing so they appear to have overlooked, or at least to have underplayed, the fact that identity formation in sport also involves the quest for self-realization and the presentation of self (Goffman, 1961; Kaelin, 1968; Gerber, 1972).

The omission by Elias and Dunning (1986) to consider the self-realization aspects of identity-formation in sport appears to stem from two sources. First, from their interpretation of the relative mixture of the elements of the mimetic sphere which characterize sport, though not leisure more generally; and secondly, I suspect, from the type of psychological and physiological research used to support their analysis. While they are right to point to the need for multidisciplinary research, the form in which they have envisaged it is too narrow; that is, they have tended to utilize forms of Freudian psychology and physiological evidence which examine the 'elemental' make-up of humans. In my view, however, there is a need to conduct a dialogue with those forms of humanistic psychology which probe such issues as 'altered states' (Murphy and White, 1978), 'peak experiences' (Maslow, 1968), and the cognitive dimensions of the sports experience (Nideffer, 1976). The psychology of happiness or pleasure, in short, is not exhausted by Freud (Argyle, 1987). In addition, there is now a growing body of literature which examines the physiological concomitants of these psychological dimensions (Riggs, 1981; Glasser, 1979). Here, interdisciplinary work examining the role of endorphins and encephalin in the lived experience of sport may be of benefit, but would require reference to an overall theory such as that provided by Elias and Dunning in order to help 'make sense' of the substantive data.

A major problem facing the symbolic interactionist and phenomenological research which has examined the self-realization dimension of the identity-forming qualities of sport is that it does so without any reference to the other dimensions which Elias and Dunning correctly highlight. Furthermore, such research is more concerned with 'micro-worlds' than with teasing out, as Elias and Dunning do, how specific interdependencies are interwoven with other sets of interdependencies. As a consequence, such research fails to grasp that 'self-realization' is not achieved alone: one does so in the company of 'others'. Furthermore, the very quest for this 'self-realization' is indicative of both the point in the civilizing process so far reached and of the main features of leisure relations to which Rojek draws attention.

But if such research has overlooked the fact that this quest is contoured by, for example, the commodification of modern culture, there is a case to be made that Elias and Dunning have also paid insufficient attention to this process and its effects when examining sport and the emotions. In addition, the dimension of sport and leisure experiences referred to by symbolic interactionists does deserve greater consideration than that so far given to it by Elias and Dunning. These observations lead me on to consider some lines of enquiry and areas of dialogue from which the figurational or process-sociological perspective could benefit.

SPORT AND THE EMOTIONS: LINES OF ENQUIRY AND DIALOGUE

In this final section I wish to examine three lines of enquiry and dialogue which may assist the general task of providing a more adequate sociological theory of emotions. These are: symbolic interactionist research on sport and the emotions; research on the commodification of pleasurable emotions; and studies of the body in consumer culture. I will argue that, while accepting the general model of sport, leisure and the emotions outlined by Elias and Dunning, reference to each of these areas can enhance the nature and range of that model. Let us discuss these areas in more detail.

While it is not appropriate to detail to any great extent the basic assumptions on which symbolic interactionism rests, a number of key points need stating. According to this position, meaningful behaviour emerges out of interaction with others. Meaning, say its adherents, constructs the social world of the individual. Social life is also a kind of drama which individuals act out and thus everyday interaction involves the presentation of self. Working within this tradition, Shott (1979: 1323) has argued for a symbolic interactionist theory of emotion which assumes that:

Within the limits set by social norms and internal stimuli, individuals construct their emotions: and their definitions and interpretations are critical to this often emergent process. Internal states and cues, necessary as they are for affective experience, do not in themselves establish feeling, for it is the actor's definitions and interpretations that give physiological states their emotional significance or nonsignificance.

Considered in this light, emotions involve a 'performance' situated in time and space. Primarily concerned with the construction of emotion by the actor, symbolic interactionist research focuses on the actor's definitions and interpretations and on the emergent, constructed character of much human behaviour. Both are seen by Shott as central to the actor's experience of emotion. Similarly, for Zurcher (1982: 2) 'the performance of emotions is enacted by individuals in terms of their understanding of appropriate emotional behaviours in a particular situation'. Sets of emotions are engendered by specific situations. They are also co-produced and, while they are an essential part of the presentation of self, they also reflect structured events.

Utilizing this overall framework, Zurcher (1982) views sports events as involving the orchestrating of emotions. This orchestration entails a scripted phasing which begins with the arousal of expectations for an emotional experience. These expectations generate a diffuse emotional state which is directed into a series of discrete and identifiable emotional displays. Zurcher's study of American football was followed by Gallmeier's (1987) study of professional ice-hockey which reached similar conclusions.

Their work is not without value. It clearly demonstrates the need for a theory of the emotions to pay greater attention to the construction and performance of emotion by people. From an Eliasian perspective there are, however, two main problems. Though Shott (1979: 1320) correctly acknowledges that 'there is a social framework that modifies the actor's experience, interpretation, and expression of emotion', in the accounts which have dealt with sport the emphasis is on the 'micro-world'. No sense of how such small-scale interaction is, at one and the same time, part of more long-term and enduring social interdependencies is evident. In addition, though Shott (1979: 1318) argues that physiological arousal and cognitive labelling 'are necessary components of the actor's experience of emotion', in symbolic interactionist work on sport the need to dovetail this level of the problem into the analysis is not usually recognized. Zurcher (1982: 3), for example, writes: 'I will not address the physiological bases of the emotions I describe, but will assume that for sociological purposes a consideration of emotions can be abstracted from physiology.' As a consequence, symbolic interactionist research again compartmentalizes the social actor. In this way, such research stands in one of the traditions examining the emotions critiqued by Elias. Attention is paid to the cognitive side of the person rather than examining people 'in the round'.

Nevertheless, the emphasis placed on dramaturgical analysis in the work of symbolic interactionists does afford the opportunity to examine both the construction and the performance dimension of human emotions and the identity-forming qualities of sport. As such, analysis along these lines would enhance the exploration of the experience of emotions in the mimetic sphere. This should not be taken simply as an injunction that ethnographic work needs to be done. The construction and performance elements of emotionality certainly need careful consideration, but ethnographic work alone will not suffice in that connection. Probes into the construction and performance of emotions need to be tied in with analyses of how such everyday interaction is part of wider, longer-term chains of interdependency. It is the probing of the interconnectedness of 'micro' and 'macro' worlds that the Eliasian perspective is better placed to examine than research within a symbolic interactionist framework as it has been conceived of and conducted up to now.

The study of the commodification of pleasurable emotions does, in some ways, link in with the research conducted from a symbolic interactionist perspective on the emotions. For example, Arlie Hochschild, one of the most-noted writers in the study of this area, has utilized work drawn from that tradition. Her work is of particular relevance in the present context because Cas Wouters (1989), one of the leading Dutch exponents of the Eliasian approach, has critically compared and contrasted her perspective on emotion management and the commodification of feeling with that of Norbert Elias. By examining her work in a little more detail, it will be possible to consider the more general issue of the commodification of pleasurable emotions.

Hochschild (1983) sets out to develop a 'social theory of emotions' and utilizes both a form of Marxism and the dramaturgical perspective derived from Goffman. Hochschild argues that commercialization threatens the 'real self' by organizing and structuring behaviour and feeling and by demanding of the person that they 'emotion manage' their 'self'. In probing this issue, Hochschild focuses on the 'costs' of emotion management and how such 'costs' are exacerbated by the commercialization of feeling. In detailing the 'costs' involved, she distinguishes between the 'true' and the 'false' self and the 'public' and the 'private' self. The 'public' self becomes processed, standardized, subjected to hierarchical control and corresponds to the 'false' self. In contrast, the 'private' self focuses on the preservation of personal wellbeing and pleasure and is, in fact, the 'real' self. It is not necessary, in this context, to go into the the details of Hochschild's argument; it is enough to note that Wouters sees such a conception as based on a false dichotomy. In reality, Wouters (1989: 98) argues, public and private selves are located on a continuum. By avoiding such a crude dichotomy, the analyst is better placed to grasp that there exist enabling and constraining features at both ends of this continuum.

For Hochschild, however, in the public world – particularly of work – individuals have to emotion-manage themselves in the light of the corporate needs of the organization they work for. She examines the work experiences of flight attendants and notes how one visible expression of this is the 'company smile'. But Wouters demonstrates how Hochschild has once again introduced a false dichotomy into her analysis. In proposing such a rigid differentiation between a 'company' and a 'private' smile, Wouters argues that Hochschild fails to recognize that workers, customers and managers do, to some extent, have common interests and that her overall model ends up depicting workers as perfect 'company robots' (Wouters, 1989: 100). But Wouters does not only take exception to such substantive aspects of Hochschild's work. In addition he suggests that the 'social theory of emotion' developed to explain the issues examined is as artificial as the dichotomies between private and public selves. Because Hochschild's argument is based on the idea that the public world exploits the private world, she develops a theory of 'transmutation' in which the 'private emotional system' comes to 'fall under the sway of large organizations, social engineering and the profit motive' (Hochschild, 1983: 19, cited in Wouters, 1989: 101).

In critiquing her theory of emotions for its failure to consider the learned, internalized control of emotions, Wouters offers three additional points which have implications for the study of sport, culture and the emotions. First, while the issues raised by Hochschild require serious consideration, such consideration is blocked if only short-term time-scales are adopted. A developmental and comparative dimension is required. Secondly, developments in standards of behaviour and feeling do not stop at the borders of either private or public life. There is an overall pattern of self-regulation and emotion management. Thirdly, changes in personal and social standards of behaviour and feeling are not exclusively determined by commercial factors. Processes of individuation and pacification, for example, play a part as well.

Despite the shortcomings of studies such as that of Hochschild, the study of the commodification of pleasurable emotions does require greater attention than has so far been given it by Elias and Dunning in their analysis of the controlled decontrolling of emotions in the mimetic sphere. Notwithstanding Wouters's criticisms of Hochschild's case study of Delta's flight attendants, a study of how élite sports-people or musicians involved in, for example, the global pro-tennis circuit or a concert tour, emotion-manage their lives in a highly commercialized setting, would be of use in adding to our cumulative knowledge of sport, leisure and the emotions. Having said that, any such study which did not take on board Wouters's observations regarding KLM flight attendants, might well be characterized by the same weaknesses as those which have been identified in Hochschild's work.

Research conducted on sport subcultures also highlights a number of issues which are relevant in this connection. Studies of professional wrestling, for example, while revealing the 'identity work' needed to become a successful member of the subculture, are complemented by studies of ice-hockey and baseball which emphasize the existence of 'back-regions', the non-public aspects of subcultures, in which those involved can find ways in which to humanize potentially alienating work situations (Donnelly, 1985). Work on subcultural responses would complement the general framework on sport, leisure and emotions being proposed here.

If studies of the spare-time spectrum and, in particular, of the mimetic sphere have so far neglected the need to consider in detail the commodification of pleasurable emotions so, too, have Elias and Dunning overlooked the need to give due attention to an examination of the use of the body in consumer culture. In one sense, this omission is rather surprising. In

Elias and Dunning's analysis (1986: 96), reference is made to one aspect of the spare-time spectrum as involving the 'routinized catering for one's biological needs and care of one's body'. Unfortunately, this point is not developed and its connections with the mimetic part of the spare-time spectrum are not explored. Let me spell out why a study of the body in consumer culture is relevant both to this issue and to the task of developing a theory of sport and the emotions. In considering the body in consumer culture, Featherstone (1983: 18) remarks:

> Consumer culture latches onto the prevalent self-preservationist conception of the body, which encourages the individual to adopt instrumental strategies to combat deterioration and decay . . . and combines it with the notion that the body is a vehicle of pleasure and self-expression. Images of the body beautiful, openly sexual and associated with hedonism, leisure and display, emphasize the importance of appearance and the 'look'.

In consumer culture, the emphasis placed on 'body maintenance' and 'appearance' suggests to Featherstone two basic categories, namely, what he calls the 'inner' and the 'outer' body. Within consumer culture these basic categories become 'conjoined', that is, the 'prime purpose of the maintenance of the inner body becomes the enhancement of the appearance of the outer body' (Featherstone, 1983: 18).

The implications of this observation for the study of sport and the emotions are considerable. It suggests, for example, that activities in the 'spare-time spectrum' devoted to 'body maintenance' and those involving 'mimetic' events may not solely be devoted to a controlled decontrolling of emotions, but are also bound up with the tendency in consumer culture for the maintenance of the inner body to be undertaken primarily in order to contribute to the enhancement of the appearance of the outer body. This appearance is, in fact, contoured and shaped by images derived from consumer capitalism. What we may be witnessing is a shift to 'display' in which, as Featherstone remarks, the 'performing self' plays a crucial part.

Clearly, recognition of bodily appearance also has implications for the study of the forms of emotion management which people perform in tune with the tone of consumer lifestyles. The staging of emotions thus involves not only the creation of tension-balances in which a pleasurable controlled decontrolling of emotions takes place but also reflects the concomitant need to enhance appearance and thus maintain one's status within the mainstream of consumer culture. Within the logic of consumer culture, Featherstone (1983: 25) argues:

fitness and slimness become associated not only with energy, drive and vitality but worthiness as a person: likewise the body beautiful comes to be taken as a sign of prudence and prescience in health matters. . . . Body maintenance is firmly established as a virtuous leisure activity which will reap further lifestyle rewards resulting from an enhanced appearance; body maintenance in order to look good merges with the stylised images of looking good while maintaining the body.

Featherstone also correctly argues that these images 'do not merely serve to stimulate false needs fostered onto the individual'. As Elias and Dunning observe with regard to their study of sport, leisure and the emotions, such needs are 'genuine'. What needs to be grasped in a more embracing analysis, however, is that the mimetic activities which exist to allow the expression and fulfilment of such emotional needs are, in late-twentieth-century Western societies, bound up in the consumer culture to which Featherstone directs our attention. We need studies of how contemporary cultural tastes and desires are created and sustained and how they relate to genuine bodily needs and desires. But up to now, the work of Elias and Dunning and, in the main, that of other researchers working within a figurational or process-sociological perspective, has focused more on long-term changes. Exponents of this perspective now need to complement such research by pushing the time frame forward and dealing with issues of continuity and change in sporting and leisure tastes as we approach the twenty-first century.

DISCUSSION

In this chapter an attempt has been made to highlight the distinctive contribution that a process-sociological perspective on sport, leisure and the emotions can make. In doing so, however, this contribution has also been evaluated in a relatively detached manner, highlighting where greater clarification and refinement are required. Reference has hence been made in this connection to other work on the emotions. While certain criticisms have been offered, most notably with regard to symbolic interactionist research and of work that examines the commodification of the body and pleasurable excitement, I have also argued that the process-sociological perspective must take on board some of the issues raised by these other approaches. In concluding, let me highlight two points which I feel the process-sociological or figurational perspective must pay greater heed to. These two points reflect the need for theoretical and substantive work to probe both enabling and constraining features of the structured processes in which sport and leisure are located.

In examining the identity-forming qualities of sport, I have argued that the manner in which Elias's theory of the emotions had been applied to sport is rather lop-sided: while due attention had been paid to the affective dimension, insufficient prominence had been given to the 'self-realization' dimension involved in identity-formation in sport. By probing the issue of the construction and presentation of emotions, in which, up to now, symbolic interactionist research has been exclusively involved, a more adequate grasp of the emotional experience of sport would be possible. However, as I also argued, such research on its own is not without weaknesses. Reference was therefore also made to the need to examine how the body and the quest for and experience of pleasurable excitement are constrained, hemmed in and contoured by commodification processes. There is a need to probe how, for example, consumer culture penetrates the terrain of the mimetic sphere, but also, at one and the same time, to examine how specific sub-cultures have the potential to provide 'back-region' resistance to such penetration. An examination of the dynamics of contemporary cultural relations is needed, with an especial interest paid to the formation of taste. In this regard what is needed above all is a radical critique of culture which avoids both the cultural élitism of 'mass society' theory and the blindness of 'critical' theory to the fact that 'insider' consumption in the mimetic sphere can involve active appropriation of meanings and not just passive surrender to the meanings imposed by powerful 'outsider' groups (Maguire, 1990).

The need for a theory of the emotions and a form of historical sociology in order to come to terms with the issues raised in this chapter is crucial, and Elias and Dunning are to be complemented for providing an overall framework within which to begin. It is necessary to examine how the present emerged out of the past and how the present is continuing to change. But it is also necessary to probe how the modern quest for exciting significance is enabled and constrained by more recent figurational developments. As has been argued here, reference needs to be made to three interrelated aspects. First, to the body as a vehicle for pleasure and self-expression; secondly, to face-to-face interactions in which the presentation of self and the management of impressions are central; and thirdly, to the organization, technologizing and surveillance of disciplined bodies (Hoberman, 1988). Such a re-emphasis, however, also requires one to recognize that the modern quest for 'exciting significance' is bounded and contoured both by interdependency chains inherited from the past and by contemporary cultural relations. Eliasian writers have pointed to long-term trends such as pacification, privatization, commercialization and individuation (Rojek, 1985). The task now is to demonstrate substantively how these trends find expression in the present day. Common ground can be made in this respect with other writers who offer a radical critique of contemporary culture.

Emotions are not something abstract, some steady-state or reified phenomenon. There is, for example, a sociogenesis, and not simply a bio-genesis or psychogenesis, of grief or anxiety. When we examine grief-stricken or anxiety-ridden people what we need to do is to locate them in the context of a funeral or of parents anxiously pacing outside the room of their sick child. We need to examine both the culturally relative and the cultur-ally universal aspects of emotions, patterned as they are along class and gender lines.

Let me conclude by saying that we are dealing here with a relatively unexplored landscape. What I have attempted to do in this revision of the work of Elias and Dunning is to suggest some promising routes to follow. The analysis seeks to open up a dialogue between different perspectives in the sociology of sport and leisure. But it does so on the basis of a striving for detached critique, not one ideologically predisposed to dismissal of alternatives. Therefore, while the analysis presented here remains attached principally to the figurational perspective, it takes Elias at his word and sees what has been accomplished so far as nothing more than a 'symptom of a beginning'.

Notes

1. This is a revised version of a paper presented at the ninth annual conference of the North American Society for the Sociology of Sport, Cincinnati, Ohio, 9–13 November 1988.

2. Moorhouse (1989) makes a similar point, but in mapping out the alternative to the work–leisure dichotomy favoured both by Parker and by Clarke and Critcher, he fails to recognize that Elias and Dunning have provided a far superior conceptualization of the issue than that of Pahl and that the explora-tion of pleasure he identifies as being central has been an integral part of the study of sport and leisure which Elias and Dunning have undertaken over the past twenty years. This observation will also lay to rest the idea proposed by some of those reviewers who assert that a Glasgow–Leicester axis somehow exists.

References

Argyle, M. (1987), *The Psychology of Happiness* (London: Methuen).

Biddle, S. (1985), 'The Study of Emotion in Sport: an Attribution Perspective Paper', presented at 28th International Council of Health, Physical Education and Recreation World Congress proceedings, July–August 1985.

Bourdieu, P. (1986), *Distinction: A Social Critique of the Judgement of Taste* (London: Routledge & Kegan Paul).

Brookes, C. (1978), *English Cricket* (London: Weidenfeld & Nicolson).

Clarke, C. and Critcher, C. (1985), *The Devil Makes Work* (London: Macmillan).

Denzin, N. (1984), *On Understanding Emotion* (Washington: Jossey-Bass).

Donnelly, P. (1985), 'Sport Subcultures', in R. Terjung (ed.), *Exercise and Sport Sciences Reviews* (New York: Macmillan) pp. 539–78.

Dunning, Eric (1979), 'The Figurational Dynamics of Modern Sport', *Sportwissenschaft,* 4: 341–59.

Durkheim, E. (1976), *The Elementary Forms of the Religious Life* (London: Allen & Unwin).

Elias, N. (1978a), *What is Sociology?* (London: Hutchinson).

_____ (1978b), *The Civilizing Process* (Oxford: Blackwell).

_____ (1982), *State Formation and Civilization* (Oxford: Blackwell).

_____ (1987), 'On Human Beings and Their Emotions: a Process Sociological Essay', *Theory, Culture and Society,* 4: 339–61.

_____ and Dunning, E. (1986), *Quest for Excitement: Sport and Leisure in the Civilizing Process* (Oxford: Blackwell).

Featherstone, M. (1983), 'The Body in Consumer Culture', *Theory, Culture and Society,* 1(2): 18–33.

Ferguson, J. (1981), 'Emotions in Sport Sociology', *International Review of Sport Sociology,* 16: 15–23.

Gallmeier, C. (1987), 'Putting on the Game Face: the Staging of Emotions in Professional Ice-hockey', *Sociology of Sport Journal,* 4: 347–62.

Gaskell, G. and Pearton, R. (1979), 'Aggression and Sport', in J. Goldstein (ed.), *Sport, Games and Play* (Hillsdale, N.J.: Erlbaum).

Gerber, E. W. (ed.) (1979), *Sport and the Body* (Philadelphia, Pa: Lea & Febiger).

Glasser, W. (1979), *Positive Addiction* (New York: Harper & Row).

Goffman, E. (1961), *Encounters* (New York: Bobbs-Merrill).

Goudsblom, J., Gleichmann, P. and Korte, H. (eds) (1979), *Human Figurations* (Amsterdam: Amsterdams Sociologisch Tijdschrift).

Hargreaves, J. (ed.) (1982), *Sport, Culture and Ideology* (London: Routledge & Kegan Paul).

Hargreaves, John (1986), *Sport, Power and Culture* (Cambridge, Polity Press).

Harre, R. (ed.) (1986), *The Social Construction of Emotions* (Oxford: Blackwell).

Hoberman, J. (1988), 'Sport and the Technological Image of Man', in W. Morgan and K. Meier (eds), *Philosophic Inquiry in Sport* (Champaign, Ill.: Human Kinetics).

Hochschild, A. (1983), *The Managed Heart: Commercialization of Human Feeling* (Los Angeles, Cal.: University of California Press).

Kaelin, E. F. (1968), 'The Well-played Game: Notes Toward an Aesthetics of Sport', *Quest,* 10: 16–28.

Kemper, T. (1981), 'Social Constructionist and Positivist Approaches to the Sociology of Emotions', *American Journal of Sociology,* 87: 336–62.

Maguire, J. (1986), 'Images of Manliness and Competing Ways of Living in Late Victorian and Edwardian Britain', *British Journal of Sport History,* 3: 265–87.

_____ (1990), 'More than a Sporting Touchdown: the Making of American Football in England, 1982–1990', *Sociology of Sport Journal,* 3: 213–37.

_____ (1991), 'Science, Sports Sciences and Process Sociology', *Quest,* forthcoming.

Maslow, A. H. (1968), *Toward a Psychology of Being* (New York: Van Nostrand).

Moorhouse, B. (1989), 'Models of Work, Models of Leisure', in C. Rojek, (ed.), *Leisure for Leisure* (London: Macmillan).

Murphy, M. and White, R. (1978), *The Psychic Side of Sports* (Reading, Mass.: Addison Wesley).

Nideffer, R. M. (1976), *The Inner Athlete* (New York: Crowell).

Riggs, C. E. (1981), 'Endorphins, Neurotransmitters and/or Neuromodulators and Exercise', in M. H. Sacks and M. L. Sacks (eds), *Psychology of Running* (Champaign, Ill.: Human Kinetics).

Rojek, C. (1985), *Capitalism and Leisure Theory* (London: Tavistock).

_____ (ed.) (1989), *Leisure for Leisure* (London: Macmillan).

Scheff, T. (1983), 'Towards Integration in the Social Psychology of Emotions', *American Review of Sociology,* 9: 333–54.

Shott, S. (1979), 'Emotions and Social Life: a Symbolic Interactionist Analysis', *American Journal of Sociology,* 84: 1317–34.

Turner, B. (1984), *The Body and Society: Explorations in Social Theory* (Oxford: Blackwell).

Wouters, C. (1989), 'The Sociology of Emotions and Flight Attendants: Hochschild's Managed Heart', *Theory, Culture and Society,* 6: 95–123.

Zurcher, L. (1982), 'The Staging of Emotion: a Dramaturgical Analysis', *Symbolic Interaction,* 5: 1–22.

5 Sports and Civilization: Is Violence the Central Problem?

RUUD STOKVIS

INTRODUCTION

In sociological discussions on sports, defining the term 'sport' remains a recurring problem. In general, it is best not to deliberate upon the matter for too long and to raise the specific subject one has in mind. After all, each and every one of us understands what we are talking about.

However, when I disagree with the interpretation of the term implied in the studies of Norbert Elias and Eric Dunning, I must question its meaning. In 'The Genesis of Sport as a Sociological Problem' (Elias and Dunning, 1986) Elias compares the terms 'sport' and 'industry'. Both terms can be used in a wider and a narrower sense (Elias and Dunning, 1986: 129). In the narrower sense they are used in relation to the specific characteristics developed by industry and sport during the last two centuries. According to Elias, these characteristics of sports consist in the fact that the violence in game contests is 'relatively restrained' and 'representative of a comparatively high sensitivity against playfully inflicting serious injuries on others for the delight of spectators' (Elias and Dunning, 1986: 131; see also 19, 20). In other words, modern sports represent a specific stage in the process of civilization and their development can be understood in terms of Elias's theory of the civilizing process.

I do not believe this view of modern sports to be totally wrong but I should like to demonstrate that it is too limited, and because of this, it leads sociological research on sports too often to matters of violence and its control, whereas more important areas for research, such as its formal organization and standardization, its diffusion in national societies and throughout the world, its professionalization and commercialization, remain beyond its scope. A viewpoint on sports will have to be found which will enable us to understand changes in their levels of violence as well as these other important developments.

In the first part of this chapter I shall demonstrate how misleading it can be when we fix our attention exclusively on the control of violence in

121

sports. In the second part I shall in more general terms expound my objections to Elias's and Dunning's ideas on modern sports and outline a wider viewpoint. I shall argue that the main characteristics of modern sports are their organization on national and international levels and their accompanying standardization. These are also the main differences between modern sports and traditional sport-like pastimes. Based upon this viewpoint, the third and final part of the chapter offers a short evaluation of Elias's and Dunning's work on sports.

PARLIAMENTARIZATION AND FOX-HUNTING

In 'An Essay on Sport and Violence' (Elias and Dunning, 1986), English fox-hunting is discussed in terms of the theory of the civilizing process. According to Elias, the development of fox-hunting is relevant to our understanding of the interpretation by the English upper class of the term 'sport'. From the eighteenth century onwards, fox-hunting became their most favourite 'sport'. Characteristic of this form of hunting is, as Elias states, the restriction of violence which is implied by the way the hunting is performed. Hounds are used that have been trained to chase only the specific fox to whose scent they have been introduced and no other animals they may come across. The hunters are unarmed and are restricted to riding behind the hounds. They get their pleasure from riding the countryside and from the tension arising from the hounds hunting the fox. The killing of the fox is left to the hounds. The thought of eating the quarry would not enter the hunters' minds. During the eighteenth century the development of this restrained way of hunting was related to other changes in English society, according to Elias. In that same period, as far as political decisions regarding English society as a whole were concerned, Parliament became the dominating institution. Elias calls this a process of 'parliamentarization'. In his view, this process had a civilizing influence on the aristocracy since they were the most involved. They were forced to regulate their conflicts, not by using physical violence but by party formation and debate. This contributed to a process of personality formation characterized, among other things, by a taste for pastimes that were less violent than they had previously been; that is, a taste for non-violent competition. Before the eighteenth century English hunting was much more violent, according to Elias. In those days the actual killing of the quarry offered the climax of excitement, whereas in fox-hunting the pleasure and excitement were aroused during the time the hounds were chasing the fox. Besides this, the earlier forms of hunting were less restricted as to the kinds of animal being hunted.

If we take a closer look at the development of hunting in England, we shall see that the civilized traits in fox-hunting to which Elias refers existed long before the process of parliamentarization began. In fact, they developed in France during the rise of the absolute monarchy independently of any form of parliamentarization. During the reign of James I (1603–25), English hunting practices were adapted to the French model. I shall briefly describe the civilization of hunting in France and demonstrate how the development of English fox-hunting fits into this process.

In France, the civilization of hunting partly corresponds with Elias's depiction of the process of state-formation and its connected changes in behaviour, attitudes and feelings. Hunting, as described in an early source from 1375, *Les Livres du roy Modus et de la royne Ratio,* still had many of the uncivilized traits that Elias attributes to all forms of hunting before the process of parliamentarization in England had begun: it was 'crude' and warlike and the meat of the hunted animal was used for food. Nearly 200 years later, in 1561, Jacques du Fouilloux published his book *La Vénerie.* This was the first written codification of courtly hunting practices. It was meant for those who did not hunt for the sake of obtaining food, but who liked hunting for its art (Duchartre, 1973: 549). Instead of the earlier crude slaughtering of, mainly, deer the favourite form of hunting consisted of selecting a deer by its scent by a special hound. The deer was then chased by a pack of hounds trained for this purpose, while the hunters, male and female, followed on horseback until it became exhausted or the hounds had lost its scent. The hunters had to be able to ride their horses well and anticipate the ruses of the chased animal. The pleasure was gained from the able performance of these 'tasks'. In France, and later in England, this style of hunting – the hunting 'par force' – became the general way in which the élite hunted.

The typical sport-like characteristics Elias observes in English fox-hunting can already be seen in this way of hunting. It was considered the most 'courtly' form of hunting, because the animal had a chance of surviving if it possessed enough endurance and intelligence (Duchartre, 1973: 172, 173). The *'chasse par force'* as developed in France during the sixteenth century offered the hunters enjoyment and tension gained from the competition between the hounds and the deer, while the violence involved in the killing of the deer was reduced to a minimum.

As we have said, this way of hunting was adopted in England during the reign of James I at the beginning of the seventeenth century. James had no liking for the 'unmanly slaughter of released animals in enclosed parks' which had been common practice during the reign of his predecessor, Elizabeth I (1558–1603) (Brailsford, 1969: 28, 110). Its diffusion from France to England may be explained in the same way by which English sports were adopted in other countries some centuries later. In the seventeenth century France became the dominant power in Europe. Manners of the French élite became a prestigious model to be followed by the élites of neighbouring countries. James I hired French riding masters and specialists in hunting to teach the French techniques. French hounds were imported and, just like the French, the English élite went hunting 'par force' (Cuddon, 1980: 436). As in France, their favourite quarry became the deer.

However, in England deer became scarce during the seventeenth century. After the Civil War wild deer could be found in only five areas (ESS, 1968: 557). So few deer were left that, in the 1660s, Charles II brought deer across from Germany to restock the royal parks. He encouraged other landowners to do the same (Cuddon, 1980: 437). This scarcity was a result of the extension of arable land and of the production of timber. Lack of order and control during the Civil War probably encouraged poaching and contributed to the reduction in deer numbers in England. This situation might also explain the many complaints made at the time about foxes killing lambs (ESS, 1968: 557). Several kinds of fox-hunting had already been practised in England during the sixteenth century (Longrigg, 1977: 52), sometimes even using hounds specially trained for hunting foxes (Carr, 1986: 36n). When deer had become scarce, the obvious alternative quarries were hares and foxes, of which there were plenty (Thomas, 1983: 164). Consequently, the English élite was forced to transpose their civilized French way of hunting deer into hunting hares and foxes. During the seventeenth and eighteenth centuries most of the hunts were probably for hares (Longrigg, 1977: 131; Carr, 1986: 25). To adapt the *'chasse par force'* to the typical behaviour of hares and, later, foxes, all kinds of technical changes had to be made in the practice of hunting. These changes, however, had nothing to do with levels of violence and restraint and sport-like or 'courtly' behaviour towards the quarry. Just like the deer, the hares and foxes also received a fair chance if they possessed enough endurance and intelligence.

In the late eighteenth century English fox-hunting was adopted in France. This adoption might be explained by a change in the balance of power between England and France at the time. Whereas France was the dominating power and the cultural centre of Europe in the seventeenth century, England took over its position in the following century.

The interest of the English aristocracy in the French way of hunting during James I's reign demonstrates that they had already acquired a taste for pastimes in which the level of violence was relatively restrained before Parliament acquired its leading role in politics. The watershed in the history of mediaeval and modern England should be placed between 1580 and 1620. In this period, the central government firmly established its monopoly on violence and the aristocrats lost the last traces of their past as practically independent warriors (Stone, 1965: 15, 16, 200). *There is no indication that the experience of non-violent competition between opposing parties in Parliament had anything to do with the development of the typically English way of fox-hunting.* This conclusion is an argument against the kind of relationship that Elias suggests exists between parliamentarization and fox-hunting. It has, however, little bearing on the more general theory of the civilizing process.

Comparison of developments in the different forms of hunting in European countries shows us a very complicated and interesting picture. They are worthy of receiving far more historical and sociological attention than they have so far been given. One line of development seems to be the stylization of cruelty in hunting in societies with a dominating royal or princely court. It is evident that the relatively sport-like '*chasse par force*' first developed in France during the sixteenth century. However, during the reign of Louis XIV (1643–1715) the '*chasse royale*' became less sport-like. The etiquette that came to control all aspects of life at court was extended to the way in which hunting was practised. It became much more ceremonialized and ritualized. This was probably not easy to combine with the uncertainty of success inherent in the '*chasse par force*'. In the '*chasse royale*' the involvement of many servants was required to ascertain that the quarry, usually a deer, was driven to a particular spot in the wood which had been specially prepared and surrounded by nets, where it could be killed in the presence of the king and his courtiers.

German princes and their courtiers had an even crueller taste. Whereas in the '*chasse royale*' some elements of the '*chasse par force*' were maintained – in particular, the identification of the animal one wanted to kill – German aristocrats amused themselves by having all the animals in a certain area driven before their guns or into an enclosed area where they could be slaughtered easily (Cuddon, 1980: 436).

This tendency to have relatively cruel forms of hunting in societies with dominating courts may also, as I have already stated, be observed in England during the reign of Elizabeth I. In England in the seventeenth and eighteenth centuries the prominence of the relatively sport-like hunting 'par force' for deer, and later for hares and foxes, might be related to the relatively independent position of English aristocrats *vis-à-vis* the royal court after the reign of Elizabeth I. This position also influenced the process of parliamentarization, but in order to understand the evolution of fox-hunting and other sports in England, one should look at this position more generally.

If the interpretation of the origin of English fox-hunting I have given proves correct and refutes that of Elias, how is his misconception to be explained? In my opinion, it might be related to too much reliance upon a well-proven theory, in this case, his own theory of the civilizing process. One may be too easily satisfied with a few facts about a certain phenomenon that will fit the theory. Elias's sources of his statement on fox-hunting are two nineteenth-century encyclopaedias and one more-or-less contemporary source: a book by a very rich and famous non-aristocratic huntsman, Peter Beckford, written in 1796 when fox-hunting had been fashionable for some time (Longrigg, 1977: 120). From sources such as these one can hardly hope to obtain a reliable view of the development of fox-hunting.

A related risk in using a well-established theory is selective perception. According to Elias and Dunning, the predominant characteristic of the development of popular pastimes into modern sports was the restraints on the violence of the participants involved in the activities. Their favourite example is the development of hurling. They could also have chosen boxing; and in sixteenth-century France, hunting would be a good example. Yet there are many other sports that were once popular pastimes which developed into modern sports without ever having had any problems concerning violence. I shall comment on this in the next section. As to fox-hunting, it was not changes in the level of its violence that made it an early example of modern sport, but the formation of clubs and great aristocratic hunts which came to use a standardized version of fox-hunting, the so-called Meynellian system (Carr, 1986: 45–65).

FORMAL ORGANIZATION OR CONTROL OF VIOLENCE?

Not all popular pastimes had a violent character before they were transformed into modern sports. Violence was only involved in those pastimes whose competition brought the participants into close physical contact. Besides hurling and boxing, one might think of wrestling and fencing. Violence – according to modern standards we should say cruelty – was involved in a great many pastimes involving animals, such as cock-fighting, dog-fighting, bullbaiting and so on. Nearly all these sports were suppressed during the nineteenth century; they either entirely disappeared or were illegally practised in obscure places. Most of the pastimes that evolved into modern sports, such as cricket, golf, bowling, tennis, archery, horse-racing and all the other sports involving racing, did not have a violent character.

The reader of Elias's essay 'The Genesis of Sport as a Sociological Problem' (Elias and Dunning, 1986) who is aware of the non-violent character of most of the pastimes that turned into sports, will share my disagreement. As I have stated before, his essay makes a distinction between the broader and the narrower sense of the word 'sport', and then begins to demythologize the idea that modern sports can be interpreted as a revival of ancient Greek sports. The argument is that the level of violence in Greek sports was incomparably higher than in modern sports. The difference can only be explained by taking into account the virtually constant state of war between the various cities in Greece. As a matter of fact, this part of the essay is, on its own, very interesting and valuable indeed. However, it strongly suggests that the main difference between modern sports and other pastimes is a matter of the control of violence. Given the fact that so many modern sports evolved from non-violent pastimes, this simply cannot be true. Changes in the level of tolerated violence observed in some sports should be interpreted as aspects of a more general development of pastimes into modern sports.

The need for a more general interpretation certainly does not imply that the theory of the civilizing process and its underlying figurational approach become superfluous. One should merely avoid the tendency to restrict observations on the development of sports to changes in the control of violence. Looking at Elias's study of the civilizing process, we see that the basic phenomena he examines are networks of interdependency. In Europe, from the Middle Ages onwards, these networks became larger and more complex. Changes taking place on the level of the personality of the people involved must be related to the developments of these networks. The development of nation-states, being pacified and centrally governed territories, and the accompanying changes in attitudes and feelings towards violence are one concrete manifestation of the general process of the increase in scale and complexity of interdependencies between people. My proposal is to regard the development of modern sports as another manifestation of this same general process.

The difference from Elias's and Dunning's approach to sports is that its development is not predominantly interpreted as an aspect of the process of state formation and the control of violence. Of course, one must take these processes into account, but the rise of modern sports should, however, primarily be interpreted as another manifestation of the increase in the scale and complexity of social life in Europe and the USA.

What does this mean for the explanation of the rise of modern sports? The approach I propose directs attention first of all to the development of interdependencies in the field of pastimes and sports. *Then the main trend becomes one from locally organized pastimes varying from place to place, to internationally standardized sports.* An important initial stage in this development was the organization on a national level of some local pastimes in England during the seventeenth, eighteenth and nineteenth centuries. This took place in Newmarket, when the great horse-races were first organized (1605) and later when the Jockey Club was founded (1751). Also in the eighteenth century cricket clubs and golf clubs were established to regulate these games nationally. As for rowing, the organization of the Henley Regatta in 1839 was of national importance. Restraining violence was not an issue in the organization and standardization of these sports at a national level. A violent sport such as boxing also became somewhat more standardized during the eighteenth century. But the rules Jack Broughton proposed in 1743 had just as much to do with the standardization of the way matches had to be organized as the control of its violence. Only one out of the seven rules he introduced concerned the regulation of violence in this sport (Fleischer and Andre, 1966: 12). Here, standardization and the control of violence went together.

As Dunning and Sheard point out (1979: 85), in the case of football the main problem for the pupils of each public school was to agree common rules for their school game. When the contacts between the schools became more frequent, the problem of standardization arose at the interschool level. The control of violence, in the form of whether or not to accept 'hacking', became an issue, not on its own, but in relation to the more fundamental dispute between the proponents of the dribbling and the handling game (Green, 1953: 33, see para. 4). It contributed to the division of football into soccer and rugby. But this issue was only one, although an important one, among many to be decided upon, in order to arrive eventually at nationally standardized versions of soccer and rugby.

The relatively early increase in the scale and complexity of life in England could also be seen in the fields of trade, industry, politics and cultural life. In the eighteenth and early nineteenth centuries England became the wealthiest and most powerful country in the world. Everything that furthered this development stimulated the increase in scale and complexity in the field of sports also. This showed itself in early organization and standardization on a national level.

This lengthening of the chains of interdependence (Elias) did not stop at the frontiers of England. Especially during the nineteenth century, relations between the European countries intensified. They all had to cope with the competition from England, the first industrializing nation (Landes, 1969: 126). Wanting to strengthen their countries, the élites of the other European nations were orientated towards the way of life of the English élite: they thought it was one of the secrets of the economic and political power of England (MacAloon, 1981: 80). Sports clubs were established according to English examples. These clubs formed national organizations and, in a surprisingly short period, international organizations were also established, among them the International Olympic Committee (1894). The leaders of these organizations were responsible for the world-wide standardization of sports.

It is unlikely that anyone will dispute that certain of the origins of modern sports are to be found in England. But it was the process of national and international organization that made sport the internationally standardized phenomenon that we know today. As part of this process the restraining of violence took place in some sports but not in all of them.

Returning to the origins of sport in England, one can ask why, if parliamentarization was not an important influence, were aristocrats the first to organize local pastimes into nationally standardized sports? To answer this question one has to consider the social position of the English aristocracy in the seventeenth, eighteenth and nineteenth centuries. Elias makes the same point. But if organization and standardization on a national and international level are regarded as the central characteristics of modern sports, different aspects of this position become of interest. A relevant aspect of their position was their greater autonomy, compared with France, in relation to the king and the central government (Stone, 1965: 503). The king did not force them to live at his court and did not undermine the regional power of the landowners. In England there was no official like the non-aristocratic *intendant* in France, who represented the central government at regional level and usurped the administrative and juridical powers that were once held by the big landowners. In England, as Elias also observes, many aristocrats lived for part of the year on their estates and for part of the year, during the 'season', in London. The 'season' was linked with parliamentary sessions. This is probably the only connection between parliamentarization and the origin of sports. It is unnecessary to speculate about its possible influence on the increase in aristocratic preference for relatively non-violent competition. The 'season' was associated with sport-like activities and aristocrats from all the different regions of the country had to agree on the rules of these events. This is one side of the English setting in which nationally standardized sports were realized.

The other side is the relation between the aristocrats and the people of their region. As the regional position of the nobility was defunctionalized to a lesser extent than that of their French counterparts they were in closer contact with the regional population (Carr, 1986: 49). They had no need to separate themselves from the population because their social position had been firmly established. In this situation they could learn to appreciate local pastimes and could afford to participate to some degree without risking their prestige. They also organized some of these pastimes when they were in London. Here they had to agree on a common version. These agreements led to the rise of the first nationally standardized pastimes: sports.

During the seventeenth and eighteenth centuries the relatively restrained violence and cruelty in English hunting practices compared with those in countries having dominant courts is probably related to the position of the aristocrats in their regional environment. The absence of a very exclusive court society that encompassed their whole lives probably made the English aristocrats susceptible to the opinions of 'well-to-do townsmen' and 'educated country clergymen'. During the seventeenth century these groups were the first to develop a new compassion for animals (Thomas, 1983: 183).

Without doubt, this analysis needs more elaboration. The English landowners formed a well-differentiated class. The smaller landowners, the squires, probably played an important role in the relationship between the big aristocratic landowners and the common people. How these relations were structured and what role sports and hunting played in them should be researched more fully.

If we take the development of clubs, national and international organizations and the accompanying process of standardization as fundamental to the rise of modern sports, the question remains: how should we interpret the restriction in the level of tolerated violence which can indeed be observed in some sports? According to the ideas presented so far, the answer is that as long as sports remained local pastimes no important objections were raised against their possible brutality. Hurling games, boxing and wrestling matches were not frequently held. They were generally one among many events at some local festivities. In these local situations the division of labour was not yet very complicated. Many people worked for themselves or were involved in work which did not crucially depend on that of others. People could be absent without impeding the work of others. These pastimes were standardized when they came to be practised by wider groups of participants on a more regular basis, independent of local activities. In the process of standardization measures were taken to control the violence. These activities came to be practised by people with interdependent jobs in organizations who could not afford to get regularly hurt (Dunning and Sheard, 1979: 110). These developments should be interpreted as aspects of a general process of social change to which employers, churches and the police made active contributions (Bailey, 1978: 17 *passim*). Of course, Elias, Dunning and their co-authors do realize this, but in restricting their attention to attempts to suppress the violence in some sports, they do not notice the much more important processes of organization and standardization in most sports.

FIGURATIONAL SOCIOLOGY, CIVILIZATION AND SPORTS

It will be clear that these critical remarks and proposals for an alternative view of sports remain completely within the assumptions of the figurational sociological approach. They are also in accordance with the theory of the civilizing process. But they are directed against a too-narrow focus on the development of sports in which the restriction of the level of tolerated violence takes a central place. *What is only one aspect in the development of some modern sports is considered the defining characteristic of modern sports in general.* Before I trace the consequences of this misconception in Elias's and Dunning's work, it is only fair to say that it does not blemish all their work on the subject.

In 'The Quest for Excitement' (Elias and Dunning, 1986) some concepts are offered that are essential to the understanding of spectators' interests not only in sporting events but also in other kinds of amusements that try to attract a mass public. The idea of a tension-balance, which was first developed in 'Dynamics of Sport Groups' (Elias and Dunning, 1986: 200), is a sensitizing concept that directs attention to the way in which tension is built up in different kinds of sport. Connected with this is the concept of mimesis as the agreeable sensation evoked by the tension of amusements. Mimesis is a well-known term and in this chapter is connected with the theory of the civilizing process. An increasing control of nature, of interpersonal relations and of individual affects makes people's lives become routine and dull. The function of all kinds of amusements is to evoke a pleasurable tension and to present opportunities to let these tensions flow freely into spontaneous, but harmless behaviour (catharsis).

This is a much more realistic account of the functions of amusements and the needs of the public than its Marxist alternative which hypothesises that people become frustrated because of the exploitation and alienation of everyday life. They release the aggression evoked by this frustration (their version of catharsis) as spectators (Vinnai, 1970: 83). The strong point of Elias's and Dunning's ideas on this subject is that they do not only apply to soccer or other mass sports but to all kinds of amusements. These ideas enable us to understand the behaviour of people in soccer stadiums as well as of those in concert halls and theatres. This behaviour is not easily interpreted as a release of aggression. So why should this be the case with spectators at sporting events.

The main critical remarks I have made in this chapter deal with the excessive concentration on violence in Elias's and Dunning's work on sports and the empirical mistakes resulting from it. This criticism obviously becomes irrelevant to all those issues in which violence does play a central role. One of these is the phenomenon of football hooliganism. In my opinion, the work of Dunning and his colleagues Murphy and Williams offers an important contribution to the sociological understanding of these remarkable forms of disturbance at soccer games. This is a result of their long-term perspective and the emphasis they put on the interdependence of social events. As to this last characteristic, they follow Becker's advice 'to look at all the people involved in any episode of alleged deviance' (Becker, 1973: 183). The long-term perspective makes it possible to find out what is specific and needs to be explained about the period under investigation. As regards hooliganism, Dunning and his colleagues point to the attention given to fights and riots by the mass media after the World Cup Finals of 1966. They trace its consequences and the way in which it influenced hooliganism. Compared with Taylor's work, they do not need to introduce an unresearched and idealized past in which spectators and players were intimately related to analyze the present.

Yet from a more international perspective, the historical analysis of Dunning seems to be incomplete. In the whole of Europe until the twentieth century fighting used to be an unavoidable activity related to festivities of the lower and rural classes (Burke, 1978: 183). With the diffusion of soccer this custom was continued in the regular fights between supporters of soccer clubs from neighbouring communities. Today's hooligans seem to continue this custom in the modern setting of the matches between professional large-city soccer teams. This agrees with the ideas of Dunning and his colleagues that some parts of the working classes have not been incorporated as fully in 'civilized' society as most other classes (Dunning et al., 1988: 227), and have continued to adhere to the older behavioural patterns of supporters. The precise way in which this continuation was brought about is still a problem for research. Increasing opportunities for groups of supporters to travel probably contributed to it (Dunning et al., 1988: 75). In the analysis of Dunning et al. this line of inquiry could have been elaborated more thoroughly. Furthermore, it is remarkable that some of the useful concepts on spectator behaviour developed in *Quest for Excitement* are not used in the studies on hooliganism. As Elias and Dunning have indicated, mimetic characteristics of matches always involve the risk of pleasurable tensions becoming really threatening (Elias and Dunning, 1986: 80). This seems to be the case in many of the incidents in which the public attacked either the referee, players of the visiting team or each other. One should make a distinction between these cases and the behaviour of more-or-less organized groups which, with a certain degree of premeditation, aim at disturbing order before, during and after matches (Stokvis, 1989: 150).

Concentration on violence is of some use for an understanding of the initial stage of the development of sports in public schools. Relationships between general social changes, reform of the public schools and the role of team games are well analyzed in the first five chapters of *Barbarians, Gentlemen and Players* (Dunning and Sheard, 1979). But in order to understand how soccer and rugby became organized and standardized on a national level, in other words, how they became sports in the modern sense, one has to study the way in which these sports diffused, how their practitioners became more interdependent and how this resulted in their wish to organize the sports on a national level.

From the 1840s onwards, problems of standardizing football games from different public schools became the most important force behind changes in the rules (Green, 1953: 15). Questions related to the violence of the game formed one of many problem areas on which a consensus had to be reached. Dunning and Sheard do not neglect the organizational issues, but these serve merely as a background for their description of the debate on 'hacking', which was connected with the separation of soccer and rugby. In the case of these sports, the question about the level of tolerated violence was indeed an issue. In spite of this, to understand their development, the whole process of national organization should be made the central focus of study, even in the case of football. In the present state, Dunning's and Sheard's account of relations between the most influential opponents during the founding years of football is not very convincing.

One uncertainty concerns the relative importance of the issues of 'hacking' and the use of hands in football. In 1863 (the year in which the Football Association was founded) and 1871 (when the Rugby Union was founded) the fundamental dispute seems to have been between the proponents of the 'kicking' and of the 'handling' game. Those who favoured 'hacking' were generally also in favour of 'handling'. When the issue of 'hacking' entered the talks on the founding of the Rugby Union, those who had argued in favour of it and had lost when the Football Association was founded now pleaded against it (Harris, 1975: 108; Green, 1953: 33). This suggests that it was not such a fundamental issue as Dunning and Sheard consider it to be.

Dunning's and Sheard's view on the earlier stages of the relations between public schools is also debatable. They do not take into account that one of Thomas Arnold's predecessors at Rugby, Thomas James, was an Etonian who had introduced the rules of the Eton 'field game' there (Green, 1953: 12). In this game carrying the ball was not allowed. This kicking game was predominant at traditional élite public schools such as Eton (Green, p. 13). At Rugby around 1840 it became permissible to carry the ball (Harris, 1975: 123). Perhaps this innovation should be seen in the light of the competition between the public schools. But then, contrary to what Dunning and Sheard wrote, it was not the Etonians who tried to distinguish themselves from Rugbeians (Dunning and Sheard, 1979: 99). It was the other way around. The suggestion that efforts to be more civilized than the lower classes played a role at Rugby (Dunning and Sheard, 1979: 86) only cause unnecessary complications in understanding what actually happened. For example, in the interpretation offered by Dunning and Sheard it remains unexplained why at Rugby, where non-violent middle-class values had the strongest support, rugby football became established as a relatively violent sport, whereas the more traditionally orientated Etonians developed a less-violent variety of football.

The theory of the civilizing process is certainly useful in explaining the general trend towards the restriction of violence in football. But in order to understand the development of relations between the public schools and its consequences for the early development of football, the interdependences between these schools and *the struggles concerning the standardization of the game in general* should be the central focus of study.

CONCLUSIONS

The basic distinguishing characteristic of modern sports is their international organization and standardization and not, as Elias suggests, the relatively low level of tolerated violence. The process of controlling violence is only an issue in some sports and often not an important one. Even in boxing, the central problems had more to do with the organization of the sport – for example, the control of corruption – than with the control of its violence. In the case of hooliganism, the emphasis on violence is justified because violence is central to the phenomenon. But it already becomes questionable in Elias's and Dunning's interpretation of the development of football. Elias's speculations on the relationship between parliamentarization and fox-hunting show to what misconceptions this exclusive concentration on violence and its control in sports can lead.

This critique is not, as I have previously stated, intended to be a denunciation of the importance of figurational sociology or of the theory of the civilizing process in research on sports. Emphasizing the interpretation of phenomena as phases in long-term processes and their comparison in different periods is an essential contribution to the sociology of sport. So is the attention given to the interdependence of phenomena and the way in which social developments are manifested in the personality of the people involved. *My critique concerns only the tendency to reduce civilizing processes in sports to restrictions in the levels of tolerated violence.*

References

Bailey, P. (1978), *Leisure and Class in Victorian England* (London: Routledge & Kegan Paul).

Becker, H. (1973), *Outsiders* (New York: Free Press).

Brailsford, D. (1969), *Sport and Society: Elizabeth to Anne* (London: Routledge & Kegan Paul).

Burke, P. (1978), *Popular Culture in Early Modern Europe* (New York: Harper & Row).

Carr, R. (1986), *English Fox-hunting* (London: Weidenfeld & Nicolson) originally published 1976.

Cuddon, J. A. (1980), *The Macmillan Dictionary of Sports and Games* (London: Macmillan).

Duchartre, P. L. (1973), *Dictionnaire analogique de la chasse historique et contemporaine* (Paris: Chene).

Dunning, E. and Sheard, K. (1979), *Barbarians, Gentlemen and Players* (Oxford: Martin Robertson).

Dunning, E., Murphy, P. and Williams, J. (1988), *The Roots of Football Hooliganism* (London: Routledge).

Elias, N. and Dunning, E. (1986), *Quest for Excitement* (Oxford: Blackwell).

Encyclopedia of the Social Sciences (ESS) (1968), ed. David L. Sills (New York: Macmillan, 1968).

Fleischer, N. and Andre, S. (1966), *A Pictorial History of Boxing* (London: Spring Books).

Green, G. (1953), *The History of the Football Association* (London: Nadrett Press).

Harris, H. A. (1975), *Sport in Britain* (London: Stanley Paul).

Landes, D. (1969), *The Unbound Prometheus* (Cambridge: Cambridge University Press).

Longrigg, R. (1977), *The English Squire and his Sport* (London: Michael Joseph).

MacAloon, J. (1981), *This Great Symbol* (Chicago, Ill.: University of Chicago Press).

Stokvis, R. (1989), *De Sportwereld* (Alphen: Samsom).

Stone, L. (1965), *The Crisis of the Aristocracy, 1558–1641* (Oxford: Clarendon Press).
Thomas, K. (1983), *Man and the Natural World* (Harmondsworth, Middx: Penguin).
Vinnai, G. (1970), *Fussballsport als Ideologie* (Frankfurt: Europäische Verlagsanstalt).

6 Chariot Races, Tournaments and the Civilizing Process*

ALLEN GUTTMANN

AVAILABLE PARADIGMS

To the many halls, chambers, nooks and crannies of historical experience there is no single theoretical password. For some rooms, one says 'Marx' and the door swings open. For others, one says 'Weber' or 'Durkheim' or 'Freud'. For some, the magic name seems to be 'Elias'. This, at least, has been my experience. The reference to my own experience is intentional. Although positivistic social science frowns upon the use of personal pronouns, it is salutary to recall a remark by Henry David Thoreau: 'We commonly do not remember that it is, after all, always the first person that is speaking.' In this introductory section of my four-part essay, I shall comment on the role that Norbert Elias and other theorists have played in my own research in sports studies.

When I turned, nearly twenty years ago, from research in American history and literature to sports studies, I began a monograph that was supposed to demonstrate, in a manner reminiscent of Alexis de Tocqueville, that American sports are uniquely American. I concluded my research with the opposite conviction, that is, that the cultural differences between American and European sports, while undeniably real, are quite superficial compared to the extraordinary differences between modern sports and the sports of preliterate, ancient and mediaeval cultures. It was impossible for me to contemplate the cultic associations of the Greek *periodos* or the stickball games of the American Indians and not see in our modern sports a confirmation of Max Weber's theories about the *Entzauberung* ('disenchantment') of the world. It was equally impossible for me to overlook the obvious similarity between the *Verwissenschaftlichung* ('scienticization') of sports and the modern mania for rationalization in all its many forms – including bureaucratization. How can one *not* recognize in the specialization, standardization and quantification of sports an instance of the larger Weberian movement from traditional to modern society?

Before I sat down to write *From Ritual to Record* (1978), I had read Eric Dunning's brilliant essay 'The Structural–Functional Properties of Folk-Games and Modern Sports' (1973), which I found extremely helpful for the

137

kinds of distinctions I wished to make. Dunning's primary focus, however, was on ball games as they evolved from the mediaeval to the modern period. My goal was a paradigm that strove to include a wider spectrum of sports across a longer span of time. While I took notes on what Dunning had to say about *Über den Prozess der Zivilisation* (Elias, 1976) and bought a copy of the Suhrkamp edition, I laid the book aside for some months. *From Ritual to Record* appeared with references to Dunning's essay and to one of the essays he wrote in co-operation with Norbert Elias, 'The Quest for Excitement in Unexciting Societies' (Elias and Dunning, 1970), but it was Henning Eichberg's masterpiece, *Leistung, Spannung, Geschwindigkeit* (1978) that finally brought home to me the fact that Norbert Elias had produced a sociological classic that was clearly indispensable for the monograph I intended to write on sports spectators. This realization was intensified when I read *Barbarians, Gentlemen and Players,* the landmark study which Eric Dunning and Kenneth Sheard published in 1979.

Before I was able to concentrate on my historical study of the spectators, however, I had to finish a project already underway; namely, a study of Avery Brundage and his role as president of the International Olympic Committee (1952–72). Although I read Norbert Elias at this time and discussed his work with a number of historians and sociologists, it was Emile Durkheim's paradigm of mechanical and organic solidarity that lay behind my speculations about the communal forms and rituals that give the Olympic Games their extraordinary fascination. Durkheim's name never appeared in the text of *The Games Must Go On* (1984), an intentionally untheoretical book, but I emphasized Pierre de Coubertin's and Avery Brundage's efforts to constitute the modern games as a secular religion. In Brundage's case if not in Coubertin's, the games were perceived as a substitute for Judaism, Christianity, Islam and other faiths, all of which had, in Brundage's view, failed to provide an ethical basis for life in the twentieth century.

Having satisfied my desire to write a biography, I concentrated my research on the spectators, modestly determining to write a history of sports spectatorship from antiquity to the present. It was clear to me even before I began the intensive research, that Norbert Elias had provided the most useful theoretical framework and that Eric Dunning and his Leicester associates had done valuable historical and sociological work on football hooliganism and related topics.

That the figurational model is more than a methodology seems clear. Methodologically, the figurational approach concentrates upon 'historically produced and reproduced networks of interdependence' (Rojek, 1985: 158).

The stress on interdependence signals the determination to avoid 'crude economic determinism', 'prime movers' and the misguided quest for some single explanation for all social phenomena (Dunning and Sheard, 1979: 8). The historical stress indicates an equally important determination to eschew the 'snapshot at a moment in time' analysis which greatly diminishes the usefulness of many sociological studies. Employing this multi-causal historical approach, the 'figurationists' have demonstrated the applicability of their methods to empirical research by analyzing 'the civilizing process' as it occurred through various moments in European history. These demonstrations have involved Elias *et al.*, implicitly if not explicitly, despite their desire to avoid determinism, in speculations about causation. The modern centralized state, for instance, looms as a force behind 'the civilizing process', and the commitment of young working-class males to a traditional conception of masculinity explains a good deal of today's 'soccer hooliganism'.

With both the methodological and the explanatory aspects of figurational sociology in mind, I sought to understand the spectators. One of my purposes, therefore, was to see how well the Elias–Dunning approach fits the historical facts for the distant past. Specifically, how much sense does it make to speak of a 'civilizing process' in antiquity and in the Middle Ages? Can the Elias–Dunning model help us understand the chariot races of Rome and Byzantium and the tournaments of mediaeval Europe?

CIRCUS FACTIONS

Like Tocqueville, Marx and Weber, Norbert Elias and Eric Dunning are *historical* sociologists whose *magna opera* are filled with precisely noted historical data.[1] If we are to consider the chariot races of the Roman circus and the Byzantine hippodrome as a test case of figurational sociology, we have to bear in mind the basic historical facts. Fortunately, like the examples that make *Über den Prozess der Zivilisation* such a wonderful sourcebook, the facts have an intrinsic interest quite apart from their usefulness as evidence.

It is impossible to state flatly that chariot races were the most popular Roman and Byzantine sport. Although fewer days were devoted to the races than to the *munera* (human combats) and *venationes* (man–animal combats), the populace may well have lusted for more gladiators and fewer charioteers. In the middle of the fourth century the Roman calendar had ten days of gladiatorial games and 66 days of chariot races, but this ratio of nearly seven to one may not have reflected the public's preferences (Balsdon, 1969: 244–52). If we assume that sports facilities are constructed, to some degree, in response to the builder's conception of popular demand, architecture is a clue to popularity. The Colosseum, that symbol of the Roman holiday, held about 50,000 spectators while the Circus Maximus – one of Rome's five hippodromes – may have had room for five times as many spectators (Carcopino, 1940: 214–15).

That the chariot races were extremely popular is unquestionable. The fourth-century AD historian Ammianus Marcellinus (quoted in Harris, 1972: 221–2) was astonished at the passion for chariot races:

> Now let me describe the mass of the people, unemployed and with too much time on their hands. . . . For them the Circus Maximus is temple, home, community centre and the fulfilment of all their hopes. All over the city you can see them quarrelling fiercely about the races. . . . They declare that the country will be ruined if at the next meeting their own particular champion does not come first off the starting-gate and keep his horses in line as he brings them round the post. Before dawn on a race day they all rush headlong for a place on the terraces at such speed that they could almost beat the chariots themselves.

In this account, of course, one detects the intellectual's puzzlement at plebeian enthusiasms.

From the written record and from archeological remains scattered around the entire Mediterranean basin, John H. Humphrey (1986) has been able to write an architectural history of the Roman circus which is also a splendidly detailed account of exactly what happened in the typical race, but his magisterial book, *Roman Circuses*, provides more technical information than we need for our present purposes, which is to look not at the drama of the four-horse chariot race but at the attendant drama of spectator behaviour.

A word about the charioteers is relevant, however, because *they*, not the horses and certainly not the chariots, were the focus of the spectators' interest. Many of the charioteers were slaves who eventually purchased their freedom with their prize money (Cameron, 1976: 219). Those who were free men, by birth or by manumission, were officially of low status, like the gladiators, but were actually lionized by the sports-mad Roman populace. The first-century satirical poet Martial complained comically – perhaps jealously as well – about the ubiquitous portraits of a certain Scorpus: *Aureus ut Scorpi nasus ubique micet* ('The golden nose of Scorpus twinkled everywhere') (quoted in Carcopino, 1940: 219). Golden because he was richly rewarded in monetary terms? There is no question about the rewards reaped by the sixth-century Byzantine charioteer, Porphyrius, one of antiquity's most famous athletes. The idol of Constantinople, he was honoured by at least 32 epigrams in the *Greek Anthology* (Cameron, 1973: 1). His stone figure, towering over the four horses of his *quadriga,* is still visible on a monument in the hippodrome (Hoenle and Henze, 1981: 103, Pl. 71). Behind him one can see the carved figures of the enthusiastically cheering spectators.

At the chariot races, as at the gladiatorial games, specific categories of people were allotted specific sections of the hippodrome. At the Circus Maximus in Rome, Augustus and the other members of the imperial family observed the races while reclining upon their *pulvinar* (a large couch). The first-century emperor Claudius provided special stone seats for senators; his infamous successor, Nero, installed seats for the equestrian class (Carcopino, 1940: 214; Balsdon, 1969: 260). (Nero's love of the circus races was so excessive that he murdered his wife, Poppaea, because she chided him on his late return from a day at the races (Harris, 1972: 215). As long as they did not usurp the seats of the senators and knights, first-century plebeians sat wherever they pleased. With the emperor in his imperial box, 'surrounded by representatives of all ranks and classes seated in due order, the circus was indeed a microcosm of the Roman state' (Cameron, 1976: 231). Here, visibly, was a social figuration.

In the Circus Maximus in Rome, the partisans of the Blues and the Greens – the 'circus factions' discussed in Alan Cameron's (1976: 50, 79) authoritative book of that title – probably had their own sections, very much like the football fans of modern Britain. In Constantinople the partisans in their distinctive blue and green jackets sat in two sections on the north-west side of the hippodrome, directly opposite the emperor ensconced in his grand *kathisma* (the imperial box).

We can be certain that men and women sat together and that the races were an opportunity for sexual adventure. In his *Life of Sulla,* Plutarch, the gossipy second-century historian, tells how the dictator's wife first attracted his attention by sitting behind him at the games and plucking a thread from his toga. The poet Ovid (1957: 109–10), a contemporary of Augustus, giving tips to lovers in his *Ars Amatoria,* advised women to display their good looks at the races: 'Nothing is gained if you hide'. In the *Amores,* the poet (Ovid, 1957: 69) described the erotic possibilities of a rendezvous at the circus: 'You watch the races, and I watch you – what a wonderful system! Each of us feasting our eyes on the delights that we prize.' The satirist Juvenal (1958: 35), writing in the second century AD, had a different view of flirtation. His verses flayed 'the tarts who display their wares at the Circus', which is the attitude one might expect from the poet who bequeathed us the phrase, *panem et circenses*. Juvenal's reference to 'tarts' was meant literally; prostitutes commonly sought customers at the races and led them to brothels conveniently located in the arcades of the Circus Maximus (Balsdon, 1969: 253). Ovid's female spectators are more interested in *amor* than in the outcome of the races. The sixth-century historian, Procopius, was also sarcastic about female motivation, noting that the female fans sometimes joined the circus factions in their riots 'although they never even went to the games' (Cameron, 1976: 273).

Quite apart from this perennial male suspicion about female commitment to spectator sports, one can turn the tables on Ovid and Procopius and ask whether or not the *men* were well informed about the fine points of charioteering. Pliny the Younger (1963: 236), whose letters are a major source for first-century Roman life, portrayed the fans of the first century AD as a mindless mob. He professed surprise that

so many thousands of adult men should have such a childish passion for watching galloping horses and drivers standing in chariots, over and over again. If they were attracted by the speed of the horses or the drivers' skill, one should account for it, but in fact it is the racing colours they really support and care about, and if the colours were to be exchanged in mid-course during a race, they would transfer their favour and enthusiasm and rapidly desert the famous drivers and horses whose names they shout as they recognize them from afar. Such is the popularity and importance of a worthless shirt.

All we need to be convinced of the similarity of ancient and modern spectators is to hear the Romans shout *'Numerus Unus Sumus'*!

Tertullian, writing in the late second or early third century, was even more appalled by the irrationality of the fans.

Look at the people, in a state of frenzy when they arrive at the spectacle, already disordered, already blind, already maddened! For them the praetor [a Roman official] is too slow. Their eyes are already on the urn from which the jumbled lots will be drawn [to determine starting positions]. And then they wait in anxious tension for the start – one scream, one insanity! (Weber, 1983: 105)

The circus, thought Tertullian, was no place for a good Christian.

The 'childish passion' of the chariot-race spectators has sometimes been construed as political apathy, but this is a false conclusion. The sports spectators of the Roman Empire were politically involved but not in the forms presently institutionalized in modern political democracies. It was, in fact, the very *absence* of political parties which necessitated substitute forms of political expression. The political functions of the eighteenth-century English and French crowd, studied by George Rudé and others, were fulfilled – to some degree – by the sports spectators of Rome and Byzantium. In the absence of political parties, Roman sports became a mechanism for the expression, and also for the manipulation, of popular opinion (Hardy, 1977). They were, writes Traugott Bollinger (1969: 71), a 'safety-valve for dissatisfaction and a substitute for democratic assemblies'. In an age that lacked modern means of mass communications, the hippodrome brought together a significant fraction of the capital's total population and allowed for immediate symbolic interaction between the rulers and the ruled.

Sports spectators, like theatre spectators, were expected to greet emperors with worshipful shouts of acclamation. The emperors often used the circus to present heirs to the throne. The circus was also used for the punishment of criminals and for the public humiliation of cowardly soldiers. Although the emperors and their consorts lay upon the *pulvinar* (in Rome) or sat in the *kathisma* (in Constantinople), visible symbols of power and authority, they were nonetheless accessible to petitioners. They were also exposed to expressions of discontent. Since the emperors were often as partisan as anyone else, spectators voiced their political displeasure by jeering at the faction the emperor favoured and cheering for the opposition. This was not always without risk. Caracalla, who ruled from 211 to 217 AD, responded to such adverse partisanship by sending soldiers to assault the offenders (Cameron, 1976: 179–80).

The second-century AD historian Dio Cassius reports several occasions when the circus was the site for political protests. During the reign of Commodus, for instance, the plebeians were convinced that the official Cleander was hoarding grain. The races gave them the opportunity to articulate their anger:

> There were chariot races. As the horses were about to begin the seventh race, a crowd of children stormed into the Circus. They were led by a large, angry maiden, who was later thought to be a goddess. At the same time, the children cried out bitterly [against Cleander], and the people assembled in the Circus took up the insults and screamed all sorts of invectives. At length, the crowd stormed down from their seats and

approached Commodus, crying his praises but shouting condemnations against Cleander.   (Weber, 1983: 234).

The excited crowd took to the streets of Rome, threatened the emperor's villa and finally succeeded in 'persuading' Commodus to dismiss Cleander.

The protests were not always limited to shouts of disapproval and demands for the redress of grievances. The public was often violent, and this, of course, is what has attracted the attention of modern scholars anxious to understand the sports violence of the twentieth century. In Constantinople the circus factions rioted at a level that makes twentieth-century mobs seem almost non-violent. In the fifth and sixth centuries, spectator violence increased and troops were repeatedly called upon to halt the mayhem and restore some kind of order. The fans of the capital set the city's wooden hippodrome on fire in 491, 498, 507 and 532 AD, whereupon the emperor Justinian constructed a stone stadium (Guilland, 1948). After a victory by Porphyrius in 507 in the circus at Antioch, the jubilant Greens ran wild and burned the local synagogue (Malalas, 1940: 111; Cameron, 1976: 150). The worst of these many riots took place in Constantinople in January 532 when supporters of the Blues and the Greens made common cause. Prisoners about to be executed on the 13th were rescued by the mob, which subsequently ignored Justinian's attempt to appease them with the promise of additional games. On the 14th the emperor acceded to demands that he dismiss the unpopular John of Cappodocia. By 18 January the still unpacified mob proclaimed a new emperor to whom a number of senators quickly paid homage. They had cause just as quickly to regret their lack of faith in Justinian. He summoned Belisarius with enough soldiers put an end to the riots – at the estimated cost of 30,000 lives (Cameron, 1973: 277–80). In comparison with this bloodbath, the worst modern outbreaks of British and Latin American football fans, which have left as many as several hundred dead, seem relatively innocuous.

In his masterful book *Circus Factions,* Alan Cameron has shown that the unruly charioteer fans of Rome and Constantinople were neither organized into political parties nor representatives of theological positions (as earlier historians had maintained). Whether the hardcore adherents of the Blues and the Greens were 'simple supporters' clubs' and essentially non-political can, however, be debated (although at least one reviewer of *Sports Spectators* seemed to feel that *any* disagreement with Cameron was an act of unwarranted temerity) (Kyle, 1987: 209–14). Cameron asserts that the 'circus factions deserve no prominent mention in any history of popular expression'. In his view, politics merely provided a pretext for behaviour which he, drawing upon the work of Ian Taylor but not that of Dunning and his associates, compares with that of twentieth-century 'soccer hooligans'. In the civil war of 609–10, for instance, 'the political conflict became a convenient facade for the colours to fight each other openly and with impunity' (Cameron, 1976: 20, 77, 284, 311).

Although Cameron's authority is generally acknowledged, his insistence that the violence committed by the circus factions was essentially non-political is not completely persuasive. Not all political expression is institutionalized into parties. Today, no scholar believes that the circus factions were remotely similar to modern political parties, but there is good reason to agree with Bollinger's (1969: 24) contention that the spectacles were often 'gatherings of a political character'. In recent years feminists have extended the term 'politics' to cover all sorts of activity, including the sexual intercourse of a married couple. To apply the word 'political' to the spectators' cries for changes in official government policy does not seem excessive.

One of Cameron's (1976: 101) arguments is that 'partisans of both colours really moved in much the same world: young men with time on their hands – the *jeunesse dorée* rather than a representative cross section of the whole population'. To this assertion two objections can be made. The first is that the alleged upper-class status of the Byzantine spectators is unusual. Dunning and his associates at Leicester, Gunter Pilz and *his* associates in Germany and a number of American sociologists all agree that the football hooligans of the modern era are the socially deprived rather than the socially privileged (Dunning, 1981; Dunning *et al.*, 1981; Guttmann, 1986: 168–74). Modern playboys misbehave, sometimes violently, but they rarely form mobs and seldom rampage through the streets.

A second criticism of Cameron's bold assertion is that he demolishes a straw man. No one maintains that the factions or the faction-led mobs were a representative cross-section of the Byzantine population. Moreover, Cameron (1976: 101) himself concedes that there may have been 'differences in behaviour and even social class' among the faction members. If there *were* differences in social class, and it seems to me incredible that there were not, then differences in behaviour were inevitable and it is quite impossible to believe that such class-based differences were wholly unpolitical. To assert that they were is to narrow unreasonably the definition of political.

What explains Cameron's failure to detect the behavioural differences inevitably motivated by differences in social class or – to choose a related term popularized by Pierre Bourdieu – *habitus*? One explanation is that the ancients had little interest in the question and have, therefore, provided us with little documentary evidence. Among contemporaries, neither the notoriously unreliable John Malalas nor the somewhat more trustworthy but still partisan Procopius showed the concern for the relationships among sports, social class and political behaviour that are routine preoccupations for modern sociologists. It is also clear that Cameron, like most classicists, has only a minimal interest in social theory. That he read some of the work of Ian Taylor is unusual; that he did not ponder the theories and familiarize himself with the empirical investigations of Elias and Dunning is not surprising. Finally, one has to suspect that Cameron fell into the trap that lies in the path of all revisionists – the tendency to go from one extreme to another.

It is a great pity that Cameron seems not to have encountered work done from a figurational perspective because he has the command of Roman and Byzantine history that one needs adequately to test the hypothesis of a civilizing process. All I can offer are some speculations that may, ideally, prompt Cameron or some other classical scholar to test the model.

The model developed by Elias emphasizes a psychological variable, affect, and the degree to which affect is expressed, suppressed or repressed. Since we know relatively little about the emotional lives of the peoples of the Byzantine period, we are left with spectator behaviour as an approximate indicator of emotional control or the lack of it. Given this less-than-ideal situation, we can, none the less, ask if the explanatory model is compatible with the evidence. Was there, as Elias asserted in *Über den Prozess der Zivilisation,* a correlation between the centralized coercive power of the state and the 'chains of interdependence', on the one hand, and the individual control of affect, on the other? Since the Byzantine spectator riots of the fifth and sixth centuries were notably more severe than earlier ones, we seem to have the reverse of the 'civilizing process' that Elias found at work in the transition from mediaeval to early modern times. Indeed, we have what might be termed 'a barbarizing process'. (I have in mind Edward Gibbon's gibe that the decline and fall of the Roman Empire represented the triumph of Christianity and barbarism.)

The Roman Empire of the fourth, fifth and sixth centuries was centralist, bureaucratic and absolutist, but it was a weaker, less efficient, less effective state than it had been in the first, second and third centuries. The *will* of the Byzantine rulers was to exert their control over what was left of the empire, but they were apparently unable to guarantee order even in the capital. The contemporary historian Procopius (1896: 57, 61), our best source despite his bias against Justinian and Theodora, described horrendous social dislocation: 'The laws and the whole fabric of the state were altogether upset. . . . Life became so uncertain that people lost all expectation of

security. . . . The government resembled a despotism, not a securely established one, but one which was changed almost daily.' Modern historians
seem to agree that the government was unstable and that 'disorder and
destitution reigned in the provinces' (Diehl, 1925: 30; Runciman, 1956:
70).

The Greek Orthodox Church, also centred in Constantinople, also
bureaucratic and absolutist, was riven by heresy and never free from theological disputes. Indeed, the factional strife between the orthodox and the
heretics of various persuasions was what seduced earlier historians to assert
that partisanship for the Blues and the Greens was somehow correlated with
the acceptance of Athanasian orthodoxy or monophysitism. Men who murdered each other because of disagreements over the ontological status of the
Son of God were hardly role models of strict affect-control.

It is also probable that the division of labour was less minute and the
'chains of interdependence' were shorter and more fragile than in the days
of Trajan and Hadrian:

Immobility was the principal feature of the social structure of the later
Roman empire as it developed following the crisis of the third century
and the reforms of Diocletian and Constantine. Those in the country who
actually worked the fields, whether they possessed them or not, became
attached to the soil; and those in the cities who were engaged in any trade
or profession of public interest became attached to their trade or profession. In neither case was there any freedom of choice; one was legally
bound to follow the trade of his father.   (Charanis, 1944–5; 1962–3)

While the eastern half of the Roman Empire was, for a time at least, spared
the extreme social disruption of the western half, which fell victim to
various German invaders, the day-to-day experience of ordinary men and
women was probably less secure and their spatial and temporal horizons
were probably more limited than had been the case when Roman civilization offered opportunities for geographical if not for social mobility, and
Roman military might provide some guarantees about the morrow.

These speculations are *not* based on the assumption that the earlier
spectators were less passionately involved in their partisanship than the
later ones. Evidence cited from various sources makes it impossible to
believe that they were. They were, however, unless the historical record has
badly misled us, demonstrably less inclined to let their passions explode in
the form of expressive violence. The history of Roman and Byzantine circus

factions from the first to the sixth centuries does seem to fit the model developed by Elias and Dunning. There was indeed a 'barbarizing process'.

TOURNAMENTS AND TOURNAMENT SPECTATORS

Tournaments were violent. For the mediaeval knight, the line between tournament and battlefield, between mock warfare and the real thing, was thin and often transgressed. Writing in 1901, J. J. Jusserand (1901: 12, 18) commented: 'Games resembled war and war resembled games. . . . The union of warfare and games was so close that it is frequently difficult to decide if a given activity ought to be classified under one rubric or the other.' One of the most detailed studies of knighthood concludes similarly that 'tournaments began as mimic wars in the twelfth century; wars take on the appearance of mimic tournaments in the pages of Froissart in the fourteenth century' (Barber, 1974: 193; See also Haskins, 1927: 238). The warlike features of the tournament were especially pronounced in the twelfth century, when the typical tournament was a free-for-all in which parties of knights fought to capture as many rivals as possible in order to maximize their glory and their ransoms. A contemporary observer wrote that 'the fracas was such that God's thunder couldn't have been heard' (Meyer, 1891–1901: III.74). A modern judgement is that the early tournament was 'unregulated, it was not a spectacle, and there was little in the way of romantic chivalry attached to it' (Hardy, 1974: 96). Needless to say, several hundred armed men struggling for fame and fortune were liable to do considerable damage to one another. Injuries were inevitable and deaths were common. At Neuss in 1240 scores of knights were killed. The Roman Catholic Church issued one ban after another. In vain. In 1471 a tournament was held in St Peter's Square (Barber, 1974: 191; Keen, 1984: 86).

The typical site for the early tournament was a meadow or a field: 'The contests seem to have been held in open country, featured perhaps with little woods, a bridge and a stream' (Cripps-Day, 1918: 29). In other words, there was very little topographical difference between the site of a tournament and the site of life-and-death combat. The most important anticipation of the later *lices closes* was the *recet* or place of refuge, where weary or wounded knights were safe from pursuit (Jusserand, 1901: 55). The twelfth-century tournament was a spectacle in the abstract but not in the literal sense of the term; there was no provision for spectators and few spectators were present. Those who did come to watch were likely to be knights who might suddenly, with no formal notice, decide to alter their status from spectator to participant. This ambiguity of role was exploited by unscrupulous knights, like Philip of Flanders who waited unobtrusively on the sidelines and then seized the opportunity to swoop down treacherously on some exhausted, unwary, unsuspecting combatant whom the count then bore off for a goodly ransom. Historians with a nineteenth-century sense of fair play may rejoice that William Marshal played the same trick on the cunning count and captured him (Painter, 1933: 38).

In the course of time, from the twelfth to the sixteenth centuries, as the 'civilizing process' transformed the bellicose fragments of feudal society into something more organized and less violent, tournaments became more pageant and less contest. Eventually, they became 'little more than a spectacle' (Ferguson, 1960: 14; see also Anglo, 1968; I: 19–40; Keen, 1977: 1–20). In the words of Jusserand (1901: 73): 'The tumultuous battles of old, with horses galloping across fields and through villages, were gradually transformed into an elegant sport, into a spectacle where crowds of glittering aristocrats gathered'. The joust between two knights became the typical form of encounter rather than the wild free-for-all clash of groups. Weapons were modified and rules were changed to diminish the danger of serious injury: 'In the second half of the fifteenth century the differentiation between battle and tournament armour increased to such a degree that their elements became mutually exclusive' (Nickel, 1988: 220). By the sixteenth century opponents were usually separated by 'tilts', that is, by wooden barriers eliminating the risk of head-on collisions. Since knights passed left arm to left arm, with lances held in the right hand, their weapons struck their opponents' shields at an angle which made it much less likely for a sixteenth-century knight to be dangerously unhorsed. Jousts were decided not by the mere shock of lance against armour but by a rather complicated system of points whose intricacies have recently been unravelled by Joachim K. Ruehl (1986). In an obvious effort to avoid the kinds of bloodshed that had occurred at the earlier tournaments, the rules called for deductions of points for hits to vulnerable places.

Although it may be difficult for twentieth-century scholars to accept a trend apparently contrary to those of our day, the spectator's role became more important and more clearly defined as the sport became tamer, less spontaneous and more civilized. The importance of the tournament as a carefully organized spectacle can be seen in the increasingly lengthy 'lead time' between the first announcement and the actual occurrence of a tournament. The twelfth-century tournament was sometimes a 'spur of the moment' affair in a quite literal sense, and the impromptu joust never disappeared, but the grander tournaments, like modern sports championships, required months and even years of careful planning and preparation.

For the famous combat at Smithfield in 1467 the challenge was issued two years before the principals finally engaged each other – a time as long as that which elapsed between Pierre de Coubertin's formation of the International Olympic Committee and the staging of the first modern Olympic Games in 1896.

The growing importance of the spectators necessitated changes in the nature of the site as well as in the length of time needed for preparations. Venues became increasingly festive. By the sixteenth century the lists 'were surrounded by gaily coloured tents and stands were crowded with spectators' (Poole, 1958: II. 623). When a tournament was held in an urban environment, which was usually the case in the fifteenth and sixteenth centuries, spectators crowded toward the windows and even upon the roofs of adjacent buildings, which is where they can be seen in many prints. If the site was outside the city, children and young adults clambered into the treetops for a free view of the spectacle.

Stands and pavilions constructed for the benefit of the onlookers were a means of social control, but the price paid by the bourgeoisie and the aristocracy for comfort and a better view was often more than an economic transaction because the stands were apparently no safer than the temporary stands of antiquity. John Stow's *Survey of London* (1908: I. 268) records the collapse of tournament stands in 1331. The ladies fell from above and injured 'knights and such as were underneath'. King Edward III then did what his Roman and Byzantine predecessors did in similar circumstances; he ordered the construction of stone facilities 'for himself, the Queen [Philippa] and other states to stand on, and there to behold the [jousting], and other shewes at their pleasure'. There is little indication that later carpentry was better able to support the burden of the closely packed spectators. Ralph Holinshed's chronicles report on a similar accident at Westminster in 1581 in which 'manie of the beholders, men as well as women, were sore hurt, some maimed, and some killed, by falling of the scaffolds overcharged' (see Nichols, 1823: II. 302 n. 2).

In the later Middle Ages and the early Renaissance the question of who watched whom became very complex. It was not simply that the roles of participant and spectator became more clearly distinguished, it was also that distinctions among the spectators became clearer. As was inevitable in a highly hierarchical society, the spectators were socially segregated. At the tournament in Smithfield in 1467 there was a separate building for the mayor and other dignitaries of London. The stands for knights and squires and others of the nobility rose in three tiers, topped by the king's box (Clephan, 1919: 76–8). Like sculpted Byzantine representations of chariot races, in which disproportionately large stone charioteers and emperors tower over diminutive carved spectators, mediaeval illustrations often use size to symbolize social status. In a typical fifteenth-century manuscript, which shows the Earl of Warwick jousting at Calais, one sees the backs of the tiny spectators in the foreground and the faces of the much larger courtiers in the background (Keen, 1984: pl. 21).

The men and women who sat in the pavilions were obviously members of the ruling class. That others were anxious to watch is proven by chronicle and romance as well as by the visual arts. Although extremely stringent rules barred all but the nobility from actual participation in the lists, tournaments which also excluded commoners from the ranks of the spectators became quite rare. When Antoine the Bastard of Burgundy accepted a challenge from Anthony Woodville, Lord Scales, the city of London seems to have been as excited as a modern metropolis hosting a world championship. When the long-expected tournament took place at Smithfield in the spring of 1467, a public holiday was proclaimed and commoners unable to crowd into the enclosure climbed trees to obtain a glimpse of the marvellous pageantry and the rather disappointing combats (Mitchell, 1938: 1, 3, 11). At the tournament held in 1501 to celebrate the birth of Prince Arthur, son of Henry VII, there was a charge for admission, but this hardly reduced the attendance, and a contemporary chronicler reported of the standing-room-only throng that there 'was no thynge to the yee but oonly visages and faces, without apperans of ther bodies' (Anglo, 1968: I. 37).

At the tournament in Smithfield there were galleries for the ladies as well, but no one knows exactly when women began to be a part of the festivities. The long biography of William Marshal, the most famous knight of the century, describes his involvement in a dozen tournaments but mentions female spectators at only one of them (Painter, 1933: 59). If women were present they were clearly not the focus of the biographer's concern. They appear in the literature and art of the twelfth and thirteenth centuries (see Guttmann, 1986: 39–40, 44–5). They appear frequently in the historical documents of the fourteenth century. The two daughters of Edward III, for instance, made their first recorded public appearance at a tournament in Dunstable in 1342. For their gorgeously embroidered robes, eighteen workers had been employed for nine days. The workers, who used eleven ounces of gold were supervised by the king's armourer, John of Cologne (Green, 1849–55: III. 176).

The fact of women's presence at late-mediaeval and Renaissance tournaments raises a question to which there can be no definitive answer: did the arrival of upper-class female spectators help to 'civilize' the males or were the males now civilized enough for females to feel secure? Most probably there was a reciprocal figurational interaction that began with a somewhat tamer tournament which, in turn, made it possible for women to attend and to accelerate the 'civilizing process'.

Whether or not one accepts this interpretation of sequence, there can be no doubt that the presence of upper-class women at tournaments signalled a transformation in function. The perfection and demonstration of military prowess became ancillary and the tournament became a theatrical production in which fitness to rule was associated with fineness of sensibility. Discussing this theme in relation to ring tournaments in the Württemburg court, Michael Hörrmann (1989: 43) writes: 'The official and unofficial chroniclers of the duke's family celebrations judged the success of the ride more by elegant posture than by the results obtained.' *Whatever* the tournament became, it ceased to be the deadly mêlée experienced by William Marshal.

Telling of the grand entry of Queen Isabelle into Paris in 1389, Jean Froissart (1814–16: IV. 51–60) dwelt upon the elaborate pageantry. When 1200 burgesses accompany the queen from St Denis into the city, when damsels chorus their praises, when an allegorical castle is constructed at Chatelet with a figure of St Anne lying upon a bed, with twelve young maidens wandering among symbolic animals, when an effigy of Saladin's castle appears, to be attacked and defended by real knights, it is clear that the demonstration of bellicose prowess with deadly weapons has been overshadowed by the dramatic spectacle in which it has been embedded. At the famous *Pas de la bergère* which René d'Anjou staged at Tarascon in 1449, there was a thatched cottage occupied by a 'shepherdess' and there were knights disguised as shepherds riding forth from pavilions disguised as humble cottages. The chivalric combat was 'entirely absorbed into the fanciful disguisings originally designed as an adornment to it' (Anglo, 1968: I. 28). René's treatise on the tournament is a compulsively detailed etiquette book comparable to those studied by Elias in *Über den Prozess der Zivilisation*. The treatise regulates exits and entrances, lays down proper verbal formulae, legislates appropriate dress. Little is said about the joust itself (Cripps-Day, 1918: lxvii–lxxxviii). A modern authority on mediaeval leisure comments that 'King René, who adored sumptuous festivals, was essentially interested in ceremony and costume; he regulated the minutest detail; but he did not indicate how the jousts were to be carried out' (Verdon, 1980: 179).

At the *Pas de l'arbre d'or* held at Bruges in 1468 to celebrate the marriage of Margaret, sister of Edward IV of England, to Charles of Burgundy, 'the tournament had become a vehicle for fantastic, even prodigal, artistic expression' (Anglo, 1968: I. 30).

There were two entrances to the lists, one painted with a golden tree from which was suspended a real golden hammer, the other built with two towers which were filled with trumpeters during the contests. Opposite the ladies' seats was planted a pine tree with gilded trunk – the Tree of Gold itself – and a so-called *perron* with three pillars which served as a stage for the Arbre d'Or, Pursuivant, his dwarf, and the captive giant. (Anglo, 1968: I. 29)

The ceremony was, of course, as elaborate as the stage set. When the Duke of Buckingham staged a tournament at Westminster in 1501, the English showed themselves the equals of their Burgundian mentors. The pageant cars were a phantasmagoria of dwarves, giants, wild men, mountains and allegorical animals (including the obligatory unicorn who laid his head upon a virgin's lap). The actual tilting was reported to have been 'inept' (Anglo, 1968: I. 38). In the letters of the Lisle family, we read of a tournament at Brussels which took place 'not without great banquetings, where some took more hurt with the cups than at the barriers with cutting of the sword' (in Byrne, 1981: V. 46). The English tournament was, in the words of a modern authority, 'a highlight of Elizabethan courtly life, but it was a spectacle and a pageant, not a field for decisions of justice or a realistic preparation for war' (Vale, 1977: 11). Nor was it much of a sports event either.

Perhaps the best illustration of the transformation from sport to spectacle was a tournament held by Henry VIII at Westminster in 1511 to celebrate the birth of Prince Arthur. Within the vast allegorical pageant Henry himself appeared as '*Ceur loyal*' while his courtiers appeared as '*Vaillaunt desyre*', '*Bone volyr*' and '*Joyous panser*' ('Loyal Heart', 'Valiant Desire', 'Good Will' and 'Happy Thought'). The use of French was conventional. The most revealing insight into the relationship of pageantry to sports at this tournament is contained in the 36 vellum membranes of the Great Tournament Roll of Westminster, a pictorial representation of the tournament. The first membrane contains a heraldic device; the last contains another device and a poem. Membranes 24–7 show Henry VIII tilting before the pavilion in which the queen sits; the remaining 30 membranes picture the entry and exit processions (reproduced in Anglo, 1968: II). If the modern Olympic Games were to have the same proportion of pageantry to athletics, we might expect a week of opening ceremonies followed by two days of sports and another week of closing ceremonies.

In such fanciful tournaments as the *Pas de la bergère,* the *Pas de l'arbre d'or* and Henry's extravaganza at Westminster, one can detect a new relationship between literature and the tournament. The mediaeval tournament left its mark on the romance and the romance left its mark on the Renaissance tournament. The literary myths of Tudor England exerted an especially powerful influence upon what had once been a fiercely martial sport. The bloody struggles of the mêlée were transformed into dramatic enactments of the adventures of King Arthur and the knights of the Round Table, with opportunities for lords and ladies to impersonate Lancelot and Tristram, Gawain and Percival, Guinevere and Arthur (Loomis, 1959: 553–9; Cline, 1945: 204–11; Borst, 1959: 213–31). The tournament, which anxious civil and ecclesiastical authorities once attempted to ban, became an instrument of centralized rule, a demonstration of royal prowess and an allegory of English history. A parallel development took place on the continent, where English myth was often borrowed by kings and princes staging *les Tables Rondes*. When King René of Anjou played Arthur and his queen took the part of Guinivere, the tournament was a very civilized affair indeed.

The 'civilizing process' did not rob the tournament of its popular appeal. This appeal can be inferred from a print of 1570 which depicts the fateful joust in 1559 in which Henri II of France lost his life. In order to observe the tournament, held in the Quartier Saint-Antoine in Paris, the spectators filled the stands, crowded into the windows of the buildings fronting the square, and even clambered up to perch like birds upon the rooftops (see Jusserand, 1901: 155).

As the mediaeval tournament was tamed into the Renaissance spectacle, the characteristic behaviour of the spectators was also transformed. Although no sports event of the entire Middle Ages seems to have approached the level of violence reached by the destructive Byzantine chariot-race riots, crowd control was a problem. There were frequent outbreaks of a more serious nature. The chronicler Matthew Paris wrote in his *Historia Anglorum* of the ill-will between the English and their opponents at a tournament in Rochester in 1151: there was '*ira et odium inter Anglos et alienegas*' (quoted in Cripps-Day, 1918: 45). At a tournament held at Chalons in 1274 Edward I was illegally seized by the Comte de Chalons, whom he had challenged, and a brawl broke out in which several people were killed (Barber, 1974: 59). When a group of squires held a tournament at Boston Fair in 1288, the fact that one side dressed as monks and the other costumed itself as canons of the church failed to prevent a riot during which the fair was sacked and part of the town set afire (Denholm-Young, 1948: 262).

To prevent such outbreaks strict rules were promulgated. The *Statuta Armorum*, published by an English committee of the late thirteenth century (the date is disputed), reveals a high degree of official worry about spectator violence: 'And they who shall come to see the Tournament shall not be armed with any Manner of Armour, and shall bear no Sword, or Dagger, or Staff, or Mace, or Stone' (quoted in Cripps-Day, 1918: xxv; see also Denholm-Young, 1948). That the committee had expressly to ban such weaponry indicates that spectators habitually arrived with the means to commit mayhem if the mood struck them. Regulation was ineffective in England and on the continent. As late as 1376 a bloody tumult occurred in Basle when middle-class spectators, trampled by mounted noblemen, responded violently and killed several knights (Wildt, 1957: 28; Schaufelberger, 1972: 46).

Eventually, however, tournament spectators seem either to have been cowed and threatened into peaceful behaviour or to have internalized a modicum of restraint. Doubtless both. While it is unreasonable and anachronistic to assume that Renaissance tournament spectators behaved with the decorum and sense of fair play expected at Victorian and Edwardian tennis matches, the trend is that predicted by Elias in his *magnum opus*. While the knightly participants played their parts in the splendid pageantry of the Renaissance tournament, the spectators played theirs.

Does Elias also provide, by implication if not by explicit argumentation, an explanation for the evolution of the tournament from twelfth-century mêlée to sixteenth-century mimesis? Yes and no. This evolution can be seen as simply one more example of the already amply exemplified 'civilizing process'. But how, exactly, did behaviour and emotional make-up ('*Affektlage*') change? 'The question', writes Elias (1976: I. 283) in a reprinted section of his work promisingly retitled 'From Tournament to Knightly Play', is 'fundamentally the same as, how do the forms of human life change?' (see also Elias and Dunning, 1986b: 47). Clearly, this response moves us to a level of analysis at which there is no such thing as a definitive answer. The best one can hope for is an explanation that seems plausible. In my opinion, the explanation offered by Elias is the most plausible one we have; which is not to say, of course, that his model of how we went from this kind of tournament to that kind of tournament is as precise as a statistical diagram of path analysis.

No one doubts that the evolution of the tournament paralleled the gamut of other institutions discussed in *Über den Prozess der Zivilisation*. These were the centuries in which European monarchs more or less successfully imposed centralized authority upon the lordly vassals who had had considerable freedom of movement in the heyday of feudalism. Constrained both by the increased external power of the state and by their internalized realization of economic and other forms of interdependence, men and women became less likely to assault one another physically in outbursts of uncontrollable rage. They learned to mask their emotions. Appropriately, their favourite sport became a kind of masque. Perhaps they felt it best, when the ever-present possibility of renewed violence lurked below the surface, to wear disguises and to represent, not the state of civilization they had reached, but rather the one to which they aspired. The masquerade tournaments in which knights wore clerical robes or women's costumes may have expressed the realization that the more civilized forms of the Renaissance covered powerful emotions always liable to explode into violence.

The description of the 'civilizing process' is, inescapably, an easier task than the search for proximate causes. I take it as a sign of philosophical maturity on the part of Elias and Dunning that they offer suggestions and refrain in their figurational analysis from presenting us with some questionable set of final causes.

A MILD CRITIQUE

My accounts of the Roman and Byzantine chariot races and of the mediaeval and Renaissance tournament testify to my indebtedness to Elias and Dunning. I should like to conclude by offering some minor general criticisms of their sports-related work as it has been gathered together and republished in *Sport im Zivilisationsprozess* (1985) and *Quest for Excitement* (1986). Others will debate the adequacy of their model as applied to modern soccer.

Elias, among the last scholars whom one might accuse of moralistic prose, warns that the terms 'civilized' and 'uncivilized' should not be taken as 'expressions of ethnocentric value judgments' (Elias and Dunning, 1986a: 133). We should not criticize past societies 'as if members of these societies had been free to choose between *their* standards and *their* norms and ours, and having had this choice, had taken the wrong decision' (Elias and Dunning, 1986a: 135). To judge by the norms of a modern historian or social scientist is – ideally – to judge with full awareness of historical change and cultural difference. Such judgements are not ethnocentric except in the trivial sense that *all* ethical judgements are inevitably made from within the confines – sometimes broad, sometimes narrow – of one culture or another. I am troubled less by the ethnocentricity of which Elias has sometimes been accused than by his emphasis on spontaneous interpersonal expressive violence and his relative neglect of programmatic institutional instrumental violence. The period during which the tournament became milder and more civilized was also the period in which ferocious wars decimated Europe. All in all, the concept of modernization may be preferable to the concept of civilization despite the fact that the former term does have its own unfortunate connotations of linear progressive moral as well as technical development (see also Guttmann, 1988: 8–11).

Repeated reading of the famous essay on 'The Quest for Excitement in Unexciting Societies' leaves me less than wholly convinced. I continue to have doubts about its use of the concept of catharsis as it relates to sports. After all, the most 'dramatic' ballgame is very different from the experience that Aristotle analyzes in the *Poetics*. Social psychologists have done an enormous amount of research devoted to testing the catharsis theory as it relates to sports, and all the research seems to indicate that sports spectacles increase rather than decrease propensities to commit acts of violence. Although several of Dunning's essays indicate scepticism about the catharsis theory, Elias and Dunning have neither come to terms with the empirical research in this field nor worked out the inconsistencies in their work.

There are also empirical data which raise questions about the theory that the quest for excitement in sports is an escape from the routinization of modern life. If this is the case, and it certainly seems plausible, then how can we explain the well-attested fact that the advantaged rather than the disadvantaged members of society are more likely to do and to watch sports? In other words, those whose lives are least routinized – that is, professionals – are more likely to seek excitement in sports than those whose lives are most routinized: factory workers and clerical personnel. Perhaps the answer lies in the *kinds* of sports that are popular with different groups of people.

There is another criticism which is, in its way, a form of praise. The work of Elias and Dunning is so very important that one is sometimes tempted to adopt their views *in toto* just as one is tempted to accept the comprehensive paradigms of Marx, Durkheim, Weber or Freud. However, as I maintained at the start of this chapter, the temptation should be resisted because no sociological or psychological paradigm is comprehensive enough. There are concerns which Elias, and to a lesser extent Dunning, have not dealt with as fully as one might hope. The focus on violence as a discriminator, for instance, has led them to pay little attention to other discriminators; for example, the level of quantification which sets modern sports apart from those of all previous ages. The valuable emphasis on excitement, tension and catharsis is well and good, but there is also the enormously important role played by the psychological process of identification, which turns athletes into symbolic representations of social groups. That they neglect these and other topics does not diminish their accomplishment. No key turns all locks.

Notes

* Portions of this essay appeared in another form in Allen Guttmann, *Sports Spectators* (New York: Columbia University Press, 1986) pp. 28–46.
1. For a historian's criticism of Dunning and Sheard, see Reid (1988).

References

Anglo, Sydney (1968), *The Great Tournament Roll of Westminster,* 2 vols (Oxford: Clarendon Press).

Balsdon, J. P. V. D. (1969), *Life and Leisure in Ancient Rome* (London: Bodley Head).

Barber, Richard (1974), *The Knight and Chivalry* (Ipswich, Suffolk: Boydell Press).

Bollinger, Traugott (1969), *Theatralis Licentia* (Winterthur: Hans Schellenberg).

Borst, Arno (1959), 'Das Rittertum in Hochmittelalter – Idee und Wirklichkeit', *Saeculum,* 10: 213–31.

Byrne, Muriel St Clare (ed.) (1981), *The Lisle Letters,* 6 vols (Chicago, Ill.: University of Chicago Press).

Cameron, Alan (1973), *Porphyrius the Charioteer* (Oxford: Clarendon Press).

_____ (1976), *Circus Factions* (Oxford: Clarendon Press).

Carcopino, Jerome (1940), *Daily Life in Ancient Rome,* trans. E. O. Lorimer (New Haven, Conn.: Yale University Press).

Charanis, Peter (1944–5), 'On the Social Structure of the Later Roman Empire', *Byzantium,* 17: 39.

_____ (1962–3), 'Some Aspects of Daily Life in Byzantium', *Greek Orthodox Theological Review,* 8: 56.

Clephan, R. Coltman (1919), *The Tournament* (London: Methuen).

Cline, Ruth Huff (1945), 'The Influence of Romances on Tournaments of the Middle Ages', *Speculum,* 20: 204–11.

Cripps-Day, Francis Henry (1918), *History of the Tournament in England and France* (London: Bernard Quaritch).

Denholm-Young, Noel (1948), 'The Tournament in the Thirteenth Century', in R. W. Hunt (ed.), *Studies in Medieval History* (Oxford: Clarendon Press).

Diehl, Charles (1925), *History of the Byzantine Empire,* trans. George B. Ives (Princeton, N.J.: Princeton University Press).

Dunning, Eric (1981), 'Social Bonding and the Socio-genesis of Violence', in Alan Tomlinson (ed.), *The Sociological Study of Sport* (Brighton, Sussex: Brighton Polytechnic–Chelsea School of Human Movement) pp. 1–35.

_____ and Sheard, K. (1979), *Barbarians, Gentlemen and Players: A Sociological Study of the Development of Rugby Football* (Oxford: Martin Robertson).

_____ , Murphy, Patrick and Williams, John (1981), 'Ordered Segmentation and the Socio-genesis of Football Hooligan Violence', in Alan Tomlinson (ed.), *The Sociological Study of Sport* (Brighton, Sussex: Brighton Polytechnic–Chelsea School of Human Movement) pp. 36–52.

Eichberg, Henning (1978), *Leistung, Spannung, Geschwindigkeit* (Stuttgart: Stuttgarter Beiträge zur Geschichre und Politik, 12).

Elias, Norbert (1976), *Über den Prozess der Zivilisation,* rev. edn, 2 vols (Frankfurt: Suhrkamp); first edition 1939.

_____ and Dunning, Eric (1970), 'The Quest for Excitement in Unexciting Societies', in G. Lüschen (ed.), *The Cross-Cultural Analysis of Sport and Games* (Champaign, Ill.: Stipes).

_____ and _____ (1986a), *Quest for Excitement: Sport and Leisure in the Civilizing Process* (Oxford: Basil Blackwell).

_____ and _____ (1986b), *Sport im Zivilisationsprozess* (Münster: LIT Verlag).

Ferguson, Arthur B. (1960), *The Indian Summer of English Chivalry* (Durham, N. C.: Duke University Press).

Froissart, Jean (1814–16), *Chronicles,* trans. John Bourchier, 4 vols (London: J. Davis).

Green, M. A. E. (1849–55), *Lives of the Princesses of England,* 6 vols (London: Henry Colburn).

Guilland, Rodolphe (1948), 'The Hippodrome at Byzantium', *Speculum,* 22: 676–82.

Guttmann, Allen (1978), *From Ritual to Record* (New York: Columbia University Press).

_____ (1984), *The Games Must Go On* (New York: Columbia University Press).

_____ (1986), *Sports Spectators* (New York: Columbia University Press).

_____ (1988), *A Whole New Ball Game: An Interpretation of American Sports* (Chapel Hill, N. C.: University of North Carolina Press).

Hardy, Stephen (1974), 'The Medieval Tournament', *Journal of Sport History,* 1(2): 96.

_____ (1977), 'Politicians, Promoters, and the Rise of Sport: the Case of Ancient Greece and Rome', *Canadian Journal for the History of Sport and Physical Education,* 8(1): 1–15.

Harris, H. A. (1972), *Sport in Greece and Rome* (London: Thames & Hudson).

Haskins, Charles Homer (1927), 'The Latin Literature of Sport', *Speculum,* 2: 238.

Hönle, Augusta and Henze, Anton (1981), *Römische Amphitheater und Stadien* (Zurich: Atlantis).

Hörmann, Michael (1989), 'Leibesübungen in der Löfischen Gesellschaft', *Sportwissenschaft,* 19(1): 43.

Humphrey, John H. (1986), *Roman Circuses: Arenas for Chariot Racing* (London: Batsford).

Jusserand, J. J. (1901), *Les Sports et jeux d'exercice dans l'ancienne France* (Paris: Plon).

Juvenal (1958), *Satires,* trans. Rolfe Humphries (Bloomington, Ind.: Indiana University Press).

Keen, Maurice (1977), 'Huizinga, Kilgour and the Decline of Chivalry', *Medievalia et Humanistica,* n.s. 8: 1–20.

_____ (1984), *Chivalry* (New Haven, Conn.: Yale University Press).

Kyle, Donald (1987), 'A Classicist's View', *Journal of Sport History*, 14(2): 209–14.

Loomis, Roger Sherman (1959), 'Arthurian Influence on Sport and Spectacle', in R. S. Loomis (ed.), *Arthurian Literature in the Middle Ages* (Oxford: Clarendon Press).

Malalas, John (1940), *Chronicle*, trans. Matthew Spinka and Glanville Downey (Chicago, Ill.: University of Chicago Press).

Meyer, Paul (ed.) (1891–1901), *L'Histoire de Guillaume le Maréchal*, 3 vols (Paris: Renouard).

Mitchell, Rosamund (1938), *John Tiptoft, 1427–1470* (London: Longmans, Green).

Nichols, John (1823), *The Progresses and Public Processions of Queen Elizabeth*, 3 vols (London: John Nichols).

Nickel, Helmut (1988), 'The Tournament: an Historical Sketch', in H. Chickering and T. H. Seiler (eds), *The Study of Chivalry* (Kalamazoo, Mich.: Western Michigan University Press).

Ovid (1975), *The Art of Love*, trans. Rolfe Humphries (Bloomington, Ind.: Indiana University Press).

Painter, Sidney (1933), *William Marshal* (Baltimore, Md: Johns Hopkins University Press).

Pliny (1963), *Letters*, trans. Betty Radice (Harmondsworth, Mddx: Penguin).

Poole, Austin Lane (1958), 'Recreations', in A. L. Poole (ed.), *Medieval England* (Oxford: Clarendon Press).

Procopius (1896), *Secret History of the Court of Justinian* (Athens: Athenian Society).

Reid, Douglas A. (1988), 'Folk-Football, the Aristocracy and Cultural Change', *International Journal of the History of Sport*, 5(2): 224–38.

Rojek, Chris (1985), *Capitalism and Leisure Theory* (London: Tavistock).

Ruehl, Joachim K. (1986), 'Wesen und Bedeutung von Kampfsagen und Trefferzahlskizzen für die Geschichte des spätmittelalterlichen Tourniers', in G. Spitzer and D. Schmidt (eds), *Sport Zwischen Eigenständigkeit und Fremdbestimmung* (Bonn: Institut für Sportwissenschaft und Sport) pp. 82–112.

Runciman, Steven (1956), *Byzantine Civilization*, rev. edn (Cleveland, Ohio: World Publishing).

Schaufelberger, Walter (1972), *Der Wettkampf in der alten Eidgenossenschaften* (Berne: Paul Haupt).

Stow, John (1908), *Survey of London*, ed. Charles Lethbridge Kingsford, 2 vols (Oxford: Clarendon Press).

Vale, Marcia (1977), *The Gentleman's Recreations* (Totowa, N.J.: Rowman & Littlefield).

Verdon, Jean (1980), *Les Loisirs au moyen age* (Paris: Jules Tallendier).

Weber, C. M. (1983), *Panem et Circenses: Massenunterhaltung als Politik im antiken Rom* (Düsseldorf: Econ).

Wildt, Klemens C. (1957), *Leibesübungen im deutschen Mittelalter* (Frankfurt: Wilhelm Limpert).

7 Sex, Gender and the Body in Sport and Leisure: Has There Been a Civilizing Process?

JENNIFER HARGREAVES

INTRODUCTION

This chapter is intended to provide a feminist critique of analyses of sport and leisure which embody the figurational approach of Norbert Elias. This is a difficult task because, throughout the two volumes comprising *The Civilizing Process,* where Norbert Elias provides a paradigm for sociological analysis he focuses on male experiences, marginalizes females and says very little about gender relations. And, unfortunately, although he wrote a book-length manuscript concerning sexual relations, it was accidentally destroyed and all that is available now is a short, reconstructed version entitled 'The Changing Balance of Power Between the Sexes' (1987b). The problem is compounded when we look at writing about sport because Elias, in common with those who use his perspective as a framework for their research, has concentrated on male sports or male bonding surrounding these sports. However, in the collaborative work of Dunning, Murphy and Williams on football and hooliganism (1988; Williams, Dunning and Murphy, 1989), gender relations are considered in this context of male culture, and the exceptional example of a discussion about this issue is Dunning's chapter, 'Sport as a Male Preserve: Notes on the Social Sources of Masculine Identity and its Transformations' in the collection of papers by Elias and Dunning (1986a; also Dunning, 1986).

However, in spite of Dunning's claim that 'Few sociologists would disagree that the changing relations between the sexes are one of the most important issues of our time' and his recognition that sociology and sports sociology have been built on patriarchal assumptions (1986b: 79), I argue here that the figurational perspective is markedly masculinist and I look at its limitations in dealing with gender.

THE QUEST FOR DETACHMENT

The neglect of a gender dimension in figurational analyses of sport and leisure is tied up with a methodological issue. Elias argues that sociology should be speaking of 'what is or was' and should be free of social and political ideologies. He wants to transcend, as far as possible, personal interests or 'involvement' and, with relative 'detachment', to describe the 'real' world (Elias, 1956; 1978: 244–5; Elias and Dunning, 1986: 25; Rojek, 1986). This vision of a potentially accurate account of the social world has provoked criticism of other approaches – for example, Eric Dunning (Elias and Dunning, 1986) argues that the neglect by sociologists of a rigorous examination of sport reveals their 'value-commitments' and that physical education specialists, who largely created the sociology of sport, have performed poorly because of their practical involvement in the area. When referring to the need for adequately theorized work about 'gender differentiation and the increasingly problematic character of relations between the sexes in more industrialized societies', he makes the following observation: 'Feminist writers, of course, have made a number of important advances in this regard but, on account of the strength of their ideological commitments, much of what they have written *appears* at least, even to many who sympathize with their cause, to be lacking in object-adequacy' (Dunning, 1986: 79, 90). It may be because Elias's concept of detachment has no empirical basis that Dunning makes these assertions without telling us his criteria for doing so and why he fails to enter into a systematic discourse with specific sports sociologists and feminist writers.

The idea that Elias and Dunning can, exceptionally, impartially separate themselves from their own histories and consciousness is implausible. Regardless of the backgrounds of theorists, the 'evidence' used is always partial and the ways in which it is interpreted are preferred ones (Carr, 1964). Like everyone else, in choosing a focus for their research Elias and Dunning are making judgements about the importance of certain concepts, issues and situations and, by their absence, the relative lack of importance of others. For example, in *The Civilizing Process,* Elias makes relatively few explicit references to the lives of women and to relations between the sexes. In the bulk of the work, when he is looking at concepts such as culture, civilization and the state, he ignores the gender dimension, in common with much of the writing about sport and leisure in the figurational tradition. A serious weakness of the quest for detachment is that it embodies the notion of male detachment.

UNGENDERED SUBJECTS IN SPORTS WRITING

I shall look now at the effects of gender neglect in some of the papers which, collectively, compose Elias and Dunning (1986). With the exception of a section about fox-hunting, in which a limited number of upper-class women would have actively participated, the book is exclusively about *male* sports and shared traditions. The cover signals its contents: it shows a boxing match with one man knocking another out of the ring, a male referee and an all-male audience. Turn inside and there is an all-male crowd celebrating a football triumph. None the less, Elias's contributions embody ungendered subjects. For example, in the Introduction he describes the emergence of less-violent sports and the establishment of a parliamentary system as parallel aspects of a general trend towards greater pacification in eighteenth century England. He states: 'Sport and Parliament . . . were both characteristic of the same change in the power structure in England and in the social habitus of that class of people which emerged from the antecedent struggles as the ruling group.' The reality is, of course, that human beings are gendered subjects and that both Parliament and the sports referred to were based, as well as on class-differences, on a patriarchal structure of power. But Elias ignores the traditions of women in sport and also the ways in which women, however unobviously, were integral to dominantly male cultures. He is also silent about the interdependence of class and gender.

I am not arguing here that it is wrong to focus on male culture and male sport but that it is misleading to do so without accounting for the ways in which starkly uneven gender relations make possible male dominance in different spheres of culture and sport and the reasons and effects of men appropriating cultural and state power to control the usages and ways of life for both sexes. From a feminist stance, Elias fails to achieve his own objective of 'high object adequacy' on the grounds that to neglect the gender dimension is to provide a partial and distorted account of human beings and the societies they form.

The chapters entitled 'The Quest for Excitement in Leisure' and 'Leisure in the Spare-time Spectrum', written jointly by Elias and Dunning, provide further examples of gender neglect. In these papers Elias and Dunning characterize sport as a popular example of the unparalleled range of leisure activities available in modern societies which provide enjoyable experiences and opportunities for the expression of relatively unconstrained emotions. They situate leisure activities within a broad range of spare-time activities, many of which are routinized and allow limited scope for emotional pleasure. 'There is some evidence', they tell us, 'which suggests that a lack of balance between non-leisure and leisure activities entails some human impoverishment, some drying up of emotions which affects the whole personality' (Elias and Dunning, 1986: 107). But the analysis is pitched at a high level of generality, focusing on the 'functional interdependence' of leisure and non-leisure, and they fail to be specific about, or to refer to, any of the literature about variables such as gender which mediate people's leisure.

Although Elias and Dunning seek to avoid the 'false dichotomy' between work and leisure, their silence about gender masks the differences between men's and women's spare time and leisure in just the same way that talking about ungendered work and leisure fails to recognize differences and in-equalities between the sexes. It has been well-documented by feminist researchers (Deem, 1986; Green, Hebron and Woodward, 1987; Hargreaves, 1989; Wimbush, 1986; Wimbush and Talbot, 1988) that the lives of vast numbers of women in England are highly routinized to the extent that on average they have far less disposable time and far fewer choices than men to participate in non-compulsory, deroutinized activities when the regard for themselves, and in particular for their own personal and emotional satisfaction, can take priority over all other considerations.

'The heart of the problem of leisure', Elias and Dunning suggest, 'lies in the relationship between the structure of the leisure needs characteristic of our type of society and the structure of the events designed to satisfy these needs' (Elias and Dunning, 1986: 74–5). They argue that in highly differen-tiated societies state regulation of leisure has become more even and more predictable (119–20). But they fail to ask themselves such questions as: 'Who has the power to define leisure needs and satisfaction?'; 'According to what criteria?'; and 'For what reasons and in whose interests does the state regulate leisure?'. Missing from their scheme are the specific relations of domination and subordination, such as gender relations, which influence the provision and control of participation in leisure, and the ways in which gender may intersect with other variables such as age, class and ethnicity. They are silent also about the concrete economic, ideological and political arrangements which affect leisure figurations and constrain emotional pleasure and they fail to examine the complexities of and conflicts over perception and fulfilment of needs. These issues have influenced the work of feminist researchers.

NEUTRAL OR PASSIONATE OBJECTIVITY?

Dunning claims that the methodology of detachment enables the researcher to escape from the 'dominant values and modes of thinking of Western societies' and to recognize the 'homologous' character of sport, rejecting 'heteronomous evaluations' (Elias and Dunning, 1986: 3–5). The implication here is that figurational theorists can somehow escape from social ideologies. But it is not an accident that all figurational sports sociology has been written by men about male sports and, in contradiction to Dunning's claim, such a position represents an alignment with the 'dominant values and modes of thinking of Western societies'. Because it claims to be objective and uncritical, in a subtle but fundamental manner it is supporting the popular idea that sport is more suited to men than to women and represents a celebration of the world of male bonding and male sport. Together with the relative silence about female involvement, such a position produces a powerful ideological message, thus helping to perpetuate relations of domination and subordination between the sexes in sport. The 'homologous character' of sport which Dunning talks about embodies gender relations in a fundamental way – to leave them out or to marginalize them is, in the terms of figurational sociology, to fail to be scientific.

The analysis of sport is a struggle between people with different perspectives about the social implications of sport and about the nature of society. But Elias does not write in ethical or moral terms. He does not examine the deep realities of social inequalities and injustices – of economic deprivation, racism and sexism, for example. The figurational approach demands a rejection of any moral position and Elias makes explicit his view that 'the sociologist should not be required or expected to express his convictions about how society *ought* to develop' (Elias, 1978: 153). He suggests that 'A unifying developmental frame of reference without ideological encrustations, without, for instance, any built-in-postulate of a necessarily better future could be useful in sociology and in the other human sciences' (Elias, 1987a: 226). But, as Rojek has pointed out, Elias's discussion of involvement 'repeatedly shows that statements which claim "high object adequacy" to the world as it really is are very often distortions of the world which reflect personal or group interests' (Rojek, 1986: 592). So the concept of detachment is a 'slippery' one because, while claiming to be neutral, it can be said implicitly to support reactionary positions and ideas.

In contrast, theory can become a critical embrace of commitment. As MacKinnon (1989: xvi) puts it:

Situated theory is concrete and changing rather than abstract and totalizing, working from the viewpoint of powerlessness to political understanding toward social transformation. This posture places the theorist inside the world and the work, not above or outside them – which, to be frank, is where the theorist has been all along.

Feminists in general, and those working in the fields of leisure and sport specifically, have a vision of a world where differences between individuals, including those between men and women, would no longer be based on power and oppression. Although the issue of gender relations in leisure and sport is a complex one, feminists are struggling, through various social science approaches, to understand the nature of discrimination in order to remove it (Hargreaves, 1990). We not only observe inequalities between the sexes in leisure and sport but believe them to be wrong and have a shared commitment to improve women's position in these spheres. To do so, it is necessary to confront actual, existing social situations and historical processes which have produced current gender inequalities and constraints in leisure and sport. Although Elias has said: 'If I were free to choose my world, I would probably not have chosen a world where struggles between humans are found exciting and enjoyable. . . . I would probably have chosen to say: avoid struggle. Let us all live in peace with one another (Elias and Dunning, 1986: 59), there is no direction in his work about how things might improve. His espousal of non-involvement and failure to situate his work in any political and ideological framework provides a rationale for non-commitment. Elias talks of people's increasing capacities to control events more consciously, but he does not say for what reasons or in what ways. In contrast, to produce a high quality of committed research is what feminism has called working with 'passionate objectivity'.

ELIAS'S TREATMENT OF WOMEN

It is hard to understand how it can be argued that figurational sociology recognizes human beings as active agents in challenging uneven relations between the sexes and struggling to change them. Elias's idea that we all experience areas of life and culture, such as sport, in 'dynamic' figurations which embody conflicts between those who compose them is overruled by his description of this process as one which 'has a determinable structure which, in European societies since the Middle Ages, has taken the form of a "civilizing process"', a feature of which has been a long-term trend towards 'an equalizing change in the balance of power between social classes and other groups' (Elias and Dunning, 1986: 13). Elias posits an equalizing of relationships between the sexes as a reflection of the lengthening of interdependency chains in social figurations. He proposes that societies with a more centralized, advanced and differentiated division of functions, and where social life is no longer exclusively tied to militarism and explicit expressions of violence, have complex and extensive chains of interdependence between people and a greater level of equality between the sexes (Elias, 1982: 91ff.).

Elias provides specific examples of gender relations in his paper 'The Changing Balance of Power Between the Sexes' (1987b) and when he writes 'On the Sociogenesis of the Minnesang and Courtly Forms of Conduct' in volume 2 of *The Civilizing Process* (1982). In the first of these Elias argues that, until its late stages, the Roman Republic was a warrior state ruled by men. He reasons that war and other forms of violence were part of everyday life and that women depended for their survival on the fighting skills of their male relatives. The social inferiority of women at this time, he says, was 'intimately connected to their relative physical weakness'. Then, in the later period of the Republic and during the Roman Empire, Elias maintains that, with the accumulation of wealth and power in the Mediterranean and with the development of a state apparatus, Roman society went through a civilizing spurt. Women, he says, gained more independence and power at this time as a result of improved education, the ownership of property and the ability to divorce their husbands, so that men and women in marriage, though not in other spheres, became relatively equal. Elias uses this example to suggest that women's subordination was no longer based on their inferior average physical strength.

Elias claims that the unprecedented changes in the balance of power between the sexes in Ancient Rome left their mark on later societies 'when the development of a society as a whole offered the right conditions for it'. He traces the 'European tradition' as a continuous process from the time of Near-Eastern and Greco-Roman antiquity, via the Middle Ages, to the modern day – a process with several spurts and maybe, he says, 'with simultaneous or subsequent counter-spurts'. It is clear to see why Elias's theory has been characterized as evolutionary when he asserts that, none the less, in all Western societies in the long-term, 'the "trend" of the movement of civilization, is everywhere the same' (1982: 248–50), embodying civilizing restraints on sexuality and aggressiveness (1978: 189–91).

Elias argues that there is a clear connection between the structure of relationships in society at large and the personality structure of people. If, he says, there are no constraints upon men to control their drives, women are systematically abused by them, whereas in a society with organized controls against violence there is greater equality between the sexes. He writes about the positions of the knights of the ninth and tenth centuries as being inseparable from those of their wives or from women of lower rank and apart from a new élite exceptions, women were, he says, brutally subjugated, regularly beaten and raped, and treated as commodities for the pleasure of males:

> And relations between the sexes were regulated, as in every warrior society with more or less male rule, by power. . . . We hear from time to time of women who by temperament and inclination differed little from men. The lady in this case is a 'virago' with a violent temper, lively passions, subjected from her youth to all manner of physical exercise, and taking part in all the pleasures and dangers of the knights around her. But often we hear of the other side, of a warrior, whether a king or a simple seigneur, beating his wife. It seems almost an established habit for the knight, flying into a rage, to punch his wife on the nose till blood flows.   (1982: 78–9)

According to Elias, the balance of power between the sexes shifted somewhat with the development in Europe of the feudal courts and more so in the absolutist courts which 'offered women special opportunities to overcome male dominance and attain equal status with men'. But a major civilizing spurt occurred from the middle of the eighteenth century with an increase in state intervention, state monopolization of violence and, at a personal level, increased self-control over emotions and impulses. Elias is clear that 'wherever men were forced to renounce physical violence, the social importance of women increased' (ibid.: 81). He says that 'One of the conditions for lessening the inequality between men and women in a society was the growth of a state organization' (1987: 292–3) and in the more developed societies of today, the functions of fighting and pacification are vested in the government.

FIGURATIONAL CONSTRAINTS

The criticism of determinism in figurational sociology arises because, as Elias puts it: 'It is the structure of society that demands and generates a specific standard of emotional control' (1978: 201). The 'lessening of inequality between the sexes' is posed as a structural criterion of the 'civilizing process' as if men and women are products of the system, locked into 'structures of mutually oriented and dependent people' (ibid.: 261). The term gender is employed descriptively and uncritically, producing a sense that men are the vigorous, powerful agents of history and women are the passive recipients of male domination and as if the movement of history towards centralization facilitates a more 'civilized' relationship between them. Horne and Jary (1987: 100–1) argue that in Elias and Dunning's work on sport there is an ahistorical assumption about patriarchy and about the inevitability of equality. Little is made in figurational accounts of the history of the subjective choices which men and women *can* make or of the political, economic and ideological arrangements which in large part produce the values that underpin the changes in the personality structure and the supposed successful civilizing of the individual. There is a need to go beyond descriptions of observable psychological structural characteristics of societies and to relate them to the meanings, interests and values integral to specific power bases which affect, in specific ways, such behaviour as gender relations. The nature of the 'processual development' of societies could then be understood in terms of the actual struggles between groups with different and often oppositional interests.

GENDER AND SPORT

There is a strong tendency in Elias's work to generalize from limited evidence about the 'civilizing' of sexuality and relations between the sexes; he refers to gender relations as if it were possible to generalize about women as a whole from the experiences of privileged and almost certainly unrepresentative groups. This is clearly misleading if we look at the evidence of women in sport which indicates not that changing gender relations in sport have been part of a 'civilizing' process during which uneven relations of domination and subordination between the sexes have become more equal with time, but rather that women have fought, conceded, negotiated and colluded with men – and with other women – to gain improvements for themselves and that sometimes they have won and sometimes they have lost or even regressed. To posit a 'narrowing of the gap between men and women' does not take account of the fact that women (and men) are not a homologous group and there are complexities and differences between, for example, black women, disabled women, lesbians, older women and working-class women and that, in many respects, there are greater differences between women from different social and cultural groups than between men and women from the same social or cultural group. Nor does it take into account that the struggle in sport over uneven power relations, based on gender divisions, is not simply a struggle between men and women. And the contradictions to the apparent general trend towards greater equality between men and women in sport cannot simply be accounted for by the idea of 'counter-spurts' – there are just too many complexities for the generalized framework of the figurational perspective to cope with. Additionally, struggles in sport cannot be understood without reference to values and commitment. There is an assumption in the idea of greater equality between the sexes in sport that because men have more power in sport than women, then women should fit into male-dominated structures. This is the liberal position; its opposite is for women to be distinctly different from men. However, the referents for both these positions are the male and masculinity which is the case also for figurational sociology. But sport is a contested area of life and some men and women are fighting *together* for a model of sport which is qualitatively different from the aggressively competitive models which have historically been dominated by men (Hargreaves, 1990).

THE GENDERED STATE

In common with liberalism, Elias's work embodies the idea that the state is a neutral, benevolent institution and that sex inequality can be put right by legal processes. He and Dunning are opposed to Marxist claims that the state is a tool of male dominance and female oppression. But as MacKinnon points out: 'neither liberalism nor Marxism grants women, as such, a specific relation to the state', and she discusses the possibility of a feminist theory of the state which 'would comprehend how law works as a form of state power in a social context in which power is gendered' (1989: 159). The liberal state, in many ways and through different channels, performs in the interest of men as a gender and yet, as MacKinnon claims, in the US the state is acknowledged as capitalist, but not as male (ibid.: 215). This argument can be applied to other advanced industrial countries where, although the governments have provided openings for equality between the sexes, when the power of men over women subtly permeates society no legislation can produce equality between the sexes. For example, huge numbers of women are consistently oppressed outside the law in their everyday lives, in private and personal situations, in particular in the home, and in ways which militate against access to leisure and pleasure. Equal opportunities legislation can do little to change a 'whole way of life' based upon conventional gender relations in social life and in the home. Sexual violence, for example, is unchanged (ibid.: 11). The power of male gender thus links the state with other contexts.

Elias and Dunning, however, give little attention to the role of the state in contemporary society and say nothing about how state power emerged as male power and has become an organized and institutionalized form of social dominance. The concept of civilization embodies a gallant view of masculinity, treating the state as an enabling mechanism without examining its role systematically and disregarding ways in which the state has treated the sexes unequally and the complexities and contradictory features of male hegemony. The term 'state' is used descriptively in figurational sociology, but it needs examination so that we can understand its gendered character and whether it is to some degree autonomous of the interests of men or an integral expression of them. Since Elias does not address the relationship between morality, justice and power, the failure to include gender in an account of the state and to posit the idea that the state is a facilitator of long-term improved relations between the sexes could be viewed as an excuse for not engaging in a struggle to change things now.

The British government in its sex equality legislation is an example of the liberal view of inequality between the sexes. The Sex Discrimination Act was passed in 1975 as a result of a government White Paper, *Equality for Women*. 'The 1975 Act makes it unlawful to discriminate on the ground of sex in the general contexts of employment, education and the provision to the public (or section of the public) of goods, services, premises and facilities' (Pannick, 1983: 9). But although this legislation was intended to encourage equal opportunities for men and women and make it possible for individuals, with the support of the Equal Opportunities Commission, to challenge discrimination based on sex, it has been constructed in such a way as to make it very difficult to mount an effective legal challenge against sex discrimination in sport and physical education.

Although it was intended that specified exceptions to the Act be kept to a minimum in order not to weaken the principle of non-discrimination, in the case of sport and physical education this principle has been lost. In Britain much of our sport takes place in the voluntary and private sectors, and since private and single-sex clubs, as well as voluntary associations and charities, are exceptions to the 1975 Act, much of our sport is therefore insulated from the effects of sex equality legislation. Added to that, section 44 states that nothing in the Act shall 'in relation to any sport, game or other activity of a competitive nature where the physical strength, stamina or physique of the average woman puts her at a disadvantage to the average man, render unlawful any act related to the participation of a person as a competitor in events involving that activity where they are confined to competitors of one sex' (Pannick, 1983: 9). This clause has been used to sanction the exclusion of women from some sports venues or to sanction the refusal to give women full membership of clubs which provide some of the limited resources available in certain sports, such as golf and snooker. It has also been used to sanction the banning of mixed competition, not only between adult men and women, but also between pre-pubertal boys and girls at which age girls tend to mature earlier and to be on average bigger and stronger than boys. Although the Act states that, apart from specified exceptions, a person must not be discriminated against on the ground of sex but should be treated according to his or her individual attributes and not according to those assumed to be characteristic of an average person of his or her sex, none the less, because it can be argued that sport is a legitimate exception in different ways, discrimination becomes legally sanctioned. And, as Margaret Talbot (1988: 30) points out, 'the onus to prove inequality or discrimination rests with the complainant', most of whom have fewer resources than the institutions whose practices they are challenging. Individuals, she says, 'have a great deal more to lose than their case; the odds are stacked against them'.

In America, although the sex equality legislation appears to have fewer loopholes, none the less it has also failed to eliminate discrimination against women. For example, although the 1972 Title IX amendment to the US Constitution was intended to eliminate 'special or preferential treatment solely on the basis of sex', evidence has shown that when single-sex organizations lose their legal protection, women have tended to lose status and power which previously they had in all-female organizations (Talbot, 1987: 14). Similar legislation in Australia and Canada has also failed to alter radically the patterns of discrimination against women in leisure and sport (Dyer, 1989).

Not surprisingly, legislation which is not specifically for equal opportunities militates against women also. For example, the present British government's scheme for compulsory competitive tendering (or privatization) of local authority provision of leisure and sports facilities may well jeopardize the existing opportunities in sport and leisure that some women have and impede radical progress. This legislation provides an example which points to the necessity for a theory of society which can account for the relationship between the state and the commercial sector as well as for gender. Local authorities are not legally obliged to ensure that those who will run leisure and sports centres in the future, whose primary imperative will be to make a profit, must discriminate in favour of those social groups who cannot afford competitive prices. There is fear that certain groups of women, as well as other disadvantaged groups such as the unemployed, the low-waged and the elderly, will be seriously and disproportionately disadvantaged by the new legislation.

The civilizing process is claimed to be a process of functional democratization or a long-term trend towards a more equal balance of power between the classes and sexes, reflected in the women's movement and in equal opportunities legislation (Dunning *et al.* 1988: 230). Such a claim is misleading and uncritical. Central and local government leisure policy in Britain has failed adequately to understand and deal with most forms of sex discrimination. This is often because there is a failure to recognize the subtle and pervasive effects of sexism. Jean Yule (1990: 3) argues:

> Policy outcomes are not analyzed in terms of the extent to which they might reinforce or challenge patriarchal power relations. There is no exploration, for example, of the extent to which the activities developed might reinforce or challenge the dominant view that women are physically weaker and more passive than men, or that certain activities are more appropriate for women than others.

Official policy is also insensitive to gender relations of power in leisure administration, management and training which, in some instances, embody blatant forms of sexism and discrimination (ibid.: 4–5; see also Talbot, 1988). Yule suggests that what is needed is an analysis of the changing role and nature of state intervention in leisure provision which could include 'particular configurations of the state, the market and the voluntary sectors and their particular implications for gender and power' (ibid.: 6).

I have argued here that Elias's theory of the state fails to address its gendered character or the complex role of the modern state. Feminist theorists who recognize the necessity to be able to understand the complexities of the relationship between patriarchal relations and capitalist relations seem to be nearer understanding the modern world than Elias's theory of civilization and the state enables us to do.

AGGRESSIVE MASCULINITY, SEXUALITY AND VIOLENCE

Recent work by Dunning, Murphy and Williams represents a shift away from the ungendered figurational approach. 'Despite the growing power of women', they write, 'Britain remains a patriarchal society and a stress on masculinity and, correspondingly, on the subordination of women is a more or less common characteristic of all social classes' (Williams *et al.*, 1989: 212). Dunning's paper 'Sport as a Male Preserve' (1986) is specifically concerned with the masculine identities of participants in early forms of combat sports, in contemporary rugby union football, and in incidents of football hooliganism. His collaborative work with Murphy and Williams, in particular *The Roots of Football Hooliganism* (Dunning *et al.*, 1988) and *Hooligans Abroad* (Williams *et al.*, 1989), alludes to the propensity of football hooligans for physical violence and the attitudes and relationships of hooligans to and with women. Their research shows that the vast majority of football hooligans come from lower-working-class communities where their general life-styles, as well as hooligan activities, are based around the construction and expression of a violent masculine style. Dunning and his colleagues see this as a 'central life commitment' which provides meaning, gratification and status which young working-class men find difficult to achieve through other means. Many of the hooligans have extreme right-wing beliefs, are virulently nationalistic and viciously racist and fascist as well as sexist. Their aggression in fighting gangs is reinforced by their experiences at home and in the rough working-class communities where there are more public forms of violence, more aggressive physical outbursts, fewer controls either by state agencies or family and community sources, and greater pleasure and less guilt experienced by young men perpetrating violence. Common features of their lives, too, are rigid sex-segregation, male domination of women, a high rate of male violence towards women and the lack of any 'softening' or 'civilizing' female influence. 'Many women in such communities', Dunning and his colleagues tell us, 'grow up to be relatively violent themselves and to expect violent behaviour from their men. To the extent that this is so, the violent propensities of the men are reinforced' (Williams *et al.*, 1989: xxix).

The 'acceptable masculine style' of football hooligans embodies a form of aggressive heterosexuality and homophobia. It is the mixture of violence with sexual imagery – in particular, the objectification of women – which combine to produce a powerful symbol of aggressive masculinity. The authors provide examples of the hooligans' typically crude language of sexuality: 'right hard cunts', 'kicked the argies to fuck', 'matched with an Englishman's arse' (ibid: 156–7). Describing English fans in Holland in 1982 they claim:

> Young women attracted most attention of all, with the least attractive adding to the growing fund of 'evidence' of the 'racial' and cultural supremacy of the visitors. Those admired for their looks were loudly and

crudely informed of the benefits of an instant liaison with English lads. (ibid.: 131)

Soccer chants and newspaper reports provide more evidence of the hooligans' language and system of signs which symbolically vilify women and celebrate male sexual power over them. Some of the fans wear tee-shirts with sexist rhymes and shout out common soccer-terrace chants which denigrate women. In 1988 the English football fans in Stuttgart

assembled at the Bierfassle Bar opposite platform nine in shorts and teé shirts, calculating beer prices, scratching their testicles and singing 'Get yer tits out for the lads' whenever a young woman walked by. (Vulliamy, 1988)

Chants and ditties which are sexually explicit, and insulting and degrading to women and gays, have become an intrinsic feature of the repertoire of soccer hooligans, characterized by the standard:

> Liverpool boys [*sic*]
> We are here
> Shag your women
> And drink your beer.

Another popular terrace chant which objectifies females is aimed at the referee when decisions go against the supporters' team: 'Referee, referee, your old lady is a whore', or to wayward opposing centre forwards: 'You couldn't score in a brothel!'. There is the more inventive Leicester chant, 'You've got more mouth than a cow's cunt', sung to the tune of 'The Camptown Races', and a visiting goalkeeper to Leicester, whose wife had had an affair, was greeted by the chant, 'Frankie's [Worthington] shagged your missus!' And in the early 1980s when a psychopath popularly called the 'Yorkshire Ripper' was sexually abusing and murdering women, the Leeds United fans were renowned for taunting the police with the ditty 'Ripper II, Police Nil, Hallelujah!', and women walking around the pitch have been subjected to thousands of male voices shouting in unison: 'Does she take it up the arse?'.[1]

In the context of rugby football, Dunning (1986) argues that the greater controls on openly aggressive physical acts on the field of play have been transformed into symbolic expressions of machismo after the match. He describes the male 'striptease' or ritual mocking of the female stripper, accompanied by the strains of the 'Zulu warrior'. Rugby initiation ceremonies include the often forceful defilement of the genitals, mixed in with other rituals and excessive beer drinking. These obscene rituals bolster, he suggests, the flagging traditional male egos which have resulted from the growing power of women.

The hidden message common to these chants is that sex has nothing to do with sensuality, sensitivity, caring and equality, but everything to do with aggressive heterosexuality and the commodification of and power over women. The ways in which sexuality is expressed and experienced in these settings is gendered through the images of power enshrined in the male body. By indulging in actual violence against other males and symbolic violence against women, male identities are consolidated.

Although the threat of physical violence is usually treated seriously, symbolic violence, though endemic and violating, becomes normalized and accepted in popular consciousness. These examples point to the intimate association between violence and masculinity and ways in which gender embodies sexuality as a form of power. However, the work of Dunning and his colleagues fails to develop an analysis of these relations to any depth and fails to show how they are part of a general structure of power relations between men and women, specific to capitalist Britain. They are keen to 'explain away' violent outbursts as counter-spurts in a generally more 'civilized' society, rather than considering them as examples of a widespread characteristic of social life linked to and legitimating male violence in other social spheres. As Rojek (1985: 172) points out, the 'tension between the historical 'trend-maintaining' tendencies towards more 'civilized' behaviour, and the persistence of aggression in present day societies, pervades the whole figurational approach'. Dunning *et al.'s* position is that, in spite of such outbreaks of violence as football hooliganism, more and more people are living in 'pacified social spaces' which are normally free from acts of violence. They argue that there is a long-term tendency for people to become 'more sensitive towards committing or even witnessing violent acts and . . . (in competition, including between the sexes), the irruption of direct physical violence is relatively uncommon' (1988: 225–7). Feminist research contradicts such a claim. We know that incidents of violence and aggression against women are numerous, regular, varied and serious and that in 'civilized' societies men's power over women is most commonly expressed in sexual terms, through the use of physical force in cases of rape, battery, incest, child sexual abuse and in sexual harrassment, prostitution and pornography. Women's reported concerns about personal safety in public have risen to unprecedentedly high levels and it is well-documented that the home has become the most dangerous place for women. In reality, public and private spaces in 'civilized' societies are far from being 'pacified social spaces' (Kelly, 1988: Smith, 1989a, 1989b; Stanko, 1985; Walby 1990).

Following the figurational position, one would expect that, in general, the less repressive the political status quo, the less physical violence would be manifest in sport. But modern sports are still overwhelmingly dominated by men and based on the belief that aggression is a necessary and positive component. Although the rules of modern sports have placed a ban on open hacking, ritualized brutality is now built into the rules and structures of most contact sports. There must be a greater incidence of, and a greater variety of, sport-related violence then ever before, which suggests that a new definition of violence is needed to incorporate the excesses and corruptions endemic to modern sport that exploit a person psychologically and emotionally as well as physically. Violent 'masculine-style' competitive sport has impelled men and, ironically, women as well, to abuse and injure the body by, for example, over-training, attempting high-risk skills, and endangering life by drug misuse and diet manipulation. The effects of less-overt forms of violence may be much more harmful than the results of primitive hacking – for example, young boys have died after playing well-ordered games of rugby and young girls have suffered paralysis as a result of gymnastic training. The term 'battered child athletes' describes the increasing numbers of children who are psychologically damaged or physically injured by the extreme pressure of competitive sports (Bottomley, 1981; Hargreaves, 1984, 1985; Silver, 1984).

It is not that women are never violent but that, in modern societies such as Britain and the US, physical violence and aggression are mostly perpetrated by men and are seen as predominantly masculine. In our society we perceive this to be so, in part because it is men, and rarely women, who are trained and legally sanctioned, as members of the police force, the armed forces, the prison service and other agencies of law and order, to use violence. Although it is more likely that an aggressive masculine style is valued and adopted by lower-working-class males, it is not exclusive to them, but, as Lynne Segal (1990: 265) points out: 'It is part of the fantasy of life, if not the lived reality, of the majority of men enthralled by images of masculinity which equate with power and violence.' Physical violence is widespread – it occurs in the home, on the streets, on the football pitch and on the terraces. As Connell (1987: 85) articulates:

the concern with force and skill becomes a statement embedded in the body, embedded through years of participation in social practices like organized sport. . . . The meanings in the bodily sense of masculinity concern, above all else, the superiority of men to women, and the exaltation of hegemonic masculinity over other groups of men which is essential to the domination of women.

CHANGING MEN

We come again to the silence in the figurational approach about issues of morality and the lack of a connection between theory and radical politics and practice. Elias tells us that civilization is a process during which individuals learn to control their animalic behaviour and regulate and restrain instinctive and affective forms of expression into more 'pacified' forms and that the disciplining of emotions occurs in outlets like sport. But this behaviourist stance is concerned with channelling a notion of 'essential' male aggression, rather than challenging and changing it. It also implicitly supports modern sporting forms, many of which stimulate and exaggerate violent tendencies and celebrate gender difference and inequality. It is not just on the football terraces where physical aggression can lead to violence, but in the game itself, which, in common with other traditional male sports, encourages a form of masculinity which in turn encourages a form of violence. Sabo and Runfola (1980: 113) argue: 'The real and assumed propensity for violence, reinforced by sports, does much to legitimate and enforce the male dominance of other social institutions.'

Sports power is rooted in the male/female distinction because sport remains, in popular consciousness, an area where biological differences are celebrated and where women's bodily differences from men are used as a reason for their subordination to men. It is the symbolic power invested in the male body through images of aggressive sporting masculinity which are linked to more general ideas of social power. Lynne Segal (1990: 288) suggests that 'masculinity' is best understood as

> transcending the personal, as a heterogeneous set of ideas, constructed around assumptions of social *power,* which are lived out and reinforced, or perhaps denied and challenged, in multiple and diverse ways within a whole social system in which relations of authority, work, and domestic life are organised, in the main, along hierarchical gender lines.

Feminist cultural struggle can only be understood in the light of values and beliefs which underpin a vision for the future, part of which is to find ways to deconstruct ideologies of femininity and masculinity and work for a truly more equal balance of power between the sexes. To do so it is necessary to understand much more about men and masculinities, male violence and men's power, as well as about women and femininities. There has been a recent spate of writing on these topics which relates to more general developments in critical social science. Much of it is concerned not just with describing what men are, but what men might be, in specific political, economic and cultural contexts (for example, Brod, 1987; Hearn, 1988; Kimmel, 1987; Kimmel and Messner, 1989; Segal, 1990). Much of this work has been shaped by feminism and, in common with much feminist writing, incorporates the personal and political as well as 'engaging with the tension of detachment/involvement that has importantly characterized much recent feminist writing' (Hearn, 1987: 678).

Most work on men and masculinities has not been a dispassionate inquiry but has been written by men who share a belief that aggressive masculinity should be discouraged and changed because, in their words (quoted in Segal, 1990: 287):

Our power in society as men not only oppresses women but also imprisons us in a deadening masculinity which cripples our relationships – with each other, with women, with ourselves.

Figurational sociology gives insufficient attention to such contested functions of life and culture as gender, masculinity and violence. A more equal balance of power between the sexes is not inevitable, and dismantling gender hierarchies necessitates an understanding of their connections to features of the social totality and 'the pursuit of change in the economy, the labour market, social policy and the state, as well as the organization of domestic life, the nature of sexual encounters and the rhetorics of sexual difference' (ibid.: 294). Gender relations in sport and in sports writing and theorizing are examples of the general social patterning of relations between men and women which figurational sociology does not examine. And the contested, complex and confusing features of gender relations do not fit comfortably into the civilizing process.

Note

1. These examples of soccer chants have been given to me by John Williams from his research with the Sir Norman Chester Centre for Football Research.

References

Abrams, P. (1982), *Historical Sociology* (Shepton Mallet, Som.: Open Books).
Arena Review (1984).
Bottomley, M. (1981), 'School Age Sports Injuries', *Medisport*, 3 March, 88–90.
Boutilier, M. and San Giovanni, L. (1983), *The Sporting Woman* (Champaign, Ill.: Human Kinetics).
Brod, H. (ed.) (1987), *The Making of Masculinities: The New Men's Studies* (Boston, Mass.: Allen & Unwin).
Carr, E. H. (1964), *What is History?* (Harmondsworth, Middx: Penguin).
Clarke, J. and Critcher, C. (1985), *The Devil Makes Work* (London: Macmillan).
Connell, R. (1987), *Gender and Power* (Cambridge: Polity Press).
Deem, R. (1986), *All Work and No Play? The Sociology of Women and Leisure* (Milton Keynes, Bucks.: Open University Press).
Dunning, E. (1971), *The Sociology of Sport* (London: Frank Cass).
_____ (1986), 'Sport as a Male Preserve: Notes on the Social Sources of Masculine Identity and its Transformations', *Theory, Culture and Society*, 3(1): 79–91.
_____ (1989), 'The Figurational Approach to Leisure and Sport', in C. Rojek (ed.), *Leisure for Leisure* (London: Macmillan).
_____ and Sheard, K. (1979), *Barbarians, Gentlemen and Players: A Sociological Study of the Development of Rugby Football* (Oxford: Martin Robertson).
_____ , Murphy, P. and Williams, J. (1988), *The Roots of Football Hooliganism: An Historical and Sociological Study* (London: Routledge & Kegan Paul).
_____ , Murphy, P., Williams, J. and Maguire, J. (1984), 'Football Hooliganism in Britain before the First World War', *International Review for the Sociology of Sport*, 19(3/4): 215–41.
Dyer, K. (1989), *Sportswomen Towards 2000: A Celebration* (Richmond, S. Australia: Hyde Park Press).
Elias, N. (1956), 'Problems of Involvement and Detachment', *British Journal of Sociology*, 7(3): 226–52.
_____ (1978), *The Civilizing Process*, vol. 1: *The History of Manners* (Oxford: Basil Blackwell).
_____ (1982), *The Civilizing Process*, vol. 2: *State Formation and Civilization* (Oxford: Basil Blackwell).
_____ (1987a), 'The Retreat of Sociologists into the Present', *Theory, Culture and Society*, 4(2/3): 223–49.
_____ (1987b), 'The Changing Balance of Power Between the Sexes – A Process-Sociological Study: the Example of the Ancient Roman State', *Theory, Culture and Society*, 4(2/3): 287–317.
_____ and Dunning, E. (1966), 'Dynamics of Sport Groups with Special Reference to Football', *British Journal of Sociology*, 17(4): 388–402.
_____ (1986), *Quest for Excitement: Sport and Leisure in the Civilizing Process* (Oxford: Basil Blackwell).
Equal Opportunities Commission, *Sex Discrimination Decisions: no. 15 – Teacher Promotion: The Case of Meller v Strathclyde Regional Council* (Manchester: EOC, n.d.).
Felski, R. (1989), 'Feminist Theory and Social Change', *Theory, Culture and Society*, 6(2): 219–40.

Ford, D. and Hearn, J. (rev. 1989), *Studying Men and Masculinity: A Sourcebook of Literature and Materials* (Bradford, Yorks: University Printing Unit).

Green, E., Hebron, S. and Woodward, D. (1987), *Leisure and Gender: A Study of Sheffield Women's Leisure Experiences* (London: Sports Council/Economic Social Research Council).

Gruneau, R. (1983), *Class, Sports and Social Development* (Amherst, Mass.: University of Massachusetts Press).

Hargreaves, Jennifer (1984), 'Taking Men on at Their Games', *Marxism Today,* August: 17–21.

_____ (1985), 'Competition: a Question of Ethics', *Sportswoman,* 1 May: 26–9.

_____ (1986), 'Where's the Virtue? Where's the Grace?: a Discussion of the Social Production of Gender through Sport', *Theory, Culture and Society,* 3(1): 109–23.

_____ (1989), 'The Problems and Promise of Women's Leisure and Sport', in C. Rojek (ed.), *Leisure for Leisure* (London: Macmillan).

_____ (1990), 'Gender on the Sports Agenda', *International Review for the Sociology of Sport,* 25(2): 287–308.

Hearn, J. (1987), *The Garden of Oppression: Men, Masculinity and the Critique of Marxism* (Brighton, Sussex: Wheatsheaf).

_____ (1989), 'Reviewing Men and Masculinities – or Mostly Boys' Own Papers', *Theory, Culture and Society,* 6(4): 665–89.

_____ and Morgan, D. (eds) (1990), *Men, Masculinities, and Social Theory* (London: Unwin Hyman).

Horne, J. and Jary, D. (1987), 'The Figurational Sociology of Sport and Leisure of Elias and Dunning: an Exposition and a Critique', in J. Horne, D. Jary and A. Tomlinson (eds) (1987), *Sport, Leisure and Social Relations* (London: Routledge & Kegan Paul).

Jary, D. (1987), 'Sport and Leisure in the Civilizing Process', *Theory, Culture and Society,* 4(2/3): 563–70.

_____ and Horne, J. (1987), 'The Figurational Sociology of Sport and Leisure of Elias and Dunning and its Alternatives', *Society and Leisure,* 10(2): 177–94.

Kaufman, M. (ed.) (1987), *Beyond Patriarchy: Essays by Men on Pleasure, Power and Change* (Toronto and New York: Oxford University Press).

Kelly, E. (1988), *Surviving Sexual Violence* (Cambridge: Polity Press).

Klein, V. (repr. 1989), *The Feminine Character: History of an Ideology* (London: Routledge).

Kimmel, M. (ed.) (1987), *Changing Men: New Directions in Research on Men and Masculinity* (London: Sage).

_____ and Messner, M. A. (eds) (1989), *Men's Lives* (London: Macmillan).

MacKinnon, C. (1989), *Toward a Feminist Theory of the State* (London: Harvard University Press).

Maguire, J. (1988), 'The Commercialization of English Elite Basketball, 1972– 1988: a Figurational Perspective', *International Review for the Sociology of Sport,* 3(4): 305–23.

_____ (1989), 'More than a Sporting "Touchdown": the Making of American Football in Britain 1982–1989', unpublished paper.

Mennell, S. (1989), 'Sport and Violence', in S. Mennell, *Norbert Elias: Civilization and the Human Self-Image* (Oxford: Basil Blackwell).

Morgan, D. (1987), *It Will Make a Man of You: Notes on National Service, Masculinity and Autobiography* (Manchester: University of Manchester Press).

Murphy, P., Dunning, E. and Williams, J. (1988), 'Soccer Crowd Disorder and the Press: Processes of Amplification and De-amplification in Historical Perspective', *Theory, Culture and Society,* 5(2): 645–73.

Pannick, D. (1983), *Sex Discrimination in Sport* (Manchester: Equal Opportunities Commission).

Rojek, C. (1985), 'Leisure and Figurational Sociology', in C. Rojek, *Capitalism and Leisure Theory* (London: Tavistock) pp. 158–71.

_____ (1986), 'Problems of Involvement and Detachment in the Writings of Norbert Elias', *British Journal of Sociology,* 37(4): 584–96.

Sabo, D. and Runfola, R. (1980), *Jock: Sports and Male Identity* (Englewood Cliffs, N.J.: Prentice-Hall).

Scraton, S. (1987), 'Gender and Physical Education: Ideologies of the Physical and Politics of Sexuality', in S. Walker and L. Barton (eds), *Changing Policies, Changing Teachers: New Directions in Schooling* (Milton Keynes, Bucks.: Open University Press).

Shroter, M. (1987), 'Marriage', *Theory, Culture and Society,* 4(2/3): 317–23.

Silver, J. (1984), 'Injuries of the Spine Sustained in Rugby', *British Medical Journal,* 288, January.

Smith, L. (1989a), *Concerns about Rape,* Home Office Research Study no. 106 (London: HMSO).

Smith, L. (1989b), *Domestic Violence,* Home Office Research Study no. 107 (London: HMSO).

Sports Council (1988), *Sport in the Community: The Next Ten Years* (London: Sports Council).

Stanko, E. (1985), *Intimate Intrusions* (London: Routledge & Kegan Paul).

Talbot, M. (1987), 'The Contribution of Comparative Studies in Understanding the Relationships between Women and Sports Structures', unpublished paper presented at Congress on Movement and Sport in Women's Life, University of Jyvaskyla, Finland.

_____ (1988), 'The Sex Discrimination Act: Implications for the Delivery of Physical Education, Recreation and Sport', unpublished paper given at the conference on 'Legal Liability in Physical Education', Leeds Polytechnic.

Vulliamy, E. (1988), 'The March of the Two Thugs', *Guardian,* 13 June.

Walby, S. (1990), *Theorizing Patriarchy* (Oxford: Basil Blackwell).

Williams, J., Dunning, E. and Murphy, P. (1989), *Hooligans Abroad: The Behaviour and Control of English Fans in Continental Europe,* 2nd edn (London: Routledge).

Wimbush, E. (1986), *Women, Leisure and Well-Being* (Edinburgh: Centre for Leisure Research).

_____ and Talbot, M. (1988), *Relative Freedoms: Women and Leisure* (Milton Keynes, Bucks.: Open University Press).

Wouters, C. (1987), 'Developments in the Behaviour Codes between the Sexes: the Formalization of Informalization in the Netherlands, 1930–85', *Theory, Culture and Society,* 4(2–3): 405–29.

Yule, J. (1990), 'Women and Leisure Policy', unpublished paper given at the Commonwealth Games Conference, Auckland, New Zealand.

Zolberg, V. (1987), 'Elias and Dunning's Theory of Sport and Excitement', *Theory, Culture and Society,* 4(2–3): 571–5.

8 Sport, Power and Dependency in Southern Africa

GRANT JARVIE

INTRODUCTION

While much of the literature on South African sport has contributed greatly to our understanding of the close relationship between sport and politics in the South African context, there is an important sense in which many of these studies have been deficient. It is the major contention of this chapter that much of the writing on South Africa has tended to revolve around the question of race and that consequently the analysis of sport has been reduced to a question of racial prejudice or the interaction between racial and class dynamics. The questions that are raised here about South African sport are essentially theoretical and, as such, this analysis does not attempt to provide an historical or developmental narrative which attempts to situate the analysis of sport within the broader context of South African society. However, the chapter does try to outline a broad set of contours upon which such a study might rest. The questions I want to raise about South African sport emanate from several years of work with the anti-apartheid movement and as a social and political theorist attempting to map out some common ground between forms of Marxist cultural analysis and Eliasian sociology. To date, both schools of thought have tended to view each other as anathema.

With this general orientation in mind, this discussion has been divided into four sections. In the first part of the chapter I shall outline some of the current developments relating to South African politics and sport in South Africa. The essential purpose of this section is to provide some concrete background to the current state of affairs in South Africa. Sections two and three are essentially theoretical in that they evaluate divergent approaches to the question of race, power and dependency, not just within South Africa, but within and between the powerful African nations as a whole. A general framework is presented which outlines some ways in which an open-ended, as opposed to a class or racial reductionist, approach to dependency and the struggle for South Africa might proceed. In the final part of this chapter I pose some specific questions and draw together the main points that have provided the basis for my analysis. In my opinion, the relation between the position being adopted here and Marxist class theory can safely be left as an open question.

THE POLITICS OF SOUTH AFRICAN SPORT

From the vast amount of literature that has focused upon the issue of sport and apartheid, at least two popular definitions continually represent themselves (Lapchick, 1975; Archer and Bouillon, 1982; Ramsamy, 1982; Jarvie, 1985; Guelke, 1986). The established state position on sport might briefly be described as 'attacking down the right' or 'sport is free to go its own way'. Despite being regulated through the Department of National Education, the official government stance is that sport in South Africa is free from all statutory control (*South African Yearbook*, 1988, p. 659). In theory at least, the depoliticization of sport has been the objective of the Directorate of Sport and Recreation Advancement – a policy which has tended to be operationalized through the South African Olympic and National Games Association (SAONGA) and the South African Sports Federation (SASF). Yet such a current position has not merely evolved overnight. It has in fact developed as a result of historically changing tensions and conflicts both within and between established and outsider groups. Established–outsider relations in this sense refers to a process in the course of which formerly more or less independent groups become more interdependent (Elias and Scotson, 1965: 17). In South Africa, the more powerful, established group produced a policy statement on sport during the late 1950s. Dr Donges, Minister of the Interior, argued in 1956 that whites and non-whites should organize their sport separately within South Africa. In 1967 Prime Minister Vorster issued a similar policy statement, while Dr Koornhof, between 1971 and 1976, was given the responsibility for establishing a new multi-national sports policy which was compatible within South Africa's overall policy of separate development. Supporters of South Africa's official policy statements on sport have argued on a number of occasions that sport provides an essential key to the process of integration and bridge-building, while critics of this position have argued that changes are cosmetic, ideological and indeed peripheral to the lives of the majority within South Africa.

The position of the outsider group might briefly be characterized as 'attacking down the left' or 'no normal sport in an abnormal society'. Aiming to create a sporting practice free from all forms of racism, sporting resistance to government policy has, since the early 1970s, been expressed through the South African Council of Sport (SACOS) and the newly formed National Sports Congress (NSC). The NSC is as vital to the resolution of the crisis in South African sport as the African National Congress (ANC) is to the solution of the crisis in apartheid society as a whole. Yet a long heritage of struggle lies behind the emergence of the NSC. The 1940s saw the development of the non-racial table tennis board; the 1950s witnessed the inauguration of the South African Sports Association (SASA) and the transition of many black sporting federations to a position of non-racialism; the 1960s saw the formation and expulsion of the South African Non-Racial Committee (SAN-ROC) from within South Africa and the expulsion of South Africa from the Olympic Games in Tokyo and Mexico; the 1970s saw the development of the South African Non-Racial Sports Organization (SASPO) and the expulsion of South Africa from the Olympic Movement; while the 1980s involved the ANC as central to sporting discussions in Harare and the development of a new militant sports organization, namely the National Sports Congress (NSC). While a number of sporting organizations have historically compromised their demands, the strength of SACOS, SAN-ROC and the NSC lies in their refusal to separate sporting demands from the broader demands for social change. We are told, 'you cannot have normal sport in an abnormal society'. Freedom in sport, it is argued, can only materialize from true liberation which in turn necessitates the dismantling of apartheid's core statutes and policies.

It would be unrealistic not to recognize that a number of changes to apartheid legislation have in fact taken place during the 1980s. During his visit to Britain, South Africa's new National Party Leader, Mr F. W. de Klerk, unveiled a new 'Plan of Action' to Mrs Thatcher during June of 1989 (*Guardian*, 29 June 1989). The National Party, it is argued, is prepared to talk with what Mr de Klerk calls reasonable black leaders to explore the mechanisms for the creation of a new political system. At the heart of this policy change is the intention to create the mechanisms through which every South African has the right to participate in the political decision-making process. At a superficial level, it would appear that some form of democracy is about to be established in South Africa. Yet at a deeper level, the Plan of Action has a number of serious flaws which in fact mitigate against 'one person one vote' in South Africa: (a) South African democracy within this plan merely refers to the creation of certain channels through which diverse 'group' opinions and needs can be voiced; (b) the white minority are not willing to entertain any system of government which would facilitate majority rule; (c) the power of the government to define who it sees as 'reasonable' black leaders remains; and (d) the 'Plan of

Action' revolves around the principle of 'group' separation which in previous years has been referred to as the policy of separate development, multi-national development or South Africa's Bantustan policy. While the rhetoric changes, the principles remain relatively unaltered. Furthermore, in this new light of apparent liberalization it is often forgotten that the same F. W. de Klerk recently called on whites to report to the police any people of colour who broke the country's residential segregation laws (*Guardian*, 23 June 1989).

While the moderates within the minority ruling group have instigated a number of legislative changes, the real problem for F. W. de Klerk, as it was for P. W. Botha, is the power of the Afrikaner Broederbond, the secretive masonry of the Afrikaner élite. The reaction of the Broederbond to Daniel Craven's rugby negotiations with the African National Congress is but one example of the power of this small group to influence South African affairs. The trip to Harare during 1988 was an attempt by Craven and his deputy, Louis Luyt, to forge a single non-racial rugby body from two antagonistic organizations: the white-administered official Rugby Board (Sarb) and the alternative anti-apartheid Rugby Union (Saru). The unity talks, held in Harare, were refereed by ANC officials. Craven's motives in Harare lay in his belief that the future of South African sport lies 'through Africa' – a zonal world cup in which South Africans would play alongside Zimbabweans, Angolans and Mozambicans (*Guardian*, 30 March 1989).

However, what was significant about the mission to Zimbabwe was the reaction in South Africa which threatened to split the Afrikaner ruling group. For the ANC to venture into the rugby citadel was too much for the Afrikaner nationalists to bear. Impassioned warnings concerning 'the enemy within' prompted P. W. Botha to respond to the rugby initiative by saying that sport was part of the ANC's terrain of subtle subversion and that there are still politically blind moles in South Africa who fail to see this (*Guardian*, 30 March 1989). Indeed, the *Freedom Charter* of the ANC, adopted at the Congress of the People in Kliptown, South Africa, on 26 June 1955, categorically states not only that the people shall govern and that all national groups shall have equal rights, but that rent, leisure and recreation shall be the right of all and that the colour bar in sport and other cultural areas shall be abolished (Meli, 1988: 211).

South Africa is perhaps unique in that sport has become an object of civil struggle. Neither the established nor the outsider social groups are powerless. Each has a greater or lesser degree of power. Perhaps the real politics of South African sport and the real struggle for sport revolve around the monopolistic capacity of one or more groups to define what sport is and what sport should be within South African culture. The terrain of what constitutes politics is always changing but an initial agenda on the politics of South African sport would have to include some or all of the following questions: (a) where does the central balance of power lie among and within the various groups who give shape to South African social structure? (b) How has sport been affected by African development? (c) Has state involvement in sport simply been a response to various internal and external tensions between more- and less-powerful groups? (d) How do the day-to-day experiences of life in South Africa affect sporting involvement? (e) Why is it that some people's account of sport in South Africa carries more weight than others? What is particularly important about these questions is that they necessitate some discussion not only about the relationships which are figured in and through sport, but also the question of power and inter-dependency. Such factors have generally been missing from the divergent approaches to race, class and sport in South Africa.

RACE, CLASS AND SPORT IN SOUTH AFRICA

The South African situation has invariably been described as involving a unified white minority subjugating and denying an undifferentiated black majority any meaningful rights by means of an overtly racist legislation, a powerful administrative machine and the use of military force. Such a limited analysis may have sufficed until the early 1970s but since then significant challenges from below have changed the balance of power within established–outsider relations in South Africa. The strikes of 1973, the Soweto uprising of 1976–7 and the more recent phases of dramatically intensified struggle have all produced a range of ever-changing alliances and coalitions. In particular, it is no longer possible to assume that race is the sole, relatively determining, factor affecting ideology and political positions. As the balance of power has changed, new groups, new inter-dependencies and new alliances have developed which defy analysis along the old predictable faultlines of race. Various community youth movements and right-wing vigilante forces, such as the Inkatha Youth Brigade and Buthelezi's Natal-based Inkatha movement are but two examples which at least require cognizance of not just race, but also religion, class and tribal factors. It is also worth remembering that the leadership of the largest of the independent black churches, the Zionist Christian Church, which has a following of anything between 2.5 and 4 million, has a political position explicitly in support of white minority rule (*Guardian,* 21 April 1987).

If the racial analysis of South Africa fails to demonstrate the salience of conservative and right-wing black opinion, it equally misrepresents white politics as monolithic. The recent whites-only election of May 1987 returned a score of seats for the ultra-right Conservative Party thus narrowly displacing the liberal Progressive Federal Party as the official opposition. Much more saliently, it reaffirmed the power of the National Party within the limited arena of white parliamentary politics. The emergence of the United Democratic Front (UDF) in August 1983, with its commitment to non-racial politics, provided another avenue into which white and black moderate anti-apartheid activists were able to move (Pheko, 1986: 182). Like the ANC, the UDF takes its politics from the Freedom Charter of 1955. In a nutshell, those who formed the UDF and call themselves progressive democrats believe that whites are an integral part of black struggle. Those in the National Forum Committee (NFC) hold a contrary view in that they believe whites have no role to play, other than conditioning their fellow whites for the inevitability of black majority rule. The NFC rejects the Freedom Charter in preference to the Azanian People's Manifesto which categorically states that the Azanian struggle being waged by the toiling masses is nationalist in character and socialist in content. The argument here is that there can be no co-operation between oppressor and oppressed, established and outsider or dominating and dominated. The NFC principles include anti-racism and anti-imperialist policies, opposition to all alliances with ruling-class parties and the development of an independent yet nationalist working-class organization (Pheko, 1986: 185). It is worth noting that the NFC charter also includes a statement demanding the provision of sport and recreational services for the Azanian people.

In much the same way, many pluralist and Marxist accounts of South African sport and South African race relations have tended to argue that the concepts of race or class have greatest salience *vis-à-vis* other structural principles. While pluralists have preoccupied themselves with racial groups and racial conflict to the exclusion or subordination of class and class conflict, Marxists have tended to argue that in South Africa race is class and class is race. Some liberals styling themselves on the progressive democrats have tried to twist Marxism in Azania in order to confuse the Azanian National struggle. The argument is often simply expressed in terms of class struggle without due recognition of the fact that Africans in South Africa belong to the 'have not' class while whites belong to the 'have' class. The polemic conducted by theorists of the pluralist school is directed against a very mechanistic conceptualization of race and class relations whose main characteristic, according to pluralists, is a rigid undialectical view of a universal class struggle. For pluralists the Marxist concept of class is dismissed as irrelevant or, at best, of secondary importance to the analysis of Africa, because it is based upon an historical analysis of capitalism within Europe and not the unique experiences, conditions and development of the African people (Stasiulis, 1980: 465).

For example, Van den Berghe (1967: 267–88) argues that social class in the Marxian sense of the relationship to the means of production is not a meaningful reality in the South African context since colour rather than ownership of land or capital is the most significant criterion of status in South Africa. Within the pluralistic paradigm, the analysis of the South African social formation is essentially limited to a polarization of several broad themes: (a) as a plural society South Africa is best explained in terms of segmentation into corporate groups often with different cultures; (b) it has a social structure compartmentalized into analogous, parallel, non-complementary and distinguishable sets of institutions; (c) the motor of development is seen to be a sort of institutional and ethnological determinism in which institutions are viewed as autonomous in relation to one another and as functioning according to their own inner logic; and (d) as a unique social formation South Africa is polarized into two components: a capitalist economic system which is harmonious, just and functional, and a system of racial domination which, as a political factor, is seen as being dysfunctional.

When sport is viewed within the confines of the pluralist approach it is itself seen to be functionally supportive and integral to a multi-racial South African society in which a plurality of groups compete within the framework of apartheid. A core part of the pluralist thesis on sport is that South Africa is the recipient of more domestic and international pressure than any other nation because its case is deemed as not just racial but also ideological. The political ideology of apartheid mediates and relatively structures sporting participation and provision in South Africa (Lapchick, 1975, 1979; Krotee, 1988). The argument is simply that sport, while having a degree of relative autonomy, is best explained in terms of racial segregation and racial discrimination. The ultimate power of the dominant white minority is reflected through the ultimate power of the state to manipulate and determine sporting policy in South Africa. Because of the institutional power that the dominant white minority can mobilize at its behest, internal sporting resistance is reduced to a matter of inconsequence in comparison to external pressures and policies. Consequently, for pluralists sporting freedom and the dismantling of apartheid will only really be brought about through continuing the sporting boycott, the stringent implementation of the Gleneagles Agreement and further external pressures being brought to bear on South African sporting organizations.

Criticisms of the pluralist approach stem from at least two main sources. The first of these might be called a liberal structural critique and is, in part, symbolized by the work of Heribert Adam (1971). Such an approach pinpoints a number of material and political forces as having primacy over explanations revolving around race and ethnicity. While agreeing with the pluralist school that apartheid has incurred great wastes when measured in terms of individual productivity, Adam is critical of any approach that does not question the reasons for racial conflict and diversity which derive, in part, from a struggle over scarce resources. Adam rejects the pluralist assumption that economic growth will erase racial discrimination. The liberal structural approach provided by Adam is a major advance over the pluralist scenario because it outlines two of the major forms of dependency which underlie the development of Southern Africa, namely the political and economic forms of bonding which have structured Southern African relations.

The second critique of the pluralist school is to be derived from neo-Marxist writers who emphasize the degree to which the political and economic struggles among the different social groups are in fact class struggles. That is, they examine the extent to which struggles experienced by white and particularly black working-class fractions do in fact arise from the relations of production. Instead of abstracting this or that feature of racial discrimination and explaining it in terms of other racial concepts deemed as flowing from ideological and political structures, neo-Marxists argue that the South African situation may be examined as a specific set of social relations characterized by the capitalist mode of production. In recent years a number of writers have drawn on some or all of these points of orientation in attempting to reinterpret South African development. While Wolpe (1983) has argued that South Africa cannot be seen as a mere reflection of ideology, Legassic (1974) has argued that the authoritarian and racially discriminatory South African structure can only be explained in terms of specific historical processes of capital accumulation. The historical analysis of Magubane (1979) led him to conclude that the struggle of the oppressed African people has, through conflict and negotiation, won space from culturally dominant groups in South Africa. One of the strengths of Callinicos's (1981) analysis of South Africa is that he attempts to situate the complete narrative within the broader context of western domination within the emerging African nation states.

One of the major strengths of the Marxist cultural analysis of sport in South Africa has been to highlight the fact that central to the struggle over South African sport are in fact the majority of the people in South Africa themselves. That is to say sport has a significant part to play within the popular struggles in South Africa. Writers who have undertaken work on sport from a cultural Marxist standpoint have done so for a number of reasons: (a) to delve into the broader conditions and social relations in which a dominant conception of sport in South Africa is produced; (b) to examine how struggles between different groups and classes have resulted in dominant, residual and emergent sporting practice; (c) to demonstrate how a particular form of sport is consolidated, contested and maintained or reproduced in the context of the reproduction of South Africa as a whole; and (d) to highlight sport as a facet of popular culture and consequently a site of resistance to forms of white hegemony (Jarvie, 1985).

The complex interaction between racial and class dynamics is certainly a feature of much of the 1980s writing on South African sport. Archer and Bouillon (1982) have argued that football in South Africa cannot be understood purely in racial terms but that, as the most popular sport in South Africa, it draws upon a significantly black, but also facets of white, working-class culture. Willan's (1987) study of an African in Kimberley between 1894 and 1898 supports the thesis that cricket became a social training-ground that reflected a number of complex alliances and coalitions between various race and class fractions. Along the same lines, Odendaal (1984) reflects upon sport in the lives of the nineteenth-century black-Victorian middle class. SACOS's demands in 1988 included not only the evolution of non-racial sport but also a free non-racial education system in an undivided South Africa governed by the working class and its allies. All these studies and many more illustrate that the social dynamics of apartheid are much more complex than pluralists would have us believe. The cultural and class dimensions of many Marxist cultural accounts provide a major advance on the pluralist writings of the 1970s.

Yet despite the attention to historical context, the avoidance of determinism and class reductionism and due attention to popular culture, several criticisms have recently emerged in relation to Marxist cultural accounts. Briefly, these are: (a) the research emphasis within Marxist cultural analysis runs from ethnographic/historical work to various text-centred and formalist theoretical traditions; there is a danger, therefore, in seeing this work as being far more unified than it actually is; (b) popular culture does not exist in isolation nor indeed, as I have tried to show here, is any dominant group homogenous; (c) many accounts of popular culture have lost sight of the importance of political economy or even the political and economic bonds which bind people together; (d) there is a relative silence among the sport/hegemony theorists on the notion of counter-hegemonic struggle as it was originally used by Gramsci; and (e) there is an imbalance between the theoretical claims of many Marxist cultural accounts and their ethnography.

Many accounts have tended not only to overestimate the power of sport but also the space that has been won from the dominant culture.

The position being adopted here does not deny the relative importance of sport as a field of cultural struggle within the overall war of position in South Africa. Indeed class cultural analysis has moved some way beyond the simple racial reductionism of the pluralist school of thought. The complex interaction of racial and class dynamics in South Africa has often concealed the realities of apartheid. Race and racial discrimination appear to be the dominant consideration, relatively determining and affecting all aspects of life. Black people, regardless of class position, are systematically denied equality of opportunity in political, economic and cultural spheres, to name but three areas of domination and subordination. Yet what this overlooks is the multi-faceted forms of bonding which bind individuals, groups and even nations together within a general and yet specific structure. This does not imply reducing the process of bonding to simply racial or class explanations of social structure. In this sense, the term 'figuration' implies a much more open-ended approach which allows for an infinite and yet specific number of networks and forms of bonding (Elias, 1978). The point is simply this: while racial and class bonds of interdependence may in fact be relatively determining, the degree of determination is flexible and yet specific to any form of development. The social dynamics of apartheid are much more complex and necessitate a framework which allows for not only racial, class and cultural relations, but for a whole range of political, economic and emotional interdependencies which bind some people together while simultaneously dividing them from others. As such, the concept of figuration not only allows for racial and class dynamics, but also gender relations, age-group relations, tribal relations and national relations amongst others.

DEPENDENCY, POWER AND SOUTHERN AFRICA

One of the features of both pluralist and Marxist writings on a total strategy within Southern Africa has been the view that dependency and underdevelopment provide an essential key to understanding the relations between South Africa and the 'frontline' African nations. Like any relationship between a metropole and its hinterlands, the dependency paradigm directs our attention to the network of power relations between and within a multitude of figurations who may or may not form class, race or nation-state formations. In the context of the dynamic dependency relations that exist between the South African metropole and the surrounding African states, it is crucial to realize that the process of dependency actually involves issues of people, planning and power. At one level there is an uneven balance of power between the South African metropole and the surrounding hinterlands which leads to some people at another level becoming dependent upon the actions of the most powerful figuration in South Africa, namely the Afrikaner Nationalist Party. Depending on the unit of analysis, it is also important to realize that the process of interdependency between the most powerful white nation-state within South Africa and the dependent homelands such as the Transkei, Ciskei and Bophuthatswana also involves a process of planning which involves people and power and results in the less powerful homelands being underdeveloped, a process which, in practice, involves some of South Africa's most desolate land being designated as a 'homeland' for various black tribal class cultures. Forced to move to bleak and often fragmented sites, these people lose their citizenship, find few jobs and obtain minimal food, medicine and education, never mind the luxury of sporting opportunity. Only in South Africa are these homelands recognized as independent nation-states.

The dependency debate first gained impetus as a result of the extensive Latin American debate on the problems of underdevelopment which began towards the end of the 1940s when a group of Latin American economists working for the United Nations Economic Commission for Latin America (ECLA) criticized the way in which the Western world had tended to explain the developmental gap between the rich and poor countries. The crucial theoretical innovation proved to be the relational idea of core and periphery. While a great volume of words has been written concerning the core–periphery debate, by way of summary it can be said that most of the following points are common to the majority of positions within the dependency paradigm (Roxburgh, 1979; Bloomstrom and Hettne, 1984; Frank, 1984; Wallerstein, 1984): (a) that underdevelopment is closely connected with the expansion of industrial capitalist social formations; (b) that dependency is not only an external phenomenon but also an internal phenomenon within or between regions, states or nations; (c) that dependency can only be adequately explained if it turns to the examination of development and patterns of exploitation both within and between nations, regions and peoples; and (d) that dependency theorists have not paid enough attention to various aspects of cultural dependency, such as sport, tradition and cultural identity.

The notion of dependency certainly provides a useful starting point for considering the state of flux and tension in Africa in general and Southern Africa in particular. By 1980 nine of the frontline Southern African nations had formed themselves into the Southern African Development Co-ordination Conference (SADCC) – the principal objective being to minimize the negative effects of the political, economic and cultural process of dependency. I would merely add to this that such political, economic and cultural aspects are relational factors and arise out of the uneven tensile balance of power between the people involved in such planning. During the 1970s the balance of power between South African ruling groups and the surrounding nation-states became less uneven. The Portuguese-ruled buffer states of Mozambique and Angola had collapsed. The collapse of Portuguese colonialism was followed by the transformation of settler-ruled Rhodesia into dependent Zimbabwe. Revolutionary regimes emerged from below in Guineau-Bissau, Angola and Mozambique, and from above in Somalia, Ethiopia and the People's Republic of Benin and the Congo (Tordoff, 1984). While many political and ideological differences continue to exist between the African nations, there is a general agreement that in unity lies power. The Organisation of African Unity, the long-standing Union Douanière de l'Afrique Centrale and the Economic Community of West African States are but a few of the many alliances to emerge during the 1960s, 1970s and 1980s. Such coalitions have contributed to a less-uneven balance of power between those peoples who are actively involved in the process of dependency and underdevelopment.

According to Mennell (1989: 129), the main weight of any explanation of inequality must rest on how groups have impinged upon one another and the nature of their interdependence. Wallerstein (1974, 1980) and others have shown at length how, on the basis of initially very small technical, economic and social advantages, the Europeans were able to weave the peoples of Africa, Asia and Latin America into a web of dependence – in Elias's terms, very unequal interdependence – which, over centuries, greatly magnified the initial disparities. In each case Elias (1978) is careful to point out that such interdependencies may occur at different levels. The range and focus of people's political, economic, cultural and emotional bonds will differ from level to level, individual to individual and group to group. At one level, emotional, economic, political or cultural interdependency may occur between larger social structures such as villages, towns and nations integral to the overall web of interdependency within Southern Africa. Emotional forms of interdependency do not operate independently in that context. More specifically, emotional forms of interdependency do not operate independently of other spheres such as the political or the economic or the sporting sphere.

The centrepiece of any discussion on dependency must be the uneven balance of power between the various groups who enter into such a relationship. The notion of power has proved to be a fruitful analytical concept for many social and political theorists. In his earlier work Poulantzas in particular tended to view power entirely in class terms. Yet in *State, Power and Socialism* (1978) Poulantzas concedes that relations of class do not exhaust power relations and that it is necessary to go a certain way beyond class relations. One of the major advantages of the Eliasian approach to power is the open-ended framework which allows for social-class explanations of power but also a multitude of other dynamic power relations. Power in this sense is a structural characteristic of all relationships. As long as people are dependent upon one another, whether it be as a function of emotional, political or economic bonds, there will always be a balance of power within and between different social groups such as villages or nation-states including the African nations. The relational practice of power and dependency operates at a number of different levels (Elias, 1978: 93). But the crucial point is that dependency is a relational phenomenon which in practice operates at variably interpenetrating levels.

This discussion of dependency and power is far from irrelevant to the analysis of sport. Despite the idealistic hopes that forms of sport are separate and represent a respite from everyday reality, sporting relations, like all forms of relations, are constitutive of and constitute the social structure of South Africa. Sport may have a relative autonomy but it is important not to overestimate or underestimate the role of sport in producing change within South Africa. Sporting relations contribute to a much wider web of interdependencies and, as such, should not be viewed in isolation from economic, political or cultural forms of bonding. At the same time it might be argued that the forms of sport that are played in South Africa today are not independent of previous stages or phases in the development of Africa in general. As a focus of analysis, sport is capable of providing a great deal of information about various figurations, tensions and conflicts which have characterized much of South African history and the development of the African social formation. As such, I should like to map out four broad inter-connected stages in the development of sport in what is today known as the Republic of South Africa:

(a) A stage which lasted from at least 460 AD until about 1650. During this pre-colonial stage of development, the origins of many African sporting practices existed in various antecedent forms. They contributed to a somewhat violent, materially impoverished culture which, in part, revolved around an organic tribal way of life.

(b) A stage which lasted from about 1640 until about 1910. At least three important processes affected the development of sport during this stage of colonial and imperial expansion and domination: (i) a process of colonization which resulted in the relative destruction of the existing social order; (ii) a process of imperial expansion which involved the introduction of many white, 'civilizing', European forms of sport; and (iii) an initial stage of cultural marginalization during which many traditional sporting practices of the indigenous peoples were gradually eroded as a direct result of colonization. Traditional sporting practices did not simply die out, however. They were marginalized and gradually replaced by white sporting practices.

(c) A stage which lasted from about 1900 until 1960 during which both imported and indigenous forms of sport became increasingly subject to the limits and pressures of segregation and apartheid policies. During the period of Afrikaner nationalism and industrialization, rugby and cricket symbolically expressed the superiority of one group over another in terms of the social relationships and unequal power relations that were evolving in South Africa. The institutionalization of 'white' sports in school physical-education programmes served as a further mechanism of social differentiation. The period after 1948 marked the evolution of South Africa's tripartite sporting structure involving white, non-white and non-racial sporting forms.

(d) A stage from about 1950 until the present day during which time South African sport experienced a number of multifaceted developments such as incipient bureaucratization under apartheid laws, increasing commodification, processes of politicization and depoliticization, and the emergence of a highly organized non-racial sports movement which has continually challenged white sporting hegemony during the 1980s. The development of South African sport has been inextricably linked with changing race, class and nationalist alliances and coalitions. These and many other developments have taken place within the changing nexus of African dependency and nationalist development.

The analysis of South African sporting development has paralleled much broader transformations within African society as a whole. Indeed the development of sport in what is now South Africa certainly encompasses some of the most basic questions that might be asked concerning South African culture, dependency and social structure. What is the relationship between sport in South Africa and the prevailing social structure? How has South African sport been affected by the historical epoch in which it moves? What social forces have relatively shaped sporting traditions in South Africa? Who have been the most powerful people within the complex web of interdependent figurations associated with South African sport? In what complex way has this power been expressed in practice? These questions are indicative of the potential richness that may be found in a sociological analysis which takes as its main focus the development of South African sport. Yes it is crucial to realize that such processes, developments, tensions and conflicts do not exist independently of the people who constitute the very social fabric of this social formation. Society does not exist outside of the individual people who form it. At the same time, individual behaviour is only relatively autonomous in that it responds to constraints and tensions which have mediated South African sporting development.

I have suggested that the notions of dependency, culture and figurational development provide an extremely powerful explanatory basis for under-standing African nationalism and sport under apartheid. The term 'figura-tion' has a relative open-endedness which makes it a more powerful, analytical tool than that of social class, race or culture while still remaining inclusive of such categories and formations at any particular point in time. At least three crucial advantages are to be gained from any problematic which has the notion of figuration as one of the axial principles around which it revolves: (a) it provides an open-ended framework capable of explaining multi-faceted forms of interdependence, domination and sub-ordination without necessarily reproducing class reductionist accounts or accounts of social structure based on false dichotomies such as individual and society or structure and agency; (b) it is a concept which has at its core, not at its periphery, a relational concept of power; and (c) it is a concept which lends itself to redressing the inadequacies which have plagued the development of dependency theory. By this, I do not mean that the explanatory power of dependency or indeed cultural theory is not central to the analysis which has been presented here, but rather that the strengths of these approaches are complementary to the notion of figuration. Marxist cultural analysis need not view Eliasian sociology as anathema.

A POLITICAL POSTSCRIPT

The new South African politics of the 1990s has created a climate of optimism that real political change is on the agenda. Following the release of Nelson Mandela even such front line foes of apartheid as Desmond Tutu and Allan Boesak have conceded that the promise of reforms has indicated that a new plan of action is now on the negotiating table (*Sunday Corres-pondent*, 2 February 1990). Mrs Thatcher's pressure on the European Community to remove economic sanctions on South Africa and President Samaranch's plea that the International Olympic Committee (IOC) should consider welcoming South Africa back into the world of sport are but two indications of the growing international conservative support for South Africa's National Party. It is important to maintain a sense of realism about the new President de Klerk's initiative of the 1990s. Certainly a great deal of euphoria and optimism has been created as a result of the partial lifting of the state of emergency, the freeing of Nelson Mandela and the unbanning of certain exiled popular liberation movements such as the ANC and the South African Communist Party (SACP). Yet already a number of problems and frustrations are beginning to emerge which indicate that the presidential promises of the 2 February 1990 are essentially reformist as opposed to revolutionary.

First, there is the issue of F. W. de Klerk's pledges to South Africa's right-wing coalitions since his presidential address of early February. It has been consistently pointed out that majority rule within a unitary political system is not on the political agenda. In a flat rejection of the ANC demand for majority rule, President de Klerk argued that 'we' are not prepared to destroy existing rights or allow them to be destroyed. The government's position remains that, for the smaller groups in a multi-national country who run the risk of being dominated and suppressed, majority rule is totally unacceptable (*Independent,* 18 April 1990). Power-sharing in National-party terms refers to the process by which black voices may be heard and re-presented but it is envisaged that this will operate through a committee structure which protects white minority rule. The message is clear: nego-tiation, consensus and limited power are on the political agenda but majority rule is not open for discussion.

Secondly, there is the issue of national unity. Nationalism in Africa has not had a good record. Regional, ethnic and tribal loyalties have often proved stronger than national ones. Political winners have tended to wrap themselves in the national flag and to demand complete obedience in the name of national unity. Power-sharing for the sake of national unity is virtually unknown. Few people would argue that Westminster-style demo-cracy is appropriate for Africa, but a system has yet to emerge there which takes into account the traditional relationship of leader and follower, the effect of colonialism and problems of diversity both within and between national boundaries. If South Africa suddenly becomes a form of meritocracy, the educational privileges which whites have kept for themselves for decades will keep jobs in white hands. On the other hand, if there is a total transfer of power and the ANC turns itself into the state and tries to nationalize the banks and mining houses as has happened in other African nations, the outflow of capital could cause economic collapse.

Thirdly, there is the issue of the ANC strategy itself. For three decades the ANC's hierarchy in exile has formed a relatively unified focus of resistance and popular struggle. Its President, Oliver Tambo, remains ill and now veterans such as Walter Sisulu and Nelson Mandela are back in play. There are reported differences between the diplomats of the ANC embodied not only in young exiles such as Thabo Mbeki but also in no-compromise militants such as Chris Hani of Umkhonto we Sizwe. There is also the question of what role will there be for those who have carried the torch inside South Africa during the ANC's 30 years of exile. If the United Democratic Front (UDF) are to be disbanded, then how are its members to be assimilated into the ANC?

The new climate of the 1990s raises a number of questions concerning South African development, culture and politics. How should we evaluate these and other reforms which have characterized South African development? What combination of forces characterizes the ongoing struggle to overthrow the apartheid state? Are the current changes essentially reformist or revolutionary? What is particularly significant about these problems is that they necessitate not only a tight fit between theory and evidence but also some understanding of the way in which race, class and nationalism in the twentieth century affect South African dependency and development. More forcibly, it might be argued that one of the central failings of structural and cultural Marxist accounts of sporting development has been their theoretical and empirical silence on the issue of nationalism.

References

Adam, Heribert (1971), *Modernising Racial Domination* (Berkeley, Cal.: University of California Press).

Archer, R. and Bouillon, B. (1982), *The South Africa Game* (London: Zed Press).

Bloomstrom, M. and Hettne, B. (1984), *Development Theory in Transition* (London: Zed Press).

Bogner, Artur (1986), 'The Structure of Social Processes: a Commentary on the Sociology of Norbert Elias', *Sociology,* 20(3): 387–411.

Callinicos, A. (1981), *Southern Africa after Zimbabwe* (London: Pluto Press).

Dunning, Eric (1989), 'The Figurational Approach to Leisure and Sport', in C. Rojek (ed.), *Leisure for Leisure* (London: Macmillan).

Elias, Norbert (1978), *What is Sociology?* (Oxford: Basil Blackwell).

_____ and Scotson, J. (1965), *The Established and the Outsiders* (London: Frank Cass).

Frank, A. G. (1984), *Critique and Anti-Critique: Essays on Dependence and Reformism* (London: Macmillan).

Guelke, Adrian (1986), 'The Politicisation of South African Sport', in L. Allison (ed.), *The Politics of Sport* (Manchester: Manchester University Press).

Jarvie, Grant (1985), *Class, Race and Sport in South Africa's Political Economy* (London: Routledge, Kegan & Paul).

_____ (1989), 'Getting Gatting', *New Statesman and Society,* 11 August.

Krotee, March (1988), 'Apartheid and Sport: South Africa Revisited', *Physical Education Review,* 11(1).

Lapchick, Richard (1979), 'Race, Politics and Sport: South Africa in 1978', in M. Krotee (ed.), *Dimensions of Sport Sociology* (New York: Leisure Press) 63–98.

Lapchick, Richard (1979), *The Politics of Race and International Sport: The Case of South Africa* (Westport, Conn.: Greenwood Press).

Legassick, M. (1974), 'Capital Accumulation and Violence', *Economy and Society,* 3(3): 30–53.

Magubane, B. (1979), *Political Economy of Race and Class in South Africa* (New York: Monthly Review Press).

Meli, Francis (1988), *South Africa Belongs to Us: A History of the ANC* (Harare: Zimbabwe Publishing House).

Mennell, Stephen (1989), *Norbert Elias: Civilisation and the Human Self-Image* (Oxford: Basil Blackwell).

Odendaal, A. (1984), 'African Political Mobilisation in the Eastern Cape, 1880–1910', unpublished Phd Thesis, University of Cambridge.

Pheko, Motsoko (1986), *Apartheid: The Story of a Dispossessed People* (London: Marram Books).

Poulantzas, Nicos (1978), *State, Power and Socialism* (London: New Left Books).

Ramsamy, Sam (1982), *Apartheid the Real Hurdle* (London: International Defence and Aid Fund for South Africa).

Roxborough, Ian (1979), *Theories of Underdevelopment* (London: Macmillan).

Stasiulis, D. (1980), 'Pluralist and Marxist Perspectives on Racial Discrimination in South Africa', *British Journal of Sociology,* 21(4): 463–90.

Tordoff, William (1984), *Government and Politics in Africa* (London: Macmillan).

Van den Berghe, P. (1967), *Race and Racism* (New York: John Wiley).

Wallerstein, I. (1974), *The Modern World System,* vol. 1 (London: Academic Press). Macmillan).

_____ (1980), *The Modern World System,* vol. 2 (London: Academic Press).

_____ (1984), 'World Systems Analysis', *Cencrastus,* Summer, 26: 1–5.

Willan, B. (1987), 'An African in Kimberley, 1894–1898', in S. Marks and K. Rathbone (eds), *Industrialisation and Social Change in South Africa* (London: Longman).

Wolpe, Harold (1983), 'Apartheid Rule', *Marxism Today,* February, 14–16.

9 Figuring a Brighter Future
ALAN CLARKE

Over the years the discussion of football has taken a number of diverse turns ranging from the knee-jerk response of the gutter press to the erudite prose of some of the finest writers on sport. It has also attracted the attention of academics from a variety of disciplinary backgrounds but usually sharing a common interest – a love for their object of study, the game of professional football. In talking with the various authors who contributed to the collection which emanated from the First World Congress on the Science of Football (Reilly, Lees, Davids and Murphy, 1988), it was clear that the logic for their studies was, first, an unexpected passion for the game followed by the need to turn their academic talents to its analysis. This is not merely a casual observation on the idiosyncrasies of my colleagues who share my affliction but an important introduction to the argument presented here because no one has managed to identify what it is that holds the interest of such a diverse group of people under the single umbrella of 'football fans'. Yet there is an underlying assumption within the analyses that we know what we are talking about. Moreover, there is an increasing feeling that one group of scholars has come closest to solving the problems of modern football and are now being asked to define the terrain for the discussion in the future. This chapter is an attempt to question the basis of that assumption and to take issue with some of the basic theoretical and empirical evidence on which that position depends.

It is difficult to know where to begin with the writings which have emerged from the 'Leicester School', as the years have consolidated a tradition which began in the arena of sociological theorization before drifting into a predominant concern with analyses of football hooliganism. Walking in the footsteps of Elias has advantages and provides a ready-constructed theoretical framework but it also has its own 'civilizing' effect on the disciples. No one can dispute the sheer amount of work which has been undertaken at Leicester but there have been many criticisms of the position put forward over the years. These have been stoutly rebutted but the arguments persist at least at the academic level. It is less clear that there is such a dispute at the level of official policy formulation. The cynic may be forgiven for thinking that there is only one 'think tank' in the world of football and that is situated in Leicester. That it may not be only cynics who view the situation this way was given some credence when the Leicester

School officially became the Sir Norman Chester Centre for Football Research. It is clear that something approaching a hegemonic position has been established by the diligence of the workers at the Centre and this has important implications for the future development of football research in this country. However, it may be a hegemonic position in a debate which does not exist.

The 1980s witnessed many outbreaks of football hooliganism and a massive wave of antagonism against the professional sport and its supporters. Attempts to explain the 'phenomenon' were legion but the official debate focused on control mechanisms rather than on any analysis of the 'problem'. The official answer has produced a disciplining of attendance at football matches by segregation, separation and surveillance. Here is the outcome of the official debate: the accomplishments of the truly hegemonic power in the football debate. We have remorselessly followed the logic of separation. The continuation of the policies which saw supporters segregated within grounds and escorted outside grounds found its logical conclusion in proposals for control by membership cards for attendance at all games. I shall return to the problems with this 'solution' later in the chapter, but first I want to consider the failures of sociology to challenge this official discourse of containment and particularly to locate the Leicester School within this process.

It may appear to be unreasonable to align the School with these developments. Indeed, the Chairman of the Football Trust, Lord Aberdare's 'foremost academic research team' (Dunning, Murphy and Williams, 1988: vii) have regularly commented on the limitations of these official moves to control hooliganism. However, I shall argue that, although the Leicester School is fundamentally opposed to simple control solutions, their arguments have been influential in creating the space for these official discourses to operate.

In order to begin this critique it is necessary to explore how the key aspects of the figurational approach have been applied to football hooliganism. It must then be considered whether this approach meets the criteria established within figurational sociology itself and only then raise objections from other empirical and theoretical positions which may be able to make a contribution to the analysis of the future of football.

Although the definitive account of the Leicester position is to be found in *The Roots of Football Hooliganism* (Dunning, Murphy and Williams, 1988) and detailed reference will be made to that text in the subsequent discussion, there is a useful summary of the position in Dunning (1989). He presents a four-page résumé of the argument and concludes (50):

That, in a nutshell, is why football hooligans fight. They develop relatively aggressive personalities, firstly because their involvement in the complex interdependency networks of modern society does not lead to pressure to exercise foresight and restraint to the same extent as other groups, and secondly because their communities receive less protection from the monopoly of violence than other groups. Indeed, because of their structurally generated deviance from dominant social standards, they regularly experience violence at the hands of the state. Moreover, for lower working-class males, fighting provides one the few opportunities for obtaining status, meaning and pleasurable excitement. They have chosen football as one of the arenas for acting out their masculinity rituals because it, too, is an arena in which working class masculine identities are at stake. Football also provides a context where there is relative immunity from arrest and where an 'enemy' is regularly provided, the fans of the opposing team.

A number of key points are made in this summary which, for Dunning (1989: 50), shows that 'far from constituting a refutation of the theory of civilizing processes or being a form of behaviour that cannot be fruitfully explored from such a standpoint, a complete understanding of football hooliganism is only possible in its terms'.

The task of 'doing figurational sociology' has been broken down by Maguire (1988: 192) who contributed some of the research to the *Roots* book. He argues: 'The task of developmental sociology is not only to generate substantive research but also to explain the status, selection and interpretation of such "facts" as part of a more general endeavour of enlarging the understanding of the various ways in which individual people are interconnected'. This raises several issues which challenge the status of the account offered by *Roots* and which undermine Dunning's own claim to exclusivity. Initially Maguire poses a fundamental problem here by referring to a wider 'general endeavour'. There has to be a serious question asked in developmental terms of an analysis which focuses on a subcategory of the figuration being studied. Rather than following in Elias's footsteps and studying the dominant figurations in the development of the civilizing processes and in the development of sport, we are presented with an account of a marginal minority within the figuration.

To expand on this we are told (12) that the 'sociological problem is to explain why they [the fans] should behave like this'. In practice this is only the question for a small number of the fans and a far more interesting sociological problem is raised by the questions why do people become football supporters and why do the patterns of support come into being? In terms of achieving a detached view of the processes involved in the history of football, this focus on the 'football figuration' rather than the 'hooligan figuration' promises clearer insights into the patterns of support and webs of interdependence. By accepting the 'hooligan' framework, the parameters of the study are set with reference to a discourse which exists outside of football (Pearson, 1983) and gives little ground to the traditions and patterns of football itself. For a historical analysis not to challenge this terminology and not to construct a model of the wider figuration leaves significant gaps in the analysis of the narrow object of study. For, as Maguire acknowledges (1988: 189), 'the task which the figurational perspective has set itself is to explore, and to make people understand, the patterns they form together and the nature of the figurations that bind them to each other'. It is doubtful that *Roots* can lay claim to such an achievement as the patterns are so little explored. In Elias's (1983) own terms, explaining the hooligan without explaining the football is like attempting to explain Louis XIV without an understanding of court society.

Again, to develop one of the criteria advanced by Maguire (1988: 192), 'the task is to trace and analyze the significance which specific events have in time and their conjunction with other events'. In order to achieve this, an understanding of the conjuncture in which the specific event takes place, as well as the specific event itself, is necessary. In dismissing some other approaches to football hooliganism, *Roots* notes the lack of historical evidence gathered by previous authors to support their theories. This critique is by no means one-sided as the adequacy of the history presented in *Roots* is itself open to question. It may help to take the earlier aspects of the account and unpack the historical context surrounding the analysis. For in drawing together an account of the history of football hooliganism, the context in which football is located is an important element in understanding the relationship between the supporters and the game they follow. What is missing from the account in *Roots* is an explanation of the position of football in the community. Instead we are presented with a focus on a single option within the range of choices available to the community at any period in time. More specifically we are looking at an increasingly popular choice in one historical period and one which in later periods suffers from declining attendances. Part of the explanation for this pattern emerges from an analysis of professional football itself but another important element comes from the position of football within the leisure industries. At no point is football an exclusive choice for any sector of the crowd and, no matter what form of market segmentation one uses, other options exist for the supporter.

This is not the place to develop a history of the leisure industries but it is important to recognize that soccer develops alongside other forms of popular entertainment and not in isolation. Reference is made to travelling support without recognizing that the opportunity to undertake such travel fundamentally affects the conjuncture under analysis and not just the attendance at football matches. In an account which draws on the sense of identity that football teams can generate for communities, such an opening up of both the opportunities and the influences has to be considered to produce an understanding of the conjuncture. By making the object of study only the 'hooligan' it may seem that such wide-ranging social forces are beyond the scope of the analysis and yet it cannot be so. This becomes especially apparent in the discussion of the travelling armies of hooligans in the 1970s and 1980s which the authors comment on. The influence of travel and of its developments cannot be considered only where it becomes involved in the process of hooliganism. It must also be considered along the more positive dimension of official and semi-official football supporters clubs. This orderly expression of support is just as significant a development within the football figuration as 'away' support becomes for hooliganism. Indeed it is in the orderly context that travelling supporters are first mentioned when *Roots* repeats Mason's (1980) accounts of travelling supporters in the 1870s. What provokes the change within a minority of the 'football figuration' which produces the development identified as significant in *Roots*? It is not the travelling *per se* which causes the problems but the patterns which emerge around that travelling support.

Another problem facing the historical analysis of the hooliganism surrounding football matches is the nature of the documentation used. Again bearing the necessity for conjunctural specificity in mind, there has to be some doubt about the material presented in *Roots*. What are we to make of the comment that:

> none of the forty-three incidents of spectator behaviour at or in connection with Leicester City's home matches in this period to which the *Mercury* reports took exception makes an appearance in the FA minutes and that, conversely, only six of the seventy-one disorderly incidents involving Football League clubs minuted by the FA were reported in the *Mercury*. (Dunning, Murphy and Williams, 1988: 94)

This statement requires several fundamental questions to be posed about the two different but elided forms of analysis being undertaken in this reconstruction of the history of hooliganism. Let us first be clear about the two types of data being considered. On the one hand we are presented with the Football Association records as the official, if somewhat sparse, memory of crowd disorders. These minutes refer to the formal hearings of the governing body of the sport and are tabulated in the form of warnings and ground closures. As the authors note, they are difficult to contextualize because of the lack of clear information about the growth of the game and the level of support. They are also difficult to contextualize in this account because they are divorced from the process which produced them. The actual configuration of the FA, the process by which the reports came to be heard and the influence of such factors as location and specific history of the clubs involved are all absent from the account. Such factors are important in understanding the decision process and the construction of the 'official' figures (Cicourel, 1964).

On the other hand we are presented with evidence from the local newspaper, the *Leicester Mercury*. Far from being an official commentary, these reports are presented as enabling 'a more complete picture to be built up' (Dunning, Murphy and Williams, 1988: 93). Using newspaper accounts is notoriously difficult and studies of local coverage compound the problems. The authors make use of the notion of 'moral panic' and identify the media as a significant actor in the generation of the concern about football hooliganism in the 1960s and yet still cite the *Mercury* as evidence. This evokes two methodological problems in dealing with the historical accounts. We are aware of the phenomenon of football hooliganism in the 1980s taking place well away from the football grounds and still being reported in the known categories of football hooliganism. This makes the stories easily recognizable for the readership and for the analyst but how can we be sure that this is true for the 1880s? Without a preoccupation for football hooliganism in the 1980s many other acts of hooliganism would be presented differently – the behaviour of 'lager louts' on the Costa del Sol springs to mind – and nowhere do we have an account of the news values which inform the press in the different periods of study. Secondly, there arises the concern of local newspapers for their own locale and how this informs the presentation of news. It should therefore come as no surprise that the incidents in Leicester are reported in the *Mercury* rather more frequently than they make the separate hearings in the national official FA and conversely, that the dealings of the FA are of less interest to the *Mercury*. To offer these sources as definitive, despite such limitations creates doubts about the empirical basis of the study.

Understanding the processes involved in the compilation of the data presented is crucial to the construction of the historical narrative. However there is a further element in the analysis which questions the evaluation of the figurational presentation of contemporary accounts. Not only is the institutional context of the accounts ignored, but so is the cultural context of the key terms around which these accounts are constructed.

Discourse analysis may sit uneasily with figurational sociology but if the attempt to construct a history which is sensitive to the web of interdependencies is to be taken seriously, then attention must be given to the terminology used and to the contemporary significance of such terms. We are told (Dunning, Murphy and Williams, 1988: 76):

> As one can see from the accounts reported in Chapter 3, disorderly behaviour by football spectators was rarely, if ever, sensationalised by the later nineteenth and early twentieth-century press. There was the occasional dramatic headline but the incidents referred to were invariably described in a matter-of-fact and low-key way and, to the extent that moral criticism was involved, the references tended to be to 'bad sportsmanship' or to a 'disgraceful scene'. The miscreants may have been labelled as 'blackguards' – a term which carried greater opprobrium then than it would today – and occasionally as 'hooligans' but they were never described as 'animals', 'lunatics' or 'thugs'.

It is not sufficient to recognize that one term – 'blackguard' – has a historically specific meaning because all terms operate within the cultural milieu of a specific historical moment. There is no attempt to construct a categorization of 'opprobrium' for the literary of terms used or to account for the absence of other terms. Language appears to be almost unproblematic in the Leicester construction of history and there is no assessment of how far the absence of the key terms is merely a local phenomenon. Is it safe to allow the *Leicester Mercury* to be the arbiter of current usage? It can therefore be seen that there are three stages to this criticism, with the absence of the national historical taxonomy of opprobrium being compounded by the lack of consideration of local equivalences, which produces the result of reading backwards for the presence or absence of current key words. Even if it is the case that the term is not used, without a moral taxonomy we cannot comment on the power of the condemnation involved in the newspaper columns. There may well be a moral equivalent grounded in the local practice and Leicester discourse.

At this stage, it is appropriate to consider the role of violence and the idea of levels of tolerance which are built into the figurational analysis of football hooliganism. Violence and the levels of tolerance are the two main aspects of the 'civilizing processes' on British society in general and on the working classes in particular. The authors argue that 'a higher level of violence also seems to have been socially tolerated than tends to be the case today' (77). This contention is central to the very notion of civilizing processes and yet there is no significant attempt to justify the assertion, despite an alternative view of the 'evidence' of tolerance being offered by Pearson (1983). Although there is no attempt to suggest that there is a simple unilinear movement away from violence towards civilization, the demonstration of the relative moral codes which govern society is allowed to remain a grey area. This is a strange absence given the central role that thresholds of tolerance play in the account offered of the moral panic which surrounds football hooliganism in the 1960s. We are confronted with an argument that media coverage is more outraged because society generally tolerates less violence but this is difficult to assess from the evidence presented. It is possible with a careful reading of the text to find events in the 1880s similar to the ones in the 1960s which met with similar punish-ments. 'Society' is therefore indexed not by its official codes but by the public pronouncements of the media.

More importantly, the motor behind this civilizing drive is presented as the monopoly of legitimate violence maintained by the state and the lengthening chains of interdependence found in society as a whole. Again, as an explanation of football hooliganism this misconstrues patterns found throughout society, not just in football. The mechanism for relating this drive explicitly to football is the idea of matching arenas of contested masculinity which is presented in the form of Suttles's (1972) theory of 'ordered segmentation'. For Suttles (1972: 199), ordered segmentation cap-tured

> two related features of the pattern of life in such communities: firstly, the fact that, while the segments that make up larger neighbourhoods are relatively independent of each other, the members of these segments nevertheless have a tendency regularly to combine in the event of oppo-sition and conflict; and, secondly, the fact that these group alignments tend to build up according to a fixed sequence.

The exact pattern of this segmentation will be influenced by the specific form of state action. What we have is a reintroduction of the criminological arguments about gang formation and the sense of territorial identification. Using this theory Dunning *et al.* (1988: 207) argue: 'the local football ground, especially the "home end" terraces, has come to be regarded by many adolescent and young adult males from the lower working class as a location which is both their own and where exciting experiences are a regular occurrence'.

This analysis is superficially very convincing. Lower-working-class males, socialized in the values of the street, excluded from the lengthening interdependences of modern society, congregate around their football club expressing their masculinity in ways which society can no longer tolerate and therefore condemns. However this account fails to deliver an explanatory mechanism for the highly selective recruitment from only a section of these 'roughs' into the ranks of the hooligans. Moreover it also fails to account for why the football ground becomes the focus for this contestation of masculinity. Similar figurations of young 'roughs' populate the streets of St Helens and Warrington as they do Liverpool and Manchester. Rugby League and professional football offer no similarities in terms of the incidence of hooliganism. Unless scale is the deciding factor, there is an element missing from the figurational explanation. As it is, the concept of the web of interdependence cannot be broken away from its relation to the division of labour and a functional specificity which ill-serves the authors' account of the recession in working-class communities.

If the chain of interdependence is taken in its broader anthropological usage to include familial ties, then a recasting of the argument may still save the explanation. Perhaps it is where the extended family, or indeed the family itself, has broken down that the hooligan option becomes attractive. But the definitive statistics presented in *Roots* cannot be reinterpreted to allow such further investigations. More worryingly, the figures allow for no analysis of inter-generational movement and its relation to the sense of identification. What are the class backgrounds of the known hooligans rather than their current class positions? Where do they come from socially, culturally and geographically and what degree of mobility do they show along these dimensions? Here in these patterns which probe beyond the surface descriptions recounted in the text we might find (and at this stage, despite all the previous research, it remains only a hypothesis) the patterns which allow the unpacking of the hooligan figuration.

Having questioned the figurational approach in its own terms, it is also useful to consider the work of the Leicester School from the position of some of the other theories they reject. Indeed one of the criticisms of the development of the Leicester position is that they dismiss other approaches with grand gestures and generalizations which belittle the work of their rivals. Horne and Jary (1987: 101) described this as a 'onesidedness and a degree of implicit theoretical overclosure' which 'can be seen as a problem in Figurational Sociology, at odds with its own explicit stress on the open-endedness of social situations'. There is a great hostility between the figurational position and the followers of other analytical traditions. A long history of hostile exchanges between various authors is in danger of preventing the fruitful development of a coherent approach to the football figuration and its location within a political economy of leisure that draws on forces seemingly excluded from the figurationalists' theoretical armoury. This section will demonstrate that there are elements of the Marxian tradition, dismissed in the rather cavalier treatment of Taylor (1971) and Clarke (1978), that are an integral part of the unpacking of the development of professional football. It might also be worth noting that the care and attention given to the exposition of Elias is not to be found in the presentation of some of the positions criticized. Positions in *Roots* are often refuted on the basis of 'straw' presentations, none more clearly than the cultural-studies position which, ironically, has the most to offer for expanding the analysis of the football figuration.

Critcher (1988) has addressed the limitations which the Leicester School impose on themselves with the overreliance on the explanatory power of the 'civilizing process'. He argues (203) that this produces a 'damaging resort to functionalist interpretation. Social and cultural activities are interrogated for the functions they fulfil for the individual, group or society'. It should perhaps be remembered, as Horne and Jary (1987) note, that the concept of function is presented as being used in a way that differentiates the figurational use from the more conventional forms of functionalist analysis. There is an attempt to distance the term from the usual concern for the maintenance and reproduction of the social systems involved but it retains its roots in functionalist analysis and particularly Durkheimian sociology. This functionalism places two parameters on the interpretation of the hooligan figuration, in that it imposes a necessity to discover the functional logic of the actions, here argued in terms of contested masculinity, and also restricts the terms of the analysis. This criticism has been developed in relation to the wider discussions on the role of sport within society, focusing on the concerns for social order and social control evident within the writings such as *Quest for Excitement* (Elias and Dunning, 1986). However these concerns with the civilizing effect of less-violent and more-controlled confrontations in sporting arenas also frame the analysis of football hooliganism presented in *Roots*.

There has been an emphasis on football hooligans because they reflect the negative aspects of the sports world and demonstrate that the figurational approach can deal effectively with contrary evidence showing that the civilizing process is not universally effective. However as well as illustrating this point, what the example also shows is the inability of the theory to account for the actions under analysis. The issue must be confronted both in terms of the content and the style of the behaviours under examination. In arguing that civilizing processes can be overturned and that the process can be seen negatively, the authors are concerned with a hooliganism that does in fact change in character. Their concern for history demonstrates that the target of hooliganism moves from being the representatives of officialdom, the playing arena and the players, to being, in the main, the rival fans. This is presented in terms of the development of the phenomenon but the change is itself significant. This is recognized by the authors but not explained, largely because the role of 'external' social factors which influence these changes is not clearly outlined in relation to the figuration. Using Suttles (1972) to describe the difference between functional and segmental bonding in the modern era does not explain the persistence of hooliganism throughout the historical account. Nowhere is it argued that segmental bonding is a development unique to the working classes in the 1970s as the evidence is drawn from urban America, going well back into the 1950s. The historical adaptation of a segment of the working class is presented in the place of a fully formed class analysis located within a model of the political economy of the society.

To draw out the benefits of the cultural studies approach, it is important to locate the analysis within the framework of the political, economic and social forces which shape the cultural terrain of which football is a part. Although there is nothing unique in this proposition, Maguire (1988: 189) notes that for figurational sociology 'the more common analytical approach in which societies are broken down into sets of 'factors' or 'spheres', (for example, the economic, the political) is eschewed'. The danger is that by eschewing such an approach the role of economics and politics in society is effectively marginalized and although there are some references to the impact of the 'recession' they are not followed through to produce a grounded analysis of the recomposition of the working class. The concept which is most startlingly absent is that of 'power', and in the context of this analysis the particular distribution and exercise of cultural power. Taylor's (1971a and b) early analysis of the ownership of the professional football apparatus was rejected by the Leicester School because there was no empirical evidence of a 'participatory democracy' actually operating and therefore the 'bourgeoisification' of football could not be responsible for the sense of 'usurpation' felt by a 'sub-cultural rump' (Dunning, Murphy and Williams, 1988: 24–5). They raised less objection to the changes which were identified as taking place in relation to the presentation of the sport itself. The game was being repackaged for an upwardly mobile population and the competition from other forms of entertainment was clearly recognized by the football authorities. Significant changes did take place within the clubs, within the grounds and within the competitions the clubs were invited to take part in. The search for empirical evidence of participatory democracy in any formal sense may well prove elusive but there is a sense in which the football figuration depends on the illusion of participation and involvement for its popularity. The importance of the symbolic association should not be undervalued, because there is no occasion where the fans have owned the 'turf' they fight to defend either and yet this symbolic relationship is firmly accepted in the *Roots* application of Suttles's writings.

Participation may never have been in terms of any democratic controlling mechanisms or participation in the behind-the-scenes operations of the clubs but what was engendered in the local areas was a sense of association with the club. In this sense Dunning, Murphy and Williams may well be correct to say that the working classes never controlled their own football clubs and this would also be true for other traditional forms of working-class leisure, with the control of the music hall and the pub lying outside the hands of the working-class community. What was the case and remained the pattern into the 1950s was that control remained remarkably localized. The landlord of the pub may not, in class terms, be a part of the community but in terms of the interactions of the community there was a clear position of interdependence between the pub and its regulars. A similar relationship can be perceived in the more structured organization surrounding employment in the local firms, with the employers recognizing responsibilities beyond the factory walls. This relationship is important when unpacking the early financing of the professional clubs, many of which developed under the benevolent patronage of local landlords and employers. The analysis of sponsorship and the rapidly growing market in sponsorship packages can mask the impact of donations in the origins of many clubs. It is not a new phenomenon introduced by the 'marketing revolution' but is a reworking of a very old practice indeed. There is still a great deal of this relationship left in many clubs which would not be financially viable without the support of the Board of Directors who, for the majority of clubs, are still local people. What has happened is that the traditional patterns of community organization which supported these forms of communal association have been disconnected by changes far removed from the realms of the football fields but intimately connected with the developments of the game.

In presenting the thesis of the civilizing process, much is made of the lengthening chains of interdependence which come into being in the developmental process. One understanding of this process is to look at the development of the division, specialization and mechanization of labour and the reorientation of society around the cash nexus. What this process does bring about through the concentration of capital is the removal of a series of levels of decision making, moving them away from the terrain of the locality towards the control of national and international actors. If the leisure industries are examined, the patterns of control now reveal very few pockets of local ownership. Breweries, cinemas, restaurants and many forms of private sports provision demonstrate the shift of control to regional head offices of national chains of international companies. This sets real constraints on the extent of local involvement in the decision-making processes which affect the development of their own community facilities. The labour market has been more fully analyzed in these terms than the leisure industries but the impact on the community of these changes combines to break down the amount of interconnection within the community. Work no longer provides the continuity and close associations which it once did for many of the people in the workplace. Changing jobs, changing forms of work and changing the place of work are all becoming features of working class life where the idea of a job for life has begun to recede into memory. This set of changes in the labour market is destroying patterns of life which depended on the community of colleagues from the workplace and family for their continuance. Far from lengthening chains of interdependence, labour and geographic mobility combined with smaller average numbers of children per family are shortening the chains for many people. Life is increasingly an isolating experience, shorn of its traditional forms of contact. These changes can certainly be contained within the framework of the civilizing processes but the movements towards restoring a sense of community and of empowering that community are a reflection that civilizing and improving the quality of life may not be synonymous processes for the working classes.

What we can see historically is an organic growth of soccer clubs within local communities, not all 'rough' working-class areas by any means, which gave them support. This involvement was therefore not a form of control but the football team then becomes a symbolic extension or expression of the community, with a clear link between the interests of the community and the interests of the club being discernible to the supporters. It is this linkage which has been broken, the illusion of common interest has been eroded. It is this distance which Taylor catches in the notion of a lost participatory democracy and it is this notion which the Football Supporters Association is trying to rebuild with their suggestions that supporters should be represented at Board level within the clubs. That this demand can be expressed in this way demonstrates the changes which have taken place within the organization of football and which allow for the argument to be formulated in business terms, in established companies concerned with specific commodities. It is by taking the analysis back, not into the roots of football hooliganism but into the roots of football support, that we can begin to make sense of one of the unexplained factors in the figuration. The football clubs do have a symbolic position within our society, standing as standard-bearers for a particular local identity. They also now carry a sense of tradition and continuity for which many areas can find no older expressions, hence the reluctance of supporters to see their clubs move away from their 'home' grounds. Until this is satisfactorily unpacked, the sense of identity which clubs can generate for supporters will remain elusive. Moreover the attraction for supporters drawn from outside that area cannot be understood either, because it is both the product of this process and the process of commercial development around the commodification of football.

The other major factor which affects the pursuit of leisure activities is their increasing regulation by extension of the controlling powers of the state. A simplified history of leisure can be presented through the regulation of and the codification of the divergent leisure forms. Even if we only consider this in relation to the development of football, we see both the internal regulation of the game imposing structures on the way the game is played and following from this an increasing routinization to when, where and in what form the game is played. Viewed from the touchline this poses dilemmas for the spectator as the development of the game imposes structures on the role of spectator as much as that of the players.

There is a further linkage which needs to be explored to ensure the adequacy of the explanation and that focuses on the use made of theories of masculinity and male aggression. It is assumed in *Roots* that football provides an arena for the contestation of male values and, within civilized guidelines, violent confrontation. The Leicester School present the violence of the hooligan as the product of a lack of effective socialization mixed with the tolerance of violence bred on the streets of rough working-class areas. Here again the analysis stops short of unpacking the figuration it is exploring by accepting the negative case it puts forward. If the work of Willis (1977) is to be valued rather than selectively used, the methodology of his work must also be considered. In developing an ethnographic approach to youth culture Willis ensured that the context in which the youths existed came into the account in their own terms. What we never receive in *Roots* is this dimension for the hooligans. There is no closure to the argument that lack of socialization, street living and young rough masculinity breed football hooliganism. By undertaking an ethnography of football supporters, some of which is being undertaken by the unofficial historians of contemporary views of football supporters, the fanzines, it might cast some light on why it is that such a recipe fails to produce more response and why football attracts such a reaction only in phases and with a variety of styles (Lacey, 1989).

Such an analysis might also case light on the way in which patterns of support have changed over the years. By attempting to unpack the bricolage of ingredients involved in the lives of the football supporters and the minority of hooligans, it has to be seen whether the early socialization emerges as the significant determinant of behaviour. There is at least some evidence from the history of clubs up and down the country that the disconnections of other forms of association are being compensated for in the strengthening of the symbolic identification with the football clubs at just the moment when the clubs want customers far more than they want local supporters. Equally the traditional backgrounds of the local population have changed around the monoliths of the stadiums which often look like massive memorials to times long past. This in turn gives rise to another factor which can be gained from an analysis grounded in the political economy where the class analysis in the terms presented in *Roots* is too inflexible to grasp the changing dimensions of the society it is operating within. Not only must it include a consideration of the mobility between classes and geographic areas mentioned earlier, but it must also give some attention to the way that racial groupings cut across the analysis of football hooliganism they are constructing. The poor socialization, the street society and the crisis of young masculinity affect all racial groups and similar explanations have been put forward to explain the presence of young black males in the crime figures. However they do not appear in any significant way within this analysis and are indeed not mentioned in the debate condemning football hooligans. Although this will be good news for the community leaders it does pose a problem for the explanatory framework presented by the Leicester School because they cannot explain why the identification for the class fraction they identify does not also include the black sections of the fragment.

Nor is it sufficient to offer the *ad hoc* view and argue that football occupies a less-significant position within black culture (although this may be true for certain sections of the ethnic minority populations), as ethnicity has had no prior role in distinguishing separate sections of the working class. This raises a serious issue in attempting to extend community schemes around football clubs because, for many ethnic minority groups, football is not an integral part of their cultural identity and may therefore pose a barrier to participation in other activities rather than the attraction that football clubs would have us believe.

An important element in the identification of patterns of supporting has to come from the way people are introduced to watching football. With the breakdown of ties within the community there has been a breakdown in the extent of groups watching the game. Young fans can no longer expect older and more experienced members of their family to take charge of their football education for the very good reason that they are not available. This means that the patterns of supporting which were once traditional – viewing in extended family groups with a mixture of ages and sexes present – cannot be reimposed on the game when such patterns of living are being broken down in the wider society. The danger is that calls for membership schemes become seen as the answer to these problems by presenting a new location for identification and solidarity. The Leicester analysis would seem to support such a notion as it includes the prospect for re-socializing the young hooligans within the more civilized confines of their law-abiding peers in the special enclosures.

Unfortunately the analysis also exposes the unsocialized hooligan to the harsher winds of social policy reaction with the imposition of discipline from outside. Indeed the major response to hooligans has been the tightening of control measures. The grounds are now segregated arenas, with home supporters and visitors rarely meeting. You become a star of closed-circuit television as you enter the stadium and are escorted to and from the match if you attend an away fixture. Motorways are patrolled, special trains once patrolled are now removed and the grounds are caged. The face of football has definitely changed over the years. However, these measures contain the problem with no hope of providing a long-term solution. Tightening the noose of external constraints will do nothing to address the problem of a lack of internalized discipline, but then such a diagnosis leaves the official bodies with little room for manoeuvre as the answer lies beyond their realm of influence. Therefore they have no alternative but to act swiftly to deter further lawlessness by clamping down on the behaviour which has now been scientifically defined by experts. This reaction is by no means unique to the problems presented by football and may serve to hide the problem for as long as the controls remain in force. It may also divert the problem into other realms of social life and transfer the problem to less-controlled areas of society.

It is not the intention to depict a totally hopeless situation, although it is difficult to see how the control mechanisms once established can be removed (Canter, Comber and Uzzell, 1989). However, it is important to demonstrate the limitations of the Leicester analysis in being able to move beyond the situation we find ourselves in at present. The positive measures proposed to counter these moves towards containment which flow from the analysis are, at the moment, ill-defined and have been long-awaited by many of us. A recent television programme posited the 'feminization' of football but argued that this would sit very uncomfortably with the masculine definitions of the arena and indeed this avenue offers little hope of countering the violence. The view that seems to be implicit in the writings of the Leicester School assumes a pacifying role for women, relocating a traditional and unchanging definition of women's roles and characteristics into the account. This undynamic view which denies the fluidity of some of the definitions of femininity which have been advanced by feminist writers restricts the prescriptions greatly. However it is not a total surprise, for the definitions of masculinity introduced to the account suffer from such rigid and inflexible values. The proposition looks very close to creating a new form of exploitation of women, drawing them in to pacify yet another social arena. In order to make the analysis of football more adequate the same degree of attention must be given to the complexities of masculine identities as there has been into feminine identities.

The emphasis on one aspect of the traditional working-class culture distorts the process involved in the depiction of working-class life. A fully formed, located class analysis would provide a context in which this violence is seen as something more than a route to street credibility. The analysis of frustrated life-chances offered in *Roots* can only be a starting point for the development of an account of segmental behaviour and has to be associated with an evaluation of the other elements of working-class life which also provide routes and responses to the lived experience of the inner city. In the same way, the account of the rough working class cannot be dealt with only in terms of a high regard and tolerance of levels of violence. This has to be located within a consideration of the marked intolerance of violence against women in these same communities and the pursuit of extremely non-violent leisure forms by the majority. These leisure forms are also a product not of the official version of the civilizing process but of the cultural developments of the street-based socialization identified in the argument as the producer of violence.

The working class is by no means an easy object of analysis but a study which combines the specific constraints on working-class life with a sensitivity to the diversity which exists within working-class culture offers a more hopeful basis on which to develop an explanation of choices within segments of that class. Such an explanation cannot be presented outside a context of the structural changes affecting the working class and the way in which these forces shape the leisure opportunities provided within society and developed within classes. This model would have to consider the very different experiences of different class fractions in the same leisure arenas. Even this schematic would not provide an analysis of football supporters, but would provide an understanding of the context within which choices are made. An ethnography of the fans which unpacked the sense of meaning given to them by their experience within the context outlined by the political economy of leisure is necessary if we are to make a breakthrough in explaining behaviour patterns. This exploration of identification would have to challenge the taken-for-granted notions contained in their discussions and interrogate the discourse thoroughly. Mapping this in terms of mobility – geographic, educational and social – would add to the depth of the findings and begin to offer a basis for undertaking further comparative research with football supporters in other countries. The hooligan minority are a necessary part of this study but cannot be the single and exclusive focus.

This critique delivers a model which demonstrates how the concept of figuration can be used to further the study of football, without accepting that it provides the exclusive answer to the analysis of professional football. The concept of figuration does offer a basis for unpacking some of the internal dimensions of the problem but without the contextualizing concept of identification being explored there are severe limitations on how far the analysis can be taken. Unfortunately the theoretical exclusivity claimed by the figurational sociologists makes it very difficult for them to explore any broad-based analysis such as this which clearly derives much of its value from concepts beyond the immediate narrowly defined figuration. Recognition of the structuring forces of society and the grounding of these in a detailed ethnography provides a way forward. Even here it must be recognized that the hooligan figuration is only a small part of the wider football figuration and the distorting of norms occurs within this wider figuration as well as the patterns of social order. Developing a community approach to football hooliganism cannot be based on the direct confrontation of hooligan behaviour but may make sense by reorientating some of the traditional values of the community and some of the traditional values of the football figuration into a new, more positive relationship for the whole of the football world (Clark, 1987). In this way, by bringing the people back into the game, football's position as the national sport may be consolidated and the 'people's game' can continue to develop with at least its 'progressive' traditions intact.

References

Canter, D., Comber, M. and Uzzell, D. L. (1989), *Football in its Place: An Environmental Psychology of Football Grounds* (London: Routledge).

Cicourel, A. V. (1964), *Method and Measurement in Sociology* (New York: Free Press).

Clarke, J. (1978), 'Football and the Working Class Fan', in R. Ingham (ed.), *Football Hooliganism: The Wider Context* (London: Inter-Action) 37–60.

_____ (1987), 'Here We Go, Here We Go . . . er, Where Are We Going?: the Future of Football', *Leisure Studies*, 6.

Cohen, S. (ed.) (1971), *Images of Deviance* (Harmondsworth, Middx: Penguin).

Critcher, C. (1988), 'Sport and Society: A Review Article', *Leisure Studies*, 7: 201–8.

Dunning, E. (ed.) (1971), *The Sociology of Sport* (London: Frank Cass).

_____ (1989), 'The Figurational Approach to Leisure and Sport', in C. Rojek (ed.), *Leisure for Leisure* (London: Macmillan).

_____ , Maguire, J., Murphy, P. and Williams, J. (1982), 'The Social Roots of Football Hooligan Violence', *Leisure Studies*, 1: 139–56.

_____ Murphy, P. and Williams, J. (1988), *The Roots of Football Hooliganism* (London: Routledge & Kegan Paul).

Elias, N. (1983), *The Court Society* (Oxford: Basil Blackwell).

_____ and Dunning, E. (1986), *Quest for Excitement: Sport and Leisure in the Civilising Process* (Oxford: Basil Blackwell).

Horne, J. and Jary, D. (1987), 'The Figurational Sociology of Sport and Leisure of Elias and Dunning: an Exposition and Critique', in J. Horne, D. Jary and A. Tomlinson (eds) (1987), *Sport, Leisure and Social Relations* (London: Routledge & Kegan Paul).

Lacey, M. (1989), *El Tel Was A Space Alien: The Best of the Alternative Football Press*, vol. 1 (Sheffield: Juma).

Maguire, J. (1986), 'The Emergence of Football Spectating as a Social Problem, 1880–1985: a Figurational and Developmental Perspective', *Sociology of Sport Journal*, 3(3): 217–44.

_____ (1988), 'Doing Figurational Sociology: Some Preliminary Observations on Methodological Issues and Sensitizing Concepts', *Leisure Studies*, 7: 187–93.

Mason, T. (1980), *Association Football and English Society* (Brighton, Sussex: Harvester).

Pearson, G. (1983), *Hooligan: A History of Respectable Fears* (London: Macmillan).

Reilly, T., Lees, A., Davids, K. and Murphy, W. J. (1988), *Science and Football* (London: Spon).

Rojek, C. (ed.) (1989), *Leisure for Leisure* (London: Macmillan).

Suttles, G. (1972), *The Social Construction of Communities* (Chicago, Ill.: University of Chicago Press).

Taylor, I. (1971a), 'Football Mad', in E. Dunning (ed.), *The Sociology of Sport* (London: Frank Cass).

Taylor, I. (1971b) 'Soccer Consciousness and Soccer Hooliganism', in S. Cohen (ed.), *Images of Deviance* (Harmondsworth, Middx: Penguin).

Williams, J., Dunning, E. and Murphy, P. (1984), *Hooligans Abroad: The Behaviour and Control of English Fans in Continental Europe* (London: Routledge & Kegan Paul).

Willis, P. (1977), *Learning to Labour* (London: Saxon House).

10 Figurational Sociology and the Sociology of Sport: Some Concluding Remarks*

ERIC DUNNING

INTRODUCTION

A number of possibilities suggest themselves as far as the format and contents of this concluding chapter are concerned. I could, for example, indicate the areas of criticism of the figurational position put forward in this volume that I agree with and then attempt a point-by-point rebuttal of those with which I disagree. Alternatively – in line with what a number of scholars erroneously believe to be one of hallmarks of the figurational or 'process-sociological' approach[1] – I could blithely ignore what others have written and simply discuss some of my own ideas.[2] However, neither of these possibilities strikes me as a particularly good idea. Let me attempt to spell out why.

Like sociology generally at the moment, the sociology of sport is multi-paradigmatic. Inherent in such a situation – dare I call it a 'figuration'? – is the near-certainty that adherents to different 'schools' will misconstrue and perhaps even parody the work of others. It is also a near-certainty in a multi-paradigmatic subject that the protagonists of particular positions will tend to see their own work as misunderstood and caricatured by 'outsiders'.

It has certainly been the case that figurational sociologists have been accused in recent years of caricaturing others' work.[3] However, we are equally adamant that our own work has been frequently misconstrued.[4] As I hope the open-minded reader will come to see, some of the criticisms advanced in the present volume fall into that category. Indeed, outside the sociology of sport, the figurational position continues not only to be caricatured but also widely ignored.[5] Accordingly, besides responding to what I take to be some of the principal criticisms so far advanced, whether here or elsewhere, I shall take this opportunity to set forth some of the things that figurational sociologists actually say. I shall also spell out what we regard as the main strengths and weaknesses of such other positions as Marxism and 'structuration theory', and specify some of the ways in which we have attempted to incorporate the strengths and overcome the weaknesses of such other approaches. It ought not to be necessary to add in this connection that, in making this last point, I am not claiming that we have necessarily been successful in these attempts or that figurational sociology is without its own weaknesses and lacunae.

I shall start, however, with some historical/autobiographical reminiscences concerning the development of the figurational sociology of sport. I shall start in this way because, while writers such as Horne and Jary (1987) praise Norbert Elias and myself for having been among the first to see the relevance of sociological studies of sport and leisure, they arguably fail to appreciate sufficiently some of the difficulties we had to contend with. In particular, they seem not to take due cognizance of what it was like to embark on sociological studies in this area, particularly 'developmental' or 'process-sociological' studies, in the environment of British sociology in the 1950s and 1960s, the period when the groundwork for most of the research we have carried out in these areas was laid down.[6]

SOME HISTORICAL/AUTOBIOGRAPHICAL REMINISCENCES

In Aachen, West Germany, in 1977 on the occasion of his 80th birthday, Norbert Elias was presented with a *Festschrift* entitled, *Human Figurations* (Gleichmann *et al.*, 1977). He started his acceptance speech by recounting a nightmare he had recurrently experienced in the 1950s and 1960s. It involved him dreaming that he was shouting into a telephone repeatedly: 'Can you hear me?', 'Is anybody there?' He interpreted the nightmare as meaning that he felt he had something to say to the sociological community but that, in those days, few were listening. As the 1960s drew to a close, however, more and more people began to listen and the nightmare ceased. The result is that when he died in August 1990 at the age of 93, Elias had come to be a widely respected, if still in some ways controversial, figure in the sociological world. Nevertheless, recognition of his work remains patchy and his influence has penetrated less widely and deeply into the world of Anglo-American sociology than into those of such continental countries as The Netherlands, Germany, France and Italy. There is, however, one exception to this pattern. It involves not a national sociological community but a particular sub-discipline. I am referring, of course, to the sociology of sport. In this field Elias is a well-known name, even in Britain and America, so much so that some people seem erroneously to think that figurational or process-sociology, the type of sociology for which he sought to lay the foundations, is concerned solely with the study of sport!

An interesting question is posed in this connection. Why, in countries where Elias's contributions are widely ignored in 'mainstream' sociology, should they have been granted a degree of recognition in what is, in my view wrongly, generally defined by the 'guardians' of the currently dominant paradigms as one of the subject's marginal byways? ·A friend once suggested that I might have had something to do with it. It is not modesty that leads me to reject such an idea. It is rather that a sociologically more plausible explanation is ready to hand, one that does not involve according too much weight to the contributions of a single individual. This more plausible explanation relates to the fact that, as Horne and Jary (1987) have rightly noted, Norbert Elias and I were among the first to enter the field. A consequence of this was that, when the sociology of sport started to expand in the 1970s and 1980s, and particularly when, in that connection, Marxists began to develop an interest in the problems that it poses, they found themselves entering a terrain already occupied by a paradigm in some ways similar to but in others different from their own. They responded with critical gusto and it was in such a context that the figurational sociology of sport, and with it Norbert Elias, began to gain a degree of recognition if not acceptance. It was also in that context that the sorts of debates that are reflected in the present volume, debates in which Marxists are prominent but, of course, by no means alone, began to be generated.

Although he was never happy about its patchy character, Norbert Elias was pleased by the latter-day recognition accorded to his work. He was also pleased by the signs of growing maturity shown by the sociology of sport and by the debates generated in connection with our joint and separate work. I share that pleasure. It is important, though, to realize that it has taken a long time for such recognition to arrive, for when, as I suggested earlier, we started work on the sociology of sport and leisure, the general sociological climate was far from propitious and, or so it seemed to us, many of the seeds we tried to sow fell on stony ground. Let me recount some reminiscences about those early days.

In the Introduction to *Quest for Excitement,* Norbert Elias (1986) suggests that it was I who first came up with the idea that sport might represent a suitable topic for postgraduate research. However, this is not strictly speaking true. The idea was first proposed by a fellow student, David Moscow, when we graduated in 1959. Norbert latched on to it, though, quickly recognizing that sport is an important area of social life that had been neglected by sociologists up to then. He suggested that David and I might carry out related enquiries into different areas of the subject. In the event, David decided against an academic career and I was left to carry out the project on my own.

I began in a situation very different from that which prevails for post-graduate students in the sociology of sport today. My initial advice to postgraduates nowadays is the standard: 'your first task is to construct a bibliography relevant to your field'. That was Norbert Elias's first advice to me. However, even the most exhaustive literature search came up with only one unambiguously sociological item, the late Gregory P. Stone's (1971) classic essay 'American Sports: Play and Display'. There was, of course, also Huizinga's (1949) *Homo Ludens,* a handful of useful items by psychologists and some extremely valuable work by physical educationalists such as Peter McIntosh (1952). However, little of that was really sociological in the sense of being orientated around sociological and sociologically relevant concepts and theories so I decided – this really was my idea rather than Norbert's – to orientate my research around his work on 'civilizing processes'.

The decision came about in the following way. Given the lack of sociological literature dealing directly with sport, Norbert suggested that I should look up relevant items in encyclopaedias and search out histories of sports, starting with my favourite, soccer. I soon had a bibliography large enough to begin preliminary work and it quickly became apparent that something like a 'civilizing process' had been involved in the modernizing development of the game. I suggested this to Norbert and his advice was that my next task was to read his book. Fortunately, I read German and so it was that I ploughed through the two volumes of *Über den Prozess der Zivilisation* (Elias, 1939) and embarked – under Norbert's close, stimulating but never overly directive supervision[7] – on the course of research that was to lead to *Barbarians, Gentlemen and Players* (Dunning and Sheard, 1979) and most of my subsequent work. It was in that way, too, that the joint research by Norbert and myself was begun.

When, in the early and middle 1960s, the processes of data collection and analysis were sufficiently advanced for us to begin to present conference papers and publish, our work met with a mixed reception. In British socio-logy – this was, after all, the heyday of functionalist-empiricist dominance – the response was almost universally hostile. Apart from the inevitable contemptuous dismissal of sport as an area of sociological enquiry, it was a context in which even a respected Marxist like Tom Bottomore (1962) could write that use of the concept of development should be restricted solely to the growth of knowledge and control over the natural environment. Others denied the validity of the concept altogether, arguing that it is just as inherently value-laden as the concept of progress. Imagine how reference to a 'civilizing process' was received in such a context!

I well remember the heated reception given to the first paper I ever gave at a BSA Conference.[8] 'How can you talk of a "civilizing process" given events in Germany in the 1930s and 1940s', was one response? I quickly pointed out that *Über den Prozess der Zivilization* had been written by a German of Jewish descent who had been forced to flee to England and whose mother had died in Auschwitz, suggesting either that Norbert Elias must have been mad or that he might have something to say that is at least worth listening to with a reasonably open mind. Another response that I remember was: 'Your paper confuses "developmental theories" with "theories of development." The latter are consistent with the canons of science but Popper [1957] delivered the decisive blow to "developmental" sociology in *The Poverty of Historicism*'. Similar objections were raised to any form of historical sociology. I even remember a conference around the same time at which a respected sociologist screamed, 'Hobhouse! Hobhouse'! when Norbert Elias ventured to suggest that 'development' might be a viable, important and reality-congruent sociological term!

From the outset, our work met with a different – though by no means uncritical – response in the newly-emerging sociology of sport. That was the case, for example, with respect to our 'Dynamics of Sport Groups With Special Reference to Football', a paper written for the Conference of the International Committee for the Sociology of Sport in Cologne in 1966, the first of what has since become an annual series.[9] We published the English version in the *British Journal of Sociology* (Elias and Dunning, 1966) and as a result were asked to read a paper at the BSA Conference in London in 1967, the theme of which was leisure. We called it, 'The Quest for Excitement in Unexciting Societies' (Elias and Dunning, 1970), and again the dominant response was a mixture of hostility and incomprehension largely centring on the concept of a 'civilizing process'. I do not think it accidental that we were forced to publish versions of that paper in two rather obscure places, a sociology-of-sport reader in the USA and a journal published in Czechoslovakia (Elias and Dunning, 1969). Nor do I think it an oversight that the leading British figures in the sociology of leisure ignored our work then and have continued to ignore it since.[10]

This situation began to change as the 1960s drew to a close. The functionalist-empiricist hegemony was beginning to crumble and the proponents of such paradigms as symbolic interactionism, ethnomethodology, feminist sociology in different guises, and various forms of Marxist and non-Marxist historical sociology were starting to stake their claims. In such a context, the historical – strictly speaking, the process-orientated – emphasis of figurational sociology began to be accorded wider legitimacy. However, this did not mean that battle ceased. Rather, it meant it was beginning to be fought simultaneously on several fronts and, in the sociology of sport if not the sociology of leisure or the subject more generally, that the figurational approach was beginning to be recognized as a leading paradigm. Since such aspects of this paradigm as our stress on 'detachment' and advocacy of the theory of 'civilizing processes' as a 'central' or 'guiding' theory still seem to be widely misunderstood, this is perhaps an appropriate point at which to move from the autobiographical/historical level and to begin to discuss the figurational approach. In order to locate this approach within sociology more generally, I shall start by providing an appraisal of what I regard as the principal strengths and weaknesses of Marxism and 'structuration theory'.

I have singled out these two paradigms for two main reasons: partly because major claims have recently been made on behalf of their significance for the sociology of sport; and partly because critical appraisal of them will provide a useful vehicle for locating the figurational position in sociology more generally. In the hope of avoiding the charge of 'caricature' in this connection, I shall endeavour to back up any criticisms I make with reference to concrete sources. In undertaking this critical exercise, it will be necessary for me to grapple with a number of complex issues that are of general sociological relevance and not just confined to the sociology of sport. I hope the reader will bear with me in this.

MARXISM AND STRUCTURATION THEORY: A BRIEF APPRAISAL

Marxism

It is, I think, indisputable that the writings of Karl Marx have formed one of the most important bases for the development of sociology. Without the work of Marx that of Weber, for example, would have necessarily taken a different form. Similarly, without the work of Marx and Weber, Norbert Elias would have been unable to begin the task of constructing the synthesis to which he sought to contribute. In a word, John Wilson is quite right to point to Elias's debt to Marx and Marxism.[11] There have been other influences, too – perhaps most notably Comte, Durkheim, Simmel and Freud – but Karl Marx has undoubtedly been among the most important.

The sociology of sport is greatly indebted to Marx and Marxism as well. In order to appreciate that one has only to think of the contributions of such scholars as Paul Hoch (1972), Jean-Marie Brohm (1978), Bero Rigauer (1981), Jenny Hargreaves (1982), John Hargreaves (1986), Rick Gruneau (1985), Chas Critcher and John Clarke (1985), Ian Taylor (for example, 1982) and since his 'conversion' from 'Weberianism', Alan Ingham (1984, 1985).[12] Although they frequently disagree among themselves, their work is characterized by a degree of paradigmatic unity and it has enabled them to furnish a plethora of insights into the ways in which sport and leisure are contoured and constrained by economic exigencies, especially the exigencies of capitalism. This is an area into which figurational sociologists have not systematically enquired as yet. Even before such enquiries have been carried out, however, it can be said from a figurational standpoint that what helps to give such Marxist work its distinctive strength is simultaneously a source of weakness. I am referring to the belief that 'the economy' or 'mode of production' is the sole or principal determinant of regularity in social structures and, via the medium of technological development and class struggle, the sole or principal 'driving force' of history and social change. Although we have no wish to deny the fruitfulness of much of the work that has been generated in this connection, our own dependency upon it or the significance of what have come to be conventionally called 'economic' processes for the understanding of social change, it is with this belief that figurational sociologists principally take issue. Let me elaborate on some of the reasons for our doubts.

It has become traditional to distinguish between three types of Marxist approaches to sport and related problems: 'correspondence theory'; 'reproduction theory'; and 'hegemony theory'. Hegemony theory derives from a reading of the work of Antonio Gramsci and is the latest of the three. Like figurational sociologists, its proponents are critical of the tendency towards economic determinism in the other two positions. John Hargreaves (1962), for example, a leading hegemony theorist, describes 'correspondence theory' and 'reproduction theory' thus:

Correspondence theory characterizes sport as a simple reflection of capitalism: its structure and its cultural ethos are completely determined and dominated by capitalist forces and the interests of the ruling class, so that it is a totally alienating activity. Reproduction theory, on the other hand, claims that culture and sport are related to the capitalist mode of production and the dominant social relations in terms of their specificity, that is, their differences and their autonomy; and that it is precisely because of their autonomy that they are enabled to function to reproduce the dominant social relations.

The fundamental weakness of these two positions, according to Hargreaves, is that they both share 'a one-sided, deterministic and static model of capitalist society' and he offers hegemony theory as a means of overcoming this weakness while remaining within the Marxist tradition. I have no wish to deny the significant contributions made by hegemony theory to the understanding of sport or to claim that it shares the 'static' character of correspondence theory and reproduction theory. Nevertheless its seems to me that, despite the value of its undoubted contributions, hegemony theory has still failed to rid itself of the economism that bedevils the other two positions. It is difficult to see how it could do so without abandoning its Marxist roots. Thus, John Hargreaves (1962: 108) describes hegemony theory 'as an attempt to give a sense of the primacy of economic relations in social being without reducing the latter to the former'. Despite his disavowal of economic reductionism, it is surely reasonable to suppose, given this continued stress on 'the primacy of economic relations', that a commitment to some form of economic determinism, to the belief that a society's mode of production is the *fundamental,* if not the *only,* determinant of its principal structural and cultural contours, remains one of the chief defining characteristics of this as of *all* forms of Marxist sociology. Perhaps one might describe correspondence theory and reproduction theory as characterized by commitment to 'strong' forms of economic determinism, while hegemony theory is committed to an ostensibly 'weaker' form?

Counter to this, writers like John Wilson are liable to quote the note in *Das Kapital* where Marx argues that societies manifest 'infinite variations and gradations in appearance, which can be ascertained only by analysis of the empirically given circumstances', and that these are affected, not only by a society's mode of production, but also by the interplay of the mode of production with the 'natural environment', 'racial relations' and 'external historical influences'.[13] It is indisputable that Marx wrote this. But it is also indisputable that he (Marx, 1965: 81) wrote in *Das Kapital* that:

> My view . . . that the economic structure is the real basis on which the juridical and political superstructure is raised, and to which definite forms of thought correspond . . . all this is very true for our own times, in which material interests preponderate, but not for the middle ages, in which Catholicism, nor for Athens and Rome, where politics, reigned supreme. . . . This much, however, is clear, that the middle ages could not live on Catholicism, nor the ancient world on politics. On the contrary, it is the mode in which they gained a livelihood that explains why here politics, and there Catholicism, played the chief part.

As Keat and Urry (1975: 111) have expressed it, in the pre-capitalist modes of production, the relations of production may not be *dominant,* 'but such relations *determine* the way in which some other structural element, such as religion or politics, dominates'. The fundamental basis of such a position, of course, is the famous argument against Hegelian idealism put forward by Marx and Engels to the effect that people need to eat in order to live and that, in order to eat, they need to work and produce. As they, wrote in *The German Ideology* (in Jordan, 1972: 94):

> the first premise of all human existence and, therefore, of all history ... [is] that men must be in a position to live in order to be able to 'make history'. But life involves before everything else eating and drinking, a habitation, clothing and many other things. The first historical act is thus the production of the means to satisfy these needs, the production of material life itself.

It would be possible to cite many other passages from Marx and Engels to substantiate what their basic position was. Nothing sums it up better, though, than Marx's famous *Preface to the Critique of Political Economy* (in Jordan, 1972: 198) where he wrote that 'the anatomy of civil society is to be sought in political economy'. For present purposes, the most relevant aspect of this fragment reads as follows:

> In the social production of their life, men enter into definite relations that are indispensable and independent of their will, relations of production which correspond to a definite state of development of their material productive forces. The sum total of these relations of production constitutes the economic structure of society, the real foundation, on which rises a legal and political superstructure and to which correspond definite forms of social consciousness. The mode of production of material life conditions the social, political and intellectual life process in general. It is not the consciousness of men that determines their being but, on the contrary, their social being that determines their consciousness.

There was some equivocation on the part of Marx and Engels over precisely how strong they supposed the influence of the mode of production to be. They used different words – 'correspond', 'condition', and 'determine', for example – to express the relationship between, on the one hand, the 'economic structure' and, on the other, the 'legal and political superstructure' and 'forms of social consciousness'. Nevertheless, it is surely undeniable that what was being argued for was some notion – stronger or weaker as the case may be – of economic determinism. Figurational sociologists object to such a position in both its stronger and its weaker forms. Principal among our objections to 'economic determinism' or, if you like, the notion of 'the primacy of economic relations', are these:

(a)   As Norbert Elias suggested, the elaboration by Marx of a materialist theory of history served as a valuable corrective to the idealism of Hegel. It constituted, according to Elias (1977), 'a highly decisive step on the road from philosophy to sociology'. In fact, it is understandable how, writing in the context of a society that was still in the early stages of industrialization, a process of social transformation in which what have come to be seen as 'economic' elements – for example, the shift to factory production and wage labour – were perhaps the most readily visible aspects of what was going on, that Marx should have concluded that these were the underlying determinants of the overall changes that were occurring. His materialist theory represented a useful early attempt at conceptually capturing the notion of social determination, of the idea that human societies are not 'divine' creations or forged according to the will of powerful kings but subject to their own, relatively autonomous dynamics. However, while recognizing it as a step forward, figurational sociologists argue that we are now in a position to see that, while some aspects of Marx's schema, such as the stress on the part played by class conflict in social change, retain a degree of adequacy, they are, in fact, only specific examples of the variety of ways in which group conflicts play a part in the production of social change. It is also our contention that, despite the great value of Marx's original insight, his theory *qua* theory was flawed in certain respects as a result of his struggle with Hegel. Let me spell out some of the ways in which this seems to have been the case.

It is arguable that Marx was not – perhaps at the time when he was writing could not have been – sufficiently thoroughgoing in his materialism, with the consequence that traces of idealism continued to vitiate his analysis in various ways. This is perhaps most evident in the categorization of the 'economic structure' as the 'real foundation' or 'material base', and in the conceptual separation of this 'structure' or 'base' from the 'legal and political superstructure' and 'forms of consciousness' which are held to 'correspond to' or, alternatively, to be 'conditioned' or 'determined' by it. Of course, Marx did not mean by this formulation to imply that legal and political institutions and forms of consciousness are in an ontological sense less 'real' than economic relations. He was making a judgement about relative importance and recognized that ideas, non-economic institutions and economic structures all form part of the same material world. Nevertheless, to the extent that he was constrained by his immersion in and opposition to Hegelianism into perpetuating a dichotomy between 'the material' and 'the ideal', it is reasonable to suppose that there is equivocation and lack of clarity in Marx's view of the ontological status and location of ideas and non-economic institutions. Such a dichotomy has its counterpart in the equally problematic distinction between 'body' and 'mind', one of the sources of the relatively low academic status of physical educationalists and the sociologists who concern themselves with the study of sport.

More importantly for present purposes, how can the 'economic structure' of a society be said to exist independently of and to 'determine' the 'forms of consciousness' of its members? Every aspect of human relations, including 'economic structures', involves ideas. Again, Marx recognized this. But he failed to recognize that the 'base–superstructure' dichotomy is inconsistent with the logic of a full-blown historical materialism. Nor did he see the significance for his theory of the fact that the production of subsistence is by no means the only distinguishing characteristic of the human species. Another that is equally constitutive, and on which the capacity to produce subsistence in part depends, is the capacity to think and to communicate ideas through language.

The existence of this inconsistency in the work of Marx is recognized by writers such as John Hargreaves. Although he uses different terms, he is dealing with the same point when he (1962: 107) argues that, 'if we take the being-consciousness or theory-practice polarity in isolation, practice appears as undetermined, as a product purely of men's free will'. However, the only way in which Hargreaves can conceive of avoiding the problem of 'free will' is by translating the 'base–superstructure' dichotomy into what he describes as the non-reductionist idea of 'the primacy of economic relations in social being'. In a word, the economy is still conceptualized as the single most important determinant of constraint and regularity in social life. It is difficult to see what is 'non-reductionist' about this.

Nor, from a figurational standpoint, can Weber's (1956) attempt to overcome the problems of the material–ideal dichotomy by juxtaposing alongside a one-sided material emphasis an explicit and equally one-sided emphasis on the ideal be said to constitute a satisfactory solution. That is because, by posing the problem in such a fashion, the material–ideal dichotomy is perpetuated, leading to interminable and irresolvable wrangles about which side of a dichotomy which lacks reality-congruence predominates over the other.

(b)	Connected with this first objection to Marxist sociology is a second, namely an objection to the more or less explicit tendency of Marxists to seek 'law-like' explanations of social structures and processes by reducing them universally to a single dominant type of causation – the 'economic'. In part, our objection in this connection relates to Elias's suggestion that, while law-like explanations have a relatively high degree of reality-congruence regarding loosely structured phenomena such as gases, they lack reality-congruence regarding highly structured phenomena such as organisms and societies. Here, according to Elias (1974), structure and process models are required. However, our objection to this aspect of Marxist sociology takes a different form as well.

Figurational sociologists obviously agree with Marx that human beings need to eat. However, they also agree with W. H. McNeill (1979) who has pointed out that they have a need 'not to be eaten' too, that is, to protect themselves from germs, bacteria and animals of various kinds. Marx, in fact, was writing in a period when the species *homo sapiens* had been dominant on earth for a very long time. However, as Johan Goudsblom (1989) has reminded us, we were for a very long time before that, not only a hunting species but a *hunted* one as well. We probably only began to obtain our hegemony over other animals when we learned to control fire. But, of course, humans do not only have to protect themselves against other animals but from other humans too. That is why the 'survival units' that they form have always tended to take on the character of what Elias (1978b: 138–9, 155, 170, 181) calls 'attack-and-defence units'. Whether they take the form of tribes, city-states, nation-states or whatever, in order to survive such units certainly need to hunt, to gather and/or grow food and eat, but why should one argue that such functions are universally more important than, say, protection against attack (whether by humans, other animals or bacteria), the control of conflict and violence within the group, or group-perpetuation through sexual reproduction. To cite the work of Goudsblom (1977: 138) once again:

> People live everywhere in dependence of 'nature'. They need it for food, for shelter. As the very word shelter indicates, 'nature' contains not only resources but dangers as well. Very early in the development of human societies, even before people had begun to engage in the 'production' of food and clothing, they had to find certain modes of 'protection' from the dangers among which they lived. They also had to develop some means of 'orientation' enabling them to find their way, to distinguish food from bait and poison, to decide upon the best time for hunting and

gathering. The triad of functions – production, protection and orientation – has continued to be central to people's control of nature.

Each one of these functions – and the list could be added to and further refined – is essential for human survival. It is impossible to rank them in importance and certainly not if one thinks of them as separate 'factors' or 'spheres' which affect each other 'causally'. By continuing to privilege 'the economic', Marxists arguably remain locked at the stage of knowledge represented by the work of Marx himself, that is, at a stage when a socio-logical mode of thinking was still in an early stage of emancipating itself from, in this case, idealist philosophy.

(c)   A third figurational objection to one of the dominant tendencies in Marxian analysis relates to the fact that Marx's hypothesis arguably led to too great a concentration on the endogenous dynamics of societies, with a resultant downgrading of the state and state control to a secondary function of economics. Our objections here are complex. We are not suggesting that Marx and later Marxists have failed to deal with international relations. As John Wilson points out in his contribution to this volume, that is manifestly not the case. 'World systems' theorists such as Wallerstein (1974–80) are only the latest Marxists to focus on such issues. Our point is not that Marxists *ignore* international relations. It is rather that they deal with them economistically and encounter difficulties with respect to explaining phe-nomena such as national, ethnic and racial sentiments or relations between the sexes, that is, phenomena which cannot easily be reduced to class and which frequently involve patterns of unification across class boundaries. Moreover, while economic rivalries are certainly an important source of war and other forms of international conflict, they are not the only processes at work in that regard. Hegemonic struggles have occurred between states ever since state-organized societies first arose and such struggles tie the members of contending states together into what Elias (1987: 43–118) called 'double-bind figurations'. Such figurations have a dynamics cen-trally connected with the mutual and often mutually escalating fears of the persons involved on either side and, yet again, although economic influences are usually also involved, these double-bind figurations cannot be adequately explained in economic terms alone. The relatively autonomous feeling-states of the interdependent antagonists play a part as well.

(d)   Closely connected with this third point is a fourth, namely, that own-ership and control of the 'means of destruction' (more properly, of the means of violence) is arguably as important in social structure and social dynamics as ownership and control of the means of production. While it is never totally independent of it, the former cannot be adequately explained solely in terms of the latter. In other words, the state and state-organization are not simply a function of the economics of isolated, independent and endogenously changing social units. Occurrences associated with *inter-societal* interdependencies play a part as well, and while these are always in part economic – obviously, only living people who eat can produce weapons and fight wars – relatively autonomous strategic and military influences and economically 'irrational' phenomena such as 'national pride', 'group belonging' and 'membership', together with the unplanned dynamics of double-bind figurations, tend to be at work as well. Furthermore, while they, too, obviously could not occur independently of economic pre-conditions and influences, processes of state-formation, especially the emergence of state monopolies on force and processes of pacification under state-control, have ramifications on 'the economy' that are not adequately taken into account in orthodox Marxist analyses that reduce everything to the mode of production, seeing it always and everywhere as the single most important 'driving force' in social structure and social development. Another and perhaps simpler way of expressing this objection would be to follow Elias (esp. 1982) and say that the absolute monarchies of Europe were one of the preconditions for the development of modern capitalism and that the rise of such 'social formations' cannot be adequately accounted for in solely economic terms.

(e)   Figurational sociologists also take issue with what is perhaps the keystone of Marxian political economy, namely Marx's version of the 'labour theory of value'. Our objection here is that Marx's critical stance towards the modern bourgeoisie arguably contributed to a failure on his part to theorize adequately one of the distinctive features of modern capitalism, namely, that the modern bourgeoisie are, in Elias's (1982) words, the first *working* ruling class in history and that they, and not just the 'proletariat', actively contribute through their entrepreneurial, organizational and other forms of labour to the creation of value. In other words, Marx's involvement in social critique arguably hampered his ability to follow through to its logical conclusion his quintessentially sociological insight that production is social and involves forms of interdependence, however asymmetrical these may be and however heavily unequal the distribution of wealth and rewards.

(f)   Another figurational objection to the work of Marx, the last I shall mention in this context, relates to his typically nineteenth century belief that it is possible on the basis of an understanding of the past to predict the future, more particularly that the dynamics of capitalism are propelling us 'with the necessity of an iron law' towards a socialist future. Of course, many present-day Marxists dispute this interpretation of Marx or claim to have abandoned this form of determinism, preferring to believe that it is possible through 'the praxis' of political struggle to advance to a higher and preferable stage of social development. Figurational sociologists have doubts about the adequacy of both these positions. More particularly, we think the future is more open-ended than many Marxists allow and that a principal desideratum at the moment is greater knowledge.[14] Who, forty or fifty years ago, would have predicted the ecological crisis that is being produced by the 'greenhouse effect'? Who, nine or ten years ago (these words were written in September 1990), would have been able to foresee *perestroika,* the collapse of the Soviet Empire and the end of the 'cold war' that we have known since the late 1940s? Who can predict at present whether humanity will be able to control or reverse the greenhouse effect? Who knows whether we are about to enter an era of unprecedented peace or whether, perhaps partly in conjunction with the effects on human populations of ecological catastrophe, other sources of international tension – some new, some older – are about to come to the fore: between the West and Islam, for example, between 'first-' and 'third-world' countries, or between the countries of Eastern and Western Europe? At present nobody knows. Yet in their different ways each of these actual and potential processes is wholly or partly a consequence of the unplanned interweaving of myriads of individual human decisions and it is the view of figurational sociologists that greater understanding of the structure of such aggregate effects is a necessary precondition for exerting greater control. Our view is that people at present – including ourselves – have only rudimentary knowledge of such processes and their effects. That is why we call for further theorizing and research. By contrast, many Marxists seem to treat Marx's theories as 'the end of the road of discovery'. According to Elias (1989), however, they are better viewed as just 'one symptom of a beginning'.[15]

Structuration Theory

'Structuration theory' is the label used by Anthony Giddens (1984) to describe his attempt to produce a synthesis of the diverse traditions of sociological theory. Apart from the fact that it is widely – and rightly – recognized as a remarkable intellectual construct, there are two main reasons for discussing structuration theory here. The first is the fact that the first eight years of Anthony Giddens's academic career – the years 1961 to 1969 – were spent as lecturer at the University of Leicester. They were years in which the Leicester Department of Sociology was at the forefront of the expansion of the subject in Britain and in which Norbert Elias was the central figure in the production of a stimulating and richly rewarding sociological environment. Giddens became acquainted with the work of Elias in that context, orally though and not through reading. That was necessarily the case because, apart from a bad translation of Volume 1 of *Über den Prozess der Zivilisation* of which only a few typewritten copies were available, little of Elias's work had then been published in English. In fact, although he had written a great deal, it was only in that period that Elias started regularly to publish. The relevance of this for present purposes is the fact that, although this is rarely acknowledged (Giddens and Mackenzie, 1982: Introduction), the influence of Elias on Giddens's work is apparent in a number of ways. There are, however, a number of critical differences and divergences as well. Discussion of these will help me to clarify further the specificity of Elias's 'project'.

The second reason for considering the work of Tony Giddens in this context is the fact that a number of scholars, prominent among them Richard Gruneau (1985: 63–6, 85–8), Peter Bramham (1984), and John Horne and David Jary (1987), have recently utilized aspects of structuration theory in an attempt to elucidate particular problems of sport. Indeed, although they are critical of Giddens for what they call his 'abstract formulations', Horne and Jary (1987: 108–9) are centrally dependent on one of Giddens's conceptual innovations when they write:

> Our contention is that alternative approaches to figurational sociology, while retaining an emphasis on historical sociological analysis and on 'structure and agency', can now provide a fuller elaboration of the 'duality' of structure and agency than figurational sociology has typically managed.

I could not disagree more strongly for, as I hope to show, Elias has arguably contributed more to a 'resolution' of the so-called 'structure-agency dilemma' than have the 'abstract formulations' of Anthony Giddens. But let me become more concrete.

The work of Anthony Giddens constitutes a remarkable achievement. However, it is probably fair to say that, while Norbert Elias's greatest strength lay in his capacity as an original thinker and in the synthesis he began to forge of sociology, psychology, history and biology, and that his greatest weakness lay in the secondary comments he made on the work of others, with Anthony Giddens the balance of strengths and weaknesses arguably lies the other way around. That is, Giddens's considerable talents are most evident in his lucid presentation and critical exposition of the work of others but his attempts at developing an original synthesis are arguably less successful. That said, there are some marked similarities between the sociological approaches of Elias and Giddens. Both, for example, share a commitment to an historical and comparative approach to the subject. Both acknowledge a dependency on Marx and Marxism, yet are simultaneously critical of it and seek, in their different ways, to move beyond it. For example, Giddens as well as Elias sees 'the state' as relatively autonomous from 'the economy' and argues that pacification under state-control was one of the preconditions for the development of modern capitalism (Giddens, 1985). Both are concerned to seek a better way of handling problems of 'structure and agency' than has proved possible in the past. And both reject Talcott Parsons's claim to have made a decisive epistemological break-through, and both seek to locate their contributions within the heritage of classical sociology. Principally under Elias's influence, these were all central topics of discussion at Leicester in the 1960s and it seems hardly conceivable that Giddens's 'project' was not considerably influenced by that fact.

It is precisely in their relations to the classical tradition, though, that the differences between Elias and Giddens begin to become apparent. For example, while Giddens (1971) identifies Marx, Durkheim and Weber as having been the most significant 'founding fathers', Elias (1978b: 33–49), whilst acknowledging his debt to this famous 'trinity' and to others such as Simmel, Freud and Levy-Bruhl, self-consciously identified as one of the most important influences on his emergent synthesis the work of August Comte. That helps to explain the attention devoted by Elias to what philosophers call 'epistemological' concerns, while Giddens deliberately focuses primarily on questions of what they call an 'ontological' kind.[16] In short, unlike Giddens, Elias has a theory of knowledge. It is, moreover, a developmental theory and as such offers insights into how Elias saw his own work and how he thinks it should be viewed by others.

This is an issue I shall return to later. For the moment it is enough simply to note that Elias's theory of knowledge – together, of course, with his experience as a philosophy doctoral student in Germany after the First World War – led him to believe that the Western Kantian and neo-Kantian philosophical tradition is irremediably flawed and that sociologists should fight against the claims of philosophers locked into this tradition to be arbiters of scientific method. Giddens, by contrast, believes that what Elias would have described as a 'flight into philosophy' is an essential precondition for the development of the subject.[17] Perhaps this helps to explain why

Giddens has, for the most part, eschewed empirical research while Elias constantly immersed himself in and wrestled with the theorizing of empirical data? Nowhere is this difference more apparent than in their treatment of 'agency' and 'structure'. It is to this thorny issue that I shall now turn.

Giddens claims to have 'resolved' the 'agency-structure dilemma' by means of the 'theorem of the duality of structure' and he is widely seen as having been successful in this attempt. In *The Constitution of Society* (1984: 25), he summarizes his basic argument thus:

> Structure, as recursively organized sets of rules and resources, is out of time and space, save in its instantiations and coordination as memory traces, and is marked by an absence of the subject. The social systems in which structure is recursively implicated, on the contrary, comprise the situated activities of human agents, reproduced across time and space. Analysing the structuration of social systems means studying the modes in which such systems, grounded in the knowledgeable activities of situated actors who draw upon rules and resources in the diversity of action contexts, are produced and reproduced in interaction. Crucial to the idea of structuration is the theorem of the duality of structure. The constitution of agents and structures are [sic] not two independently given sets of phenomena, a dualism, but represent a duality. According to the notion of the duality of structure, the structural properties of social systems are both medium and outcome of the practices they recursively organize. Structure is not 'external' to individuals: as memory traces, and as instantiated in social practices, it is in a certain sense more 'internal' than exterior to their activities in a Durkheimian sense. Structure is not to be equated with constraint but is always both constraining and enabling.

While Giddens's stress on structures as enabling as well as constraining certainly represents an advance relative to many earlier formulations, it is doubtful – as numerous critics have already pointed out[18] – whether 'the theorem of the duality of structure' can be said, in any sense, to 'resolve' the 'agency-structure dilemma'. In fact, it appears to be a particular expression of it. There are a number of reasons for saying this:

(i)   unless it is an unnecessarily complex way of saying something to the effect that 'structure' does not exist as such, independently of its particular manifestations, the idea of structure as 'out of time and space' is a non-testable, literally metaphysical construct;

(ii)　the idea that structure exists only in its 'instantiations' and as 'memory traces' seems to be little more than a complex way of saying that it exists only in the behaviour and memories of individuals. The impression that this is what Giddens means is reinforced when he writes that: 'structure is not "external" to individuals . . . it is in a certain sense more "internal" than exterior to their activities in a Durkheimian sense'. This is a highly nominalist or subjectivist formulation. As such, it fails to capture what one might call the 'relational dimensions' of social structures, for example, those implied by such concepts as 'interdependency chains' and 'social networks'. Although nothing tangible or concrete links the individual human beings who form structures of these kinds, they are as 'real' as the individual human beings who form them and are not reducible to their individual components. For example, they involve properties such as the *length* of interdependency chains, and the degrees of *openness* or *closure* of social networks which, as Elias[19] and Elizabeth Bott (1957) have shown, are crucial determinants of the personality and behaviour of individuals;

(iii)　while rules play an important part in the production and reproduction of the patterned character of social life, they are not exhaustive of social structure in that sense. For example, as Durkheim (1964) recognized when he wrote of increasing 'material density' as a necessary though not sufficient condition for an increase in the division of labour, and as Simmel grasped when he wrote of 'the significance of number in social life' (for example, in Wolff, 1950: 87), factors such as group or population size and density are important influences on social patterning at both what are conventionally called the 'micro' and the 'macro' levels of social integration. In fact, in tying his concept of structure so closely to rules, Giddens appears to be endorsing a variant of the 'Parsonian' or 'normative functionalist' notion of social structure. In any case, structure in the sense of 'order', 'pattern' or 'regularity' exists even in the absence of rules as Durkheim (1952) showed through the concept of 'anomie' and as Elias (1978b: 76–80) demonstrated through his discussion of 'the primal contest';

(iv)　the idea that structures are both medium and outcome of the practices they recursively organize seems to be little more than a tautology. What has to be explained is how the normative and non-normative dimensions of structure are generated, how they interact, and how, under specific conditions, they are reproduced in relatively unchanging forms and how, under others, they are transformed;

(v)　the idea that agents and structures are not 'independently given phenomena, a dualism, but represent a duality' seems to be little more than a play on words, perhaps even a form of 'word magic'. If this line of reasoning has any substance, it means that the 'theorem of the duality of structure' cannot be held to constitute a 'resolution' of the 'agency-structure dilemma'. That is, it does not and cannot tell us anything about the relationships between agents and structures because, at least if Elias was working along fruitful lines as I believe to have been the case, such a task cannot be accomplished by means of philosophical discourse, only by means of scientific theorizing and research. That is to say, in order to contribute to an *advance* in the understanding of such issues – not a once-and-for-all 'resolution' – what is required is the kind of detailed, painstaking, theoretically guided and informed observation undertaken by Elias of the ways in which the structure of human personalities and individual behaviour are formed and change over time in conjunction with changes in social organization, and vice versa;

(vi)   not only does Giddens, by providing a subjectivist definition of structure, arguably reduce structure to agency, he also arguably reproduces the 'agency-structure dilemma' by introducing a dichotomic distinction between 'structure' and 'system' (Giddens, 1984: 25).[20]

(vii) Giddens's concept of human agency is too rationalistic and does not pay due attention to emotional life. That this may help to explain his neglect of subjects such as sport was recently suggested by John Urry (1990) when he wrote that:

> Giddens' conception of human activity is too routinized, too boring, and it is difficult in his framework to conceptualize pleasure-producing activities such as travel, leisure, holiday-making, sightseeing, playing sport, visiting friends and so on.[21]

It was precisely these sorts of issues that Elias and I tried to grapple with in our essays on leisure and excitement (Elias and Dunning, 1986). This is perhaps an appropriate point at which to undertake a brief examination of Elias's approach to questions of 'agency' and 'structure'.

'AGENCY' AND 'STRUCTURE' IN THE WORK OF NORBERT ELIAS

In their recent critique of the figurational sociology of sport, John Horne and David Jary (1987) approvingly quote an argument put forward by Zygmunt Bauman (1979) that there is a clear affinity between 'the idea of figuration and such other household notions as "pattern" or "situation"'. This is arguably a misconception. One can talk of a 'figuration of human beings' but one cannot use the terms 'pattern' or 'situation' in this way. One has to refer to a pattern 'formed by' human beings or to a situation 'in which they find themselves'. In other words, these more standard sociological terms separate the structures formed by human beings from the human beings themselves with the consequence that, in using them, it is comparatively easy to reify the structures, to give the idea that they are 'things' that exist in their own right, independently of the constituting human beings. 'Figuration' could, of course, be used in such a reifying way but, for reasons which it is relatively easy to make clear, Elias arguably succeeded in pointing the way towards a non-reifying usage. Let me elaborate on how that is so.

The concept of figuration refers simultaneously to acting human individuals and their interdependence. That is, it implies a reference both to action and to structure. Given this, it arguably contributes *per se* to a more adequate 'resolution' of the 'agency-structure dilemma' than that proposed by Giddens. To say this is not 'word-magic' of the kind I have suggested may be involved in Giddens's claim that 'agency' and 'structure' constitute a 'duality' rather than a 'dualism'. That is because 'figuration' is a concept which was not only carefully chosen because of its linguistic properties compared with those of 'structure', 'pattern', 'situation', 'system' and so on, but also because it was forged in the context of a programme of research into how 'agents' and 'structures' are mutually produced and mutually transformed over time. This research also points to a possible explanation of why the 'agency-structure dilemma' arose in the first instance and of why it persists. It will help my exposition of this rather complex issue if I focus the discussion around the critique of figurational sociology published by my colleague Derek Layder (1986).

According to Layder, the concept of figuration was held by Elias to represent what Layder (1986: 373) calls 'a complete characterization of social ontology'. However, the term was not intended, *qua* concept, to bear such a heavy 'explanatory load'. Expressing it in the most general terms, one could rather say that it comes in some ways close to being what Herbert Blumer (1969: 149; quoted in Goudsblom, 1977: 100–1) called a 'sensitizing concept', one that obtains its concrete functions and contents only in the context of particular empirical-theoretical investigations. It is not, that is to say, a 'definitive concept' circumscribed by a definition in terms of attributes or fixed bench-marks but 'shapes up in a different way in each empirical instance'. In other words, the concept of figurations serves as a signpost for the process of research in the sense that it is intended to direct the attention of researchers to the interdependency chains and networks formed by acting human beings without prejudging the contents, or as Layder would presumably say, the 'ontological properties', of the particular interdependencies being researched.

Although it was not formulated in this rather formalistic way – for better or worse, formalism was one of the things he regularly eschewed – this 'sensitizing' function of the concept of figurations was proposed by Elias in *What Is Sociology?* (1978b), a book where he saw his task as primarily didactic. It was Derek Layder's focus on the concept as defined in that context that led him to what is probably his principal misinterpretation of the figurational genre. More particularly, he failed to realize that the concept of figurations is tied in with Elias's critique of the conception of 'the person' as *homo clausus* ('closed individual') which, in turn, is dependent on his studies of the European 'civilizing process';[22] that is, the concept had its foundations in Elias's investigations into the ways in which the personality structures of people in Western Europe changed between the eleventh and the twentieth centuries in the course of a long-term social process. The concept of figurations, that is to say, cannot be properly understood in abstraction from Elias's empirical-theoretical work. Layder makes a relevant point when he berates Elias for not acknowledging that Cooley (in Layder, 1986) prefigured his (Elias's) 'complaint about the false dichotomy between the individual and society when he [Cooley] state[d]: "a separate individual is an abstraction unknown to experience and so likewise is society when regarded as something apart from individuals"'. This is an argument with which Elias would not have disagreed. However, because Cooley's formulation contains no terms with an explicit connotation of structure, it is difficult to see it performing the function with respect to the 'agency-structure dilemma' which, if my earlier argument holds good, is one of the hallmarks of the concept of figurations.

Layder was wrong, moreover, to suggest that there is nothing new in Elias's concept. That is not the case, at least relative to writers such as Cooley and Giddens, because, unlike the latter, Elias provided a reasoned *explanation* of *why* people in the modern West recurrently experience themselves as *homo clausus* and thus fail to recognize the sociologically self-evident fact articulated by Cooley. According to Elias, the 'subject–object split', including as one of its crucial variants the tendency to split 'agency' from 'structure' and 'individual' from 'society' while simultaneously reifying the latter, corresponds to a *real* experience. That is a central reason why it is difficult to avoid. There is insufficient space here for me to probe this complex issue in the detail it deserves. It must be enough to illustrate the distinctiveness of Elias's view by citing a short passage from *What Is Sociology?* (1978b: 122) where he wrote:

> As human society develops, people experience themselves increasingly strongly as separate beings, distinct both from other people and from natural objects. Reflection and conscience increasingly interpose themselves through the process of social training as controlling and taming influences between people's own spontaneous impulses to action and other people, other natural objects. So it is anything but easy to combine the insight that the feeling of a dividing line between the 'inner self' and the 'outside world' is very genuine, with the insight that the dividing line is non-existent. In fact, it requires a further effort at self-distancing. This is essential if people are to recognize that the apparently real partition between self and others, the individual and society, subject and object, is in fact a reification of the socially distilled disengagement of their own self-experience.

So Elias formulated both a concept which can arguably contribute to a more adequate understanding of the relationship between individuals and the societies they form than that proposed by Giddens, the concept of figurations, and he proposed an explanation of why people recurrently experience this particular form of 'subject–object split'. In putting these arguments forward I am not suggesting that Elias was necessarily right. It is simply my contention that what he wrote is deserving of more serious attention than it has been given hitherto. Nor do I think I am being disingenuous when I say that the late Philip Abrams was one of the few sociologists, in my opinion, to have grasped the measure of Elias's contribution in this regard. Abrams (1982: 230–1) wrote that:

> The most remarkable recent attempt to contain the social and the individual within a unified scheme of sociological analysis is probably that made by Norbert Elias. In *The Civilizing Process* Elias gives us both a principled critique of the dualism of conventional social analysis and, by way of a minutely documented case study of the 'history of manners', a thoroughly substantiated presentation of an alternative theoretical position. Just because his work offers us such an exceptionally bold and direct assault on the credentials of dualism coupled with a powerful empirical demonstration of an alternative it must command attention as a crucial point of reference. . . . [I]n place of the sterile pursuit of the

formal interrelation of individual and society he proposed the historical analysis of what he calls 'human figurations'.

It is important to realize at least one more thing in this connection. Unlike Anthony Giddens, Elias never presented his work as having 'solved' or 'resolved' the 'structure-agency dualism' or anything else. Rather, he offered it as a 'breakthrough', that is, as a means for helping sociological theorization and research to be *more* fruitful in relation to such issues than has often been possible in the past. Because it ties in with his theory of the development of knowledge, mention of this idea provides an appropriate point at which to introduce a discussion of Elias's work on 'involvement and detachment', another subject on which he has been widely misunderstood.

PROBLEMS OF INVOLVEMENT AND DETACHMENT

Just as Norbert Elias never claimed to have 'solved' the problem of 'structure' and 'agency', neither did he profess to have produced research which is 'detached' in any absolute sense. Nor for that matter – for the simple reason that such an idea runs totally counter to some of the key tenets of our position – does any other figurational sociologist make such a claim. What Elias attempted to do in relation to 'structure' and 'agency' was to work out a way of approaching the problem which it is hoped, if it gains a degree of acceptance, will facilitate research into and theorizing of the relationships between human individuals and the societies they form which is more fruitful than has proved possible by treading in the footsteps of a sterile neo-Kantian philosophy which, according to one of Elias's most strongly held beliefs, has outlived its usefulness. His view on questions of involvement and detachment was similar. *Pace* such critics of figurational sociology as Horne and Jary (1987: 102, 108) who translate the concept of detachment into a straight equivalent of 'value-neutrality', it was Elias's contention that sociological research and theory are hindered rather than helped by thinking in terms of such simple dichotomies as those between 'subjectivity' and 'objectivity', 'irrationality' and 'rationality', or 'value-bias' and 'value-neutrality'. It is better, he maintained, to think in terms of fluid and complex balances. Let me elaborate on this. It will be useful to start by comparing Elias's position on these issues with that of 'critical theory', of the writers of 'the Frankfurt School'.

The position of critical theory on questions of involvement and detachment has been cogently summed up by Robert Bocock (1983: 22). He writes:

> Epistemologically critical theory stresses the importance of sociology and social theory being critical of scientism in the realm of methodology. Scientism means here the uncritical attempt to copy the methods of the natural sciences in doing social science. Critical theory tries to retain links between social philosophy and ethics, rather than severing them in order to make sociology appear more like a natural science – something which it is in principle impossible to do anyway as far as this epistemological position is concerned. The social world is *appraised* in the very language used to describe, analyse, explain and understand it. Neutral scientific-sounding language does not avoid such an appraisal, it merely suggests that there is nothing in that which it is analysing to get too worked up about either politically or morally. Critical theory developed its epistemology under the shadow of the Nazi regime, and it has always held that liberal, well-intentioned value-neutrality in the social sciences aided the rise of Nazism by appearing to students and others to be unable to offer any political values worth caring for, thus providing a gap which fascism filled.

Norbert Elias was assistant to Karl Mannheim in the Sociology Department at the University of Frankfurt from 1929 to 1933, a time which coincided with the early days of Horkheimer and Adorno's privately funded Institute for Social Research, the institutional setting of the Frankfurt School. In fact, the University rented rooms for the Sociology Department from the Institute in the so-called 'Marxburg' (Mennell, 1989: 14), and Elias related to me once how, at considerable personal risk, he had been instrumental in helping Adorno to escape the Nazis. I mention this only to reinforce the fact that Elias too developed aspects of his 'epistemology' – he preferred to call it simply a 'theory of knowledge' – under the shadow of the Nazis. Yet despite his contacts with members of the Frankfurt School and exposure to similar dangers, Elias came to different conclusions on the issues of involvement and detachment. He shared Adorno *et al.*'s opposition to 'scientism' but not, as I have suggested already, their embrace of an unreformed philosophy. What he urged instead was that, for sociology to be a 'science', it had to develop methods appropriate to its own subject-matter. And although, to my knowledge, he never criticized their position explicitly or at length, Elias also parted company with the Frankfurt School over what he regarded as their too simple and in many ways non-developmental view of language and values. He did not seek to deny that the language of some forms of social science, while making a claim to be 'neutral', can mask an 'appraisal' of the social world. It was his contention, however, that 'appraisal' is not a simple 'either–or' matter but a question of degrees. According to Elias, that is to say, there are *degrees* of 'scientificity' or, to put the same thing the other way round, *degrees* of 'objectivity' and 'value-bias'. Ideo-logies, too, differ in their degrees of reality-congruence but, Elias contended, they always – even those with which one sympathizes person-ally and Elias's sympathies were always with the political left – contain a mythical component and he was firmly of the opinion that a *sine qua non* for effective social reconstruction is a larger fund of knowledge about ourselves and the societies we form (Elias, 1978b: 68–70). In fact, his position in this regard was a complex one, intricately bound up with his emergent theory of knowledge and social development. Let me try to unpack it step by step.

According to Elias (1987: xxxvi), 'the capacity for detachment is a human universal'. That is, it is a constitutive feature of *Homo sapiens* and involved in such ostensibly simple activities as making tools or weapons. That is the case because, in order to undertake such tasks, 'human beings have . . . to detach themselves to some extent from their immediate internal or external situation'. In other words, making artefacts of these kinds is not, as such, a means of stilling hunger. It involves 'the capacity for distancing oneself from the situation of the moment, for remembering a past and for anticipating a possible future situation where the work of one's hands . . . might be of use'. These operations, said Elias, 'are essentials of the variety of self-regulation described here as detachment' (1987: xxxvi). In other words, a greater or lesser capacity for detachment is a property of all human beings, part of the condition of being human. It is not just a property of scientists in their research.

This universal human capacity for detachment is dependent in part on the biological constitution of the species, above all on the co-ordinating func-tions performed by the cerebral cortex. It is also dependent on the related fact that this organ crucially depends on learning from what Elias called 'the social fund of knowledge' (1987: 50ff). However, detachment is necessarily always blended with involvement. As Elias (1987: 3) put it:

One cannot say of a person's outlook in any absolute sense that it is detached or involved (or if one prefers, 'irrational', 'objective' or 'sub-jective'). Only small babies, and among adults perhaps only insane people, become involved in whatever they experience with complete abandon to their feelings here and now; and again only the insane can remain totally unmoved by what goes on around them.

I think Elias would have agreed that, apart from babies and the insane, the only completely detached human beings are dead ones! Adult behaviour – in *all* human societies – normally lies between the two extremes. It is a question of balances and blends. As Stephen Mennell (1989: 160) has pointed out, Elias's 'emphasis on this point is in clear contrast to Talcott Parsons's notion that the distinction between *affectivity* and *affective neutrality* . . . is a clear-cut, dichotomous, mutually-exclusive choice between opposites'.

Mennell has constructed the following diagram as a device for clarifying Elias's complex arguments on this point:

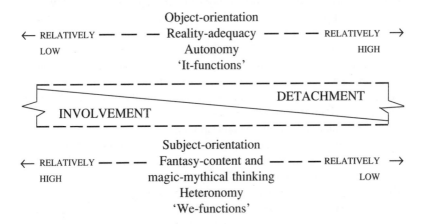

Object-orientation
←— RELATIVELY — — — Reality-adequacy — — — RELATIVELY —→
LOW   Autonomy   HIGH
'It-functions'

DETACHMENT

INVOLVEMENT

Subject-orientation
←— RELATIVELY — — — Fantasy-content and — — — RELATIVELY —→
HIGH   magic-mythical thinking   LOW
Heteronomy
'We-functions'

Implicit in this diagram is the idea that, even though the capacity for detachment is a human universal, the balance between it and involvement varies both among individuals and societies and groups. It is this second side of the equation – that of group and societal variations – that is of principal interest to sociologists. By what criteria, according to Elias, is it possible to measure people's patterns of speech, thought and activity on the continuum between higher and lower degrees of detachment or involvement? Stephen Mennell (1989: 161) sums up Elias's suggestions on this issue thus:

> The criteria are neither purely 'psychological' nor purely 'social'. Elias chose the terms 'detachment' and 'involvement' . . . precisely because 'they do not fall in line with linguistic usages which are based on the tacit

assumption of the ultimate independence of psychological and social properties of humans'. At all costs, Elias wishes to avoid the mode of thinking in which psychological attributes and social attributes are conceived of as separate entities standing in some metaphysical cause-and-effect relation to each other.

Why this should be avoided is that 'The way in which individual members of a group experience whatever affects their senses, the meaning it has for them, depends on the standard forms of dealing with, and of thinking about these phenomena gradually evolved in their society.'

Crucial in this connection is the degree to which a society's fund of knowledge is expressed primarily in 'magical-mythical" or in more reality-congruent, scientific terms. Again, this is a question of balances and degrees: even the most 'advanced' societies contain layers or residues of magical-mythical thinking and no society, no matter how 'primitive', could survive without a measure of reality-congruent knowledge. However, for most of humanity's existence, magical-mythical forms of thinking have prevailed and the level of knowledge remained, correlatively, low. There have been two main breakthroughs from the 'double-bind' experienced in this connection: in Ancient Greece a limited breakthrough towards science which subsequently drowned, and in Renaissance Europe a more substantial and enduring process in which we are still caught up today.

As one can see, Elias's position on questions of scientific method did not take the form of a simple treatise on 'objectivity' or 'value-freedom'. As I said earlier, it is bound up with a theory of the development of knowledge. This theory is based partly on the observation that, over the millennia, but with quickening pace especially since the Renaissance, people have been able to build up larger funds of more reality-congruent knowledge. They have been able, as Elias put it, to construct 'small islands of certainty in the vast oceans of their ignorance'. However, this development has occurred faster with respect to physical and biological processes than regarding human beings and the societies they form. In Elias's (1987: 50–1) own words once again:

Over the millennia, human groups, with the help of the growing social fund of their knowledge, have been busily building into the undiscovered and uncontrollable universe a widening safety area for themselves – an area of known connections which they can more or less control. As a result, people are now able in certain areas to steer their way through the flow of blind and unmanageable processes better than their forebears –

at least at the physical levels, if less so at the human levels, just as people aboard ships steer their way through the unmanageable waters of the ocean or, in spaceships, through the uncontrollable processes of the sun-system. In that way, by expanding their control within the uncontrollable flow of events, humans, in the more advanced societies, have managed to provide themselves with a larger protective shell designed, as far as possible, to keep out the dangers that emanate from the non-human levels of the overall process. They have not yet managed to develop an equally comprehensive and realistic fund of knowledge at the human or social levels. Hence, they are not yet able to bring under control the dangers that·human beings constitute for each other and themselves.

One of Elias's central hypotheses in this connection is that the growth of knowledge since the Renaissance has been, in part, a function of the 'civilizing spurt' which began around that time. In other words, one of the preconditions for the growth of modern science, he suggested, was an increase in specific (but later widening) groups in the socially instilled capacity of their members to exercise self-distanciation and self-restraint. However, by consolidating the experience of the self as *homo clausus,* this same process which facilitated the growth of the physical sciences acted as a blockage to the emergence of their social counterparts. Hence, in part, the slower, later and lesser growth of the latter. However, the social sciences *have* grown to a degree and, as Mennell (1989: 180) again observes, Elias recognized his own debt to 'the practical example of the three great figures he always acknowledges as pioneers of process theories: Darwin, Comte and Marx'.

It was not, however, only the slow emergence of sociology and the other social sciences which led Elias to suggest that people – especially in the more 'advanced' societies – are slowly coming to adopt a more detached approach towards themselves. Such an approach, he argued, is to an extent also inherent in the predominantly secular ideologies of our age.[23]

It is inherent in them by virtue of the very fact that they are predominantly secular as opposed to religious. It is also inherent in the fact that these ideologies are based on the idea of societies as kinds of 'wholes' or 'systems'. That said, however, present-day ideologies, whether of the left, right or centre, continue to contain such 'voluntaristic' ideas as the belief that it is possible on the basis of current knowledge to construct 'Utopias' in the real world, but, according to Elias, voluntaristic thinking about human relations is akin in many ways to magical-mythical thinking. Beliefs of this kind may provide a degree of comfort and emotional warmth in a cold, impersonal, complex and rapidly changing world but, when translated into action, they are likely to produce unanticipated and, in the main, undesired and undesirable consequences. It is for such reasons that Elias believed it to be vital for sociologists to strive for greater autonomy in relation to political and similar ideologies. Even though they represent a development towards greater detachment in certain respects, present-day belief systems of a predominantly ideological kind continue to place questions of unexamined faith at the forefront of the agenda whereas, in Elias's view, our greatest need is for a larger fund of reality-congruent knowledge about ourselves and the societies we form.

Earlier I quoted Elias's comment that many present-day Marxists appear to treat Marx's theories as 'the end of the road of discovery', whereas they are better seen, according to Elias, as 'one symptom of a beginning'. In other words, such Marxists and others who seem similarly to believe there is not an urgent need for greater knowledge about ourselves appear guilty of a kind of hubris. By contrast, Elias never ceased to talk about our still in many ways rudimentary sociological knowledge at the current stage.

While Elias never explicitly said so, it would, I think, be consistent with his view of the present development of sociology to say that, if Marx's work constituted one symptom of a beginning, his own constitutes another. Because he was able to build on the spadework of Marx (and others), it may be in some ways more advanced but it is a symptom of a beginning none the less. All sociologists, that is to say, are workers in a fledgling science. It follows from this and my earlier arguments that Elias nowhere claimed that any of his theories, including his joint and individual work on sport and leisure, are either completely 'detached' or constitute anything more than small, hopeful breakthroughs in the process of growing knowledge about ourselves. 'Complete' or 'absolute' detachment is a chimera. So likewise, at the present level of sociological development, is a 'fully-fledged' or 'final' theory of civilization, knowledge, sport, leisure, football hooliganism or anything else. As Elias (1987: 6) put it:

> The aim of [scientific] inquiries is to find the inherent order of events as it is, independently not of any but of any particular observer, and the importance, the relevance, the value of what one observes is assessed in accordance with the place and function it appears to have within this order itself.
>
> In the exploration of nature . . . scientists have learned that any direct encroachment upon their work by short-term interests or needs of specific persons or groups is liable to jeopardize the usefulness which their work may have in the end for themselves or for their own group. The

problems which they formulate and, by means of their theories, try to solve, have in relation to personal or social problems of the day a high degree of autonomy; so have the sets of values which they use; their work is not 'value-free', but it is, in contrast to that of many social scientists, protected by firmly established professional standards and other institutional safeguards against the intrusion of heteronomous evaluations.

As one can see, Elias was opposed to those who argue that sociology should be the tool of some particular class or interest group. He did not accept the glib idea that 'if you are not for us, you must be against us'. That is to say, he did not accept the notion that a sociology which is not expressive, say, of the interests of the working class is *ipso facto* expressive of the interests of their rulers. Rather, he urged sociologists to strive for autonomy and against heteronomy, against interference in the determination of their aims and objectives by any outside group or its real or nominal representatives. To this end he advocated the development of standards, institutions and modes of proceeding similar to those in the 'natural' sciences but moulded to the specific properties of human beings and societies. Adding to knowledge *per se* should be paramount over short-term interests and concerns both in research and in deciding the merits of particular pieces of work. That advances in knowledge of a relatively non-ideological character about human societies are possible is shown, for example, by the work of Marx relative to that of Hegel, by the fact that the former contributed decisively to the initial development of sociology out of philosophy. However, Elias was equally clear that, in striving to achieve these aims, sociologists cannot and *should not* abandon their political interests and concerns. As Elias (1987: 16) expressed it:

> The problem confronting [social scientists] is not simply to discard [their more involved, political] role in favour of . . . [a more detached, scientific one]. They cannot cease to take part in, and to be affected by, the social and political affairs of their group and their time. Their own participation and involvement, moreover, is itself one of the conditions for comprehending the problems they try to solve as scientists. For while one need not know, in order to understand the structure of molecules, what it feels like to be one of its atoms – in order to understand the functioning of human groups one needs to know, as it were, from the inside how human beings experience their own and other groups, and one cannot know without active participation and involvement.

The problem confronting those who study one or the other aspects of human groups is how to keep their two roles as participant and as enquirer clearly and consistently apart and, as a professional group to establish in their work the undisputed dominance of the latter.

It was for reasons such as these that Elias always encouraged students to carry out research in areas in which they were directly interested and involved, while urging them to strive as hard as possible when they were engaged in the research process to distanciate themselves from the objects of their research, to take the 'detour via detachment' in order to maximize the degree of reality-congruence of their findings, that is, to make these findings correspond as far as possible to the objects themselves rather than to their personal fantasies and feelings or to personal and/or group interests and myths of various kinds. This, then, in broad outlines was Elias's position on problems of involvement and detachment. Let me now respond to what some of the critics have written.

SOME COUNTER-CRITICAL COMMENTS

Chris Rojek argues that 'figurational sociologists have produced no rules, no drill, to accomplish self-distancing from the object of study'.[24] Although it is not expressed in terms of the need to achieve a balance between involvement and detachment, of Elias's contention that a specific blend of both is required for effective research, this is a charge, I think, which has some substance. The undeniable gap in this regard results, in part, from the fact that Elias's work on involvement and detachment was neither simply nor mainly a treatise on sociological methods, but was bound up, as I have said, with a contribution to the theory of knowledge. One would not necessarily expect a theory of that kind to concern itself with the details of rules regarding procedures for individual researchers. That said, however, Elias's work on involvement and detachment may not be quite so devoid of practical rules as Chris Rojek implies. Here are some of the rules of procedure which he propounded:

(a) Avoid the 'retreat to the present'. Locate the objects of your research historically and in the wider system of social interdependencies in which they are embedded. Simply trying to do this will force you into greater detachment.

(b) Explore connections and regularities, structures and processes for their own sake. By attempting as dispassionately as possible to contribute to knowledge rather than to help in the achievement of some short-term goal, you will increase your chances of avoiding bias as result of personal interests or because of your membership of or identification with a particular group or groups.

(c) Attempt to see yourself and your work as far as possible through the eyes of others. Stop perceiving yourself as a '*wirloses Ich*' – an 'I without a we'. As Elias (1987: lxi–lxii) also wrote; every step of enlarging the social fund of knowledge presupposes the acquisition by the individual subject concerned of a social fund of knowledge, including knowledge of a language, from others'. Relate your work to the existing body of knowledge in your field.

(d) In connection with (c) above, always relate your observations to a body of theory and your theories to a body of observations. As Elias (1987: 20) expressed it: 'it is a characteristic of . . . scientific . . . forms of solving problems that . . . questions emerge and are solved as a result of an uninterrupted two-way traffic between two layers of knowledge; that of general ideas, theories or models and that of observations and perceptions of specific events. The latter, if not sufficiently informed by the former, remains unorganized and diffuse; the former, if not sufficiently informed by the latter, remains dominated by feelings and imaginings.' Theories, in short, are vital to the continuity and the systematic character of knowledge. Observation is vital to its reality-congruence, to its detachment from the fantasies of individual men and women. Because, at their best, scientific theories are inherently more 'object-orientated' than ideologies, concern with testing them will help your work to be more detached in this sense. Of course, theories can count as 'scientific' which come later to be recognized as false starts or fantasy constructions. There is no escape in this connection from the scientific equivalent of 'the struggle for survival' or from the fact that theories become fashionable for a greater or lesser period of time for extra-scientific reasons. This is more likely to happen in sciences such as sociology which are in their early stages of development and which lack the sorts of standards and institutional procedures specified by Elias. It nevertheless holds good that, even in such subjects, an orientation towards the 'two-way traffic' between theory and observation is one means for moving in the direction of that blend between involvement and detachment which is most conducive to reality-congruent knowledge.

(e)   in order to help ensure that your detachment is suitably tempered by an equally necessary involvement, always work in areas in which you are personally interested and involved and in which you have detailed practical experience.

I realize that these five 'rules' do not add up to much of a practical guide. Elias recommended us to gain distance from our objects of research and from ourselves, and then to 'get back in' through what he called 'secondary re-involvement'. A prerequisite for gaining distance from ourselves is a high degree of self-understanding, perhaps furthered by psychoanalysis or some other form of depth psychology. But apart from the above 'rules' and from showing how we are all dependent on the long-term development of knowledge, language and wider social conditions, and suggesting that we should model our standards and institutional procedures on those of the natural sciences, Elias had little advice to give to sociologists regarding practicalities in this connection. In other words, despite my quibbles around the margins, Chris Rojek's criticism in this connection is one that holds good. He has correctly identified an area to which figurational sociologists need to devote a great deal more attention.

Let me turn now to the criticisms offered by Jenny Hargreaves. They merit attention next because they centre to a large extent around problems of involvement and detachment. They also highlight some of these problems in a particularly clear, lively and impassioned form.

FIGURATIONAL SOCIOLOGY AND FEMINIST CULTURAL STUDIES

It is, I hope, clear from the discussion so far that at least some aspects of the critique of figurational sociology and the figurational sociology of sport offered by Jenny Hargreaves in this volume are based on a misreading of our work. That said, her critique is one that has to be taken very seriously indeed. What is principally at issue is our view of sociology as a subject primarily concerned with adding to the social fund of knowledge – in the hope that such knowledge will be of practical value, if not now, then in the longer term – and the view of feminist cultural studies according to which the principal task is contemporary critique with a view to changing things here and now. I am impressed by the power, cogency and evident passion and commitment with which Jenny Hargreaves advances her case. As far as I can tell, I share many of her goals and values regarding relations between the sexes, whether in sport or elsewhere. However, I share fewer aspects of her vision of what sociology is and ought to be. Moreover, her critique has not led me seriously to doubt the value of the figurational approach. Let me spell out some of my reasons for saying this.

I accept – as I am sure the majority of figurational sociologists do – that we have in the past been too silent on questions of gender. We needed feminists like Jenny Hargreaves to point out the unexamined masculinist assumptions in our work. An example would be the failure of Elias and me to explore the dependency of so much sport on the exploitation of unpaid and poorly paid female labour. That we did not pursue such avenues of exploration in our early work on sport and leisure is not in doubt and some of us are striving now to rectify the balance.[25] What is at issue is whether the simple replacement of an unexamined masculinist problematic by what seems to me to be in many respects an equally unexamined feminist one is a route to desirable social change or, indeed, whether such change will be possible without greater knowledge.

Implicit in Jenny Hargreaves's position is, I think, the idea that critique and political action using existing ideologies will be sufficient on their own to secure desirable social change. However, the history of political struggle suggests that we are dealing here with an area where knowledge remains rudimentary. Think how frequently undesired and unintended consequences have resulted from intended political actions. Think how frequently revolutions have been betrayed. I am not making this point as a call for avoiding political action. I am making it as part of an argument *about what sociology is and ought to be.* Just like everybody else, figurational sociologists are at present dependent in their political actions to a large extent on ideologies and values which lack an adequate scientific base. Just like everybody else, there are political differences among us. What unites us is our view that our primary concern *as sociologists* should be to contribute to knowledge in the hope that it will facilitate an improvement in the efficacy of political action by changing the balance between its knowledge-based and ideological contents in favour of the former. We agree in large measure with the conventional Weberian position that political action and critique belong to the role of citizen, not that of scientist. Where we differ is in believing it to be wrong to treat 'value-neutrality' (detachment) and 'value-bias' (involvement) as simple, dichotomous opposites. Accordingly, it is our view that the 'scientific' and the 'critical' traditions in sociology need not necessarily be quite so incompatible as they are sometimes supposed to be. That is, social critique is likely, in our view, to be enhanced by incorporating good sociological theory and research, and sociological theory and research are likely to be enhanced by assimilating good social critique. Difficulties are likely to arise between representatives of the 'scientific' and 'critical' traditions, however, to the extent that they misrepresent and caricature each other's work, and I want to contend that some aspects of Jenny Hargreaves's critique of figurational sociology do just that. More particularly, it seems to me, such is the strength of her commitment to critical feminism that she: (a) fails to respond to aspects of our case that are potential threats to that commitment, at least in its presently articulated form; (b) asserts as facts a number of things which are consistent with a feminist ideology but which have not yet been backed up by research; and (c) uses these ostensible facts as 'disproof' of a caricatured version of the theory of civilizing processes. Let me attempt to substantiate these charges.

I have suggested elsewhere (Elias and Dunning, 1986: 268–70) that the balance of power between the sexes is polymorphous and multi-determined. However, instead of responding in detail to my case, Jenny Hargreaves remains content with a few one-dimensional, economistic assertions about patriarchy and capitalism. In pointing this out I am not trying to suggest that relations between the sexes are unaffected by capitalism. That would be obvious nonsense. What I am suggesting is that aspects of the 'social totality' other than the mode of production and patterns of economic ownership and control have to be taken into account in order to understand patriarchy; for example, ownership and control of the means of violence. I am also suggesting that such aspects cannot be adequately explained by reducing them simply to 'the economic'. In addition, I am inviting Jenny Hargreaves to respond to the details of my case and that she has patently so far failed to do.

Jenny Hargreaves also rests her critique in part on such blanket assertions as the following: that, especially for women, 'public and private spaces in "civilized" societies are far from being "pacified" social spheres'; that 'women's reported concerns about personal safety in public have risen to unprecedentedly high levels'; and that 'the home has become the most dangerous place for women'. Comparative statements about processes over time of the kind made by Elias and other figurational sociologists are replaced here by empirically unsupported assertions. How, independently of back-up from painstaking historical research, can Jenny Hargreaves maintain that women's concerns about their public safety have risen to *unprecedentedly* high levels? How can she assert that the home has become *the most dangerous* place for women? What sort of time period does she have in mind? The last ten years? The last fifty? The last thousand? Is the home in Britain today more dangerous for women than its equivalents were in the Middle Ages or Ancient China? And what about the 'homes' of slaves in Ancient Rome or, for that matter, the American South? Is it more dangerous for them independently of social class? Could not the expression by women of rising concern about public safety be, in part at least, a consequence of higher expectations and not simply of rising violence *per se*? Could it not be, again at least in part, a consequence of unrealistic fears engendered by sensationalizing media of mass communication which give rise to and reinforce the idea that society today is more violent than it is in fact?

I have deliberately framed these questions in a rhetorical and provocative way because of what I take to be the rhetorical and provocative character of some aspects of Jenny Hargreaves's critique of the theory of civilizing processes. In raising them I am not suggesting that her arguments are necessarily wrong. It is simply my point that, as yet, they are empirically unsupported. That, from a figurational standpoint, is what is urgently required: *historical research* into these complex issues so that concrete data can be supplied in place of unsubstantiated assertions. That is one of the principal ways available to us at present of moving towards greater detachment. Moreover, contrary to a popular misunderstanding of the theory of civilizing processes which Jenny Hargreaves evidently shares, it would not necessarily be inconsistent with that theory if a rise in violence against women – or, for that matter, any other group – were currently occurring. The theory is not evolutionist in the sense of claiming to have identified a necessary and irreversible unilinear trend. In the more 'scientific', as opposed to the critical, sides of her sociological work, Jenny Hargreaves has added greatly, by means of a well-tempered balance between involvement and detachment, to our understanding of women in sport.[26] Unfortunately, that balance deserted her in her response to the theory of civilizing processes. Let me now spell out in some detail exactly what that theory does and does not say.

THE THEORY OF CIVILIZING PROCESSES[27]

It would be silly to pretend that the theory of civilizing processes is anything but controversial. Figurational sociologists cling stubbornly to the belief that it is a fruitful 'central theory', a co-ordinating guide to and stimulator of research in a wide number of fields.[28] They respond vigorously to the many and varied criticisms that are offered. For their part, critics of the theory stick equally stubbornly to the belief that the theory rests on dubious foundations. Clearly, one encounters here a failure of communication of massive proportions, a failure precisely of the kind that is liable to occur in a multi-paradigmatic subject. So in the hope that it may be of help in getting us out of the current impasse and into a situation where both more fruitful dialogue and – most desirable of all – actual *testing* of the theory can begin, let me once again respond to the critics and attempt to set the record straight.

I must hasten to add that it is not my intention in expressing the matter in this way to be simply dismissive of the critics. Our difficulties are mutual and inherent in the current situation. That is because all of us – Marxists, critical feminists, figurational sociologists and others – are trained in the assumptions, values and concepts of a particular paradigm and hence find it difficult to respond to what the proponents of different paradigms say without reading nuances and ideas into their words which they do not intend or do not believe are there.

That is certainly our reaction to what is perhaps the most common charge laid against the theory of civilizing processes, namely that it is 'evolutionary', a throwback to the discredited theories of the nineteenth century. We have repeatedly denied that (see, for example, Dunning, 1989). Yet, echoing the earlier criticisms by Otto Newman (1986), James Curtis (1986) and Ian Taylor (1987), Jenny Hargreaves writes in the present volume: 'It is clear to see why Elias's theory has been characterized as evolutionary when he asserts that . . . in all Western societies in the long-term, "the 'trend' of the movement of civilization is everywhere the same, embodying civilizing restraints on sexuality and aggressiveness"'. This statement by Elias is an empirical one and it stands or falls as such. It would only be meaningful to class it as 'evolutionary' by means of a critical analysis of the aetiology Elias employed and that Jenny Hargreaves signally fails to do. As I hope in a moment to show, Elias's view of the dynamics, or 'sociogenesis', and 'psychogenesis', of the civilizing process in Europe is far from 'evolutionary' in any conventional sense of that term.

A similar critique was offered by Horne and Jary (1987: 99–100) when they wrote that:

> the focus on cultural and sporting phenomena embodied in Elias's concept of the 'civilizing process', whatever its productiveness in some respects, can[not] . . . escape criticism. It can be seen as an amalgam of fruitful notions and those whose utility is more questionable, including the apparent contradictions in the central methodological prescriptions of figurational sociology, especially a tendency to 'latent evolutionism'. On the positive side . . . the concept of the 'civilizing process' is responsible for the focus on 'combat sports' and the codification and

domestication of these in their modern forms. It provides a systematic –
if only one – rationale for focus on class, class emulation and class
conflict. Against this, however, and variously at odds with some of
figurational sociology's own methodological self-definitions, functionalist, evolutionary and related assumptions associated with the concept
of the 'civilizing process' have been rightly questioned, for example:
'the apparent irreversibility of the process' (Lasch, 1985), its 'irrefutabil-
ity' (Smith, 1984), its explicit or implicit reference to 'societal needs'
and 'functional requirements'.

I have already indicated the ways in which Horne and Jary seem to me in
crucial respects to misconstrue the figurational position on 'methodology',
so I shall say no more about that issue here. The other charges, though, are
deserving of some response. I welcome the praise that Horne and Jary give
to the figurational contributions to the sociology of sport. I welcome, too,
the very fact that they see them as worthy of being singled out for systematic critique. However, I find it difficult to see how even 'implicit' notions
of 'societal needs' and 'functional requirements' can be read into Elias's
work. He was always dismissive of the work of Parsons – sometimes,
admittedly, on the basis of a reading that was less than thorough – and
would certainly have endorsed the judgement of Robert Merton (1957: 52)
that the concept of 'functional needs' or 'requirements' is 'one of the
cloudiest and empirically most debatable concepts in functional theory'. It
is true that Elias insisted that a concept of functions is essential in a science
like sociology that is concerned with relationships. However, his definition
of it was reality-orientated and centred around power-differentials and,
above all, very different from the harmonistic usage of Talcott Parsons
(Elias, 1978b: p. 75ff.). Perhaps Horne and Jary read the concepts of
'societal needs' and 'functional requirements' into Elias's concept of 'blind'
or 'unplanned' long-term social processes; processes which, although they
result unintentionally from the aggregate effects of the interweaving of the
intentional acts of pluralities of individuals, were nevertheless held by Elias
to have a structure and direction which can be retrospectively determined.
However, it is difficult to see how concepts of 'societal needs' and 'functional requirements' could be read into this idea, for what Elias was, in
effect, attempting was to lay the foundations for a testable concept of social
development which grasps the patterned but reversible character of such
processes, while simultaneously avoiding the elements of teleology and
inevitability found, for example, in the theories of Hegel, Comte and, on
certain readings, Marx. That this is the case and that it is to say the least

misleading to attach the label 'latent evolutionism' to Elias's theory, will I hope become clear from the following exposition. I shall discuss his approach to the concept of 'civilization' first.

The concept of civilization

It seems to me that part of the difficulty that many English-speaking sociologists appear to experience in appreciating the theory of civilizing processes may stem from the vicissitudes of translation. In English even the titles of Elias's *magnum opus* have been changed in several ways. The overall German title is, *Über den Prozess der Zivilization: Soziogenetische und Psychogenetische Untersuchungen.* Volume 1 is subtitled *Wandlungen des Verhaltens in den weltlichen Oberschichten des Abendlandes*; and volume 2 is subtitled *Wandlungen der Gesellschaft: Entwurf zu einer Theorie der Zivilisation.* In English, volume 1 is rendered simply as *The Civilizing Process,* and against Elias's vigorous but unsuccessful opposition the subtitle, *The History of Manners,* has been added by the publisher.[29] Volume 2 is translated, perhaps less inappropriately, as *State Formation and Civilization.* In the translation the modesty and much of the subtlety of Elias's original German have been lost. More accurate translations would read as: *On the Process of Civilization: Sociogenetic and Psychogenetic Investigations,* volume 1, *Changes in the Behaviour of the Secular Upper Classes in the West;* volume 2, *Changes of Society: Outline of a Theory of Civilization.*[30] From these translations one gets a better idea of the fact that Elias saw his theory as a *contribution* to the understanding of Western civilization and its development rather than as a theory which is fully fledged and complete. That is lost in the bald English title. Also lost is the delimitation to the secular upper classes and, perhaps more importantly, the ambiguity of the term *Prozess,* a word which in German means 'trial' as well as 'process'. Writing as he did in exile after the Nazi rise to power and on the eve of the Second World War, Elias wanted to convey the connotation of civilization, not only as a process but, particularly at that historical conjuncture, as massively on trial as well. In short, his work was centrally concerned from the beginning with civilizing controls as a fragile shell and with civilizing processes as developments that are liable, under specific conditions, to go into reverse.

Elias started by observing that 'civilization' is such an all-embracing term that it is difficult if not impossible to define it. Its function, however, is easier to discern. 'Civilization' is a concept, he wrote, which has come to express the self-consciousness of the West. As Elias (1978a: 3, 4) put it, it is a term which sums up everything in which Western society of the last two or three centuries believes itself superior to earlier societies or 'more primitive' contemporary ones. By this term, Western society seeks to describe what constitutes its special character and what it is proud of: the level of *its* technology, the nature of *its* manners, the development of *its* scientific knowledge or view of the world, and much more.

According to Elias (drawing on the work of Lucien Febvre and others), this modern usage of the term dates from the second half of the eighteenth century. It is a usage which lacks a connotation of process. It expresses the self-confidence of the dominant groups in the late eighteenth-, nineteenth- and early twentieth-century West that their own civilization was complete and that it was their mission to 'civilize' both the peoples of 'barbaric lands' and their own lower classes. Originally, however, 'civilization' had been a term associated with moderate social critique. It was first used by the Physiocrats as part of a protest against the excesses of absolute rule. For them, it had connotations of progress and social reform. They had derived it from *civilité,* the word used since the sixteenth century to describe courtly behaviour, partly to distinguish the latter from the more rough-and-ready standards of mediaeval nobles which had been signified by the term *courtoisie.* This terminological, conceptual and social development took place in France, Elias suggested, because French society began to undergo processes of state-formation and unification under state-control compara- tively early on and because the French court was more open to bourgeois outsiders than its counterpart in Germany.

By comparison with France (and Britain too), Germany emerged as a unified nation-state comparatively late. The members of its French-speak- ing court circles were also highly socially exclusive and contemptuous of the German language. In that context, 'civilization' became a term for bourgeois intellectuals – the first *national* middle class in Germany – which signified superficiality, ceremony and politeness in contrast with the inner depth and solidity which they regarded as their own principal virtues. They expressed the latter through the term *Kultur.* The antithesis in Germany between *Zivilisation* and *Kultur* was solidified when the country became nationally unified in the second half of the nineteenth century and when, correspondingly, the power of bourgeois strata – including now larger commercial and industrial segments – grew. This residue of ambivalence towards 'civilization' and all it signifies was further strengthened when the First World War was fought against the Germans in its name. In that way, a degree of disdain for 'civilization' became for a while a prominent strand in Germany's specific strand of nationalism.

As one can see, Elias's theory starts out from a concern with the sociogenesis of the term 'civilization' and its changing value-content. He also paid attention to the different meanings the term came to acquire in different European countries, most notably in France and England on the one hand and Germany on the other.

It is, I think, relevant in this connection to draw attention to the fact that, in its recent pamphlet 'Anti-Racist Language: Guidance For Good Practice', the British Sociological Association has the following entry:

Civilized/civilization:
This term derives from a colonialist perception of the world. It is often associated with social darwinist thought and is full of implicit value judgements and ignorance of Third World history. However, in some cases, such as the work of Norbert Elias, civilization takes on a different meaning without racist overtones.

The BSA were right to single out Elias's work for this exemption. His theory is fully attuned to the dangers of racist language and seeks to shed light on the underlying processes involved in the production of this specific variant by examining key developments in a Western European context, that is, by means of an investigation of the concrete processes in the course of which the dominant groups in Western Europe came to view themselves and their cultures as superior.[31] According to Elias, specific developments at the level of personality as well as in social structures were involved in these processes. These developments at the levels of personality and social structure were also interdependent.

What Elias attempted in this connection was an exploratory theorization of a mass of empirical data about the different, interdependent levels of the European *'civilizing process'*. Just as other sociologists employ terms such as 'class' and 'bureaucracy' in a sense that is more detached than their everyday usage, so Elias used the concept of civilizing processes in a more technical sense. The concept is derived, that is to say, from a testable empirical base and has shed the value-laden connotations that 'civilization' and 'civilized' have in popular usage. As such, it directs attention away from the moral and political questions associated with national and class claims to superiority and towards such scientific questions as whether the evidence supports Elias's claims and whether his theorization has begun to shed light on identifiable sociogenetic and psychogenetic connections. One might call such connections 'causal', though Elias was crystal clear about the specificity of patterns of determination in social relations and, therefore, avoided such scientistic and reductionist terms. Let me briefly summarize this aspect of the theory.

The Sociogenesis and Psychogenesis of the Civilizing Process in Western Europe

The bedrock on which the theory of civilizing processes is built is the observation that, in the societies of Western Europe between the Middle Ages and the early twentieth century, a more or less continuous refinement of manners and social standards took place, together with an increase in the social pressure on people to exercise stricter, more even and continuous self-control over their feelings and behaviour. As part of this unplanned process there occurred, according to Elias, a shift in the balance between external constraints and self-constraints in favour of self-constraints and, at the level of personality, an increase in the importance of 'conscience' or 'super-ego' as a regulator of behaviour. That is, social standards have come in the course of the European civilizing process to be internalized more deeply and to operate, not only consciously, but more beneath the level of rationality and conscious control; for example, by means of the arousal of internally generated feelings of guilt, anxiety and shame. According to Elias, furthermore, throughout the period under consideration members of the upper and middle classes were the main originators of social standards and, when and where conditions were appropriate, standards tended to diffuse downwards from the top of the social scale.

If this analysis has a degree of reality-congruence, an aspect of the European civilizing process that has been of central relevance for the development of modern sport has consisted of a tightening in the normative regulation of violence and aggression, together with a long-term decline in most people's propensity for and capability of obtaining pleasure from directly taking part in and/or witnessing violent acts. Elias referred in this connection to a 'dampening of *Angriffslust*', literally to a curbing of the lust for attacking, to a taming of people's desire and capacity for obtaining pleasure from attacking and inflicting injury on others. Psychologically, this has entailed at least two things; first, a lowering of the 'threshold of repugnance' regarding bloodshed and other direct as well as symbolic manifestations of physical violence. As a result, people nowadays tend to recoil more readily and to show greater sensitivity in the presence of such manifestations than was the case with people in the Middle Ages. Secondly, it has entailed the internalization of a stricter taboo on violence as part of the super-ego. A consequence of this is that guilt-feelings are liable to be aroused whenever this taboo is violated. At the same time there has occurred a tendency – perhaps revealed most dramatically in the abandonment of public executions – to push violence behind the scenes and, as part of this, to describe people who openly derive pleasure from violence in terms of the language of psychopathology, punishing them by means of stigmatization, hospitalization, imprisonment or a combination of all three.

Elias also traces in considerable detail the European civilizing process with regard to behavioural standards generally, paying particular attention to the changing normative regulation and social control of such biological functions as sex, defaecation, urination, spitting, blowing one's nose and sleeping. These subjects take up the bulk of his attention in volume 1. How did he account for the civilizing process overall? In popular understanding, the terms 'violence' and 'civilization' are usually taken as antitheses but Elias holds that the long-term civilizing of the West occurred unintentionally and in conjunction with violent elimination struggles among kings and other feudal lords. These led – at different times and rates – to the establishment within each of the emergent European nation-states of relatively stable and relatively effective monopolies on the twin, mutually supportive major means of ruling: the right to use force and the right to impose taxes. In other words, far from being simple antitheses, violence and civilization are characterized, according to Elias, by specific forms of interdependence. More particularly, it was his contention that a civilizing process depends on the establishment of an effective violence-monopoly at the centre and that this, in its turn, facilitates internal pacification, a lengthening of what Elias called 'interdependency chains', an equalizing change in the balance of power between classes and other groups – Elias later referred to this as 'functional democratization' – and economic growth. Forms of reciprocity between these 'part-processes' were involved as well. For example, economic growth increases the revenue available to the state through its tax monopoly, thus enabling the state to buttress its monopoly over violence. At the risk of some oversimplification, one could express Elias's theory by saying that he held a civilizing process basically to be a function of state-formation, growing social differentiation, growing equality of power chances and growing wealth.

As is characteristic of social processes generally, because of the part played in them by the innovativeness and learning capabilities of more or less knowledgeable and reflexive human actors, none of these part-developments should be mechanistically read as always and everywhere occurring in identical fashion. One can speak of probabilities in that connection but not of law-like, cast-iron certainties (Elias, 1974). Moreover, although, with the exception of the process of 'feudalization' that occurred correlatively with the collapse of the Carolingian empire, Elias focused primarily on 'progressive' or 'civilizing' developments, his theory is attuned to the occurrence of shorter- and longer-term 'counter-civilizing' developments or 'de-civilizing spurts' as well (Elias, 1978a: 13–66; Mennell, 1989: 227–50). For example, he wrote (1978a: 253):

> this movement of society and civilization certainly does not follow a straight line. Within the overall movement there are repeatedly greater or lesser counter-movements in which the contrasts in society and the fluctuations in the behaviour of individuals, their affective outbreaks, increase again.[32]

One can add that, although Elias never dwelled on this, the theory also implies a theory of 'de-civilization'. That is the case because it leads one, *ceteris paribus,* to anticipate that 'counter-civilizing' developments will occur in a society which experiences (absolute?) economic decline, a shortening of interdependency chains, diminishing state monopolies over force and taxation and growing inequality in the balance of power between groups. Contemporary examples might be provided by the Lebanon, in some parts of Northern Ireland, and in those areas of the former Soviet empire where the state has lost control. Of course, since social processes always depend upon the capacity for learning and innovation of more or less knowledgeable and reflexive human actors, any such 'regressive' change, however long its duration and great its extent, is unlikely to replicate in reverse the details and phasing of its 'progressive' counterpart.

Nor, even though Western societies in the nineteenth and twentieth centuries established forms of dominance on a global scale, did Elias regard these societies as particularly advanced. He (1978a: 57) denied that they represent a 'pinnacle', described their members as 'late barbarians', and speculated that future historians may come to see the present era as part of what we call 'the middle ages'. It was nevertheless his contention that we are, today, in certain identifiable respects *more* 'civilized' than our mediaeval forebears. However, for Elias this is a question of fact, not of value-judgement, praise and celebration. How, he asked, can the people of today praise themselves for being the beneficiaries of an unplanned process? To do that would make no more sense than to blame the people of earlier stages for living, equally unintentionally, in societies which were domestically more violent than those of the present-day West.

This, then, in outline form is basically what Elias's theory claims. As I have said, it is presented as a contribution towards the understanding of civilization and civilizing processes and not as a fully fledged and final answer. It undoubtedly has its weak points and lacunae but, whatever these may be, it is difficult to see how the theory can be characterized as 'functionalist' or 'evolutionary', at least in so far as these terms have come to be conventionally understood. As I hope I have also made clear, Christopher Lasch is simply wrong to refer to 'the apparent irreversibility of the process'. Horne and Jary are similarly wrong to speak of an 'explicit or implicit reference to "societal needs" and "functional requirements"'. For Elias, both these terms involve an unacceptable and sociologically misleading reification. That is, while it may make sense to describe human individuals as having 'requirements' or 'needs', it is manifest nonsense to project such concepts on to constructs such as human 'societies' or 'social systems' because the latter refer to aggregates of interdependent individual human beings. In Elias's view, it is the task of sociology to shed light on the structure and dynamics of the chains of interdependency in which, as human beings, we always find ourselves unintentionally enmeshed from birth to death. It is also sociology's task to illuminate the unplanned but nevertheless patterned consequences that follow in the longer term from the interweaving of the intentional acts of aggregates of individuals. The theory of civilizing processes is fundamentally about the latter kind of interweaving.

Pace Dennis Smith, moreover, the theory of civilizing processes is not 'irrefutable' but testable on different levels and in a variety of ways. For example, Stephen Mennell has attempted a limited test of the theory by means of his study of the development of eating and taste in England and France. Similarly, Elias and I attempted to test it in a limited sphere through our studies of the development of sport. Of course, as progenitor of the theory and one of his students, we might not have had the same kind of interest in seeking disconfirming instances as the supporters of a rival theory would have had. Nevertheless we tried to search for evidence with an open mind and did not know prior to these investigations that our results would appear largely consistent with the theory. Elias's conclusions could also be tested by examining a wider range of societies than the three – England, France and Germany[33] – on which he principally focused. Non-western societies such as China[34] and Japan might be particularly apposite in this connection in the sense that they might be conducive to the development and refinement as well as the simple testing of the theory.

In order to be adequate, though, any such tests would have to distinguish between at least two aspects of Elias's theory: his conclusions regarding the overall direction of the European civilizing process and his conclusions regarding its sociogenesis and psychogenesis. In the former connection Elias's theory would be refuted if it could be shown empirically that the *overall* trend of the European civilizing process in the time-frame he considered – roughly from the Middle Ages up to about the First World War – was in a de-civilizing direction. De-civilizing developments since that time would not refute the theory or require it to be substantially modified unless it could be shown that they have occurred as a result of changes that Elias's theorization would lead one to expect to have produced consequences of a civilizing kind. This brings me to the second aspect. In this connection, in order to test the theory particular attention would have to be paid to Elias's theorization of the relationships among state-formation, lengthening of interdependency chains, functional democratization, growing wealth and civilization. But, of course, in a sense such testing has already been taking place. It has been taking place not simply by ourselves but by others with less of a vested interest in securing a vindication of Elias. I am referring to the fact that, like any science, sociology is social and that published results become subjected to critical scrutiny in the competitive arena of academic discourse. The present volume represents part of that competitive process. Only time will tell whether and how far those of us are right who believe that Elias's theory represents an advance in the understanding of civilization, and whether and how far we are right to defend it and attempt to build on it.

Let me turn now to an attempt in the present volume, not simply to criticize a figurational theory, but explicitly to test it, build on it and offer the outlines for a better alternative. I am referring to the challenging essay by Ruud Stokvis, 'Sports and Violence'. Although his understanding of the figurational perspective is arguably in part defective, Stokvis sympathizes with that perspective and its objectives and does not seek to reject the theory of civilizing processes wholesale. Instead, using the history of hunting as his main example, he claims to have falsified on empirical grounds some of Elias's conclusions on that subject. He then goes on to suggest that Elias and I made too much of the control of violence in our work on sport and that Kenneth Sheard and I got some aspects of the development of football wrong. Finally, he uses this critique as the basis for developing a less violence-centred theory of sport. As I hope to show, Ruud Stokvis has probably succeeded in falsifying part of Elias's work on the development of fox-hunting. I am not so sure about the other parts of his argument, though. But, whether Stokvis or I is judged in the end to be right, his essay is refreshing because it involves an attempt to *test* propositions about sport advanced by figurational sociologists, rather than a simple dismissal of the *genre* by the application of pejorative labels. For that reason and because it is so well and powerfully argued, his essay is worth singling out for detailed examination.

TESTING ELIAS'S THEORY OF SPORT: THE CASE OF
FOX-HUNTING

According to Norbert Elias (1986; Elias and Dunning, 1986: 26–40), the
initial development of modern sport – what he referred to as the 'sportization
of pastimes' – took place fundamentally in eighteenth century England in
conjunction with the 'parliamentarization of political conflict'. In his so-
far-published work on this subject,[35] Elias took the emergence of fox-
hunting as the primary example by means of which to illustrate this process.
Ruud Stokvis is rightly critical of him for relying for his empirical evidence
in this connection on a limited number of sources. According to Stokvis,
this led Elias to fail to recognize that this peculiar, more ritualized and
civilized form of hunting first developed in the court society of sixteenth-
century France. It was called there '*la chasse par force*' and, in that form,
was adopted in England during the reign of James I (1603–25). As Stokvis
puts it:

> If we take a closer look at the development of hunting in England, we
> shall see that the civilized traits in fox-hunting to which Elias refers
> existed before the process of parliamentarization began. In fact, they
> developed in France during the rise of the absolute monarchy independ-
> ently from any form of parliamentarization. . . . There is no indication
> that the experience of non-violent competition in Parliament between
> opposing parties had anything to do with the development of the typi-
> cally English way of fox-hunting.

Stokvis goes on to point out that it was deer that were primarily hunted in
'*la chasse par force*' and that it was a combination of deforestation and the
over-hunting of that animal in England which contributed to the choice of
foxes as the quarry. In this and other respects we are dealing here with what
is, in part, an empirical question. It seems highly plausible in the absence of
further research that Stokvis may have correctly identified that – probably
as a result of his reliance on a limited number of sources – Elias has wrongly
truncated a more long-term social process. That said, however, Stokvis has
misinterpreted Elias in an important respect. More particularly, he interprets
Elias as having posited a *causal* relationship between 'parliamentarization'
and 'sportization', whereas it was Elias's argument that these were twin
manifestations of one and the same overall development in a civilizing
direction. In short, *pace* Stokvis's interpretation, Elias's point was not that
'the experience of non-violent competition in parliament between opposing parties had [something] to do with the typically English way of fox-

hunting', but more subtly that, as the cycle of violence which had character-ized English society in the seventeenth century began to cool down, a more civilized ruling class began to emerge which developed less-violent ways of behaving in both the political and the leisure spheres. Moreover fox-hunting, Elias suggested, was just one among a number of more-civilized leisure-forms to emerge in this connection. Others were cricket, horse-racing and boxing, all of which began in eighteenth century England to develop re-cognizably modern forms of organization and competitive action.

In any case, again *pace* Stokvis, Elias was able by reference to the spe-cific pattern of state-formation in England – a process in which parliamentarization was one of the decisive features – to explain why independent clubs and similar forms of association were able to develop in this country, whereas in absolutist France such a development was impos-sible. This helps to explain why fox-hunting became a much more central part of the way of life of the English landowning classes than was the case with their counterparts in France. It also seems plausible to suppose that, while the development of this peculiar form of hunting may have started in French courtly circles, the English variants of the ritual may have repre-sented a further development in a civilizing direction. More particularly, it seems from the evidence Ruud Stokvis presents that the hunting nobles in France may still have participated directly in the kill. If this is a correct interpretation of Stokvis's data, then the formation of clubs may not have been the only significant development to have taken place in England. The practice of killing 'by proxy', that is by the hounds instead of the hunting humans, may have been a development that took place here too. In short, the validity of Elias's hypothesis about parliamentarization and sportization may be restricted as far as fox-hunting is concerned to this latter innovation and the emergence of clubs rather than to the development of this peculiar hunting ritual as a whole. Its adequacy in relation to cricket, boxing and horse-racing is an issue which remains to be explored.

Present indications are thus that Ruud Stokvis may have falsified part of Elias's thesis on empirical grounds. However, I am afraid that the same cannot be said regarding his more general contention that, in our work on the development of modern sport, Norbert Elias and I have placed too much emphasis on the control of violence. According to Stokvis, 'the main characteristics of modern sports are their organization on national and international levels and their accompanying standardization'. 'The rise of modern sports', he writes, 'should be interpreted as another manifestation of the increase in the scale and complexity of social life in Europe and the USA.' And thirdly, he suggests that:

not all popular pastimes had a violent character before they were transformed into modern sports. Violence was only involved in those pastimes whose competition brought the participants into close physical
contact. . . . Most of the pastimes that evolved into modern sports, such
as cricket, golf, bowling, tennis, archery, horse-racing and all the other
sports involving racing, did not have a violent character.

Although they are clearly adequate to a certain degree, these contentions are
nevertheless arguably deficient on a number of grounds. For example, if, as
I believe to be the case, Elias's work has generally pointed us in the right
direction, sports could not have become organized nationally without the
prior occurrence of substantial national unification – the emergence of
more-or-less unified nation-states – processes which empirically involved
the monopolization of violence under state control and which involved what
Elias called violent 'elimination struggles' among contenders for the royal
position. Nor, again if Elias's theorization points us in the right direction,
could increases in the scale and complexity of social life have taken place
independently of processes of pacification under state-control. The work of
Anthony Giddens on the nation-state and violence supports Elias on this
point.[36] Similarly, the existence of international rules of sports presupposes
at least a degree of peaceful collaboration between the representatives of
different nations. International sports bodies were not formed in times of
war, and international competitions such as the World Cup and the Olympics tend to be suspended at such times. Indeed, they are sometimes even
threatened when an escalation of tension between major powers which
stops short of actual war takes place, as was shown by the US boycott of the
Moscow Olympics as a result of the Soviet action in Afghanistan.

   This argument can be taken even further. While Ruud Stokvis would
have been right if he had suggested that not all the popular pastimes which
developed into modern sports were *equally* violent intrinsically and that the
chances for violent interaction probably always tend to be greatest in the
physical contact sports, his arguments in this regard are oversimplified in
some respects and arguably simply wrong in others. In fact, they involve
treating sports as if they exist(ed) to some extent in a social vacuum. For
example, he overlooks the fact that aggressive feelings are liable to be
aroused in *any* competitive activity and can lead to violent outcomes where
norms demanding self-control over violent impulses have not been deeply
internalized. In a word, it seems reasonable to suppose that the level of
violence even in non-contact sports is likely to depend, *ceteris paribus,* on
the level of civilization of the participants and of the societies to which they
belong. It may even be the case, as the research of Richard Sipes (1973)

suggests, that the more violent and aggressive a society overall the greater will be the tendency of its members to favour violent and aggressive sports. Ruud Stokvis also overlooks in this connection the copious opportunities for violent physical interaction that exist in horse-racing and the various forms of competitive running that involve humans alone. Under present conditions, these sports may not often involve large-scale physical confrontations or escalate to a level of seriousness which threatens their existence as sports, but think, for example, of the frequency of pushing, jostling and even deliberate 'spiking' in such events. Finally, although it would clearly be ludicrous to suggest that a game like golf or, to take an example that Ruud Stokvis does not mention, croquet had violent origins – unless, that is to say, it could be shown that the latter is a distant relative of polo – he seems completely unaware of the fact that cricket is a quintessential example of a war-game. Perhaps his inclusion of it in his list of 'non-violent' sports derives from an acceptance of the non-cricket-playing foreigner's image of the game. But whether or not that is so, cricket involves hurling an extremely hard projectile at a mock castle, 'the wicket'. In fact, being bowled is still sometimes referred to as 'being castled'. One of the central tactics in the game also involves deliberately aiming the ball directly at the heads of opposing players, ostensibly in the hope of intimidating them and increasing the chances that they will play a false stroke. Of course, cricket involves the guile and deceptiveness of the slower bowlers and not simply the intimidatory tactics of their faster counterparts. (To say this is not to imply that the latter do not use guile and deceptiveness too.) It also involves eating cucumber sandwiches during the tea-interval and a whole series of 'gentlemanly' rituals between opponents. However, none of this should be allowed to divert attention from the fact that cricket simultaneously involves, as a central ingredient, opportunities for aggressive behaviour at a much more basic level. Nor should it be forgotten that, even though the game began to develop its modern form under the aegis of a ruling class that was under-going a 'civilizing spurt', individual members of that class were still capable of cruelty to social subordinates and were engaged, at the same time as they were involved in the early development of cricket and other sports, in the predatory build-up of the largest empire – at least in the formal sense of being named as such – that the world has ever known.

By way of concluding this response to Ruud Stokvis, it is worth pointing out that, while he is right to criticize Norbert Elias for having relied on a small number of sources, he can himself be charged with a similar shortcoming regarding his critique of aspects of Kenneth Sheard's and my work on the development of football. I am referring to Stokvis's use in this connection of the work of H. A. Harris and – most dubious of all – the journalist Geoffrey Green. Norbert Elias's sources were at least primary! More particularly, while Thomas Arnold's late eighteenth century predecessor at Rugby, Thomas James, was certainly an Etonian, Geoffrey Green – on whose work Ruud Stokvis so unquestioningly relies – presents no evidence for his argument that James may have taken the Eton 'Field Game' to Rugby. It is nothing more than a speculation and a dubious one at that. There are a number of reasons for saying this. There is, for example, no mention of the 'Field Game' in James's account of the boys' leisure activities during his own days as a pupil at Eton. Not even football gets a mention. The closest, in fact, is an obscure reference to a game called 'goals' (Ogilvie, 1957: 75, 104; 1973: 64–86). Furthermore, while, when James was headmaster at Rugby, he certainly seems to have encouraged the boys to exercise – swimming, cricket and hare-and-hounds are mentioned in that connection but again not football (Ogilvie, 1957: 106) – it would have been uncharacteristic for a public-school master at that stage to have used sport as a means for improving relations between staff and students. That was the sort of strategy employed after the 1840s in the era of the so-called public-schools 'games cult' (see Dunning and Sheard, 1979: 76, 100, 103). In any case, the Field Game did not become fully codified in the sense of being based on written rules until 1849. Given that, a process of diffusion of the kind hypothesized by Green would have been difficult though not impossible. If it did occur, that would, of course, be consistent with the divergent development of the Rugby and Eton games. It would not, however, explain the development of such diametrically opposite practices as carrying and scoring over the bar in the Rugby game, and scoring under the bar and an absolute taboo on handling in its counterpart at Eton. Further to this, James was at Rugby from 1778 to 1794, that is, in the period of maximum disorder in what were, in the late eighteenth and early nineteenth centuries, generally disorderly schools. Rugby, in fact, experienced at least one full-scale pupil rebellion under James's headship – in 1786. It is difficult to conceive of such a situation being conducive to the orderly spread of a game-form from one public school to another.

What Ruud Stokvis appears to have done in this connection is to have accepted at face-value a journalist's projection into the past of a game-form that he loved – soccer, of which the no-handling Eton Field Game is prototypical – in order to increase the length of its pedigree. There can, however, be no reasonable doubt on the basis of the currently available evidence that a relatively undifferentiated kicking and handling game such as rugby has more in common with the folk-antecedents of the modern game than does the more differentiated game of soccer with its specialization around the use of feet and absolute taboo on handling for all players except the goalkeeper. There are no grounds for believing this taboo to be anything other than a comparatively recent development. In any case, Ruud Stokvis shows his misunderstanding of the argument proposed by Kenneth Sheard and myself when he says that: 'contrary to what Dunning and Sheard wrote, it was not the Etonians who tried to distinguish themselves from Rugby. It was the other way around.' This completely misses the point of our hypothesis that the incipient bifurcation of rugby and soccer appears to have been in part a consequence of status rivalry between Rugbeians and Etonians in which each group was trying to distinguish itself from the other (Dunning and Sheard, 1979: 98–9). Ruud Stokvis did not need such a misconstrual of our hypothesis to sustain his argument, probably in large measure valid, that Norbert Elias got some aspects of the development of fox-hunting wrong. Nor did he need to expand his case into what, if my arguments here have any substance, is mainly a faulty critique of Elias and myself for concentrating too much on the control of violence in our work on the development of sports.

Although I disagree with much of it, Ruud Stokvis's critique represents, in my opinion, a step forward for this area of the sociology of sport.[37] It does so for the simple reason that it attempts to strike at the empirical and theoretical core of what Elias and I have written and constructively to develop a counter-case. It does not, that is to say, treat our work simply dismissively by the use of labels such as 'functionalist' and 'evolutionary'. That is why I have singled it out for detailed treatment. I look forward to seeing Ruud Stokvis's reply to my counter-critique.

CONCLUSION: FUTURE DEVELOPMENTS OF FIGURATIONAL SOCIOLOGY AND THE SOCIOLOGY OF SPORT

There are many other criticisms of the figurational sociology of sport advanced by the contributors to this volume that I could have responded to. I could, for example, have pointed out in relation to Allen Guttmann's claim that Elias and I failed to come to terms with the critiques of catharsis theory that, whatever other failings and lacunae there may be in our work – and they are undoubtedly legion – it is precisely our point relative to the proponents of conventional views of catharsis that a principal *raison d'être* of sport and leisure events is the *creation* rather than, in any simple sense, the relief of tensions. It would have been similarly possible for me to respond at length to Jenny Hargreaves's assertion that, in the preface to *Quest for Excitement* (Elias and Dunning, 1986: 2), I argued that physical educationalists who have contributed to the sociology of sport have tended to perform 'poorly'. That was not my point at all. It was rather that such scholars have tended to focus on sports-related issues first and foremost, and that their work sometimes displays a lack of organic embeddedness in central sociological concerns. With the proviso that Jenny Hargreaves is one of the growing number of physical educationalists to whom it does not apply, that is a judgement that I stick to. However, I stick to it only if it is coupled with my related point that sociology as a whole shows its continuing dependency on 'heteronomous evaluations' rather than its orientation towards scientific concerns by the failure of so many of its leading advocates to appreciate either the growing significance of sport as an area of social life or its importance as a subject for sociological enquiry.

Many of Alan Clarke's arguments could also have been subjected to detailed scrutiny. I shall content myself, however, with a few brief comments. The first thing worthy of note is the 'startling absence' of the concept of power in figurational sociology that Alan Clarke claims to detect. This is in itself a rather 'startling' observation. Our concept of power may not be sociologically adequate or the same as that employed by Alan Clarke but it is, in fact, one of figurational sociology's *central* concepts. As Norbert Elias wrote: 'Power is a structural characteristic . . . of *all* human relationships' (1978b: 74; see also 37ff, 65ff, 80ff, 81–91, 92–4, 139ff). In other words, it is not only 'radical' sociologists who are attuned to problems of power. Nor, as I argued earlier specifically in relation to Marxists, can their understandings of power be said to be sociologically unproblematic.

On a more positive note, I agree with Alan Clarke when he writes that the figurational explanation of football hooliganism fails

> to account for why the football ground becomes the focus for this contestation of masculinity. Similar figurations of young 'roughs' populate the streets of St Helens and Warrington as they do Liverpool and Manchester. Rugby League and professional football offer no similarities in terms of the incidence of hooliganism. Unless scale is the deciding factor, there is an element missing from the figurational explanation.

Along with such things as degrees of media exposure and intensity of support as measured, for example, by the frequency of away-match travel, scale may well be one of the elements that explain this lacuna in our case regarding the differential occurrence of hooliganism at soccer and Rugby League. I suspect, though, that there may be socio-cultural differences in the kinds of support that these two games attract as well. This is an issue which will be resolvable only through further research. I fully agree with Alan Clarke that such research ought ideally to focus on 'the football figuration' rather than just the 'hooligan figuration' but am acutely aware of how difficult it is under present conditions to get funds for research which is not orientated towards issues that are perceived as 'social problems' by the 'funding fathers' and their 'masters'.

Research is needed, too, on the social construction of gender roles. Although I cannot agree that our conceptualizations of masculinity and femininity are 'static', I sympathize with Alan Clarke when he writes that some of our arguments about women and football come 'close to creating a new form of exploitation for women, drawing them in to pacify yet another social arena'. My colleagues and I are acutely aware of the dilemmas posed here. All I can say is that, while we regard such issues as the part played by sport in the reproduction and change of gender roles as, by and large, still-open questions and as requiring a great deal of further *inter-disciplinary* theorizing and research, I suspect that writers such as Alan Clarke are happy, for the most part, to remain at the level of ideology in this regard.

This brings me to the final points I want to make. I suspect that one of the sources of opposition to the theory of civilizing processes may be a feeling on the part of some of the critics that, despite our avowals to the contrary, a combination of class and ethnocentric hubris lurks somewhere within our work. I hope I have said enough in this chapter to dispel any such notion. According to Norbert Elias, as I have said, even people in the 'advanced' societies of the contemporary West are 'late barbarians'. Furthermore, he maintained that our knowledge of ourselves and the societies that we form remains in many ways rudimentary. It strikes me as possible, indeed, that in a sense it may not be figurational sociologists but some of our critics who display a tendency to hubris. At least that appears to be a possibility with those – Marxists, critical feminists and others – who seem to believe that present theories and ideologies provide an adequate basis for effective social action. Despite the welcome convergences that are detectable, for example in the work on sport of figurational sociologists and hegemony theorists, I suspect that this issue is likely to remain a major bone of contention. They appear to think they have 'the answers' and believe in the efficacy of action here and now. We believe we are still only in the early stages of gaining useful sociological knowledge. We acknowledge that, as citizens, we are constrained to act largely in ideological terms but, as *sociologists,* our fundamental commitment is to the increase of knowledge because knowledge, we believe, is a *sine qua non* for effective action in relation to the range of problems and dilemmas that currently face humanity whether in sport or elsewhere. We also believe that action on the basis of ideologies is likely to produce unintended consequences and that, on balance, these are likely to be of an undesirable rather than a desirable kind. Hence our research concern, on the one hand with the unintended interdependences within which human action always takes place and, on the other, with the unintended aggregate consequences that tend to follow from the interweaving of the intentional actions of pluralities of interdependent human beings.

I noted earlier that, according to Norbert Elias, Marx's work represents 'one symptom of a beginning'. I also suggested that Elias regarded his own work as another such symptom. The same holds true regarding the work of figurational sociologists in the fields of sport and leisure. That is to say, while we hope it represents a contribution to knowledge and understanding in these fields, it has never been presented as any kind of definitive, complete or final answer. That is because, in our view, 'definitive' answers are, in the main, impossible at the present stage of knowledge. All that is possible for the most part is preparatory spadework. In other words, it is simply our hope that our use of a figurational perspective has enabled us to contribute to the laying of firm foundations in the sociology of sport and elsewhere.

It is also my personal hope that the critique and counter-critique provided by the essays in *Sport and Leisure in the Civilizing Process* will prove conducive to the furtherance of constructive debate and fruitful research in the field. Above all, I hope that the essays in this volume will help to clear up some of the confusions and to clarify some of the misunderstandings that have grown up regarding figurational sociology, in that way helping to pave the way for debate about its *real* strengths and weaknesses and for research into the various propositions advanced by its advocates.

As far as the future of the figurational sociology of sport is concerned, we are, as I said, only at the beginning. The research programme that lies ahead is, correspondingly, a large one. Only a few aspects of the pressing tasks that face us can be singled out for mention here. The part played by sport in the social construction and change of gender roles is a project that will certainly loom large. Then there are such questions as those posed for sport by developing European integration, the decline of the Soviet empire, the rise of the Far East, the collapse of apartheid in South Africa, and the continuing travails of African, Middle Eastern, Central and South American and other 'less-developed' countries. Problems are also posed by the gathering – in large part media-fuelled – global competition between European and American sport-forms. What is the likelihood of sports such as baseball and 'gridiron' football really catching on in the European context and of

sports such as soccer catching on in North America? What will the consequences of such processes of diffusion be for traditional sports on either
side of the Atlantic? Can they prosper side by side or is one set likely to
push the other to the margins? Does American world hegemony imply the
probability of hegemony for American sport-forms? And what about Japanese
financial power? What will be the consequences of this for the spread of
Japanese sports and other cultural forms?

Figurational work on what are conventionally called sport and 'the
economy', sport and 'politics' and sport and 'the state' is also urgently
required. So is further work on football hooliganism, player violence, drug
dependency, and racial, national and ethnic tensions, prejudice and discrimination as manifested in and through sport. As I have said repeatedly in
this chapter, nothing that figurational sociologists have done so far – including
our work on football hooliganism – represents anything more than a beginning. We hope to build on what we have done so far. I hope that others
will join us in this quest and also help by pointing out constructively where
we have gone wrong and in what ways our work can be improved.

Let me finally express the hope that the essays in this volume will help
to persuade more sociologists that the sociology of sport is a field which is
vibrant and alive. I hope too, that *Sport and Leisure in the Civilizing Process* will help to persuade more of them of the growing world-wide significance of sport and leisure, and of the urgent need that there is for constructive research into and debate about the manifold and complex issues that
this raises. It is my belief that we have a golden opportunity at the moment
to raise the status of the sociology of sport within the subject as a whole.
However, if we continue to be ostrich-like in relation to paradigms that are
different from our own and engage in sterile name-calling instead of
meaningful debate and *meaningful* research, I am afraid that such an opportunity may pass us by.

Notes

*   My friends, Joop Goudsblom, Richard Kilminster, Stephen Mennell, Pat
      Murphy, Chris Rojek and Ivan Waddington read an earlier draft of this
      chapter and I have benefited greatly from their critical comments.
1.   'Figurational sociology' is a term coined by Norbert Elias in the 1960s as a
      replacement for the term 'developmental sociology' which he had used
      earlier. However, towards the end of his life, he came to prefer the term
      'process sociology' as a means of conveying the distinctiveness of his ap-
      proach. Horne and Jary (1987) have suggested that figurational sociology is

not really distinctive – they misleadingly say we claim to be 'unique' – but simply consists in 'the raising of classical sociological questions, and . . . recourse to sociological "best practice", in an area where these had hitherto been conspicuously absent'. No figurational sociologist would disagree with this except in the sense that identifying labels are arguably necessary in a multi-paradigmatic and competitive field. We certainly do not claim that our approach is 'unique'. Nor do we claim 'exclusivity' as Alan Clarke implies.

2.   It is to me remarkable that figurational sociologists are often accused of ignoring others' work and of not locating what they write in the context of central sociological concerns when the very people who make such claims are guilty of ignoring an attempt to survey the whole of sociology from a figurational standpoint. I am referring to Johan Goudsblom's excellent *Sociology in the Balance* which came out as early as 1977 and which, to my knowledge, has been unjustly ignored by virtually all British and American sociologists. I sincerely hope that the same fate will not befall Stephen Mennell's equally excellent *Norbert Elias, Civilization and the Human Self-Image*. It provides a masterly exposition of virtually the whole of the figurational genre and deserves to be widely read.

3.   See, for example, Horne and Jary, 1987: 86–112.

4.   I hope that, having read this chapter, the open-minded reader will come to see that many aspects of Horne and Jary's critique of the figurational sociology of sport involve responding to a caricature of our position rather than to what we actually say.

5.   The work of Anthony Giddens is a prime candidate in this regard. For example, his *The Nation-State and Violence* (1985) contains arguments that are remarkably similar to some articulated by Elias as early as 1939, yet Elias merits only one mention by Giddens and that is dismissive (p. 195). The 1939 argument by Elias I am referring to related to the significance of the central control of violence and pacification under state control for economic growth and the emergence of modern capitalism. In fact, Giddens fails even to mention Volume 2 of *The Civilizing Process* in his bibliography.

6.   I can see now that Norbert Elias and I made a mistake when preparing *Quest for Excitement* (1986) for publication in not relating what we had written in the 1960s to work done in the sociology of sport since that time. Much of it is excellent and reference to it might have helped to avoid some of the hostility to figurational sociology of figures working in the field.

7.   One of Norbert Elias's pieces of advice to students was: 'fight your teachers. That is one of the preconditions for the advance of knowledge. But always fight them in a well-prepared and non-aggressive way.'

8.   The paper was given at a meeting of the now defunct 'Teachers' Section' of the BSA held at the London School of Economics in late 1965 or early 1966. It was on the concept of development and attempted to demonstrate the reality-congruence of this concept by means of discussions of the civilizing process and the early development of football. With some modifications, it was later published as 'The Concept of Development: Two Illustrative Case Studies' (1966).

9.   The Conference Proceedings were published in 1966 under the title *Kleingruppenforschung und Gruppe im Sport* (Köln und Opladen: Westdeutscher Verlag). The conference was organized and the proceedings

edited by Günther Lüschen. I should like to take this opportunity to record the debt to Günther of all who work in the sociology of sport. Without his seminal academic and organizational contributions the field could never have risen to its present standing.

10. I am thinking in this connection of the work of my good friends, Stan Parker and Ken Roberts. See, for example, S. R. Parker (1971) and K. Roberts (1978). Interestingly, Bert Moorhouse has recently criticized the work of Parker and Roberts along lines which overlap to some extent with the figurational critique. Nevertheless, Moorhouse (1989) still writes as if *Quest for Excitement* had never appeared!

11. See pp. 65 ff. of the present volume.

12. As with Ian Taylor, I could cite many of Alan Ingham's articles in this connection. For present purposes it must be enough just to cite these two.

13. See p. 69 of the present volume.

14. See Norbert Elias (1978), esp. Ch. 6, 'The Problem of the Inevitability of Social Development', for a discussion of this issue.

15. It is probably worth pointing out in this connection that Norbert Elias failed to foresee the end of the 'cold war' and that in his most recently published book, *Studien über die Deutschen*, he told the Germans that they would have to learn to live with the division between the Federal and Democratic Republics.

16. Giddens (1984: xx) has expressed this emphasis thus: 'concentration upon epistemological issues draws attention away from the more "ontological" concerns of social theory, and it is these upon which structuration theory primarily concentrates'.

17. According to Giddens (1984: xvii), 'The social sciences are lost if they are not directly related to philosophical problems by those who practise them.' Elias took the opposite view, regarding the work of scholars like Giddens as journeys into a blind alley.

18. See, for example, Callinocos (1985). See also Held (1989) and Bryant and Jary (1990). If for no other reason, the volume edited by Bryant and Jary is of note for its inclusion of an excellent critique of Giddens from a figurational standpoint by Richard Kilminster of the University of Leeds. Richard Kilminster's chapter deserves to be very widely read.

19. Giddens's equivalent for the concept of interdependency chains is that of 'time-space distanciation' or 'time-space stretching' (see Giddens, 1984: 258–9). While it may have a degree of spurious scientificity, such a concept arguably lacks the clear-cut structural connotations of the concept of interdependency chains. Against that, the latter may not adequately capture the balance between enablement and constraint, containing too much of an implied emphasis on the latter pole.

20. Giddens's attempt in this connection to overcome the tendency towards dichotomizing the 'micro' and 'macro' levels of sociological analysis is welcome. It is another aim that he shared with Norbert Elias and was, in fact, a central topic of discussion in the Leicester Sociology Department when Giddens was there (see Giddens, 1984: 139ff). Although I do not agree with all of it, see also Nicos Mouzelis's excellent, 'Restructuring Structuration Theory' for a lucid and cogent critique of some of Giddens's central conceptualizations on this score.

21. It is perhaps worth recording in this connection that the MA thesis submitted by Giddens to the London School of Economics in 1961 was on the subject of sport. Given that, this lacuna in his later work represents something of a contradiction.

22. See, apart from the discussion in *What is Sociology?*, Norbert Elias's Appendix 1 to the English translation of *The Civilizing Process* (1978) pp. 221–63. This was the Introduction to the 1968 German edition.

23. This is not to deny the fact that processes in a 'de-secularizing' direction are currently dominant in some parts of the Moslem world. From a figurational standpoint, one of the interesting problems that are posed in this connection is that of the interdependence of these processes with the predominantly secularizing developments in the West and with the fluid and shifting balance of global power.

24. See p. 19 of the present volume.

25. See Dunning (1990). Along with my colleagues, Patrick Murphy and Ivan Waddington, I am currently seeking funds for a project on sport and gender.

26. I could cite many sources in this connection but, for present purposes, Hargreaves (1984) will have to suffice.

27. I have referred here to 'civilizing processes' in the plural in order to convey the idea of the specificity within the general movement of, for example, the English, French and German civilizing processes. The plural connotation also conveys Elias's idea that the concept of a civilizing process can also be used with reference to the socialization of single individuals.

28. A good idea of what has been achieved in this connection is conveyed in Mennell (1989).

29. The publishers in question were the German firm Urizen Books, the publishers of the first translation. Stephen Mennell has reminded me that the title they employed for the American edition of volume 2 was *Power and Civility*. The substitution of 'civility' for 'civilization' and 'civilizing process' is, of course, a classic instance of precisely the 'process reduction' that Elias constantly urged sociologists to avoid in their modes of concept-formation.

30. The German word '*Entwurf*' could be equally well translated as 'sketch' or 'draft'.

31. For an interesting recent application and development of Elias's work on this subject, see Bleicher (1990).

32. See also Mennell (1990).

33. For an attempt to test Elias's theory in the context of German social development, see Krumrey (1984).

34. In vol. 1 of *The Civilizing Process,* Elias (1978a) refers to the Chinese practice of eating with chopsticks, and quotes the Chinese view of Westerners as 'barbarians' because 'they eat with swords' (p. 126). He speculates that the disappearance of the knife from the Chinese table may have been connected with the early dominance in Chinese society of scholarly officials over the warrior segment in the ruling class.

35. Among Elias's unpublished work on this subject is a brilliant fragment on boxing. Unfortunately, he was unable to locate it when we were preparing *Quest for Excitement* for publication.

36. See the analysis in the first half of Giddens (1985).

37. I have not mentioned it in the text but I want to draw attention in this

connection to the work of Frank Kew. He has imaginatively combined a modified ethnomethodology with the figurational perspective in order to shed light onto the development of the rules of sports and games. Among other things, what he shows very successfully is how Elias and I, in our work on the dynamics of sport groups, did not pay sufficient attention to the tensions and struggles between players and legislators as a determinant of changes in the rules (see Kew, 1990). Like the work of Ruud Stokvis, Frank Kew's constructive, but by no means uncritical, approach to the ethnomethodological and figurational perspectives represents, in my view, a positive and very welcome development in the sociology of sport.

References

Abrams, Philip (1982), *Historical Sociology* (London: Open Books).

Bauman, Zygmunt (1979), 'The Phenomenon of Norbert Elias', *Sociology,* 13: 117–35.

Bleicher, Josef (1990), 'Struggling with *Kultur'*, *Theory, Culture and Society,* 7: 97–106.

Blumer, Herbert (1969), *Symbolic Interactionism: Perspective and Method* (Englewood Cliffs, N.J.: Prentice-Hall).

Bocock, Robert (1983), *Sigmund Freud* (London: Tavistock).

Bott, Elizabeth (1957), *Family and Social Network* (London: Tavistock).

Bottomore, Tom (1962), *Sociology: A Guide to Problems and Literature* (London: Allen & Unwin).

Bramham, Peter (1984), 'Giddens in Goal: Reconstructing the Social Theory of Sport', in P. Bramham, L. Haywood, I. Henry and F. Kew (eds), *New Directions in Leisure Studies,* Papers in Applied and Community Studies no. 1 (Bradford, Yorks.: Bradford and Ilkley Community College) pp. 5–30.

British Sociological Association, *Anti-Racist Language: Guidance for Good Practice* (London: British Sociological Association, n.d.).

Brohm, Jean-Marie (1978), *Sport: A Prison of Measured Time* (London: Ink Links).

Bryant, Christopher and Jary, David (eds) (1990), *Giddens' Theory of Structuration* (London: Routledge).

Callinicos, A. (1985), 'Anthony Giddens: a Contemporary Critique', *Theory and Society,* 14(2): 133–66.

Clarke, John and Critcher, Chas (1985), *The Devil Makes Work: Leisure in Capitalist Britain* (London: Macmillan).

Curtis, James (1986), 'Isn't It Difficult to Support some Notions of "The Civilizing Process"? A Response to Dunning', in C. R. Rees and A. W. Miracle (eds), *Sport and Social Theory* (Champaign, Ill.: Human Kinetics) pp. 57–66.

Dunning, Eric (1966), 'The Concept of Development: Two Illustrative Case Studies', in Peter I. Rose (eds), *The Study of Society* (New York: Random House) pp. 879–93.

_____ (1989), 'The Figurational Approach to Leisure and Sport', in C. Rojek (ed.), *Leisure for Leisure* (London: Macmillan) pp. 36–52.

_____ (1990), 'Sport and Gender in a Patriarchal Society', paper delivered at the World Congress of Sociology, Madrid.

_____ and Sheard, Kenneth (1979), *Barbarians, Gentlemen and Players: A Sociological Study of the Development of Rugby Football* (Oxford: Martin Robertson).

Durkheim, Emile (1952), *Suicide: A Study in Sociology* (London: Routledge & Kegan Paul).

_____ (1964), *The Division of Labour in Society* (Glencoe, Ill.: Free Press).

Elias, Norbert (1939), *Über den Prozess der Zivilisation*, 2 vols (Basle: Verlag Haus zum Falken).

_____ (1974), 'The Sciences: Towards a Theory', in R. Whitley (ed.), *Social Processes of Scientific Development* (London: Routledge & Kegan Paul) pp. 21–42.

_____ (1977), 'Zur Grundlegung einer Theorie Sozialer Prozesse', *Zeitschrift für Soziologie*, 6(2): 127–49.

_____ (1978a), *The Civilizing Process* (Oxford: Basil Blackwell).

_____ (1978b), *What is Sociology?* (London: Hutchinson).

_____ (1982), *The Civilizing Process*, vol. 2: *State-Formation and Civilization* (Oxford: Basil Blackwell).

_____ (1986), 'An Essay on Sport and Violence', in N. Elias and E. Dunning, *Quest for Excitement* (Oxford: Basil Blackwell) pp. 151–74.

_____ (1987), *Involvement and Detachment* (Oxford: Basil Blackwell).

_____ (1989), *Studien über die Deutschen* (Frankfurt: Suhrkamp).

_____ and Dunning, Eric (1966), 'Dynamics of Sport Groups with Special Reference to Football', *British Journal of Sociology*, 17(4):

_____ and _____ (1969), 'The Quest for Excitement in Leisure', *Society and Leisure*, 2: 388–402.

_____ and _____ (1970), 'The Quest for Excitement in Unexciting Societies', in G. Lüschen (ed.), *The Cross-Cultural Analysis of Sport and Games* (Champaign, Ill., Stipes).

_____ and _____ (1986), *Quest for Excitement* (Oxford: Basil Blackwell).

Giddens, Anthony (1971), *Capitalism and Modern Social Theory* (Cambridge: Cambridge University Press).

_____ (1984), *The Constitution of Society* (Cambridge: Polity Press).

_____ (1985), *The Nation-State and Violence* (Cambridge: Polity Press).

_____ and Mackenzie, Gavin (eds) (1982), *Social Class and the Division of Labour: Essays in Honour of Ilya Neustadt* (Cambridge: Cambridge University Press).

Gleichmann, Peter, Goudsblom, Johan and Korte, Hermann (eds) *Human Figurations: Essays for Norbert Elias* (Amsterdam: Stichting Amsterdams Sociologisch Tijdschrift).

Goudsblom, Johan (1977), *Sociology in the Balance* (Oxford: Basil Blackwell).

_____ (1989), 'Human History and Long-Term Social Processes: Towards a Synthesis of Chronology and "Phaseology"', in J. Goudsblom, E. L. Jones and S. Mennell, *Human History and Social Processes* (Exeter: University of Exeter Press) pp. 11–26.

Gruneau, Richard (1985), *Class, Sports and Social Development* (Amherst, Mass.: University of Massachusetts Press).

Hargreaves, Jennifer (ed.) (1982), *Sport, Culture and Ideology* (London: Routledge & Kegan Paul).

_____ (1984), 'Action Replay: Looking at Women in Sport', in J. Holland (ed.), *Feminist Action* (London: Routledge & Kegan Paul) pp. 125–46.

Hargreaves, John (1962), 'Sport and Hegemony: Some Theoretical Problems', in H. Cantelon and R. Gruneau (eds), *Sport, Culture and the Modern State* (Toronto: University of Toronto Press) pp. 104–5.

_____ (1986), *Sport, Power and Culture* (Cambridge: Polity Press).

Held, David and Thompson, John B. (eds) (1989), *Social Theory of Modern Societies: Anthony Giddens and his Critics* (Cambridge: Cambridge University Press).

Hoch, Paul (1972), *Riff Off the Big Game* (New York: Anchor Doubleday).

Horne, John and Jary, David (1987), 'The Figurational Sociology of Sport and Leisure of Elias and Dunning: an Exposition and Critique', in J. Horne, D. Jary and A. Tomlinson (eds), *Sport, Leisure and Social Relations* (London: Routledge & Kegan Paul).

Huizinga, Johan (1949), *Homo Ludens: A Study of the Play Element in Culture* (London: Routledge & Kegan Paul).

Ingham, Alan (1985), 'From Public Issue to Person Trouble: Well-being and the Fiscal Crisis of the State', *Sociology of Sport*, 2(1): 76–98.

_____ and Hardy, Stephen (1984), 'Sport: Structuration, Subjugation and Hegemony', *Theory, Culture and Society*, 2(2): 85–103.

Jordan, Z. A. (ed.) (1972), *Karl Marx* (London: Nelson).

Keat, Russell and Urry, John (1975), *Social Theory as Science* (London: Routledge & Kegan Paul).

Kew, Frank (1990), 'Constituting Games: an Analysis of Game Rules and Game-Processes', unpublished PhD thesis, University of Leeds.

Krumrey, Horst-Volker (1984), *Entwicklungsstrukturen von Verhaltensstandarden* (Frankfurt: Suhrkamp).

Lasch, C. (1985), 'Historical Sociology and the Myth of Maturity: Norbert Elias's "Very Simple Formula"', *Theory and Society*, 14: 705–20.

Layder, Derek (1986), 'Social Reality as Figuration: a Critique of Elias's Conception of Sociological Analysis', *Sociology*, 20(3): 367–86.

McIntosh, Peter (1968), *Physical Education in England since 1800* (London: Bell).

McNeill, W. H. (1979), *Plagues and People* (Harmondsworth, Middx: Penguin).

Marx, Karl (1965), *Capital* (London: Lawrence & Wishart).

Mennell, Stephen (1989), *Norbert Elias, Civilization and the Human Self-Image* (Oxford: Basil Blackwell).

_____ (1990), 'Decivilizing Processes: Theoretical Significance and Some Lines of Research', *International Sociology*, 5(2): 205–23.

Merton, Robert (1970), *Social Theory and Social Structure* (Glencoe, Ill.: Free Press).

Moorhouse, H. R. (1989), 'Models of Work, Models of Leisure', in C. Rojek (ed.), *Leisure for Leisure* (London: Macmillan).

Mouzelis, Nicos (1989), 'Restructuring Structuration Theory', *Sociological Review*, 37(4): 613–35.

Newman, Otto (1986), Review of Chris Rojek, *Capitalism and Leisure Theory* (London: Tavistock), *Sociology*, 20(2): 322.

Ogilvie, Vivian (1957), *The English Public School* (London: Batsford; 2nd edn, 1973).

Parker, S. R. (1971), *The Future of Work and Leisure* (London: MacGibbon & Kee).

Popper, K. R. (1957), *The Poverty of Historicism* (London: Routledge & Kegan Paul).

Rigauer, Bero (1981), *Sport and Work* (New York: Columbia University Press).

Roberts, K. (1978), *Contemporary Society and the Growth of Leisure* (London: Longman).

Sipes, Richard (1973), 'War, Sports and Aggression', *American Anthropologist,* 75: 64–86.

Smith, D. (1984), 'Norbert Elias: Established or Outsider?', *Sociological Review,* 32: 367–89.

Stone, Gregory P. (1971), 'American Sports: Play and Display', in E. Dunning (ed.), *The Sociology of Sport: A Selection of Readings* (London: Frank Cass) pp. 47–65.

Taylor, Ian (1982), 'On the Sports Violence Question: Soccer Hooliganism Revisited', in J. Hargreaves (ed.), *Sport, Culture and Ideology* (London: Routledge & Kegan Paul).

_____ (1987), 'Putting the Boot into Working-Class Sport: British Soccer after Bradford and Brussels', *Sociology of Sport Journal,* 4: 171–91.

Urry, John (1990), 'Time and Space in Giddens' Social Theory', in C. Bryant and D. Jary (eds), *Giddens' Theory of Structuration* (London: Routledge) pp. 160–75.

Wallerstein, Immanuel (1974–80), *The Modern World-System,* 2 vols (New York: Academic Press).

Weber, Max (1956), *The Protestant Ethic and the Spirit of Capitalism* (London: Allen & Unwin).

Wolff, Kurt H. (ed.) (1950), *The Sociology of Georg Simmel* (Glencoe, Ill.: Free Press).

Author Index

285

Subject Index